D1561632

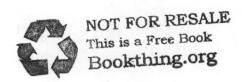

Intentions and Intentionality

Intentions and Intentionality
Foundations of Social Cognition

edited by Bertram F. Malle, Louis J. Moses, and
Dare A. Baldwin

A Bradford Book
The MIT Press
Cambridge, Massachusetts
London, England

Set in Sabon by The MIT Press.
Printed and bound in the United States of America.

Library of Congress Cataloging-in-Publication Data

Intentions and intentionality: foundations of social cognition / edited by Bertram F. Malle, Louis J. Moses, and Dare A. Baldwin
p.   cm.
"A Bradford book."
Includes bibliographical references and index.
ISBN 0-262-13386-5 (hc: alk. paper)
I. Intentionalism. I. Malle, Bertram F. II. Moses, Louis J. III. Baldwin, Dare A.

BF 619.5.I58 2001
153.8—dc21   00-064590

Contents

Foreword

The concept of intention had a rather checkered, indeed a somewhat scandalous history in the twentieth century—more so in the human sciences, perhaps, than in philosophy. It was typically neglected and caricatured as a topic for empirical research, rarely finding its way much beyond formal philosophy. Intention seemed an embarrassing idea to hard-nosed psychological theory. This volume goes a long way toward bringing intention back as a focus for empirical psychological research and theory. But, beyond that, it also marks a turning point: in these pages, philosophical and psychological issues are treated not as if they were separate, from different worlds, but as two related perspectives on the same set of issues. The analytic concerns of the philosopher can no more be ignored by the psychologist than the psychologist's empirical findings can be ignored by the philosopher.

What has produced this change? The chapters that follow have much to say on this matter, but it might help to add a brief, rather more historical perspective to the interesting conceptual perspectives the various chapters bring to the matter.

The fact is that there was little room for a concept like intention in the self-professed "tough" psychological theorizing of the twentieth century. For the very idea of intention implies that somebody carries out an act in the light of some preconceived goal that he or she has in mind, and that the person who has so acted can therefore supply proper or "correct" reasons for having done so. But invoking intention in this way violated most the self-imposed taboos that psychology thought it had to honor to become a full-fledged member of the natural sciences.

For one thing, the very notion of intention gave a special pride of place to "mental states" as determining behavior. The new objectivism that had come to dominate much of academic psychology in the twentieth century—whether inspired by American behaviorism or by Pavlov—put mental states into the category of the "subjective," which, in the newly emerging objectivism, could have no explanatory power. The subjective was either epiphenomenal or simply ignorable.

In that atmosphere, moreover, intention smacked of teleology, and it was precisely such teleology that psychology was seeking to shed in its efforts to explain behavior "scientifically." And this brings us to still another side of the "scandal of intention"—a rather surprising one.

Paralleling twentieth-century psychology's anti-teleology was a new anti-rationalism that stemmed principally from psychoanalytic theory. It was not that people did not strive for goals or ends, but that, more often than not, they did not know what their "real" intentions were. Real intentions were "unconscious" and not accessible to the actor. The task of psycho-analysis, as it were, was to help the person surmount his or her "defenses" in order to discover what he or she really intended. Thus, although the concept of intention was central to psychoanalytic theory, the transparency of intentions was seen as deeply problematic.

In an atmosphere dominated by objectivism and anti-teleology on the one side and by psychoanalytic "crypticism" on the other, most psychologists (whatever their adjectival identity) stayed away from the study of intention, substituting concepts like "need" and "motivation" in its place. Not even Elizabeth Anscombe's elegant analytic study *Intention*, with its exemplary account of the presuppositions implied by the term, was able to overcome their reluctance—even in 1957, just as the Cognitive Revolution was being born.

What turned the tide? Answers to that question can be found in virtually every chapter of this book. But the history that one is living through is not easy to see clearly. Indeed, there is an irony among Italian intellectuals that is apropos here. Italian history after the Second World War is not part of the curriculum even of secondary schools in that country, its absence justified by that same lame excuse about being too "close" to understand. But the real reason, intellectual wits like to tell you, is that Italians still find it difficult and divisive to face the excesses of Fascism, much as Americans find it difficult to face slavery or the British the exploitativeness of their country's colonialist past. And similarly, we psychologists often still refuse to look squarely at the issue of mind, still embarrassed by our earlier anti-mentalistic excesses even though we began moderating them in the 1960s. So what indeed turned the tide?

My own view is that we are living through an intellectual revolution—call it "the information revolution" or "the inward turn"—that has returned mind to center stage not only in our efforts to understand the human mind but also in our efforts to construct "artificial human intelligence." One central problem that has emerged in this new revolution is the classic one of Other Minds—how we understand them, how we manage to communicate about our own or others' states of mind, what it takes to learn about what others have in mind, and so on. Much of the new research on these topics, both in psychology and in philosophy—on intersubjectivity, as it is now referred to—is lucidly reviewed in the chapters of this book, so there is no need to go into any detail about them here. But there are two particular research topics that have emerged in this work that deserve a special word, for they throw new light on the changed direction of psychological research and theory.

The first has to do with development and elaboration of our beliefs and knowledge about Other Minds. Crucial to this discussion is the question of how and when we come to understand what others intend. Also crucial is the question of what it is that is understood when a child behaves "as if" he or she grasped another person's intention. Does the child have "theories" about the intentions of others and how they are expressed? Or, rather than have theories, is the child able to make actuarial predictions about how others will behave based only on how they behaved in the past, or on how people "usually" behave in particular situations? Or is our view of others' intentions based on a primitive normative conception of what is "appropriate" in given social, interpersonal settings? And do very young children have some primitive form of "intention recognition," or does the very concept of "intention" have to be acquired in some experiential way? Of course, these questions go well beyond the sheer "having" or "recognizing" of material intentions to *do* things, for there are also "communicative intentions" to take into account, with their conventionalized illocutionary force and felicity conditions. In view of how modern theories of sociolinguistics have moved away from the simple nativism of Chomsky, the recognition of another's communicative intentions becomes a sine qua non for language acquisition itself.

But let me turn to the second research topic that has provided an especial goad to psychological theorizing. If the first one is principally ontogenetic in emphasis, the second is phylogenetic. Can higher primates indeed read one another's minds? And do they do so in the same "conceptual" way that ordinary humans do, or are they limited to some less abstract, more actuarial way of reading one another's intentions? In short, does the emergence of human culture depend upon an elaborated system for grasping the intentions of one's conspecifics? Questions of this order have infused a new vitality into studies of the origins of human culture, and they are well represented and scrupulously argued in the chapters of this book.

The nature of intention and the means whereby we recognize one another's intentions has become a central issue not only in philosophy but also in psychological theory and research—and not just in psychology "in general," but in enriching our understanding of how the growing child comes to know his or her social world and, indeed, how *Homo sapiens* managed to take the crucial step of developing human culture. This book will serve well not only in making this new approach accessible to the general reader, but also in clarifying some of the deep and ancient issues that are still unresolved.

Jerome Bruner

Preface

This volume emerged from a series of expanding collaborations. All three of us had been occupied with issues of intentions and intentionality for some years. Bertram Malle had worked on the role of intentionality in adult social perception and folk explanations of behavior, Lou Moses on the place of intentional concepts in preschoolers' emerging theory of mind, and Dare Baldwin on the roots of intentional understanding in infancy and its significance for early language development and knowledge acquisition more generally. Our shared belief that intentionality is critical to how people interpret action and interaction in their daily lives led us to undertake several related projects, eventually culminating in the present volume.

The first of these projects was a joint graduate seminar on intentionality, held during the fall of 1997.[1] Central topics of this seminar—the conceptual components of intentionality, how intentions are detected, the role of intentionality in behavior explanations, and the relations between intentionality and responsibility—became the guiding questions of the present volume. We are grateful to the seminar participants (Jodie Baird, Joanna Bulkley, Diego Fernandez-Duque, David French, Kristi Klein, Richard Littman, Vicki Luu, Matt O'Laughlin, Mark Sabbagh, and Meg Saylor) for helping us to isolate what was known and, especially, what was not known about these topics. The seminar convinced us that, although important work was being carried out on intentions and intentionality in developmental psychology, in social psychology, in psycholinguistics, in philosophy of mind and action, in anthropology, and in law, a satisfactory account could arise only from an interdisciplinary perspective on these matters. For instance, much of the work in psychology had proceeded without the ben-

---

1. http://darkwing.uoregon.edu/~bfmalle/intentionality.html

efit of important conceptual distinctions drawn by philosophers; conversely, many of the philosophers' claims were made without the benefit of available psychological data.

Our second project, then, was to bring together a group of eminent scholars, all working on aspects of intentionality, for an interdisciplinary conference at the University of Oregon in October 1998.[2] Our central aim at the conference was to encourage intellectual dialogue across disciplines, a goal that is often cherished but rarely accomplished. The conference was funded by the Institute of Cognitive and Decision Sciences at the University of Oregon[3]; the National Science Foundation provided supplemental funding. We are especially grateful to Sarah Douglas and John Orbell (the directors of the institute at the planning and implementation phases of the conference, respectively) for their advice and encouragement throughout. We would also like to thank Vonda Evans for invaluable secretarial and logistical support.

The presentations and discussions at the conference were so stimulating that we decided to make them the starting point for a third project, the present book. Our overarching goal was to showcase perspectives from various disciplines on how folk conceptions of intentions and intentionality affect social cognition. Almost all of the scholars attending the conference contributed to this volume, and many of the chapters reflect a boundary-crossing, interdisciplinary agenda.

Our editorial work was supported by the National Science Foundation under CAREER Grant 9703315 to Bertram Malle and New Young Investigator Award 9458339 to Dare Baldwin, and by a John Merck Scholars Award to Dare Baldwin. The volume was completed while Dare Baldwin was a fellow at the Center for Advanced Study in the Behavioral Sciences in Stanford. We are grateful for the financial support provided by the Center and for that provided by the William T. Grant Foundation through award 95167795. We are indebted to Jerome Bruner for writing the foreword, to Josef Perner and three anonymous reviewers for providing insightful comments, to Amy Brand for her immediate excitement about the book proposal and her constant encouragement as we put together the early drafts, and to Paul Bethge for helping us to bring the book to fruition.

2. http://darkwing.uoregon.edu/~bfmalle/conference/
3. http://hebb.uoregon.edu/institute

Intentions and Intentionality

Introduction: The Significance of Intentionality

Bertram F. Malle, Louis. J. Moses, and Dare A. Baldwin

Considerations of intentions and intentionality permeate human social life. Picture a first date, in which the partners try to find out their own and the other's desires, or a business negotiation, in which proclaimed intentions must be separated from hidden ones. Scan the human affairs columns for stories about conflicting desires and surmised intentions, or for legal cases about intent and insanity. Or simply read literature to see that human social interaction fundamentally requires that people infer and avow intentions as well as probe and affirm the intentionality of actions. If one took a Kantian approach to social cognition, searching for the fundamental concepts without which such cognition is impossible, intentionality would be one of those concepts, on par with space, time, and causality in the realm of non-social cognition.

Intentionality is a foundation for social cognition in several ways. For one, the concept of intentionality unlocks a central part of the folk ontology of mind, because intentionality's constituent components represent basic mental categories, such as belief, desire, and awareness. Moreover, the concept of intentionality brings order to the perception of behavior in that it allows the perceiver to detect structure—intentions and actions—in humans' complex stream of movement. Further, the intentionality concept supports coordinated social interaction by helping people explain their own and others' behavior in terms of its underlying mental causes. And intentionality plays a normative role in the social evaluation of behavior through its impact on assessments of responsibility and blame.

Intentionality is thus a tool with manifold functions, ranging from the conceptual to the interpersonal and even to the societal, and it is a tool with various domains of application, ranging from perception to explanation to interaction. Contemporary research on the role of intention and intention- ality in human social cognition has touched on all these functions and domains, but findings from this research are often discussed in isolation from one another. For example, much philosophical work has been devoted to analyzing the conceptual components of intentional action, but these analyses have rarely guided psychological research on the social perception of intentional behavior. Within psychology, the role of intentionality in explanations and in assignments of responsibility has been studied in devel- opmental psychology within the paradigm of "theory of mind" and in social psychology within the paradigm of "attribution theory," but little communication has occurred between these paradigms. The central aim of this volume is to bring together the various disciplines, approaches, and tra- ditions that have examined intentions and intentionality and to integrate current knowledge of this central facet of human cognition.

With this integrative aim in mind, we have organized this introductory chapter and the book by the major research questions being asked about intentionality across disciplines. A first set of questions concern how the concept of intentionality is defined within the folk theory of mind, what components make up this concept, how the components are related, and how they are acquired between infancy and adulthood. Earlier attempts to answer these questions can be found both in philosophy (e.g., Brand 1984; Mele and Moser 1994; Schueler 1995; Searle 1983) and in psychology (e.g., Astington and Gopnik 1991; Malle and Knobe 1997a; Maselli and Altrocchi 1969; Moses 1993). A second set of questions concern how peo- ple perceive human action and detect its underlying intentions and motives. These issues, which are a major focus of current research in developmental psychology (e.g., Barresi and Moore 1996; Baldwin and Baird 1999; Zelazo, Astington, and Olson 1999), have attracted considerable attention in philosophy (Bogdan 2000; Carruthers and Smith 1996; Davies and Stone 1995), as they did in early social psychology (Heider 1958). A third set of questions concern the role of intentionality in people's explanations of behavior, and especially its role in distinguishing "reason explanations" from "cause explanations." Here, too, pertinent work spans the disciplines of development (Bartsch and Wellman 1989; Kalish 1998), social psychol- ogy (Buss 1978; Malle 1999; White 1991), and philosophy (Audi 1993; Davidson 1963; Lennon 1990). A final set of questions concern the role of judgments of intentionality in the evaluation of human action in terms of responsibility and blame. These issues have been explored in legal, philosophical, and psychological writings (e.g., Duff 1990; Hart 1968; Shaver 1985; Wallace 1994; Williams 1993).

Conceptual Elements of Intentionality

If the study of intentionality is to be a successful cross-disciplinary enterprise, it will require conceptual clarification to establish a common conceptual language and a shared map with which to scout the territory. This is not merely a methodological desideratum. Conceptual clarity represents a necessary step toward a model of what intentionality consists of, what it means to people, and how it functions in the social world.

Intentionality has two quite different meanings. Brentano (1874) introduced it as a technical term that could be used to refer to the property of all mental states as being directed toward something. Desires, for example, may be directed toward attractive objects, and beliefs toward states of affairs (Searle 1983; Lyons 1995). Second, intentionality is the property of actions that makes ordinary people and scholars alike call them purposeful, meant, or done intentionally. The focus of this volume is on this second sense—more specific, on people's conceptions of this sense of intentionality.

Another important distinction is that between *intentionality* and *intention*. The two terms are sometimes equated in psychological writing, even though folk use and philosophical analysis mark them as distinct. Intentionality, as we have mentioned, is a quality of actions (those that are intentional or done on purpose), whereas intention is an agent's mental state that represents such actions. This type of mental state often precedes its corresponding action or even occurs without it. One can therefore ascribe intention to an agent without making a judgment of intentionality. The reverse is not true, however: The judgment of an action's intentionality typically implies the ascription of an intention to the agent. Whether this implication holds under all circumstances is still debated among philosophers (Adams 1986; Bratman 1987; Harman 1976; Mele, this volume), but studies of folk use have thus far supported it (Malle and Knobe 1997a).

Both intention and intentionality are complex concepts in that people apply them only when a number of conditions are met. The ascription of an intention to A requires minimally that one grants the agent a desire for some outcome O and a belief that A will likely lead to O (Malle and Knobe 1997a). But an intention cannot be reduced to this belief-desire pair nor are intention ascriptions just shorthands for elaborate desire ascriptions. Three chapters in part I explore what unique conditions underlie people's ascriptions of intention and how these conditions distinguish the folk concepts of intention and desire.

In chapter 2, Bertram Malle and Joshua Knobe contend that the two concepts are distinguished by three features: First, intentions are directed at the intender's own action whereas desires can be directed at anything. Second, intentions are based on some amount of reasoning whereas desires are typically the input to such reasoning. Third, intentions come with a characteristic commitment to perform the intended action whereas desires do not. Malle and Knobe provide conceptual arguments and empirical data to support the validity of this tripartite model. They also speculate about the psychological functions of the folk distinction between desire and intention.

In chapter 3, Louis Moses argues that, although preschool children have some appreciation of motivational aspects of intention, they are not especially cognizant of the fact that agents' beliefs constrain their intentions. Such belief constraints further distinguish intentions from desires. For example, although agents cannot intend what they believe to be impossible (Davis 1984; Grice 1971; Velleman 1989), there is nothing that prevents them from desiring it. Moses concludes that children aged 3 and younger may collapse desire and intention within a generic pro-attitude concept.

Janet Astington, in chapter 4, also traces developmental stages in mastering the folk concept of intention and disentangling it from desire. Paradoxically, intention can be thought of as either an early-arriving or a late-arriving concept within children's developing theory of mind: Infants seem to be able to detect intentions by age 1 (see part II), but not until age 5 do children reliably master the distinction between intentions and desires. The complex adult concept of intention must therefore be acquired gradually, with some aspects (e.g., object-directedness) acquired well before others (e.g., self-referentiality). Genuine understanding of intention, Astington hypothesizes, depends on the emergence of "metarepresentational" understanding—the child's understanding that people's beliefs and desires are mental representations of the world that mediate their actions in the world (Bartsch and Wellman 1995a; Perner 1991). Astington's hypothesis converges here with Moses's claim that an intention concept requires a belief concept, as the latter also rests on metarepresentational understanding.

The importance of metarepresentational understanding after age 3 poses a puzzle, however. Even 2-year-olds seem to have an understanding of mental states like goals or desire (Bartsch and Wellman 1995a; Wellman and Woolley 1990); thus, either children have already acquired a representational theory by age 3 or else their early understanding of desire, although mentalistic, is not representational. The latter would be an unusual combination of features in light of the philosophical tradition of defining mental states as representational states (Brentano 1874; Chisholm 1981; Searle 1983). In chapter 10, as one part of his larger argument, Alvin Goldman challenges the evidence and logic in support of such a non-representational desire concept.

The conditions for ascribing intentionality are even more complex than those for ascribing intention, as Alfred Mele demonstrates in chapter 1. Following Aristotle and Hume, philosophers have focused on desire and belief as primary features of intentionality; however, the mere presence of appropriate belief and desire states is not sufficient for an action to be intentional. For one thing, intentions are considered an additional condition of intentionality. A behavior may be performed in accordance with a belief-desire pair, but it would not count as intentional unless it was brought about by an intention grounded in that belief-desire pair (Brand 1984; Bratman 1987; Searle 1983; Thalberg 1984). Suppose Brenda fouls an opponent during a basketball game. Suppose further that we are certain Brenda wants to win the game and believes that fouling her opponent would help her win. Still, we can't be certain that she committed the foul intentionally unless we know of Brenda's specific intention, her *decision* to act on her desire and belief. Moreover, even a behavior that was based on appropriate desires and beliefs plus an intention may not count as intentional: The intention must also cause the action via skill rather than luck. For instance, a golf novice may (at most[1]) intend to hit a hole in one, but few would call the accomplished feat *intentional*. Both conceptual analyses and empirical studies have converged on identifying skill as a further necessary condition for intentionality (Malle and Knobe 1997a; Mele and Moser 1994). Finally, the folk concept of intentionality appears to require a particular kind of awareness on the part of the agent, namely, the awareness of acting as intended (informants call it "knowing what she is doing" (Malle and Knobe 1997a)). This condition shares some similarity with Searle's (1983) notion of an "intention-in-action" even though, somewhat surprisingly, Searle did not characterize intentions-in-action as conscious. Future research should address the stringency of the awareness condition as it applies to habitual and automatic daily actions (e.g., eating or driving). In his analysis of these conditions of intentionality, Mele poses a number of additional questions about the intentionality concept that invite further research, such as the generality of the intentionality-intention implication, the boundaries of skill, and the relevance of moral considerations for judgments of intentionality (as opposed to the relevance of intentionality considerations for moral judgments—see chapter 16).

Despite some disagreement over details, there is consensus across disciplines that intention and intentionality are complex states that are ascribed only if a set of simpler component states are present (in contrast to models of "direct perception" of intentionality, which are discussed in the following section). The ascription conditions for intention minimally include the presence of desire, belief, and some form of commitment; those for intentionality minimally include the presence of desire, belief, intention, skill, and awareness. This does not mean, of course, that perceivers always compute each and every component before they ascribe the resulting complex state. Many routine actions and familiar social contexts permit the spontaneous judgment of intentions or intentionality without explicitly checking as to whether each component is present. However, the constituent components are very likely to be considered when such judgments are difficult to make, or when they are debated (as in interpersonal conflict or in a court of law).

Analysis of the components of intention and intentionality offers many advantages. For one, it helps us to separate concepts and phenomena that adult social perceivers distinguish, such as desires, intentions, and intentionality. As a result, we can ask precise questions, such as "How does children's theory of mind develop from broad category distinctions to differentiated component concepts?" Moreover, unlike the full-blown concepts themselves, their constituent components can be relatively easily grounded in lower-order precursors, such as belief in perception, desire in bodily needs, and intention in acts of reaching—precursors that children may perceive both in themselves as agents (Russell 1996) and in others through social interactions (Bruner 1981; Dunn 1991). Analysis of components also sharpens our understanding of extraneous variables that influence judgments of intention and intentionality, among them emotions and stereotypes. Stereotypes may provide default assumptions about certain components, such as expectations about an agent's stable desires or beliefs, which may bias the perceiver toward or against ascribing intentions and intentionality. Finally, component models highlight a fundamental feature of folk theories of mind: that they consist of conceptual networks systematically relating beliefs, desires, intentions, and other mental states to one another and to observable behavior (Gopnik and Wellman 1994). These networks provide tools for parsing and organizing what might otherwise be a chaotic stream of mental experiences (in the case of self) and behaviors (in the case of both self and others).

Traditionally, intentions have been regarded as private mental states that one ascribes to individual persons. However, intentions can also be ascribed to pairs or groups of people, who may have a joint intention to see a movie together, win a game, or publish an edited volume. Recent work in philosophy and psychology (e.g., Abelson, Dasgupta, Park, and Banaji 1998; Bratman 1993; Gilbert 1989; O'Laughlin and Malle 2000; Searle 1990; Velleman 1997) has begun to explore the nature of such joint intentions and the intentionality ascribed to whole groups and even nations. In addition, psycholinguists have examined the emergence of shared meaning out of individual intentions, a necessary process for successful conversation and social coordination (Clark and Brennan 1991; Gibbs 1998; Krauss and Fussell 1996). Interesting questions about the "location" of joint intentions and the "location" of shared meaning arise. One wonders, for example, whether there actually exist group minds that "have" mental states or whether social perceivers merely metaphorically extend their folk ascriptions of mental states to group agents. These puzzles notwithstanding, the ascension from individual to shared mental phenomena is essential to human relations. Along these lines, Raymond Gibbs (chapter 5) examines the function of shared meaning in communication and argues that at least some intentions are not in the head but rather are emergent social phenomena. In addition, Daniel Ames, Eric Knowles, Michael Morris, Charles Kalish, Andrea Rosati, and Alison Gopnik (chapter 15) review recent psychological evidence that people comfortably apply their theory of mind to individual agents as well as to group agents and, moreover, that cultures seem to differ in their tendency to designate either groups or individuals as the primary agent category.

Reading Intentions and Intentionality

People typically read the intentions underlying the behavior of others readily and with little conscious effort. Of course failures occur, and these are sometimes serious enough to give rise to argument, legal action, or international conflict. However, such interpretive failures are rare when measured against the countless actions to which perceivers smoothly assign relevant intentional meanings—actions such as tooth brushing, newspaper reading, and kitchen cleaning. Even actions motivated by complex and potentially obscure intentions, such as the casting-about behavior occasioned by a search for a television remote control, often pose little interpretive difficulty for perceivers. The same can be said of novel actions. On first viewing a skiboarder in action, for instance, it is easy to recognize the intention of thrill seeking.

How do people so effortlessly detect intentions within the dynamic behavior stream and so readily apprehend their content, and how is such skill acquired in children's development? Surprisingly, these questions received little systematic examination before the relatively recent attempts by social psychologists. For example, following ideas that Asch (1952) borrowed from gestalt psychology, Newtson and his colleagues (see, e.g., Newtson 1973; Newtson and Engquist 1976) argued that people *directly perceive* others' intentions on witnessing their actions. Intentionality, and the specific intentions at play, are thought to be there within the behavior stream, waiting to be detected. Working within a similar direct-perception framework, Premack and his colleagues (see, e.g., Premack 1990; Premack and Premack 1995) provided nativist speculations about the origins of the human ability to read others' intentions. They suggested that infants arrive in the world biologically prepared to perceive certain kinds of animate motion (in particular, self-propelled motion) as intentional, and that infants and can recognize at least a small set of specific intentions (e.g., helping vs. hurting) on the basis of the different behavioral patterns associated with them.

Here it is important to separate possible claims about detecting intentionality (how perceivers recognize *that* an intention is being enacted) from those concerning the *content* of an agent's intention (how perceivers recognize which specific intention, or set of intentions, is being enacted). The direct-perception framework seems at least potentially fruitful in accounting for the former, but seriously flawed as an approach to the latter. Let us consider these points in turn. Concerning the detection of intentionality, organisms wired to read "intentional" anytime they encounter self-propelled motion would be off to something of a start, because of the correlation between such motion and intentional action (see also Mandler 1992 and Wellman and Phillips in this volume). Of course, they would then need to learn to suppress an intentionality reading for countless important exceptions involving self-propelled motion or the appearance of it: involuntary behaviors such as sneezing, accidental and incidental motions such as the inadvertent knocking of objects off counters, and the motion of many inanimates for which the cause of motion has either been missed or is not yet understood (e.g., feathers and leaves blown by the wind, falling rocks, cars and trains, computer cursors). Clearly, then, the direct-perception framework requires substantial embellishment to successfully account for the full spectrum of intentionality judgments that adult perceivers actually make. Nonetheless, it might well capture the essence of how infants get their start in the business of detecting intentionality.

In contrast, the direct-perception framework seems fundamentally unworkable as an account of how perceivers detect the *specific* intentions motivating others' behavior. Behavior patterns and intentions stand in a many-to-many relation (Baird 1999; Baldwin and Baird 1999; Searle 1984): One and the same action (e.g., pressing a hypodermic needle into another's arm) admits of multiple intentional interpretations (e.g., the intent to heal vs. harm), and one and the same intention (e.g., to heal) can give rise to many possible actions (e.g., referral, advice, medication, surgery). Moreover, an infinite number of possible intentions are consistent with any given action, yet only one of these candidates (or at most a very small set) is actually relevant and usually considered by perceivers. Searle (1984, p. 58) captures this beautifully:

> If I am going for a walk to Hyde Park, there are any number of things that are happening in the course of my walk, but their descriptions do not describe my intentional actions, because in acting, what I am doing depends in large part on what I think I am doing. So for example, I am also moving in the general direction of Patagonia, shaking the hair on my head up and down, wearing out my shoes, and moving a lot of air molecules. However, none of these other descriptions seems to get at what is essential about this action, as the action it is.

Searle's example makes obvious that the content of agents' intentions cannot be recovered directly from the behavior stream itself; too many possible intentions are recoverable in any given case. In other words: From the standpoint of the perceiver, the content of agents' intentions is radically underdetermined by their behavior.

An alternative approach views the detection of intentions and intentionality as the outcome of an inferential system. (See, e.g., Baldwin 1993b; Baldwin and Baird 1999; Dittrich and Lea 1994; Meltzoff 1995; Tomasello, Kruger, and Ratner 1993.) Unlike the direct-perception account, this inferential framework readily accommodates, at least in principle, our ability as perceivers to deal with the complex link between actions and intentions. The specific intention motivating a given action is thought to be inferred not just from the flow of behavior itself but also from external information, including other cues in the immediate context (e.g., a medical setting such as a clinic, the presence of doctors, nurses, and medical supplies), prior knowledge about the agent (e.g., a physician vs. a violent offender), and the script within which the agent's motions are embedded (e.g., a physical exam vs. a session of interrogation and torture). Sensitivity to such "extra-behavioral" characteristics could enable perceivers to constrain their inferences about intentions in the face of the limitless possibilities.

In addition to providing a possible account for the ability to interpret the content of agents' intentions, the inferential approach seems amenable to explaining how people distinguish intentional from unintentional or incidental behavior. Because behaviors from these different classes seem structurally different in many cases (e.g., self-propelled motion is often intentional whereas motion caused by direct physical contact with another moving body rarely is), processing of the behavior stream can play an important role in making these distinctions. This is why the direct-perception framework also can offer something in accounting for such ability. However, the inferential approach again has the advantage in that it also has the potential to explain the finer judgments about intentionality that social perceivers make—for example, the ability to recognize the behavior of sleepwalkers and "zombies" as unintentional despite the surface similarity of such motion to that of conscious agents. In such cases, an inferential account would point to information external to the behavior stream (e.g., night-time setting, history of night-time talking and walking, lack of response to questions, known ingestion of mind-altering substances) as crucial in shaping the perceiver's inferences about the agent's intentionality.

The chapters in part II all speak (at least implicitly) to the inferential framework. Each offers new ideas and new evidence regarding the processes involved in detecting intentions. In chapter 9, Jodie Baird and Dare Baldwin highlight some of the qualities requisite to an inferential system for intentional understanding. In particular, they propose that such an inferential system crucially depends on the operation of a low-level structure-detection mechanism capable of analyzing the dynamic behavior stream into relevant units—units coinciding with the initiation and the completion of intentions—for further analysis. Moreover, they present new evidence that adults as well as 10–11-month-old infants spontaneously parse continuous intentional action in terms of just such "intention-relevant" units.

To date, the preponderance of work within the inferential approach has focused on development, exploring infants' and young children's emerging abilities to detect and interpret the intentions motivating others' behavior. Many of the chapters in part II reflect this trend, as they deal primarily with developmental evidence. In chapter 7, Amanda Woodward, Jessica Somerville, and José Guajardo present research indicating that infants as young as 9 months understand the goal-oriented quality of some intentional actions and can distinguish between intentional and unintentional action in at least some cases. Further, they find that at this early age infants already use information external to the behavior stream to determine the relevance of a goal object. For example, previously provided information about an agent's interest in the contents of a box led infants to construe a subsequent box-grasping action as goal-oriented; in the absence of such prior information, infants failed to register the action's goal-oriented quality.

This "action-in-context" effect meshes nicely with the predictions of the inferential framework described above, which is grounded in the idea that intentions are inferred by interpreting action within its larger context.

Inferential theorists concerned with how children come to detect intentions and intentionality typically think in constructivist—as opposed to purely nativist—terms. To the extent that judgments about intentions are derived through complex inferential processes depending on experience and world knowledge, conceptual change within this arena is to be expected as development proceeds. Many of the chapters in part II manifest this partiality for constructivist speculation regarding the origins of intentional understanding. For example, in discussing the origins of early intentional understanding, Henry Wellman and Ann Phillips (chapter 6) offer an analysis of the kind of input regarding intentions and intentionality that might be available to infants through observation of others' behavior. They go on to present new evidence that infants as young as 12 months are sensitive to two perceptible features of behavior—object-directedness and action-connectedness—that are typical of intentional action. As Wellman and Phillips suggest, early recognition of these features may not actually reflect a genuine understanding of the agent's intentions; rather, it may represent crucial steps toward such understanding. In a similar vein, Woodward and colleagues (chapter 7) have found that infants at 9 months process some actions (such as grasping) in ways that are relevant to intentions but fail to process other actions (such as pointing) in these terms. This is among the first evidence suggesting that abilities enabling the detection of intentional content are constructed through infants' world experience. In chapter 9, Baird and Baldwin suggest that a low-level mechanism for analyzing action plays a crucial role in making possible developmental change of the kind that Woodward et al. demonstrate.

In chapter 8, Andrew Meltzoff and Rechele Brooks provide important ballast to the constructivist stance by embracing a hybrid account that credits newborns with crucial skills for interpreting others' actions. Such an account helps to explain how typically developing children so easily and naturally come to understand others' intentions. Meltzoff and Brooks propose a "starting-state nativism" that consists of innate foundations that are modified by extensive development and practice in social interactions. The innate foundations are at work, for example, when a newborn imitates someone's actions, thus translating a perceived act into an act of its own. This imitation relies on a mapping between others and self—at birth, on the level of actions. By 18 months, this mapping occurs on the level of goals. Meltzoff and Brooks describe experiments in which infants observed another person engaging in action that failed with respect to goal attainment (e.g., an attempt to open a device was unsuccessful) but nevertheless inferred the goal and spontaneously performed the action that successfully led to the goal (opening the device). Meltzoff and Brooks argue that the pivotal element in early imitation, in later goal inference, and in many other achievements of infant social cognition is the "like me" analogy—the tendency to see others' acts as being like acts the infants can produce themselves. As they experience their own attempts to control behavior, infants build maps that link effort experiences, goals, and their own actions, and they use these maps to infer others' goals from observed actions.

The idea of an innate analogical process shares important similarities with a simulation theory account such as the one suggested by Alvin Goldman in chapter 10. Like Meltzoff and Brooks, Goldman offers his account as an alternative to a purely inferential framework. A key element of his model is the distinction between first-person and third-person attributions of mental states. Goldman argues that first-person attributions are based not on inference but rather on a form of direct perception, or introspection. He defends this proposal against recent skepticism regarding the possibility of introspection (e.g., Gopnik 1993). Goldman goes on to argue that social perceivers make third-person attributions of mental states with the help of first-person access, using simulation processes to re-create and thereby represent others' mental states. He then musters various lines of evidence for the plausibility of simulation as a core mechanism of intention reading. This evidence includes the intriguing possibility of "mirror neurons" in primates that seem to fire both when the organism perceives certain actions performed by others and when it performs that action itself—a mechanism not unlike the supramodal representation system discussed by Meltzoff and Brooks in chapter 8.

Any attempt to account for the ability to read others' intentions must grapple with the extent to which such skill is special to humans. On the one hand, there is an obvious gulf dividing humans from other species in terms of the complexity of reasoning about others' intentions. Imputing to others complex intentions with multiple subparts, such as intentions to embezzle funds for charitable purposes or to run for president of the United States in good faith but with little hope of success is everyday fare for humans, but as far as we can tell nothing of comparable complexity has ever been seen in other species. On the other hand, behavior that powerfully suggests the essence of intention-reading ability is ubiquitous in interactions between humans and other species and in interactions among members of other species. A dog's suspicion at signs indicating an intention to bathe him and his ecstasy when he notes preparations for a walk are examples familiar to many. Other examples are easy to find throughout modern literature, even at the academic level; witness two influential volumes concerning the social understanding and the "Machiavellian intelligence" of higher primates (Byrne and Whiten 1986; Whiten and Byrne 1997).

In chapter 11, Daniel Povinelli describes a substantial body of work investigating these issues. Based on the evidence, he suggests that chimpanzees lack a genuine appreciation for the intentions motivating others' actions, despite their evident skill at processing such actions in ways that enable them to predict and influence others' behavior. To account for this apparent paradox, Povinelli proposes the operation of two independent mechanisms. One is the skill of analyzing, correlating, and predicting complex patterns of behavior on the merely behavioral level; the other comprises genuinely mentalistic reasoning about intentions and intentionality underlying behavior. On this proposal, both humans and chimpanzees are skilled at behavior analysis but only humans are capable of mentalistic reasoning. And Povinelli speculates that the developmental progress from infants' behavior analysis to preschoolers' mentalistic reasoning may be a qualitative step—the emergence of a separate mechanism—rather than a gradual elaboration of a single mechanism from its incipient to its mature stage.

Intentionality and Explanations

Explanations of behavior are regarded by many as a key function of folk psychology, and the concept of intentionality plays a pivotal role in the construction of such explanations. Behavior explanations take cognitions of behavior (including judgments about the behavior's intentionality) as input and render as output a model of what generated the behavior, often including reference to mental states such as beliefs, desires, and intentions. Such a model, in turn, influences judgments of responsibility, predictions of future behavior, and attempts to change the behavior.

Various traditions of explanation research across disciplines can be organized along two dimensions: whether or not the role of intentionality in explanations is considered, and whether or not explanations are studied in their natural context of conversation and social interaction. Figure 1 shows the resulting four combinations.

The first cell contains approaches to explanation that do not consider the role of intentionality and analyze explanations independently of the interactive context in which they occur. According to this *causal judgment* approach, explanations are cognitive processes (often unconscious) that apply equally to all objects of explanation, be they physical or behavioral, intentional or unintentional events. Prime representatives of this approach include Kelley's (1967) ANOVA model of causal attribution and its variants (e.g., Hewstone and Jaspars 1987), the cognitive study of causal reasoning (Spellman 1997; Cheng and Novick 1990), and normative models of scientific explanation (Hempel and Oppenheim 1948). The strength of this approach is that it focuses on the common cognitive principle of all explanations: that they identify causal antecedents of the explanandum according to rules of logic and evidence. At the same time, this focus is also its major weakness, because distinctions among explananda (e.g., actions vs. physical events) and corresponding distinctions between causal models

ROLE OF INTENTIONALITY

INTERACTIVE CONTEXT

	not considered	considered
not considered	Causal Judgment Approach	Intentional Approach
considered	Communicative Approach	Folk-Theoretical Approach

Figure 1
Four approaches to the study of explanation.

are overlooked, as is the social context that gives explanations their function, regardless of how they are cognitively (or physiologically) realized.

The second cell contains paradigms that still analyze explanations independently of their interactive context but that consider the role of intentionality by distinguishing between two types of explananda (intentional human action vs. all other events) and their corresponding types of explanation (often labeled *reasons* and *causes*). Representatives of this *intentional* approach include the hermeneutic movement in the social sciences (e.g., Gadamer 1989; Harre and Secord 1972; von Wright 1971) and the substantial contingent of philosophers who consider reason explanations of intentional action to be unique and irreducible (e.g., Audi 1993; Davidson 1963; Mele 1992a; Taylor 1964). The strength of this approach is that it recognizes important conceptual differences between two types of explanation and tries to work out the implications for theories of science, motivation, and action. However, the psychological reality of the two types of explanation has not been explored within this tradition, because it regards explanations primarily as logical entities rather than as verbal behaviors. Philosophers of action sometimes assume that ordinary people, too, distinguish between reasons and causes, but no systematic empirical data are ever mustered in support of this assumption.

The third cell contains the *communicative* approach, which emphasizes the social context and function of explanations, especially their dialogical nature in both everyday and scientific settings (Antaki 1994; Bromberger 1965; Hilton 1990; Kidd and Amabile 1981; Turnbull and Slugoski 1988). Explanations are seen as answers to why-questions, filling a knowledge gap exhibited by the questioner. (The explainer and the questioner are typically separate individuals, but in the case of private explanations they are identical.) Scholars within this approach—e.g., Slugoski, Lalljee, Lamb, and Ginsburg (1993)—have recognized that causal judgments are responsive to the social demands created by why-questions, such that explainers search for and present different explanations depending on their inferences about the questioner's background and the particular knowledge gap that is to be filled. For example, when Q asks E "How come Mary bought a Mercedes?" E might answer "Because it's a good car." However, if E considers that Q asks the question because Q knows Mary is poor, a more appropriate answer would be "Because she inherited a load of money" (McClure and Hilton

1997). Variations in explanations are therefore understood not just in terms
of different causal perceptions but also in terms of different social demands
that the explainer tries to meet (Malle, Knobe, O'Laughlin, Pearce, and
Nelson 2000). Perceived gaps in knowledge present the most obvious
demands; authority and accountability have also been examined (Edwards
and Potter 1993; Scott and Lyman 1968; Tedeschi and Reiss 1981).

The communicative approach shares with the causal-judgment approach
its major strength and its major weakness: It identifies general principles of
explanation but does not distinguish between different types of explananda;
hence, it still assumes that humans have a uniform conceptual model of
causality. The consideration of social context, however, is a distinct strength
of the communicative approach. Important questions follow from this consideration, such as whether the "truth" of an explanation depends solely on
a speaker's and an audience's assumptions and to what extent social demands
may modify not only verbal behavior but actual causal perceptions.

The fourth cell contains approaches emphasizing both the role of intentionality in explanations and the social-interactive context in which explanations are embedded. We call this the *folk-theoretical* approach because it
considers explanations as an integral part of folk theories for core domains
of cognition, such as psychology, physics, and biology (Carey 1995; Malle
1997; Wellman, Hickling, and Schult 1997). Within folk psychology, explanations heavily implicate the concept of intentionality in that all human
behavior is classified as either intentional or unintentional and (depending
on the classification) explained in conceptually distinct ways (Buss 1978;
Locke and Pennington 1982; Kalish 1998; Malle 1999; Read 1987; White
1991). In particular, unintentional behavior is explained by mere causes,
which are seen as simply bringing about the effect in a mechanical way (sadness causes crying; sunshine causes happiness). In contrast, intentional
behavior is explained by reasons—the beliefs and desires in light of which
the agent formed an intention to act.

Unlike scholars who take the intentional approach, those who endorse
the folk-theoretical approach do not try to clarify the nature of explanation
in a philosophical sense, nor do they necessarily postulate the objective
existence of intentionality. Instead, they analyze explanations and intentionality as cognitive tools that guide people's perception, prediction, and control of their environment. Explanations are thus assigned a psychological

reality that is grounded in a shared folk-conceptual framework. In addition, and in agreement with the communicative approach, some researchers consider explanations also to be a social tool, expressed and strategically used in social interaction (Bartsch and Wellman 1995a; Malle and Knobe 1997b; Malle et al. 2000).

A possible weakness of the folk-theoretical approach is that, in appreciating the complexity and the variability of explanations in particular domains, it may lose the generality that other approaches seek. However, domain specificity is not incompatible with generality. Some functions of explanations (e.g., the need to anticipate and control one's environment (Heider 1958) and the desire to propel one's theoretical understanding of it (Gopnik 1998)) hold across domains; other functions (e.g., the face-saving and evaluative character of behavior explanations) are specific to particular domains. The same might be said of the cognitive processes underlying explanations, of which some may be domain-general (e.g., considerations of temporal order in causal processes) and others domain-specific (e.g., considerations of rationality in explanations of intentional behavior). Future research will have to clarify the exact similarities and differences among different types of explanation, but the contribution of the folk concept of intentionality to some of these differences is already apparent.

Several recent advances in folk-explanation research are driven by the assumption that people learn to master not one but a variety of modes of explanation (e.g., Kalish 1998; Malle 1999; McClure and Hilton 1997; Wellman et al. 1997). One question to be settled is whether these modes of explanation can be distinguished solely by their domain of application (Wellman et al. 1997; Schult and Wellman 1997) or whether they exhibit distinct conceptual structures (Kalish 1998; Malle 1999). Broad domain distinctions (e.g., physics, biology, psychology) provide useful approximations of explanatory types, but they may be less helpful for distinguishing modes of explanation within the richest of domains: that of human behavior. Because humans can be characterized as physical, biological, and psychological systems, explanations of human behavior encompass all the forms of explanation employed in other domains but also make use of unique modes that apply only to intentional action.

All the chapters in part III deal in one way or another with the interplay and the distinctions among the various modes of explaining human behavior. In chapter 12, G. F. Schueler takes a close look at the tension between two ways of explaining intentional action: by means of the agent's own reasons, and by means of objective causal processes that seem to leave no room for genuine reasons. He argues that reason explanations are distinct from and not reducible to standard causal explanations because they fundamentally incorporate normative features. Even reason explanations offered by an observer must mimic the normative reasoning process the agent went through when deciding to act.

In chapter 13, Bertram Malle argues that folk explanations of intentional behavior encompass three different modes, with *reason* explanations the primary one and *causal history of reason* explanations and *enabling factor* explanations the secondary ones. Malle proposes a model that distinguishes these modes by their conceptual, linguistic, and functional features and contrasts this model with alternative theories of attribution and explanation. He also explores what implications this plurality of explanation modes has for the well-known debate between "theory theorists" (who assume that people ascribe mental states by relying on an organized set of generalizations) and "simulation theorists" (who assume that people ascribe mental states by relying on their capacity to simulate these states in their own mind).

In chapter 14, Andrea Rosati, Eric Knowles, Charles Kalish, Alison Gopnik, Daniel Ames, and Michael Morris explore the possible reconciliation between behavior explanations referring to the agent's mental states and behavior explanations referring to the agent's enduring traits. Rosati et al. identify mental-state components in trait concepts and demonstrate that trait inferences rely crucially on mental-state inferences. In the past, mental-state explanations were featured in the theory of mind tradition and trait explanations in the social-psychological attribution tradition. Rosati et al. attempt to integrate these rather disparate paradigms of research into social cognition.

Intentionality, Responsibility, and Social Context

Interpersonal perception encompasses not only cold assessments of others' mental states but also affective and moral responses to those states and to the social actions the states generate. These responses, which include praise, blame, pride, shame, resentment, and gratitude, may well be unique to humans. They stake out the evaluative and corrective functions of the folk theory of mind, and they place issues of intentionality in a larger societal context. Moral responses are inextricably linked to the constituents of intentionality, to mental-state inferences, and to explanations of action, the topics discussed in parts I–III of this volume. But exactly how these connections should be understood—that is, exactly how intentionality relates to moral responsibility—is a matter of some debate in psychology, philosophy, and the law. Below we provide a conceptual framework for studying the intentionality–responsibility connection, and we locate some recent literature as well as this volume's contributions within that framework.

Responsibility has many meanings (cf. Frey and Morris 1991; Hamilton and Sanders 1992; Hart 1968), and so the role of intentionality in responsibility will differ depending on the meaning in view. *Responsibility* or *being responsible* always refers to a socially ascribed relation that holds either (1) between an agent and a specific action or outcome, (2) between an agent and that agent's general capacity for acting, or (3) between a cause and an effect. The third relation casts responsibility merely as causality (e.g., "The hurricane was responsible for 10 deaths"[2]), a derivative meaning that exports the first (agent/outcome) meaning of responsibility from the psychological realm into the realm of natural events but removes its implication of intentional agency. We therefore focus here on the two principal meanings, which might be labeled *normative responsibility* and *responsibility as agency*. (For similar distinctions, see Bratman 1997, note 7.)

Normative responsibility establishes a normative relation between an agent and a specific action or outcome. This relation is cast either as *duty* ("Mulder and Scully are responsible for investigating every paranormal event in the country") or as *liability* (liableness to blame[3]) ("That constitutes child neglect and the parents should be held responsible!"). Duty and liability are normative in that they refer to social rules or expectations that dictate what the agent should do or should have done (Hamilton 1978). Responsibility as duty is typically used in a forward-looking manner to direct the agent's future actions ("What are your responsibilities at your new job?"). One *has* such responsibilities because they are *given* or *assumed*. Responsibility as liability is typically used in a backward-looking manner to respond to negative outcomes ("Police and public officials are not responsible for the attack"). One is *held* responsible or *accepts* responsibility for those outcomes (which usually means that one is blamed or accepts blame). In practice, the two normative relations are often blended, as pre-existing duties are considered when assigning liability (Haidt and Baron 1996; Hamilton 1978).

Responsibility as duty presupposes the capacity for intentional action. Assigning specific duties to a person is pointless unless one assumes that the person can intentionally fulfill them. Responsibility as liability, too, pre-supposes the capacity for intentional action: Liability is assigned when the agent could and should have acted so as to prevent the outcome but didn't (Hamilton and Sanders 1992; Weiner 1995). "Could have" corresponds to an assumption of preventability or intentional controllability; "should have" corresponds to an assumption of duty. Liability does not, however, presuppose factual intentionality—agents can be liable to blame even for outcomes they did not bring about intentionally but rather caused through negligence or recklessness (Duff 1990; Hart 1968). Intentionality amplifies liability, to be sure, and lack of intention can ameliorate it (Heider 1958; Schlenker, Britt, Pennington, Murphy, and Doherty 1994). But liability holds even for unintentionally caused outcomes, as long as the agent had the intentional capacity and duty to prevent that outcome.

Beginning with the classic work of Piaget (1932), research on children's developing moral reasoning has emphasized the transition from judgments based solely on outcome severity to judgments incorporating or even focusing on the agent's intentions and motives. This transition occurs in the preschool period (Nelson-LeGall 1985; Yuill and Perner 1988), apparently after a child begins to distinguish intentional from unintentional behavior (Shultz 1980) and to ascribe motives to agents (Bartsch and Wellman 1995a). Not surprisingly, it seems to take a child some time to learn to apply the intentionality concept to the new function of distinguishing a blame-worthy from a blameless state of mind.

An even more complex step occurs when a child learns that sometimes even unintentional behaviors leave the actor subject to blame. In chapter 17, Michael Chandler, Bryan Sokol, and Darcey Hallett explore this intriguing developmental step. As was mentioned above, adults hold agents responsible when they are perceived to have been capable of preventing the behavior and to have a duty to do so. Chandler et al. demonstrate that by age 5 children begin to take these counterfactuals into account when making judgments of blame. Furthermore, they argue that this advance in moral reasoning is tied to the onset of a "constructivist" theory of mind—one that fully appreciates that human agents interpret and construct what they know about the world but that their interpretations and their ensuing moral conduct can be more or less justified.

Responsibility as agency, the second principal meaning of responsibility, refers to an agent's general capacity to perform autonomous, rational action (e.g., "The successful performance of chores is another way that patients can demonstrate they are ready for greater financial responsibility"). To act with responsibility in this sense requires the ability to consider the consequences of one's actions and to choose an action with desirable consequences ("Taking responsibility means accepting the consequences of your own choices"). Responsible agency thus presupposes intentionality in the form of planning, deliberation, and reasoning (Bratman 1997; Hart 1968). Indeed, these planning features of intentionality define a particular version of responsible agency: acting with good judgment ("If you choose to drink alcohol, drink responsibly"). However, exactly what goes into the concept of responsible agency beyond the capacity for intentional action is still debated among philosophers (see, e.g., Bratman 1997; Fischer 1994; Wallace 1994). Proposed criteria include rationality, communicative capacity, and responsiveness to reasons. The choice of these criteria has great practical importance; for example, it affects sentiments and decisions about the responsibility of children and that of mental patients. However, there have been no empirical studies exploring what the criteria for responsible agency might be. Psychological research (see, e.g., Fincham and Jaspars 1980; Shaver 1985; Weiner 1995) has focused almost exclusively on the conditions under which people assign liability, leaving discussions of factors that constitute responsible agency to legal and philosophical scholars.

Normative responsibility, responsibility as agency, and intentionality are closely intertwined concepts. Responsible agency presupposes intentionality (the capacity to deliberate about and choose one's course of action). Normative responsibility in turn presupposes responsible agency (hence intentional capacity), for unless one considers an agent equipped with responsible agency in general one cannot assign to this agent any specific duties or any liability for specific outcomes. Thus, the folk-psychological assumption that humans are capable of intentional action underlies both of the principal meanings of responsibility; as a result, judgments of intention and intentionality permeate the social practices of praise, blame, reward, and punishment (Marshall 1968; Williams 1993).

The fundamental role that the assumption of intentionality plays in responsibility is further highlighted when we consider the social role and function of responsibility attributions. The practice of assigning responsibility—in all its meanings—serves the coordination and organization of social activities, the maintenance of social order, and the enforcement of social rules (Heider 1944; Schlick 1966; Semin and Manstead 1983). Normative responsibility, in particular, lays the foundation for a social feedback system in which desirable outcomes yield a premium and undesirable outcomes are sanctioned. But this normative system applies only to those outcomes that are in principle controllable by intentional agency (excluding, for example, natural disasters) and involves only those agents who are equipped with responsible agency (excluding, for example, young children and some mental patients). This feedback system has often been discussed in theoretical terms, but few scholars have explored it in detail. In chapter 16, Bernard Weiner does exactly that, detailing some of the system's cognitive, emotional, and behavioral elements and using a model centered on the concept of controllability to account for moral sentiments (such as anger or pity), philosophies of punishment, and individual differences in political ideology.

Two chapters put intentionality and responsibility in their larger social and cultural contexts. In chapter 15, Ames, Knowles, Morris, Kalish, Rosati, and Gopnik try to integrate considerations of norms and context into the often purely cognitive models of social perception. They examine, in particular, how people's social and cultural contexts shape their judgments of intentionality and responsibility as well as their mental-state ascriptions and their behavior explanations. In chapter 18, Leonard Kaplan analyzes how conceptions of intentional agency and responsibility interrelate and, more important, how they are in tension with expectations of justice in the modern state. Kaplan examines several models of moral action and identifies their varying assumptions about intentional agency, responsibility, and justice. Because all these models center on responsibility as the ethical duty to be responsive to another's needs, classic issues of social cognition arise when the models specify to what extent an individual is capable of recognizing the suffering of others and distinguishing it from deception or exploitation. Even though the particular ethical problem of enabling justice in the modern state must remain unsolved, Kaplan's analysis illustrates how ethical discourse presupposes the agent's capacity to act intentionally and to perceive and interpret the social world and other beings within it.

Conclusions

Theories and research programs on the role of intention and intentionality in social cognition are distributed over many scholars, traditions, and disciplines. These individual efforts, though united by the goal of elucidating interpersonal understanding, have often remained isolated from one another. A unifying theory of how humans understand other humans will have to emerge from communication and collaboration across the traditional boundaries of paradigms and disciplines. The research brought together in this volume, we hope, both attests to the fundamental role of intentionality in human social cognition and offers noteworthy progress toward a broad and interdisciplinary account of human social relations.

Acknowledgments

Preparation of this chapter was supported by a National Science Foundation CAREER award (No. 9703315) to Bertram Malle and by a National Science Foundation New Young Investigator Award (No. 9458339) and a John Merck Scholars Award to Dare Baldwin. The chapter was prepared while Dare Baldwin was a fellow at the Center for Advanced Study in the Behavioral Sciences; she is grateful for the financial support provided by the William T. Grant Foundation under award 95167795.

Notes

1. On the appropriateness of ascribing to such an agent only an intention to try to A, not an intention to A, see Mele 1989.
2. Quoted examples were found by searching the World Wide Web and various newspapers for sentences containing the words *responsibility* or *responsible*.
3. This meaning of responsibility is also labeled accountability, answerability, or blameworthiness in the literature. Its legal version is liableness for punishment.

I
Desires, Intentions, and Intentionality

1
Acting Intentionally: Probing Folk Notions

Alfred R. Mele

What is it to do something *intentionally*? Philosophical work on this question is motivated by a variety of interrelated concerns. In trying to understand and explain human action, a project that is as old as Plato and Aristotle, philosophers of action are concerned primarily with intentional actions. In discussions of freedom of action, intentional action also naturally occupies center stage. And although people are morally accountable for some unintentional actions, as in cases of negligence, moral assessment of actions is focused primarily upon intentional actions.

In my opinion, any adequate answer to my opening question will be anchored by common-sense judgments about particular hypothetical or actual actions. One can test attempted philosophical analyses of intentional action partly by ascertaining whether what these analyses entail about particular actions is in line with what the majority of nonspecialists would say about these actions. Although I doubt that common-sense *theories* about philosophical issues are likely to be much more successful than common-sense theories about topics in physics, economics, or psychology, I believe that we have good reason to take seriously common-sense judgments about whether an adequately described action is or is not intentional. Making plausible judgments of this kind normally is not a terribly demanding task; it certainly is far less demanding than constructing a plausible theory about the nature of intentional action. It is also worth noting that if there is a widely shared concept of intentional action, such judgments provide evidence about what that concept is, and a philosophical analysis of intentional action that is wholly unconstrained by that concept runs the risk of having nothing more than a philosophical fiction as its subject matter.

In a ground-breaking paper, Bertram Malle and Joshua Knobe (1997a) report the results of some empirical studies of the "folk concept" of intentional action. They write (p. 111):

In people's folk concept of intentionality, performing an action intentionally requires the presence of five components: a desire for an outcome; beliefs about an action that leads to that outcome; an intention to perform the action; skill to perform the action; and awareness of fulfilling the intention while performing the action.[1]

In the first section, I will argue that this statement of necessary conditions for intentional action needs refinement. In the second and third sections, I will identify some additional issues one would need to explore in constructing a statement of individually necessary and jointly *sufficient* conditions for intentional action. I will conclude with a brief discussion of the conceptual analyst's task.

Testing Malle and Knobe's Five Conditions

The Desire and Belief Conditions

Is it true that performing an action intentionally requires "a desire for an outcome and beliefs about an action that leads to that outcome"? Consider the following case. While happily doing some carpentry work in his workshop, John whistles a happy tune and enjoys his whistling. He is quite conscious both of his whistling and of his enjoying it. Is John whistling intentionally?

I believe that the great majority of speakers of English would answer this question affirmatively. (Obviously, we can ask people about this and see what they say.) But does John's intentionally whistling the tune require that he have a desire for a relevant outcome and a belief to the effect that his whistling, or his whistling this tune, is a means to that outcome? Elsewhere (Mele 1992a, chapter 6), I have argued that the answer is No. Some of our intentional actions are not directed at any further goal—that is, any goal external to the action itself. John's whistling may well be a case in point. Even if most intentional actions are directed at some further goal and therefore are plausibly explained in part by a desire-belief complex of the sort Malle and Knobe have in mind, we have no assurance that *all* intentional actions are like this.

Now, if we were to ask nonspecialists whether performing an action intentionally requires "a desire for an outcome and beliefs about an action that leads to that outcome," we might well find that the great majority say Yes. But that finding, I suggest, should not carry nearly as much weight in the project of constructing an analysis of "the folk concept" of intentional action as the finding that the great majority deem John's whistling intentional. After all, the general question about the dependence of intentional action on desire-belief complexes is more deeply theoretical than the question whether John's whistling is intentional, and in thinking about the general question nonspecialists may focus exclusively on paradigmatic cases of action—that is, "instrumental" intentional actions, actions directed at a further goal.

In discussing their five conditions, Malle and Knobe indicate that desires and beliefs of the kind they mention contribute *indirectly* to intentional action: Desires and beliefs influence our intentional actions by influencing what we *intend* (p. 108). If my suggestion about John's case is correct, it may be that some intentions are not produced by a combination of desire and instrumental belief, and that Malle and Knobe's instrumentalist desire and belief conditions are dispensable in the case of intentional actions that execute these intentions. I should emphasize that the present worry is specifically about the *instrumentalist* nature of Malle and Knobe's belief-desire constraint on intentional action—the idea that every intentional action requires a desire for an outcome and a belief that links the action performed to that outcome as (roughly) a means to an end. Plainly, if John's end or goal in his intentional whistling act is the whistling act itself and he does not whistle for the sake of a further goal, then his intentional whistling act is not explained by a desire for a further goal and a belief that links his whistling to that goal. This leaves it open, of course, that there are alternative desire and belief conditions that accommodate intentional actions of the kind at issue.[2]

Some philosophers would object to Malle and Knobe's desire and belief conditions on grounds having to do with "double effect." (See, e.g., Bratman 1987; Harman 1976; 1986.) I myself am not such a philosopher, but the issue certainly merits attention. Consider this example (Harman 1976, p. 433): "In firing his gun, [a sniper who is trying to kill a soldier] knowingly alerts the enemy to his presence." Harman claims that, although the sniper "does not intend to alert the enemy to his presence," he nevertheless *intentionally* alerts the enemy, "thinking that the gain is worth the possible cost." Plainly, it is false that the sniper alerts the enemy because he has a desire for some relevant outcome and a belief that his alerting the enemy is a means to that outcome.

If Harman is right in claiming that the sniper intentionally alerts the enemy in this case, then not only is it false that Malle and Knobe's belief and desire conditions are required for intentional action; it is also false that their *intention* condition is required—that is, intending to A is not a necessary condition for intentionally A-ing. But is Harman right? I doubt it. To be sure, Harman's sniper does not unknowingly or accidentally alert his enemy. For that reason, many people may deny that the sniper *unintentionally* alerts the enemy. But that denial does not, in any *obvious* way, commit one to holding that he *intentionally* alerts the enemy. Perhaps there is a middle ground between intentional and unintentional action. Arguably, actions that an agent in no way aims at performing but that are not performed unknowingly or accidentally are properly located on that middle ground. They might be *non*intentional, as opposed to *un*intentional (Mele and Moser 1994, p. 45; Mele and Sverdlik 1996, p. 274).

Empirical data on how people respond to cases of double effect would be useful in testing Malle and Knobe's statement of necessary conditions for intentional action. Even if their instrumentalist belief and desire conditions are undermined by cases in which an intentional action is not directed at a further goal, these conditions—and their intention condition—may be quite consistent with common-sense judgments about what is done intentionally in cases of double effect. In any case, a comprehensive empirical investigation of the folk concept of intentional action should tell us whether that concept includes or excludes actions such as Harman's sniper's alerting the enemy.

The Intention Condition
Does performing an action intentionally require "an intention to perform the action"? If asked, I suppose, most people would say Yes. But a more reliable test of what the folk concept of intentional action implies about the connection between intention and intentional action would feature judiciously selected examples of action.

I begin with some conceptual background. The conceptual connection between intention and intentional action obviously depends not only on what it is to do something intentionally but also on what it is to *intend* to do something. A relatively popular claim among philosophers is that agents intend at a time t_1 to do something A at a time t_2—where t_1 and t_2 may or may not be identical—only if they believe at t_1 that they (probably) will do A at t_2.[3] The proposal is designed to capture, among other things, the *confidence* in one's success that intending allegedly involves. A less demanding claim—one that I have defended elsewhere (Mele 1992a, chapter 8)—is that intending at t_1 to do A at t_2 requires that, at t_1, one *lack* the belief that one (probably) will *not* do A at t_2.[4] (The person might have no belief on the matter.) If there is a folk concept of intention, what it has to say about various alleged belief or "confidence" constraints on intention may be tested by eliciting lay responses to an appropriate range of cases.[5]

Consider the following scenarios:

(1) Because Karl would like to become an instant millionaire, he buys a lottery ticket. He knows that the odds against his winning the big prize are astronomical.

(2) Although there are no lotteries in Lydia's state, there is a weekly million-dollar contest for amateur golfers. Contestants pay a dollar for the privilege of taking a single shot at making a hole in one from a distance of 180 yards. Lydia has never hit a golf ball, but, desperately wanting to become a millionaire and thinking that there is a remote chance that she will make a hole in one, she enters the contest. She has seen golf on television, and she estimates her chances of holing her shot at about one in a million. As Lydia eyes the ball, she deliberates about how she might achieve her goal of making a hole in one, giving special attention to what club to use. She selects a three wood, lines up the shot, and then swings hard, with the goal of making a hole in one and winning the big prize. (Mele 1997a, pp. 22–23)

(3) Mary steps up to the free-throw line of a basketball court, knowing that her success rate from there is about 30 percent and believing that she is no more likely to make her next free throw than any other. She tries to sink her shot.

(4) Ned, in a practice session, is about to attempt to bench press 400 pounds. He has never bench pressed more than 390 pounds, although he has tried to do so many times, and he believes that his chance of successfully completing the present lift is quite small.

Leave it open, for now, whether these agents were successful. Did they *intend*, at the time at issue, to perform the featured actions?[6] What would nonspecialists say? There are a variety of ways of seeking lay responses to this question. Consider the following method (keeping in mind that I would defer to psychologists about technical details of an appropriate test). Subjects are given instructions of the following form regarding these cases (and some other cases in which agents are justifiably confident about their chances of success).

Instruction set 1 Please rate the appropriateness of the following responses on a scale from 1 to 7 (where 1 signifies "highly appropriate" and 7 signifies "highly inappropriate"):

(a) S wanted to A.

(b) S hoped to A.

(c) S intended to A.

(d) S would be pleased if she (or he) were to A.

(e) S does not care whether he (or she) As.

(f) S would be relieved if she (or he) were not to A.

(S is a placeholder for the agent's name. A is a placeholder for the action at issue—i.e., buying a prize-winning lottery ticket, hitting a hole in one, sinking this free throw, or bench pressing 400 pounds.)

My guess is that, in each of the four cases I have described, responses a, b, and d would receive significantly higher ratings than response c. Suppose that my guess were confirmed. Its confirmation would provide evidence that the state of mind of our imaginary agents fits the folk concepts of wanting and hoping better than it fits the folk concept of intending. If, as I should think, we would not find a similarly broad gap between wanting and hoping, on the one hand, and intending, on the other, in cases in which the agents are very confident of success, that would be evidence that agents' assessments of the likelihood of the success of their attempts are relevant to the folk concept of intention.

Some readers may contend that it would be more productive simply to ask subjects whether the agents in my cases did or did not intend to perform the actions in question (e.g., buying a winning lottery ticket or hitting a hole in one) I think not. There is an unfortunate tendency to read and hear statements like "S does not believe that the Yankees will win" and "S does not want to run into Bill today" as entailing "S believes that the Yankees will not win" and "S wants not to run into Bill today." (Plainly, S might not believe that the Yankees will win while also not believing that the Yankees will not win. It is not as though, with respect to every proposition that we entertain, we must either believe that it is true or believe that it is false. Similarly, S might be indifferent about running into Bill today, in which case he neither wants to run into him nor wants not to run into him.) And a sentence like "Karl did not intend to win the lottery" might wrongly be read or heard as implying that he was somehow averse to winning it.

I return to intentional action. If there is a confidence condition on intention, even if it is only the "negative" one that I identified earlier (i.e., people intend to A only if they *lack* the belief that they (probably) will not A), the door is open to cases in which agents A intentionally even though they lack an intention to A. This is illustrated by the following two-part story.

Earl's story, part A Earl is an excellent and powerful bowler. His friends tell him that the bowling pins on lane 6 are special 200-pound metal pins disguised to look like normal pins for the purposes of a certain practical joke. They also tell him that it is very unlikely that a bowled ball can knock over such a pin. Apparently as an afterthought, they challenge Earl to knock over a pin on lane 6 with a bowled ball and offer him $10 for doing so. Earl believes that his chance of knocking over a pin on lane 6 is very slim, but he intends to try.

(I interrupt the story here. Does Earl intend to knock down a pin? A plausible answer is that he does not, since he believes that his chances of doing so are very slim.)

Earl's story, part B Earl rolls an old bowling ball as hard as he can at the pins, hoping that he will knock down at least one. To his great surprise, he knocks them all down! The joke, it turns out, was on Earl: the pins on lane 6 were normal wooden ones.

Now, if intending to A entails lacking the belief that one (probably) will not A, then it is false that Earl intended to knock over a pin. Even so, other things being equal, I conjecture that most people would count Earl's knocking over some pins as an intentional action.[7] If there is a "belief" constraint of the kind at issue on intending, and if my conjecture is right, the folk concept of intentional action would seem not to entail that agents intentionally A only if they intend to A. Perhaps in some cases agents who intended to *try* to A and succeeded in A-ing are properly said to have intentionally A-ed, even if it is false that they intended to A.[8]

To be sure, sentences of the following sort have a jarring ring: "S intentionally A-ed, but it is false that S intended to A." Even so, it is plausible that Earl hoped and tried to knock down a pin while lacking an intention to knock down a pin. It is plausible, as well, that he intentionally knocked down some pins, given that he tried to knock some down, the pins and lane were normal, he used his relevant, excellent bowling skills in his attempt, and luck was not a factor.[9] People who would confidently reject sentences of the sort in question at first sight may be led to a considered endorsement of some such sentences after due reflection on cases.

Suppose that people presented with Earl's story in its entirety and tested for an assessment about intentional action favor saying that he intentionally knocked down some pins. If these people are then tested for an assessment of intention, they may infer from their previous answer and a (tacit) theoretical belief about the connection between intentional action and intention that Earl intended to knock down a pin. Would the effect of the hypothesized (tacit) theoretical belief be as strong in people who are first tested for an assessment of intention (using something like instruction set 1 above) and then tested for an assessment about intentional action? My hunch is that it would be less strong, but I would like to know. It should also prove instructive to give one group of subjects only part A of Earl's story and test for an intention assessment while giving another group of subjects the entire story and testing for an assessment of intentional action. My guess is that on symmetrically constructed tests conducted in this way the score on "Earl intentionally knocked down some pins" would significantly outstrip the score on "Earl intended to knock down some pins." At any rate, how lay folks would respond to Earl's case is empirically testable, and further tests may show that Malle and Knobe's claim about the intention component in the folk concept of intentional action is in need of modification.

The Skill Condition
Malle and Knobe claim that, according to the folk concept of intentional action, performing an action intentionally requires "skill to perform the action." I agree. In a paper offering an analysis of intentional action, Paul Moser and I argued for a skill condition on intentional action (Mele and Moser 1994). Now, on our view, the ordinary concept of intentional action is what philosophers call a "vague" concept. That is, it—like the concept of baldness, for example—lacks precise boundaries. There are clear cases of bald people and clear cases of people who are not bald, but there also are borderline cases. It is quite natural to think that, in cases of this last sort, the ordinary concept of baldness simply is not precise enough to tell us whether or not the individuals in question count as bald. Similarly, Moser and I argued that the ordinary concept of intentional action is not sufficiently precise to sort all actions into those that are intentional and those that are not. And one of the dimensions on which the ordinary concept of intentional action is vague, we argued, is the skill dimension.

If, under normal conditions, a basketball player with a 90 percent success rate on free throws tries in his normal way to sink a free throw and tosses the ball directly though the hoop, most people would say, I believe, that his sinking that free throw was an intentional action. Now consider my uncle Joe, an athletic blind man. Joe sinks about 2 percent of his free throws. Suppose that, under normal conditions, he tries in his normal way to sink a free throw during a contest with me and tosses the ball directly though the hoop. Did Joe intentionally sink the shot? I conjecture that most people would say No. What about Shaquille O'Neal, who sinks about 50 percent of his free throws? If he were to toss the ball straight through the hoop on his next attempt, would most people say that he sank that shot intentionally? I, for one, would like to know. And if most people were to say that Shaq intentionally sank the shot, would they be as confident about that as they are in a parallel scenario featuring a superb free-throw shooter? In any case, the connection between "degree of skill" and intentional action merits investigation in a full-blown study of the folk concept of intentional action.

The Awareness Condition

Malle and Knobe contend that, according to the folk concept of intentional action, performing an action intentionally requires "awareness of fulfilling the intention while performing the action." I am not certain how they intend this condition to be read. Is the required awareness meant to include the awareness of the intention *as* an intention, for example? If so, there is a problem. Consider the following case. Upon seeing Nancy return from work, her 10-month-old son Otis excitedly crawls to her. Does he intentionally crawl to her? My guess is that the great majority of people would answer affirmatively. Was Otis aware of "fulfilling the intention [to crawl to her] while performing the action"? If the prevailing view that 10- month-old children do not have the concept of intention is correct, then Otis (an ordinary baby) is not aware of this intention *as* an intention. This leaves it open that he is aware of his intention as something or other. But is Otis aware of *fulfilling his intention*? That depends on how much conceptual sophistication such awareness requires. If it requires possession of the concept of fulfilling an intention and Otis lacks the concept of intention, he is not aware of fulfilling his intention. In any case, the awareness condition itself requires some analysis or explication.

Suppose that the awareness condition that Malle and Knobe have in mind is a very modest one. Imagine that being aware of fulfilling one's intention to A, as they mean this to be understood, requires nothing more than intending to A now and being aware that one is A-ing now. Even then, their awareness condition is problematic. For example: Al knows that funny jokes and cartoons about cows have consistently made his young daughter laugh. When Al composes and sends a funny e-mail message about cows to his daughter with the intention of making her laugh, he is not then aware of making her laugh (although he is aware of composing and sending the message). Even so, under normal conditions and assuming Al's expertise in making his daughter laugh, if he succeeds in making her laugh with his e-mailed joke he intentionally makes her laugh. More cautiously, I conjecture that most people would count Al's making his daughter laugh in the present scenario as an intentional action. Of course, my claim leaves it open that intentional action requires awareness of *some* relevant activity.

Sufficient Conditions for Intentional Action?

Malle and Knobe do not make the bold claim that the conditions they present as necessary for intentional action are collectively *sufficient* for intentional action. A search for sufficient conditions would lead us to some issues that I have not considered thus far in this chapter.

Consider the following case. Al intends to make his daughter laugh and has the necessary "skill to perform the action." He plans to make her laugh by composing and sending her a funny e-mail message, but he accidentally sends the message to his wife's e-mail address. As luck would have it, his daughter's e-mail connection is temporarily out of order and she is using his wife's e-mail account at the time (a rare occurrence); she sees the funny message from Al and laughs (cf. Mele 1992a, p. 151).[10] I believe that most people would deem the following sentence false: "Al's making his daughter laugh is an intentional action." The success of Al's attempt owes too much to *luck* (and hence is too accidental), I believe, for his making his daughter laugh to count as something he did intentionally.

Malle and Knobe rightly identify the need for a skill condition on intentional action. But even when relevant skills are used (e.g., comedic and e-mailing skills), "lucky success" may render the pertinent action unintentional. A full-blown study of the folk concept of intentional action requires an investigation of the role played by considerations of luck in common-sense judgments about cases of action, including cases in which the agent has the relevant skills.[11]

Assumptions about agents' background beliefs may play an important part in shaping common-sense reactions to some instances of lucky success. Consider the following case (Mele and Moser 1994, p. 51):

Young Thor grew up in a distant land in which a game, 'hoops', remarkably similar to basketball is the national pastime. The chief difference is that hoops is played without a backboard. On a visit to Los Angeles, Thor encounters basketball for the first time, noticing some skilled young men playing a hoops-like game in a park. He is surprised by the wooden slab to which the hoop is attached. It strikes him as simply a device to minimize running after wayward balls. He has not seen a shot banked off the backboard; nor does it occur to him that the wood can serve this purpose. After joining the game, Thor is fouled and goes to the foul line with his standard hoops plan—a plan involving his shooting the ball *directly* into the hoop. He misses by a foot, hitting the backboard above the basket, and the ball bounces smoothly through the hoop. Thor is dumbfounded.

Did Thor intentionally sink his free throw? I would be curious to see how nonspecialists respond. It would also be revealing to compare lay responses to this case with lay responses to a related case in which an equally skilled *basketball* (as opposed to hoops) player shoots a foul shot with the plan of tossing the ball directly through the hoop but banks the ball in instead. Even if Thor and his counterpart (who is very familiar, of course, with relevant properties of the backboard) are equally lucky, the counterpart's sinking of his free throw may well get a significantly higher intentionality rating. If it does, it may be that the folk concept of intentional action is sensitive to agents' appreciation—or lack thereof—of ways in which modest departures of their actions from their plans do not preclude the success of their attempts.

Of course, luck, like skill, raises the issue of vagueness. A little luck need not stand in the way of an action's being intentional. Unbeknownst to Alex, there is a glitch in his phone that produces a mismatch between the number he dials and the number he contacts about one in a thousand times. So at least a little luck was involved in his contacting the person he intended to contact on his last call. However, this certainly seems consistent with his having intentionally contacted this person. If the probabilities were reversed, Alex's contacting the person he intended to contact would seem to be too lucky to be intentional. I doubt that there is a clear point of demarcation between intentional and nonintentional contact of the intended party in this "glitchy phone" scenario. The relevant vagueness would have to be accommodated in a full-blown analysis of intentional action.

Intentional Action and Morality

Might the folk concept of intentional action treat morally significant and morally insignificant actions differently?[12] Might it have a lower threshold, for example, for the intentionality of "lucky" actions deemed morally wrong than for the intentionality of equally lucky actions deemed morally neutral? If so, this would complicate the project of capturing the folk concept of intentional action in terms of individually necessary and jointly sufficient conditions of an agent's performing an action intentionally.

Consider the following four cases.[13]

Case 1 Fred, who has never fired a gun, is offered $100 for hitting a distant bull's-eye that even experts normally miss. With a view to winning the money, he takes careful aim at the bull's-eye, fires, and hits it dead center. Fred has no natural talent for marksmanship, however. He fires 200 additional rounds at the target—with equal care and for larger cash prizes—and does not even come close.

Case 2 In a variant of case 1, two details change. Fred's first shot ricochets into the bull's-eye off a rock situated 50 feet in front of the target. (Again he aimed carefully at the bull's-eye.) He fires half of the 200 additional rounds at the bull's-eye and half at the rock. (They all miss the bull's-eye, and the rock as well.)

Case 3 Fred, who has never fired a gun, is offered $100 for shooting a distant horse that even experts normally miss. The horse has been chained to a post in a field. With a view to winning the money, he takes careful aim at the horse, fires, and hits it in the head. Fred has no natural talent for marksmanship, however. He fires 200 additional rounds at another chained horse at the same distance—with equal care and for a larger cash prize—and does not even come close.

Case 4 In a variant of case 3, two details change. Fred's first shot ricochets into the horse's head off a rock situated 50 feet in front of the horse. (Again he aimed carefully at the horse.) He fires half of the 200 additional rounds at the other horse and half at a rock 50 feet in front of that horse. They all miss the horse, and the rock too.

Imagine a study in which untutored subjects are asked to rate the appropriateness of an intentionality ascription on a seven-point scale. Half of the subjects (group A) are presented with cases 1 and 2 and asked about the appropriateness of the claim that Fred intentionally hit the target, and half (group B) are presented with cases 3 and 4 and asked about the appropriateness of the claim that Fred intentionally hit the horse. Suppose that the subjects are *not* given the impression that the experimenters are studying the folk concept of intentional action. My hunch is that case 3 would evoke a significantly higher intentionality rating than case 1, that the same would be true in a comparison of case 4 with case 2, and that, even though case 4 involves more "luck" than case 1, it would evoke a significantly higher intentionality rating than case 1. If my hunch were confirmed, would that show that the folk concept of intentional action has a lower threshold for the intentionality of "lucky" actions deemed morally wrong than for the intentionality of equally lucky actions deemed morally neutral? Not necessarily. Most people, I conjecture, would feel inclined to pin some blame on the horse shooter. I conjecture, also, that, if the experimental design is such that the *only* way subjects can express blame is by means of an ascription of intentionality, there will be a significant inclination to make that ascription. Imagine a new group of subjects (group C) presented with the same cases as group B but given the following instructions about each case:

Instruction set 2 Please rate the appropriateness of the following claims about this case on a 1 to 7 scale (where 1 signifies "highly appropriate" and 7 signifies "highly inappropriate"):

(a) It was wrong of Fred to shoot the horse.

(b) Fred deserves blame for shooting the horse.

(c) Fred's hitting the horse was more a matter of luck than of skill—good luck for Fred and bad luck for the horse.

(d) Fred intentionally shot the horse.

(e) Fred tried to shoot the horse.

(f) Fred should be excused for shooting the horse, since his shooting it was just a case of beginner's luck.

My hunch is that group C would give Fred's shooting the horse a significantly lower intentionality rating than group B. If this hunch were confirmed, we would have reason to be suspicious about the reliability of the initial test.

Earlier, I said that an adequate analysis of intentional action—of what it is to do something intentionally—will be anchored by common-sense judgments about particular hypothetical or actual actions. However, an adequate analysis cannot simply be "read off" from such judgments. People occasionally make theoretical errors that taint their judgments about cases. For example, until they are caused to think with some care about the matter, many people may (tacitly) assume that an agent is blameworthy for doing something only if he or she did it intentionally. Such an assumption obviously may influence a person's assessment of the "horse" cases, for example. And it is easy enough to show most people that, upon consideration, they themselves would *reject* the assumption.

Consider the following case: Bob got rip-roaring drunk at a party after work. When the party ended, he stumbled to his car and started driving home. He was very drunk at the time—so drunk that he eventually lost control of his car, swerved into oncoming traffic, and killed a family of five. Now, did Bob intentionally crash into this family's car, or intentionally kill these people? The great majority would say No, and I believe they would also say that Bob is blameworthy for crashing into the car and for killing these people. Once this point is brought home to people who make these claims about this all-too-familiar scenario, they see that the assumption at issue is false—and false by their own lights rather than by the lights of an externally imposed theory. Subjects who have recently been led to see this point would, I believe, be more reliable judges about the "horse" cases than subjects who have not. It would be interesting to compare the responses of groups like B and C above to the "horse" cases to the responses of a group that had recently discussed the "drunk driver" case.

Stalking Folk Concepts

Must any attempt to locate the (or a) "folk concept" of intentional action rest on unacceptable presuppositions about human beings? An opponent of the search for folk concepts may suggest that the project presupposes that people have tidy analyses or definitions of these concepts in their heads. However, the suggestion is mistaken. For example, one need not be in possession of a detailed analysis of intentional action in order to make reasonable judgments about whether particular (actual or hypothetical) actions are intentional. An imaginary "conceptual analyst" attempting to formulate a particular person's conception or understanding of intentional action would proceed by asking that person about the intentionality of a wide range of judiciously selected cases of action, including cases of the various sorts considered here. The analyst would then attempt to formulate a tentative statement of necessary and sufficient conditions for "S did A intentionally" that coheres with the person's judgments about cases. If such a statement were to be formulated, the analyst would proceed to test it by asking questions of such a kind that certain answers would provide disconfirmation and others confirmation. (If significant inconsistencies were found, the analyst might look for their source. A *Socratic* conceptual analyst would make the person aware of his or her inconsistencies and see whether—and if so, *how*—the person found a way to resolve them.)

The procedure followed by a conceptual analyst in search of a collective conception or understanding of intentional action would be quite similar. Once again, there would be no presumption that any member of the group is in possession of a detailed, well-formed account of intentional action. Nor, obviously, would there be a presumption of a "group mind" that houses an analysis. Of course, a conceptual analyst will not find complete agreement about all cases of action, but thank heaven for statistical analysis!

Acknowledgments

I am grateful to Bertram Malle for useful written comments on a draft of this paper and to Jim Friedrich for helpful discussion.

Notes

1. In this volume, Gibbs argues that "many aspects of intentional . . . behavior are, at least partly, products of dynamic social interactions and not solely the result of privately held, internalized mental representations." Notice that dynamic social interactions can influence a person's intentional behavior by influencing her or his desires, beliefs, and intentions.

2. For example, it may be claimed that all intentions to A encompass a desire to A and, accordingly, that John desires to whistle the tune. On this idea, see Mele 1992a, pp. 169-70. I will return to belief shortly.

3. The proponents—some of whom omit the parenthetical qualifier—include Audi (1973, 1986, 1991), Beardsley (1978, 1980), Davis (1984), Harman (1976, 1986), and Velleman (1989). See also Moses, this volume.

4. Other alternatives include the requirement that S believe to a "degree" (even a degree associated with a subjective probability significantly less than 0.5) that he will A (Pears 1984, p. 124; cf. Pears 1985) and the requirement that S believe that "there is some chance that he can" A (Davidson 1985, p. 215).

5. Malle and Knobe (this volume) develop differences between folk concepts of intention and desire, some of which bear on the confidence issue (cf. Moses, this volume). Astington (this volume) offers evidence that 5-year-olds have a relatively good grip on both concepts.

6. In chapter 8 of Mele 1992a, largely on functional grounds, I defend an account of intention that portrays this mental state, roughly, as an executive attitude toward a plan (which plan, in the limiting case, is a simple representation of a simple action, e.g. flexing one's right wrist). But, on nonfunctional grounds, I argue for a modest, negative belief constraint on intention. On this negative belief constraint, also see Malle and Knobe this volume. (Incidentally, in that chapter they seem to have a more robust notion of a plan than the one I just alluded to.)

7. This conjecture is subject to a qualification voiced in the final paragraph of this subsection.

8. For discussion of a distinction between intending to A and intending to try to A, see Mele 1992a, pp. 132–135 and 147–150.

9. I take it that it was not a matter of luck that the pins were normal wooden pins.

10. This is a simple case of "causal deviance." For a variety of more complicated cases, and distinctions among types of causal deviance, see Mele and Moser 1994.

11. As I have observed elsewhere (Mele 1992b, n. 20), lucky success of a kind inconsistent with the relevant action's being intentional is not always improbable success. "Bart, a normal agent, will win $20 for throwing anything other than 'snake eyes' (two ones) on his next roll of a pair of normal dice. The chance of his throwing a non-snake-eyes roll is high. Still, assuming that Bart, hoping to throw such a roll, does throw one," people would be disinclined, I believe, to claim that he intentionally throws non-snake-eyes. A plausible diagnosis of the disinclination (assuming that I am right about it) is that people take Bart to lack control over the dice of a kind required for the intentional throwing of a non-snake-eyes roll.

12. For discussion of a closely related issue, see Mele and Sverdlik 1996.

13. Cases 1 and 2 are from Mele 1992b, p. 363.

2

The Distinction between Desire and Intention: A Folk-Conceptual Analysis

Bertram F. Malle and Joshua Knobe

Brian seems to be interested in asking Lisa to marry him, but Lisa is not sure how serious he is. He has been discussing the issue with friends, writing about it in his diary, and his face takes on a special glow whenever the topic of marriage comes up in conversation. As the days progress, Lisa may begin to ask herself whether he only has a *wish* to propose to her or whether he has he actually *decided* to propose.

Like Lisa in this example, people in general distinguish between desires (expressed in English with the verbs *wish*, *hope*, and *want*) and intentions (*decide, plan, intend*). People are often faced with the task of classifying a person's mental state into one of these two categories. In this chapter we propose a psychological theory about what people do under these circumstances—what criteria they use to classify mental states and how they use the resulting classification.

Philosophers have developed various analyses of the distinction between desire and intention (Audi 1988; Brand 1984; Bratman 1987; Davis 1984; Mele 1988; Velleman 1989). Typically, the aim of these philosophical analyses is to reach a more adequate understanding of what desires and intentions ultimately *are*—to better understand the nature of these mental states as they actually exist in human agents. We put these questions aside. Our aim is to understand how social perceivers use the concepts of desire and intention to interpret other people's behavior. Thus, our inquiry is one part of the broader attempt to better understand what has been called "naive psychology of action" (Heider 1958), "theory of mind" (Gopnik and Meltzoff 1997; Premack and Woodruff 1978; Wellman 1990), or "folk psychology" (Greenwood 1991)—the conceptual framework that helps people perceive, explain, predict, and change human behavior by reference to mental states. We will be concerned with the specific question of how people come to treat certain mental states as desires and others as intentions. Developmental research has begun to explore how and when children distinguish these two mental states (Astington and Gopnik 1991; Astington, this volume; Moses, this volume; Perner 1991; Phillips, Baron-Cohen, and Rutter 1998; Schult 1996). However, a systematic account of the endpoint of this development—the adult distinction between intention and desire—has not been offered.

In providing such an account, we blend conceptual analysis with empirical study. We begin with a rough sketch of the desire-intention distinction, then construct specific hypotheses about the features that social perceivers use to distinguish desires from intentions. Each of these hypotheses is tested empirically, using naturally occurring data and controlled experiments.

A Rough Sketch

Desires and intentions are both representational states, and they both express a pro attitude toward the state of affairs they represent, frequently propelling the agent to act in such a way as to bring about that state. However, there is an important difference. When we say that an agent has a desire, we are not saying that she[1] has actually decided to do anything. She might have a desire for world peace even if she doesn't plan to take any steps to make this desire a reality. Similarly, an agent might have a desire to start screaming at her boss even though she has specifically decided not to do so. When, however, people adopt an intention, they are actually deciding to perform the action in question.

One might say, speaking roughly, that desires and intentions occupy different positions in the path that (typically) leads to action. Desires stand in the very beginning of the process. Before making a decision about how to act, the person needs to consider various desires, balancing them against each other and asking which of them can potentially be fulfilled. In the course of this reasoning process, the person arrives at an intention. This intention is an all-things-considered decision that takes into account the person's various desires. The intention, then, is just one step away from the action; all that remains is to put one's decision into motion.

To clarify these initial intuitions, we constructed specific hypotheses about three criteria that social perceivers use to distinguish intentions from desires. These criteria are the *type of content*, the *function in reasoning*, and the *degree of commitment*.

Type of Content

A number of philosophers, including Baier (1970) and Castañeda (1972), have argued that, whereas desires can have many different types of content, intentions always have as their content an action performed by the person who holds that intention. As Aristotle remarks (1962, 1111b25), people may "wish for the victory of a particular actor or a particular athlete," but "no one chooses such things, for we choose only what we believe might be attained through our own agency." Thus, a person may want a lot of money, but she cannot intend a lot of money. What people intend is always their own action (to go jogging, to write a letter, to cook a nice meal) or an event directly controlled by their own action (to be polite, to be at the party tonight). People may intend to bring it about that an athlete be victorious (e.g., by paying for a world-class coach), but they cannot literally intend another person's action or an event outside of themselves.

But what about such statements as "I intend to be the next president," "I intend you to marry my cousin's son," or "We intend Alex to go to kindergarten next fall"? Are these intention avowals not blatantly violating the proposed rule? And would not social perceivers who strictly adhere to the rule be utterly confused by these statements? As we will see shortly, such statements are extremely rare—in the vast majority of intention avowals, their content designates the agent's own action. The few exceptions may be addressed in various ways. One is to say that these expressions do not strictly follow the rules of proper English. A second option is to say that the English words in question (e.g., *decide*, *intend*) almost always refer to a single folk concept—here, the folk concept of intention—but that there are occasional cases in which they don't refer to this concept. These occasional cases may turn out to be extended or metaphorical uses of the standard term. For example, when a person says "I intend to be the next president," social perceivers may consider the claim to mean "I really want to . . . and

I will try everything I can to. . . ." The uses may also be shorthands for some longer sentence that involves the folk concept of intention in the standard way (e.g., "I intend you to marry my cousin's son" is a shorthand for "I intend to bring it about that you marry my cousin's son"). It may turn out that all of these options are valid, each applying to a different sort of counterexample. But the fundamental point is, we think, that a few cases in which people's uses of the words depart slightly from conceptual rules should not lead us to abandon the whole theory that identifies these rules. Surely, if a few years from now people invented a sport in which the word *intend* was used in a somewhat unusual way, we would not have to completely revise our theories of the folk concept of intention.

Our first hypothesis is, then, that people use the content of a pro attitude to identify it as a desire or an intention, with desires representing any content and with genuine intentions representing what we call *action content*. A pro attitude has action content when the content of the attitude is an action performed by the same person who holds that attitude. Linguistically, this content is most clearly displayed in English *that*-constructions, such as "Jones hopes that he will go jogging," but more commonly (Rosenbaum 1970) it is expressed in *to* + infinitive constructions, such as "Jones plans to go jogging."[2] What evidence do we have for the claim that desires can have any type of content whereas genuine intentions always have action content?

The content difference between intention and desire has grammaticalized in English such that there is a systematic difference in the syntactic complementation patterns for the verbs *want* and *intend*. According to a study by Aarts and Aarts (1991), the verb *want* is realized in three different ways: with *to* + *infinitive* (55 percent of the cases; e.g., "I just want to know"), with a direct object (28 percent; e.g., "Employees want a greater say at work"), or with a noun phrase (NP) and various complements (17 percent; e.g., "He wanted Browne dead"; "He wanted us to get going"—see Erdmann 1993). In contrast, the verb *intend* is primarily realized with *to* + *infinitive*. In a sample of 110 occurrences of *intend* or *intended* in American newspapers and magazines (extracted from the NEXIS database), we found that 97 percent of the active verb forms of *intend* were paired with *to* + *infinitive*.

In the realization of *intend* with *to* + *infinitive*, the grammatical subject of the *intend* verb is identical to the grammatical subject of the infinitive, guaranteeing identity between the agent who intends and the agent of the intended action, as in "I intend to drive" (= I intend that I drive). Such identity is violated in occurrences of *want* when it is paired with NP complements (which are typically referring to another person or state of affairs). Thus, it is unproblematic to state "I want them out of this room right now" but problematic to state "I intend them out of this room right now" (except perhaps, metaphorically, to express an unusually strong desire or stern command).

To strengthen this point, we collected linguistic data on the distribution of contents for intention verbs (*intend, plan, decide*)[3] and desire verbs (*want, wish, hope*). Using the NEXIS database, we selected active-voice occurrences of each of the above verbs (30–100 per verb) and coded them for their content—referring to the agent or not. (For a subset of the verbs, two coders independently coded the agent/not-agent variable and reached an agreement of 93 percent.) The content of intention verbs referred to the agent in 98 percent of the cases,[4] whereas the content of desire verbs referred to the agent in 63 percent of the cases; $\chi^2(1, N = 396) = 82.4, p < 0.001$.

In addition, two coders also rated the controllability of the verbs' content (on a five-point scale from –2 to +2), for which they reached an agreement of $r = 0.87$. (The ratings were made while blind to the original verb; i.e., all verbs were replaced by the generic term *represent*.) The average controllability for all three desire verbs was uniformly low (from $M = -0.28$ for *wish* to $M = 0.24$ for *want*), whereas the average controllability for all three intention verbs was uniformly high (from $M = 0.94$ for *plan* to $M = 1.46$ for *decide*). The contrast of the three desire verbs against the three intention verbs was highly significant, $F(1, 391) = 104.9, p < 0.001, \eta^2 = 21$ percent. A strict test comparing only those verb forms that had action content still showed desire verbs to be paired with significantly less controllable actions ($M = 0.62$) than intention verbs ($M = 1.24$), with $p < 0.001$.

One implication of the rule that intentions refer to action content is that one cannot intend another person's actions, only one's own (Baier 1970; Brand 1984). To test this implication, we collected a small set of experimental data, using a multiple-choice verb completion design. Participants (109 college students) read several sentences that normally would contain a desire or intention verb, but the verb's position was left blank. Participants were asked to choose the most appropriate verb from a list of five: want, hope, intend, plan, and decide. The results were as follows.[5]

(1) *Enja* _____ *her husband to pick up their daughter from the airport.*

wanted	85%	
hoped	0%	desire: 85%
intended	8%	
planned	6%	
decided	0%	intention: 15%

(2) *"I am serious: I* _____ *you to be back by midnight!"*

want	93%	
hope	2%	desire: 94%
intend	3%	
plan	3%	
decide	0%	intention: 6%

It should be noted that these items were presented as part of a 40-minute mass-testing questionnaire that certainly did not engage all participants. Moreover, the participants included about 5 percent (unidentified) non-native speakers. Thus, one should not overinterpret the small number of people who chose an intention verb to complete these sentences. What seems clear is that the vast majority of informants preferred the verb *want* to refer to a non-agent action content. This is particularly impressive for the second item, where the sentence was constructed to express a strong desire ("I am serious . . ."), conceived by some, including Rundle (1997, chapter 5), as closer to an intention. That same marker of intensity, when coupled with a content that describes *agent-controlled* action, led to 82 percent intention verb choices:

(3) *"I am serious: I* _____ *to be back by midnight!"*

want	15%	
hope	3%	desire: 18%
intend	45%	
plan	37%	
decide	0%	intention: 82%

We have argued that intentions are pro attitudes with action content[6] whereas desires may have any content (one's own action, another's action, an unlikely outcome, etc.). Thus, if the social perceiver sees that a pro attitude does not have action content, he can immediately assume that the attitude is a desire.

Now we would like to speculate briefly about why desires and intentions have different types of content. In folk psychology, intentional action is interpreted and explained in terms of mental states (Malle 1999). Some mental states are felt to be very close to action: They affect an action directly, without the intermediation of any other mental states. Intentions serve precisely this role. An intention to perform action A might lead directly to action A. The social perceiver need not posit an intermediary mental state that is affected by the intention and in turn affects the action. Other mental states are felt to be very distant from action: They can affect an action only through a long chain of causes and effects—e.g., by affecting another mental state, which then affects another mental state, and so on, until ultimately one reaches a mental state that affects the action directly. Thus, a desire for world peace does not directly cause the person to perform a particular action. It can lead to action only in conjunction with a number of other mental states (e.g., beliefs about which actions tend to promote world peace).

If we wanted to map out the whole process that leads to an action according to folk psychology, we might begin with fairly general beliefs, desires, and values. These mental states would serve as inputs to a reasoning process that ultimately led to an intention. The intention would then typically lead directly to an action. Now, the mental states that affect the action indirectly (the beliefs, desire, and values) may have any type of content. Even if they don't have action content, they can indirectly affect the agent's actions by affecting other mental states, as long as they eventually affect a mental state that specifies a particular action to be performed. However, the mental states that directly affect the action must always have action content. The content of these states is precisely the action they lead to. That is, in the chain of mental states that leads eventually to action A, the state just preceding A must specifically represent the action A. This final state is an intention.

Role in Reasoning

A person might have many pro attitudes with action content, but most of these will never be transformed into intentions. Maybe the person wants to devote her life to charity. Maybe she wants to slap her annoying co-worker. Social perceivers need to know whether these pro attitudes with action content are just desires or whether they are genuine intentions (which are more predictive of action). To do so, they make use of additional criteria.

One of the additional criteria is the role that the attitude plays in the agent's reasoning. For example, a desire to eat chocolate is not based on any reasoning, but it may set into motion a reasoning process about how to acquire some chocolate. An intention to go to the corner store, in contrast, is likely to be based on reasoning about what one needs (e.g., chocolate) and whether the store carries it. These prototypical cases suggest that desires are typically inputs to reasoning, whereas intentions are typically outputs of reasoning. At least that is how people treat desires and intentions: According to the folk concept of intentionality, the reasoning process underlying intentional action takes desires as input and uses them to generate intentions (Malle and Knobe 1997a). By looking at a pro attitude's role within the agent's reasoning, then, social perceivers can distinguish between intentions and desires (even if both of them have action content).

Philosophers have argued that, in actual fact, intentions are sometimes inputs to reasoning (Bratman 1999) and desires are sometimes outputs of reasoning (Harman 1976; Schueler 1995). This, however, is no objection to the hypothesis we are advancing. We do not say that each attitude can occupy one and only one predetermined role in reasoning. Our point is simply that there is a tendency for social perceivers to infer that an attitude is a desire if it is the input of reasoning and to infer that it is an intention if it is the output of reasoning. The pro attitude's role in reasoning thus serves as a *clue* for perceivers as to the nature of the attitude.

To explore this hypothesis, we again used people's verb choices as measures of their desire or intention inferences. We held the action content of the stimulus sentences constant but varied the linguistic and conceptual context to indicate either a reasoning input phase (deliberation) or a reasoning output phase (decision). A sample of 206 undergraduate students completed these vignettes in a mass-testing questionnaire, choosing the verb they considered most appropriate from a list of six.

In the first vignette, the target sentence "Carl [verb] to make a large charity donation" was either paired with a reason explanation (4), rendering the target sentence a reasoning output, or with an indicator of early deliberation (5), rendering the target sentence a reasoning input. Clearly, people preferred intention verbs when the target sentence was a reasoning output, compared to the same sentence functioning as reasoning input.

(4) *Carl _____ to show his relatives that he is a generous person,* . . .

want	49%	
hope	8%	
need	7%	desire: 64%
intend	25%	
plan	4%	
decide	8%	intention: 36%

. . . *so he _____ to make a large charity donation.*

want	1%	
hope	1%	
need	1%	desire: 3%
intend	15%	
plan	33%	
decide	49%	intention: 97%

(5) *Carl _____ to make a large charity donation, but he didn't know much about charity organizations.*

want	52%	
hope	4%	
need	2%	desire: 57%
intend	13%	
plan	14%	
decide	16%	intention: 43%

A second vignette confirmed this difference with even stronger effect sizes:

(6) *In her dire financial situation Beth _____ to make a lot of money fast,* . . .

want	13%	
hope	17%	
need	61%	desire: 91%
plan	0%	
intend	4%	
decide	5%	intention: 9%

. . . so she _____ to buy high-risk stock.

need	0%	
hope	3%	
want	8%	desire: 11%
plan	16%	
intend	9%	
decide	64%	intention: 89%

(7) *Beth _____ to buy high-risk stock, but she was afraid of losing a lot of money.*

need	3%	
hope	4%	
want	64%	desire: 71%
plan	11%	
intend	13%	
decide	6%	intention: 30%

In a second test, we inspected naturally occurring instances of intention and desire verbs, hoping to find a similar trend that people would use desire verbs more often to describe what they consider inputs to reasoning and intention verbs more often to describe what they consider outputs of reasoning. Unfortunately, the NEXIS verb sample described above contained very few explicit indications of reasoning. Among 183 desire verbs, 15 showed explicit indications of their function in reasoning (e.g., *therefore*, *in order to*, *because*), and 9 of those were reasoning inputs (60 percent). Among 217 instances of intention verbs, 42 showed explicit indications of their function in reasoning, and 38 of those were reasoning outputs (90 percent), χ^2 (1, $N = 400$) = 16.0, $p < 0.001$. (For example, one desire-as-input expression was the following: "Amy Regan-Axelson wants you to make time to come riding with her. That is why she founded Women's Mountain Biking." One intention-as-output expression was "The government intends to introduce annual council elections to make financial decision-making more responsive to the electorate.")

From these verb distributions and from the experimental data earlier we can conclude that there is a strong trend for intentions to be treated as outputs of reasoning and a somewhat weaker trend for desires to be treated as inputs to reasoning. Both of these trends are consistent with the folk concept of intention, which requires intentions to be based on (belief-desire) reasoning whereas no such requirement accompanies the concept of desire (Malle and Knobe 1997a).

We would now like to explore why intentions and desires might perform their different functions in the practical reasoning chain, at least as seen by folk psychology. Suppose that an agent has a desire for outcome O and a belief that action A will lead to outcome O. As a result of this belief-desire pair, she might acquire a desire to perform action A. Under those conditions, why can't she simply act on her desire to A? What would be the point of further deliberation in which the desire to A serves as input to a reasoning process that ultimately yields an intention to A as output?

The answer is that, before a pro attitude with action content becomes a full-fledged intention, the person needs to ask herself (a) whether she is capable of performing the action and (b) whether she has other desires that outweigh her desire to perform the action.

Suppose that the agent wants to climb a mountain on Saturday. She will not immediately decide to climb the mountain. She must first engage in a certain amount of reasoning. She has to make sure that she is capable of performing the action in one way or another. Moreover, she has to figure out whether she has any other desires that outweigh her desire to perform the action (e.g., whether there is something else that she would rather do on Saturday). If she concludes that she is capable of performing the action and has no outweighing desires, she may form a corresponding intention (Davidson 1980b). Otherwise, she may retain her desire to perform the action even though she forms no intention to act on that desire.

According to folk psychology, then, intentions serve to fulfill desires by identifying a course of action that is feasible to implement for the agent and is compatible with the agent's other desires. Because of the closeness of intentions to actions in the world, intentions have to fit the world (in the sense that the agent would be capable of implementing them), and because of the consequences of actions for the agent's welfare, intentions have to fit the agent's desires. This fit is sometimes expressed as the "consistency criterion" for intentions (Moses, this volume). The agent's reasoning checks for such consistency, and social perceivers expect an agent to have engaged in this sort of reasoning when forming an intention.

Degree of Commitment

Even when there is evidence that an agent engaged in practical reasoning, there is no guarantee that the agent has formed an intention. Maybe she is still unsure. Or maybe she has concluded that, although there would be many advantages to performing the action, she is not going to form an intention to do so. The social perceiver needs a way to distinguish among these various possibilities. Thus, a third criterion is necessary: *commitment*.

When we say, in this technical sense, that an agent is "committed" to an action, we do not mean that the agent has made a promise to anyone else, nor even that she has made some sort of promise to herself. An agent is said to be committed when she has made up her mind, when she has settled on a particular path of action (Bratman 1987; Mele 1992a). Thus, suppose that the agent is wondering whether to order a hamburger or a slice of pizza. At first, she faces a number of competing desires, accompanied by various beliefs about the possible consequences of her action and the situation at hand. Then, after a period of reasoning, she settles on ordering the hamburger. At that point, she considers the question closed. When the waiter asks for her order, she does not begin deliberating all over again. She simply acts on the intention she had already formed. This settledness, the conclusion of the reasoning process, is what we mean by commitment.

Social perceivers consider the agent's degree of commitment to distinguish intentions from desires. However, they cannot directly perceive commitment, so they make inferences on the basis of at least three indicators. First, an agent indicates commitment by making *early investments* (e.g., buying a concert ticket in advance). Second, an agent indicates commitment by accepting *opportunity costs* of not pursuing alternative courses of action (best indicated when such alternatives become in fact available). Third, an agent indicates commitment by accepting (sometimes inviting) *sanctions* from others in case she does not fulfill the intention (e.g., public announcements of intentions, which put the agent's credibility on the line).

Take, for example, the intention to stay with a romantic partner. A strong commitment is expressed through early investments (e.g., joint purchases), accepting opportunity costs (e.g., not dating others), and inviting sanctions (e.g., introducing the partner to friends and family), whereas fear of commitment manifests itself in the absence of these signals (few joint purchases, insistence on dating others, reluctance to meet friends and family).

Now we turn to our empirical data on commitment, which illustrate people's sensitivity to indicators of commitment when inferring intention.

To begin, when a speaker is committed to a course of action, others can rely on it. In (8), a speaker tries to communicate this reliability to an addressee, and consequently social perceivers ($N = 109$ college students) judged that the speaker would use an intention verb. Conversely, in (9) an indication of *not* being committed to a course of action led people to choose desire verbs (even though the content considered was clearly an action).

(8) *Sheila* _____ *to go to the Thai restaurant on 29th Street; you can find her there.*

wanted   3%
hoped   1%   desire: 4%
intended   8%
decided   63%
planned   25%   intention: 96%

(9) *Sarah* _____ *to go to a Thai restaurant perhaps, or pretty much any Asian cuisine.*

wants   74%
hopes   19%   desire: 93%
intends   3%
plans   3%
decides   1%   intention: 7%

Speakers themselves often indicate their commitment in avowals of intention, and in (10) commitment is indicated in a global way ("seriously"), which is sufficient to convince most social perceivers ($N = 206$ college students) that an intention verb would be most appropriate. In contrast, in (11) the speaker expresses doubt about the intention's fulfillment, and perceivers are significantly less likely to infer an intention:

(10) *The teacher said "Seriously, I _____ to return your papers tomorrow."*

need	5%	
hope	12%	
want	3%	desire: 20%
plan	39%	
intend	40%	
decide	2%	intention: 80%

(11) *The teacher said "I am not sure it's going to work, but I _____ to return your papers tomorrow."*

need	0%	
hope	43%	
want	10%	desire: 53%
plan	22%	
intend	23%	
decide	2%	intention: 47%

The next item illustrates the power of a specific commitment indicator, lack of) early investments to go to a concert, which allows an inference about the agent's (lacking) intention.

(12) *He likes U2, but I doubt he _____ to go to the concert—he hasn't bought tickets yet.*

need	2%	
hope	0%	
want	15%	desire: 17%

plan	41%	
intend	34%	
decide	9%	intention: 83%

The availability of multiple indicators of commitment (investments, opportunity costs, etc.) offers the possibility that, in social perception, commitment is inferred not as an on-off state but in degrees. Thus, the more commitment an agent shows toward a course of action, the more inclined people are to infer an intention rather than a desire. Initial evidence for a continuum of commitment comes from the next vignette, in which subjects were presented with a potential action of moving to Europe under three conditions that decreased in commitment: (a) with opportunity costs clearly indicated, (b) with a time index signaling reasoning but only vague commitment, and (c) with a strong pro attitude but a lack of commitment. The results show that the corresponding inference of intention (rather than desire) drops precipitously from 84 percent to 41 percent to 15 percent.

(13a) *I know she _____ to move to Europe; she's already given notice.*

need	2%	
hope	6%	
want	8%	desire: 16%
plan	35%	
intend	29%	
decide	20%	intention: 84%

(13b) *I know she _____ to move to Europe next year.*

need	0%	
hope	17%	
want	42%	desire: 59%
plan	23%	
intend	14%	
decide	4%	intention: 41%

(13c) *I know she _____ to move to Europe some day; it's been her childhood dream.*

need	0%	
hope	55%	
want	30%	desire: 85%
plan	7%	
intend	8%	
decide	0%	intention: 15%

A Model of Desires and Intentions

We have now arrived at a three-part model of how social perceivers distinguish between desires and intentions. For one thing, they examine the content of the agent's pro attitude. If the content is not the agent's own action (but rather someone else's action, an object, or an outcome), social perceivers will assume that the attitude is a desire. If the pro attitude has action content, it may be classified as an intention. However, further information may be necessary: Perceivers also examine the role that the attitude played in the agent's reasoning. If the attitude is not based on any reasoning, it is classified as a desire; if it is based on reasoning, it may be classified as an intention (but further information might still be necessary). Finally, social perceivers assess the degree to which the agent is committed to the represented action. If the agent shows no indications of commitment, the attitude will be classified as a desire; if the agent does show commitment, the attitude will be classified as an intention.

Social perceivers might proceed through these three steps in order, always tracking content and beginning a search for other features only if the content is an action (otherwise, no search is necessary, because the pro attitude must be a desire). To warrant an intention classification, all three features must be identified, otherwise the search ends with a desire classification. At times, perceivers may look immediately at the feature of commitment and, if it is present, infer an intention (because commitment to action entails action content and is likely to be based on reasoning). This confirmatory strategy may be used when perceivers strongly expect an intention.

Alternative Distinguishing Features
The philosophical literature makes reference to additional features that potentially distinguish between desires and intentions.

A first possible criterion is the controllability of the intended behavior. Some philosophers, including Baier (1970), have argued that an agent cannot intend to perform a behavior unless it is controllable. One should distinguish, however, between the agent's belief that the behavior is controllable and the actual controllability of that behavior. An agent might decide to start her car even though, unbeknownst to her, the alternator is malfunctioning and the act of starting is therefore uncontrollable. A social perceiver who knows about the malfunction will ascribe a genuine intention to the agent, even though he is certain that the agent's intention will not be realized. If, however, the agent believes that the alternator is malfunctioning and that she therefore cannot start the car, the perceiver will not say that the agent *intended* to start it but only that she *wished* to. Here again, it is not clear precisely how confident the agent must be in the controllability of her behavior before the social perceiver will ascribe an intention. Still, we can be relatively certain that a perceiver will not ascribe an intention if the agent is confident that the behavior is uncontrollable.

Second, some scholars, including Davis (1984) and Velleman (1989), have argued that intending to A entails believing that one will A whereas wanting to A does not entail that. Others, including Anscombe (1957) and Thalberg (1972), claim that an agent can intend to A even when she is certain that she will not A. Some have taken an intermediate position: An agent need not believe that she will A (with any kind of certainty), but she cannot specifically believe that she will not A (Mele 1992a, chapter 8). Although we have no empirical data on this issue of belief, we did demonstrate that social perceivers require a certain amount of commitment before classifying a mental state as an intention, and a belief that one will not perform a particular action seems incompatible with having such a commitment. It would be perplexing for someone to say "I intend to go to the party tonight but I'm sure that I won't" (since, clearly, the speaker shows a lack of commitment). Thus, our criterion of commitment suggests that social perceivers will not ascribe an intention to an agent who simultaneously believes that she will not perform the action in question. However, further empirical research may clarify whether perceivers require a specific degree of confidence (e.g., being fairly sure that one will perform the action) before classifying a pro attitude as an intention.

Finally, some authors, including Harman (1986) and Mele (1992a), have claimed that intentions to A entail a plan for A-ing. The truth of this claim depends on the required detail of such a plan. On the one hand, during the reasoning process the agent checks for the action's controllability and its compatibility with other desires. Thus, the agent takes the first steps of planning by narrowing down the possible courses of action to a few that are feasible and compatible with other goals. On the other hand, reasoning toward an intention does not necessarily lead to a plan of action. Indeed, the very act of forming an intention may instigate the process of working out a plan of action (Bratman 1987). So we suspect that social perceivers sometimes ascribe intentions even in the absence of a plan. For example, people may say that a presidential candidate intends to reform the prison system even though they recognize that the candidate has not yet worked out a plan of how to implement these reforms. As long as the agent's intention is based on reasoning that supports the feasibility of the intended action (i.e., the agent has *some idea* of how to perform the action), social perceivers may not require plans as a necessary component of intention.

Other Meanings of Intention

The intention concept described in our model is confirmed by the clear and consistent everyday use of the word *intend* and the expression of avowed intentions ("I will A"). However, related words, such as *intended* (the passive participle or adjective) and *intention*, can have different meanings and functions, and our model suggests that they in fact refer to desires. For example, much philosophy has been written about the expression *doing A with the intention of doing B*. In some cases, the *intention of doing B* is truly an intention (consistent with the three posited features), but in many cases it is not. For example, "She bought a ticket with the intention of winning the jackpot" does not reference an intention proper, because one should not infer that she intended to win the jackpot (representing an uncontrollable action). As a result, several authors have concluded that the phrase *with the intention of* in fact refers to a goal or aim—more a desire than an intention (Harman 1986, p. 93; Mele 1992a, chapter 8, fn. 22; Velleman 1989, p. 112).

Another misleading relative of *intend* is the passive form *intended for* (synonymous with *designed for* or *designated for*), as in "These planes were intended for export." These uses take on desire content rather than intention content, reliably violating the content and commitment conditions. Similar considerations apply to the term *(un)intended consequences*. Because such consequences are by definition consequences of action and thereby outcomes, they violate the feature of action content. Of course, an agent may have thought hard about certain outcomes and may be committed to bringing them about, but that means that the agent intends to perform particular actions in order to fulfill her desire for these outcomes. Despite the etymological similarity between the verb *to intend* and the adjective *intended*, they perform different functions in the folk theory of mind and behavior. Whereas the distinction between intention and desire helps social perceivers predict other people's future behaviors, the distinction between intended and unintended outcomes assists—at least in part—in the assignment of responsibility and blame for past behaviors, and it is therefore governed by different folk-conceptual rules than the notion of genuine intentions to act.

The Function of the Desire/Intention Distinction in Social Perception
It seems appropriate here to speculate briefly about the function of the intention/desire distinction in social perception. It lies, we think, in the different roles occupied by the concepts of desire and intention in the social perceiver's attempt to predict, explain, and influence others' actions. It is useful to have information about the agent's intentions because such information allows the greatest possible predictive accuracy. If the social perceiver is trying to make predictions about what the agent is going to do next, it might be helpful to know the agent's general preferences, habits, beliefs, etc., but it would be most helpful to know what she intends to do in this specific case. Even if the social perceiver knows that the agent has a desire to perform a particular action, he still won't be nearly so sure of his predictions as he would be if he knew that the agent had actually formed an intention.

Still, the social perceiver cannot base all his predictions on knowledge of the agent's intentions, because he cannot possibly know what the agent intends to do in every specific case. In the vast majority of cases, he will have to predict the agent's actions on the basis of more general information. In any given case, this information will not give the social perceiver nearly as much predictive accuracy as he could have obtained from knowledge of the agent's specific intentions, but he will be able to use this information in a wider variety of cases. For example, Ben's knowledge that Anne wants to make a lot of money is of limited use in predicting the particular behaviors she is going to perform at this evening's party (for that, Ben would need to know Anne's specific intentions), but it does allow him to deal with her successfully in many different situations. Moreover, knowledge of desires provides a broad guideline for supporting or opposing others' actions. Rather than respond only to concrete intentions and actions, one can respond to the agent's overarching goal and, for example, suggest alternative paths to the goal or devise ways to block all paths to it.

People also use desires more often than intentions when they are trying to explain an action that has already been performed. If someone asks "Why did the agent perform action A?" it usually isn't very helpful to respond "Because she intended to perform action A." Ideally, one would want a response of greater explanatory power, i.e., a response that not only explained this one action but also provided a more general insight into the agent's goals or the demands of the situation. Precisely because desires are part of the reasoning input to intentions, they provide illuminating background information about an action's general purpose and meaning. If we hear someone say "She performed A because she wanted to obtain outcome O," we are gaining information that subsumes this action under a broader principle, which can then be used to predict, explain, and perhaps influence a variety of further actions.

Psychological Implications of the Desire/Intention Distinction

Assuming that social perceivers classify an agent's attitude as either a desire or an intention, one may ask how this classification affects social perceivers' own behaviors toward the agent. We wish to advance three hypotheses.

The Role of Intention Ascriptions in Persuasive Communication

Since information about intentions offers greater predictive accuracy, people may emphasize that the agent has formed an intention when they wish to convince others that the agent will actually try to perform the behavior: "She has made a firm decision; she definitely plans to do it." Conversely, when people wish to indicate uncertainty about the agent's future trying, they may emphasize that the agent has a desire but not an intention: "She would really like to do that, but she hasn't reached a decision yet. . . ."

Intentions Are More Open to Charges of Incoherence
If a person believes her desires to be incompatible, people don't usually feel that she is making any kind of error. They just say "Well, that's what she happens to want." Consider a person who wants to go to a colloquium at 3:00 P.M. and also wants to go running at 3:00 P.M. Even though she knows that her two desires are incompatible, she doesn't seem to be guilty of any kind of irrationality. If, in contrast, she adopts a set of intentions that she knows to be incompatible (e.g., intending to go to the talk at 3:00 P.M. and also intending to go running at 3:00 P.M.), she definitely seems to be making some sort of error (Harman 1976; Moses, this volume).

This difference between desires and intentions stems from their differing roles in the reasoning process. The agent is presumed to have a vast array of conflicting desires. In the process of reasoning, she is supposed to sift through these desires and formulate a set of consistent intentions. Any inconsistencies in the agent's intentions are therefore regarded as evidence of an error in reasoning.

Intentions Are More Open to Debate
If social perceivers want to change an agent's intentions, they may present complex arguments (pointing out inconsistencies in the agent's intentions, drawing the agent's attention to disadvantages of the action intended, etc.); if they wish to change an agent's desires, they are more likely to forgo rational arguments in favor of other techniques. This is because intentions typically function as reasoning output and are therefore amenable to rational arguments, whereas desires typically function as reasoning inputs. If, for example, an agent announces her intention to date her secretary, the social perceiver may point to the disadvantages of doing so, or he may argue that the agent would be unlikely to succeed in implementing her intention. In short, he provides a series of arguments designed to dissuade the agent from her intention, and if she retains her intention despite powerful arguments against it he may feel that she is behaving irrationally. If, however, the agent merely announces a desire ("Sometimes I feel an urge to date Harry . . ."),

the social perceiver may feel that no arguments are possible. No matter how many arguments the social perceiver amasses, the agent can always say "I understand all that, but even so, I keep feeling this urge." Social perceivers who want to influence the agent's desires are therefore likely to look beyond rational argument to other influence techniques (e.g., portraying the secretary in an unflattering way).

Further studies are needed to test and refine these hypotheses, and other psychological implications of the desire/intention distinction will have to be explored. But we hope that our more general point has been successfully argued: that any satisfactory theory of social perception must account for the distinction people make between desire and intention.

Acknowledgments

Preparation of this chapter was supported by NSF CAREER award SBR-9703315 to the first author. We are grateful to Dahlia Spektor, Sarah Nelson, and Keith Miller for help in data collection and coding and to Michael Bratman, Donald Davidson, Gilbert Harman, Alfred Mele, and especially Lou Moses for comments on an earlier draft.

Notes

1. We use feminine pronouns for agents and masculine pronouns for social perceivers.

2. Cases of intending "to be polite" or "to be at the house at 7" can also be classified as action content because they refer to events directly controlled by the agent's actions (to act politely, to come to the house at 7).

3. We excluded occurrences of *to plan* when the verb was used in the sense of planning as an activity, not as an intention state (e.g., planning around the events; planning for the next 15 years; planning a vacation). Similarly, we excluded instances of the verb *to decide* when it was used in the sense of judging or concluding (e.g., "In 1963 he decided that Macmillan should step down as premier.")

4. The exceptions were "intended his interview as an overture," "intended the bomb to be used for . . . ," and "did not intend any disrespect."

5. The results are displayed with verbs ordered by type (desire or intention) and endorsement frequency. In the original questionnaire, their order was randomized across items, with three verbs of one type never succeeding one another.

6. There is a complication that we have not discussed, and it concerns intentions of group agents. Some scholars have argued that it is natural to speak of "our intention" when, say, two people plan to sing a duet together or a football team intends

to execute a pass play together (Bratman 1997; Gilbert 1989; Searle 1995). But it is not clear whether an individual person can intend something that she knows depends significantly on others' actions (Velleman 1997), and in fact the rule of intention content we have proposed would deny such a possibility. Perhaps an individual can only *desire* that the entire group perform a certain action (Zaibert, in press) and *intend* to do his or her share. Or perhaps the entire group can say "We intend to *A*" (referring to the group, not any individual), just as social perceivers are comfortable ascribing such mental states to other groups (O'Laughlin and Malle 2000). In the case of "We intend to *A*," the agent who intends is identical to the agent who performs the intended action, in line with the proposed rule of intention content.

3

Some Thoughts on Ascribing Complex Intentional Concepts to Young Children

Louis J. Moses

One of the great successes of modern psychological science has been the discovery of a rich and largely unsuspected cache of cognitive competencies in infancy and early childhood. Concepts concerning objects, motion, causality, number, and mind that were once thought to emerge only late in development are now believed to be available much earlier, and this has revolutionized the way we think about young children and their development (Kuhn and Siegler 1997). In the wake of these scientific breakthroughs comes an altogether different kind of challenge. Even the most ardent believer in early competence must concede that, in some way, children's concepts fall short of the sophisticated and complexly interconnected concepts possessed by adults. The difficulty, then, is to find a vocabulary that does justice to children's often-impressive cognitive capacities without doing violence to the meaning of the full-blown adult concepts. This is a daunting challenge, one that is too often quickly finessed with the aid of a caveat here and a footnote there paying mere lip service to the possibility of important conceptual advances at later points in development. What is required, but rarely delivered, is some more precise analysis of the ways in which children's concepts fail to measure up to those of their adult counterparts. The goal of this chapter is to provide such an analysis with respect to the concept of intention.

The folk concept of intention is complex and multi-faceted. It is related to, but importantly distinct from, a host of other folk-psychological notions, such as desire, belief, goal, trying, planning, deliberation, and commitment. As with any mental state, the meaning of intention is in part determined by its relations to these and other mental concepts. Indeed, according to the thesis of holism (Duhem 1906; Quine 1953) the meanings of such concepts are so thoroughly interwoven that the concepts "must be introduced *together or not at all*" (Armstrong 1981, p. 24). Although this "package deal" approach to mental-state concepts is not without its critics (Fodor and LePore 1992), it remains safe to say that the interdependent nature of many mental-state concepts may well have important ramifications for how we portray children's theories of mind at various points in development. If a major constituent of the adult folk-psychological network were missing at early ages, its absence could well have rippling influence across the remainder of that network. With this in mind, I will first attempt to characterize the folk concept of intention and then to illustrate how, early in life, an appreciation of intentional matters may be limited in certain essential respects. In doing so, I will argue that the adult concept of intention is deeply intertwined with the notion of belief. An appreciation of belief, however, is widely thought to be absent from children's folk-psychological repertoire until late in the preschool period. If this is the case, any claims that toddlers or infants have concepts of intention (in their mature form) would have to be modified. Along these lines, I will argue for, and present empirical evidence in support of, the position that, although very young children have considerable insights into intention-relevant matters, they do not yet possess a concept of intention that is commensurate with that of adults.

When we say that an agent intended to perform an action in order to bring about some outcome, we are making at least three claims (Davis 1984; Heider 1958; Malle and Knobe 1997a; Schmidt 1976). The first is a motivational claim: The agent must, in some sense, have wanted to perform the action. This does not, of course, mean that the agent necessarily liked what he or she was doing. Suppose that Max is preparing for a dinner party. He might very well want to (i.e., be motivated to) clean the bathroom without enjoying it in the least. He presumably desires to clean the bathroom because doing so is a means to some other, more intrinsically valued end. The second claim is a causal one: For an outcome to have been intended, it must have been achieved in the right way. It is not enough that the outcome satisfy the agent's desires; it must have been deliberately *caused* by the agent. Some things I desire come about without intervention from me (e.g., sunny days), and I cannot be said to have intended those things (Searle 1983). The third claim is epistemic: The agent's intention must have been connected to a belief (or set of beliefs) about what would be possible given the agent's abilities and the affordances of the environment. In short, possibility is the mother of intention: I cannot intend what I believe to be impossible.

Corresponding to each of these facets of intention we can envisage children possessing a different form of intention-relevant knowledge:

understanding the motivational aspect of intention This form of knowledge centers on an appreciation of desires and their relation to actions. It requires recognition of the fact that people typically do things because they want to do them. Wellman and Phillips (this volume) convincingly argue that 2-year-olds have a beginning appreciation of the motivational component of intention. Children of this age recognize that people can have different desires that are satisfied by different objects, and that they may have differential emotional reactions depending on whether or not their desires are satisfied (Wellman and Woolley 1990). More critical in the present context is the fact that they appropriately explain actions in terms of desires and predict actions from desires (Bartsch and Wellman 1995a; Wellman and Woolley 1990).

understanding the causal aspect of intention This form of knowledge requires recognition of the fact that intentions are causally related to actions and outcomes, whereas desires need not be so related. Even when an outcome satisfies a person's desire, the outcome may not have been intended. Only those outcomes that a person was actually trying to bring about could possibly have been intended. Hence, positive outcomes can sometimes be desired without being intended. Astington (this volume) summarizes evidence indicating that children do not begin to distinguish desire and intention in this way until they are 4 or 5 years old. (See also Feinfield, Lee, Flavell, Green, and Flavell 1999; Schult 1996.) Younger children tend to think that if the outcome was desired by the agent it must also have been intended.

understanding the epistemic aspect of intention This form of knowledge requires recognition of the fact that intention is a product of beliefs as well as desires. Specifically, it involves appreciating that an intention to perform an action generally entails a belief that one will perform the action (as well as other relevant background beliefs). Much less attention has been devoted to children's understanding of this facet of intention. In what follows I describe more fully how beliefs relate to intentions and then discuss some of my own research designed to assess what knowledge young children might possess concerning this relation.

The guiding principle behind the epistemic aspect of intention is that an agent's intentions should be consistent with his or her beliefs. This consistency requirement critically distinguishes intentions from desires. For example, Nadine cannot intend to buy a Ferrari while believing that she is flat broke, but there is nothing to stop her from wanting to buy it while holding that belief. Although she can desire it, she cannot intend what she believes she cannot do. The reason for this belief constraint on intentions is readily apparent when one considers the function intentions play in organizing and controlling everyday behavior. For example, intentions are typically parts of larger plans, and these plans serve to coordinate our activities (Bratman 1987). But I can be fully successful in coordinating my activities only if my plans are internally consistent. That is, coordination will be possible only if I arrange my activities such that my plans and the intentions embedded within them can "be successfully executed given that my beliefs are true" (Bratman 1987, p. 31). Clearly, if I believe that what I intend to do is not possible, and my belief is correct, I will not get very far. My intention will fail, and any larger plan of which it is a part will at best be derailed and will at worst collapse entirely. Hence, if intentions are to play an effective role in organizing behavior, they must be consistent with beliefs.

The way in which beliefs constrain intentions is also bound up with the relation between intention and commitment. Unlike desires, intentions involve commitments to act. Clearly, if I believe that I will not perform an action, then, just as it makes little sense for me to intend to perform that action, I can hardly be committed to performing it (Malle and Knobe, this volume).

But precisely what kinds of beliefs are entailed by having an intention, and how confidently must those beliefs be held? With respect to the first of these questions, an intention to perform an action most directly requires a belief that the action will in fact be performed (an *action belief*, for short). For example, if Clive intends to fly to Lisbon he should also believe that he will do so. Clearly, it would not be rational for Clive to intend to fly to

Lisbon while believing that he will not. In addition, intentions are typically accompanied by a host of other, increasingly tacit background beliefs. Clive's intention, for instance, should be accompanied not only by a belief about what he is going to do but also by beliefs that the airlines indeed fly to Lisbon, that he can afford a ticket, that his passport is up to date, and so on. These background beliefs lay the foundation for Clive's intention and his overarching action belief, and, again, it would make little sense for him to intend to fly to Lisbon if he did not hold such beliefs.

As to the strength of the beliefs involved, there are a number of possibilities. They are listed below in order of strength.[1] If I intend to perform action A, then I must believe one of the following:

(a) I can A—i.e., that it is possible for me to A. (See, e.g., Brand 1984.)

(b) There is some chance that I will A. (See, e.g., Bratman 1987; Davidson 1985.)

(c) I probably will A. (See, e.g., Davis 1984.)

(d) I will A. (See, e.g., Grice 1971.)

Of these proposals, (a) appears to be too weak. There are many things that I can do but that I believe I will not do, and I surely cannot intend what I positively believe I will not do. Less consensus exists over proposals (b)–(d); that is, over how confidently I must believe that I will A in order to be said to intend to A. My own view here is that intending to A requires a relatively strong belief that one will A. If the relevant belief is only weakly held, then, it seems to me, one can at best be said to intend *to try* to A (Mele 1992a; Mele, this volume). For example, a novice at darts might have very little confidence in her ability to hit the bull's-eye. Under these circumstances, she could not really intend to hit the bull's-eye, but she could perhaps intend to try.[2]

In any event, there is general agreement that, whether or not my intention to perform an action must be accompanied by a strong belief that I will do so, it normally is so accompanied (Bratman 1987). And it is surely no accident that we generally intend to do things that we are very confident we will do. Just as our plans would rarely come to fruition if our intentions were utterly inconsistent with our beliefs, we would be little better off if those intentions were accompanied by beliefs that we held with little confidence. Clive's larger plan to summer in Portugal will be in serious danger of collapsing, for example, if he believes there is only a slim chance that he will fly to Lisbon.

To recap: Part of what distinguishes intentions from other motivational states, such as desires, is that intentions must be consistent with beliefs. If they were not, we would forever be off in pursuit of Utopian aims, unattainable goals, and impossible dreams. Certainly our actions are occasionally driven by such motives, but I would submit that the lion's share of everyday behavior is organized around intentions constrained by beliefs about what is possible. In this way, intentions play a critical role in practical reasoning and in guiding human action.

One implication of the foregoing analysis is that an unfulfilled intention must be accompanied by at least one false belief. Suppose, for example, that Clive's intention to fly to Lisbon had been thwarted. Suppose that his passport had expired and the authorities never let him get off the ground. In that case, not only would his intention have been unfulfilled; he also would have held a false action belief (he thought he would fly to Lisbon when in fact he did not) and a false background belief (he thought his passport was valid when in fact it was not). Thus, to understand intentions like that held by Clive it is necessary to appreciate the possibility of false belief.[3]

In view of these relations between intention and belief, a child's concept of intention could not fully emerge before the concept of belief. Yet even a cursory reading of the current literature on children's theories of mind suggests the opposite. Whereas a concept of belief (and especially false belief) is commonly thought to arrive late in the preschool period (Moses and Flavell 1990; Wimmer and Perner 1983; Wellman, Cross, and Watson, in press), an appreciation of intentions is often argued to be present as early as infancy (Baldwin and Moses 1994; Bretherton, McNew, and Beeghly-Smith 1981; Gergely, Nadasdy, Csibra, and Biro 1995; Meltzoff 1995; Tomasello, in press). Two possible resolutions of this apparent contradiction suggest themselves. On the one hand, children might actually have an appreciation of belief earlier than much of the literature suggests. In particular, they might more easily reveal an understanding of false belief in contexts in which they see someone acting on an intention that turns out to be unfulfilled. Contexts of this kind might well help children: Unless they are able to recognize the false beliefs underlying unfulfilled intentions, they will be forced to view a lot of what people do as unintelligible. That is, without some appreciation of false belief, children are likely to regard people as spending much of their time flailing away irrationally in pursuit of unreachable goals. It seems unlikely that they could proceed for long with such an implausible view of human activity, and so an understanding of intention-relevant false beliefs might well appear early. On the other hand, it might indeed be the case that preschool children entirely lack concepts of belief and false belief. If so, their intentional understanding would be much more limited than that of adults, and any claims that they or younger children possessed intentional concepts would have to be heavily qualified: Although such children might appreciate some aspects of intention-related phenomena, they would lack an understanding of the essential epistemic component.

I have explored these issues directly in studies examining whether preschoolers might more easily reveal an understanding of false belief in contexts in which the beliefs in question were highly relevant to actors' intentions (Moses 1993). Successful performance in these studies hinged on an understanding of the relation between unfulfilled intentions and false beliefs. In a first study, a group of 32 3-year-olds was shown short movies in each of which an actor tried to, and believed he or she would, bring about a desirable outcome. In each case, though, the actor was unsuccessful in achieving the outcome and was very much surprised and saddened by this failure. After each movie, children were questioned about the actor's unfulfilled intention and about one of the critical but now patently false beliefs that had underpinned the intention. In two of these movies (action-belief movies) the belief question concerned the action the actor had been about to perform, in two others (background-belief movies) it concerned the identity of an object in a container). For example, one of the action-belief movies involved a protagonist who intended to pick up some toys and books from the floor and place them on a table. After successfully placing the toys on the table, he accidentally dropped the books on the floor. Children were asked whether he had been trying to drop the books on the floor or to put them on the table, and whether he had thought that he would drop the books on the floor or that he would put them on the table. In one of the similarly structured background-belief movies, a protagonist intended to pour cereal and milk into a bowl. After successfully pouring the cereal, she attempted to pour on the milk, but the carton was full of dirt. Children were then asked whether she had been trying to get dirt or milk from the carton, and whether she had thought that there would be dirt or milk in the carton.

Three findings from this study are important for present purposes. First, children performed equivalently on the action-belief and background-belief movies. They were just as good at inferring false beliefs about actions as at inferring false beliefs about objects. Second, in contrast to many other studies of false belief, 3-year-olds actually performed at above-chance levels on the false-belief questions (73 percent correct), which was consistent with the view that intentional contexts facilitate false-belief reasoning. Many of these 3-year-olds appeared to have little difficulty appreciating that, for example, the protagonist thought there was going to be milk in the carton when in fact there was dirt in the carton. Third, 3-year-olds' performance on the intention questions (84 percent correct) was nevertheless significantly better than that on the belief questions. Children rarely had difficulty understanding that, for example, the protagonist had been trying to put the books on the table, even though he ended up dropping them on the floor.

A second study with a new sample of 24 3-year-olds yielded similar results. Because no differences had been found between the action-belief and the background-belief movies in the first study, the children were shown only background-belief movies. The study also included a baseline comparison with false-belief tasks of a kind that 3-year-olds generally fail. These standard false-belief tasks were variants of the well-known "Smarties" tasks (Hogrefe, Wimmer, and Perner 1986; Gopnik and Astington 1988), in which children are first shown that a familiar-looking box actually contains something unexpected and are then asked what a friend will think is in the box before it is opened. In this new study, children were again above chance on the intention-relevant, background-belief questions, although their performance was not as good in absolute terms as in the first study (60 percent correct). In addition, their performance on the background-belief questions was superior to that on the standard false-belief questions (44 percent correct), which ruled out the possibility that children in these studies were somehow precocious relative to those included in other false-belief studies. Finally, however, performance on the intention questions (85 percent correct) was again clearly superior to that on the belief questions.

The findings from these two studies warrant three conclusions.   First, children's excellent performance on the intention questions indicates that by age 3 they have an understanding of at least one way in which mental states can differ from reality. That is, they understand that people sometimes have goals in mind that in the end they are unable to achieve. The findings thus converge with other work (e.g., Astington, this volume; Shultz and Wells 1985; Wellman and Phillips, this volume) in suggesting that children of this age have substantial appreciation of at least the motivational aspect of intention. What the evidence does not clarify, however, is whether such children understand the causal link between intentions and actions. For example, it is possible that an understanding of desire alone could have led children to perform well on these tasks. They might simply have heard questions about what protagonists were trying to do as questions about what they wanted. They did not necessarily need to understand that the protagonists' intentions actually caused them to act in order to satisfy their desires. That said, it seems likely that by the age of 3 years children have at least some understanding of the causal power of the mind to produce action. We might expect, for example, that simple introspection would facilitate this understanding (Goldman, this volume). Children's own feelings of volition before acting, and their energy expenditure while acting, are presumably quite salient at this age. It is hard to imagine that, on at least some occasions, they would not also have some sense of why they are doing what they are doing—that is, a sense of the goals and intentions driving their efforts. Such a possibility is certainly consistent with the evidence reviewed by Wellman and Phillips in this volume, but the issue remains in need of further research.

Second, even though children performed better on the intention questions, they also responded correctly quite often to the belief questions, which suggests that they may understand more about false belief than was once thought. Of course, their performance in these studies was far from perfect. Nevertheless, the findings are inconsistent with the view that 3-year-olds have *no* appreciation of false belief. Rather, the children in these studies looked more like a group with an initial, still fragile understanding of belief that emerges only under highly supportive conditions—in this case, a rich intentional context.

Finally, 3-year-olds revealed a much stronger appreciation of the motivational aspect of intention than of its epistemic aspect (i.e., they consistently performed better on questions about what the actor was trying to do than on those about what he or she believed). This finding is congruent with other work indicating that young children generally find it easier to infer motivational states such as desires than cognitive states such as beliefs (e.g., Flavell, Flavell, Green, and Moses 1990; Gopnik and Slaughter 1991; Lillard and Flavell 1992; Wellman and Woolley 1990). Moreover, it seems likely that, if one were to examine these issues at still younger ages an even wider gap would emerge between understanding of the motivational and epistemic aspects of intention. At 2 years and younger, for example, there continues to be good evidence of desire understanding but little hint of any appreciation of beliefs (Bartsch and Wellman 1995a; Repacholi and Gopnik 1997).

In sum, the findings of these studies suggest that, although some 3-year-olds have begun to recognize the beliefs that underpin intentions, a substantial number of them have little insight into these matters. Such children could not be said to possess a full appreciation of intention. This is not to deny the impressive strides that children of this age have already taken along the path to such an appreciation: Recognizing how motivational states relate to actions is a profound achievement in its own right, and one that forms the bedrock of intentional understanding. Until their appreciation of intentional phenomena incorporates an epistemic component, however, it will remain fundamentally distinct from its adult counterpart; hence, collapsing these two conceptions may only confuse matters.

How then should we portray the intentional understanding of younger children? It appears that children of age 3 and younger may not yet have differentiated their concept of intention from their concept of desire—that at this point in development they lack an understanding of the epistemic factors (and, possibly, of the causal factors) that distinguish intention from desire. It would be a mistake, however, to assume that they have a well-formed conception of desire out of which emerges a concept of intention. Such a characterization is probably too simple. It appears more likely that they have some more amorphous, global concept that fuses aspects of the adult conceptions of desire and intention but that does full justice to neither. Their conception may be something like a superordinate-level pro attitude (Davidson 1963) that isn't entirely desire and isn't entirely intention. At the heart of this conception may be an intention/desire notion that is closely wedded to action.[4] (For a similar view, see Astington, this volume.) A child may think that if someone is acting on something then he or she must want it; conversely, if someone wants it then he or she will surely act on it. But of course people have many desires that they never come close to acting upon (e.g., Alec sometimes wants to strangle his neighbor who has a noisy leaf blower, but he never actually does). The idea that people actually carry around with them a host of desires that they never make the slightest attempt to act out is, I suspect, foreign to very young children. To be clear, I do not want to claim that children's early desire/intention concept is behaviorist (i.e., nonmentalistic). Very likely they do view themselves and others as having mental experiences that motivate actions. Still, motivational states that are divorced from action may not be so easily recognized by them. This would not be surprising if, as seems probable, the desires they perceive most frequently in their daily lives are desires that people (the children included) are attempting to act upon or already have acted upon. If children's concept of a pro attitude is indeed action centered, then it is in some sense closer to (though not the same as) a concept of intention than a concept of (pure) desire.

There are other grounds for believing that children's initial conception of desire may be limited. The very same advances in epistemic understanding that bear on children's intentional appreciation are likely to have ramifications for their notion of desire. None of the arguments presented earlier is meant to imply that beliefs are entirely irrelevant to desires. Take Nadine and her desire for a Ferrari. The fact that Nadine holds this desire doesn't require a belief that she will actually buy a car of that kind. Still, her desire must be framed by at least some beliefs. She presumably has some beliefs about what a Ferrari is and what it can do for her. She may want the car because she believes that the Ferrari is superior to its rivals in performance, comfort, styling, and status. Of course, these are not beliefs concerning whether Nadine will act on the desire or even about whether her desire will be fulfilled. Rather, they constitute some of the reasons she has for holding her desire. Specifically, they are the belief reasons underlying her desire. In addition, she will have desire reasons—e.g., she also *wants* a car with these features. Together, these belief and desire reasons motivate Nadine's desire for a Ferrari. Clearly, then, the emergence of a conception of belief will have implications not only for intentional understanding but also for children's appreciation of reason-based desires.

Not all desires are reason based (Nagel 1970; Schueler 1995). Some things we desire are ends in themselves (e.g., desires for nourishment, physical safety, sexual gratification). We don't need belief or desire reasons to support these desires. Suppose Jack has a desire for food. Beliefs might not enter into it, beyond some minimal belief about what food is; Jack's desire may be entirely driven by hunger pangs. In Malle and Knobe's (this volume) terminology, desires of this kind are not the outputs of reasoning, although they can certainly be inputs to reasoning aimed at furthering the likelihood that they will be fulfilled.

Other desires (such as Nadine's desire for a Ferrari) are not for things that are necessarily desirable in and of themselves but merely for things that are means to other, perhaps more intrinsically desirable ends. Such desires are held for reasons: They are links in chains of practical reasoning that are (or should be) constrained by agents' beliefs. In this respect they share some similarity with chains of intentions that form larger plans. At this point we know very little about when children come to appreciate how beliefs generate desires (or, more generally, about when they recognize how desires participate in extended reasoning sequences), but they would seem unlikely to do so before the age of 4 or 5 years.

Some children experienced little difficulty with either the intention or the belief questions in the studies described earlier. What can be said of their intentional understanding? Although these children certainly appeared to have a foothold on understanding epistemic aspects of intention, it would be premature to claim that they had a full understanding of these matters. Specifically, the findings do not demonstrate an understanding that intentions are *necessarily* accompanied by beliefs. Strictly speaking, all they show is that these children understood certain false beliefs that happened to be embedded in an intentional context. It is possible that they did not explicitly recognize the link between the actors' intentions and their beliefs; instead, the actors' intentions may simply have made those beliefs salient. Still, understanding such beliefs in these contexts is certainly an important step along the road to understanding belief-intention relations. Further steps remain ahead, however, before children can be said to have a complete appreciation of the epistemic aspects of intention. One facet of this appreciation concerns the consistency of our mental states. Clearly our beliefs should be consistent with one another. We generally resist holding beliefs that we know to be contradictory. But the same is true of intentions: If I intend to go to a movie and I intend to go to a party, these possibilities shouldn't be contradictory—at least, I should *believe* that I can do both things without conflict. Again, the role of intentions in everyday action and as components of larger plans makes these consistency requirements clear— if my intentions are inconsistent with one another, my plans will fall apart, just as they will if any single intention is inconsistent with my beliefs. This consistency requirement further distinguishes intentions from desires. There is no need for my desires to be consistent—I can want to go to the movie and to go to the party even if it is physically impossible for me to do both at the same time.

Related to these consistency requirements is the fact that intentions agglomerate but desires do not. If I intend to go to the movie and I intend to go to the party, then I should intend to go to both. But desires don't have to agglomerate in this way. Recall Max and his dinner party. Max might have one desire to invite his college drinking buddy and yet another desire to invite his wealthy great uncle who happens to be a confirmed teetotaler. But that doesn't mean he has a desire to invite both—if both were to come, the outcome could have disastrous consequences for Max's fiscal future.

Our intentions agglomerate because they are mental states that already involve commitments to act. In making such commitments, an agent tacitly accedes to any combination of intentions that he or she possesses: If an agent were unwilling to do so, he or she would surely not be committed to carrying out these intentions. With desires, there is (as yet) no commitment to act, and so there is no telling whether the agent would want to combine them. If the agent's desires are believed to be inconsistent or in some other way incompatible, he or she will presumably not wish them to agglomerate.

At the outset I described three kinds of understanding, corresponding to the motivational, causal, and epistemic components of intention. The more complex facets of intentional appreciation just discussed indicate a further distinction between perceiving intentions merely as the melding together of a belief and a desire to produce action (a "glue" theory of intention, as Bratman (1989) calls it) and recognizing their role in larger, possibly long-range plans involving coordinated sets of mutually consistent intentions. This more sophisticated notion of intention requires an appreciation of humans as actively constructing their mental agendas, a conception of psychological functioning that is unlikely to emerge before the close of the preschool years (Chandler, Sokol, and Hallett, this volume).

In conclusion, I hope to have illustrated some of the complexities involved in characterizing the intentional understanding of young children. The adult conception of intention is a many-sided one that is surely not mastered in a single stroke. Although some basic insight into intentional phenomena may well develop early in life, the acquisition of a full appreciation of the pivotal role of intentions in guiding human behavior is likely to be quite protracted.

Acknowledgments

Thanks to Dare Baldwin, Bertram Malle, and Josef Perner for helpful comments on an earlier draft.

Notes

1. To cover the possibility that I hold no explicit beliefs about the success of my actions, these proposals are sometimes expressed as *negative* belief constraints (Mele 1992a; Mele, this volume). Like positive constraints, however, negative constraints can also be arrayed in terms of strength—e.g., "I must not believe that I will (probably) not A" versus "I must not believe that there is some chance that I will not A."

2. Interestingly, people with low self-efficacy—i.e., those who do not believe that their actions are likely to be successful—often end up failing to act, sometimes with deleterious consequences for their well-being (Bandura 1997). It seems that, without the requisite beliefs, individuals not only cannot form intentions, but, in certain situations, they may cease trying to act altogether.

3. On the view that intentions require only weaker belief constraints, unfulfilled intentions will not necessarily be accompanied by false beliefs: Believing that there is merely some chance that I will A is quite consistent with my not A-ing. Still, even if this view is correct, it is at least not the case that I held a full set of relevant true beliefs. For example, if I intend to perform A but actually perform B, then, what-

ever I believed about performing A, I certainly did not believe that I would perform B. This point is critical with respect to the development of intentional understanding: As we shall see, many young children not only fail to ascribe false beliefs to agents whose intentions are unfulfilled; they also appear to inappropriately grant them relevant true beliefs.

4. Consistent with this hypothesis, young preschoolers appear to think that intentions are isomorphic with actions—that when two individuals perform the same actions they must have identical intentions (Baird and Moses 2000).

4

The Paradox of Intention: Assessing Children's Metarepresentational Understanding

Janet Wilde Astington

At the beginning of their landmark article "Does the chimpanzee have a theory of mind?" Premack and Woodruff (1978, p. 515) write: "As to the states of mind the chimpanzee might infer, let us look at some of those that members of our own species infer. It seems beyond question that purpose or intention is the state we impute most widely." At the end of the article (p. 526), they speculate: "Of all possible guesses, we find the most compelling one to be that inferences about motivation will precede those about knowledge, both across species and across developmental stages." From the literature of the past 20 years, it appears that primatologists and developmentalists agree with Premack and Woodruff that the attribution of intention is simpler and more commonplace than the attribution of belief and that, in general, motivational states are more obvious and more easily understood than knowledge states. I too agree—but only in part. There is something paradoxical about intention attribution. Though it is true that motivational states are more obvious and more frequently inferred than beliefs, the attribution of intention—in a precise and complete sense—is not simpler, and may indeed be harder, than the attribution of belief. The paradox might lie in the fact that, although children seem to have command over some aspects of the concept of intention early on, not until later years do they seem to have command over other aspects. Indeed, perhaps it is unwise to use the same term to refer to the early and later understanding. Intention is a complex concept, and a full metarepresentational understanding of intention is only gradually acquired.

What Is Intention?

Primatologists argue that, because of the social complexity of primate groups, selective pressure in the evolution of primate intelligence decisively favored the evolution of social intelligence (Byrne and Whiten 1997). In order to live successfully within a social group, an animal must be able to *anticipate* the actions of other animals in the group (Goody 1995). Social intelligence is thus based on apprehension of action *before it occurs*. It may be too much to claim that this entails awareness of intention—the animal may simply have a set of dispositional concepts that are behavioral but not mental (Povinelli, this volume). However, even at this level, information concerning what the other is trying to do (that is, recognition of the goal of the other's action) allows intervention in a competitive or a cooperative manner. Such intervention, to thwart or to help, is the essence of social interaction. Moreover, for adult humans these interventions do appear to entail awareness of intention. We see intention everywhere, giving meaning to what others do and say and guiding our interactions with them. Small (1990, p. 440) provides a nice example: She was walking down a country road when a car stopped and the driver asked "Are you walking for exercise?" Small replied "Yes, thank you," and the car drove on. She considered why she had said "Thank you" and not just "Yes." She concluded that she had inferred that the driver intended to offer her a ride, which she declined with thanks. Our everyday interactions are imbued with such implicit attribution of intention that we do not think about it unless we reflect on it.

From what I have said so far, intention can be seen as a pro attitude tied to action. This is true, but it does not take us far enough. We need to distinguish intention from desire, because both are pro attitudes that may motivate action (Malle and Knobe, this volume). Intentions, desires, and also beliefs can be construed as mental states that represent attitudes toward propositions (Searle 1983). Intentions and desires are alike, and are unlike beliefs, in that their satisfaction depends on events in the world coming to match the propositional content, which is a representation of the intended or desired outcome. Intentions differ from desires, however, in that the propositional content refers to the action the intention causes. Desires are satisfied so long as the desired outcome is achieved, no matter how. Intentions, on the other hand, are satisfied only if the intention causes the action that brings about the outcome. This is what Searle (1983, p. 85) designates the "causal self-reference" of intention.

Anscombe (1957) introduces her classic examination of the concept of intention by distinguishing three aspects of intention that are fundamental to a complete understanding of the concept: intentional action, intention in acting, and expression of intention for the future. That is, the concept of intention can be used to denote deliberate action (in contrast to accidental behavior), to refer to the reason or reasons why something is done, or to refer to future planned action. Searle's (1983) analysis of intention captures these three points in distinguishing between prior intention and intention-in-action. Prior intentions, which may be made explicit as expressions of intention for the future, are mental states that precede actions and that depend on one's desires and beliefs (which provide the reasons for acting). Intention-in-action, on the other hand, characterizes a current action, which consists of the intention-in-action and the bodily movement.

Malle and Knobe's model (this volume; see also Malle and Knobe 1997a) of the adult folk concept addresses all three aspects of intention distinguished by Anscombe by making a distinction between intention and intentionality: Intention is a mental state, whereas intentionality is the manner in which an action is performed. Intentions are mental states that integrate the desires and beliefs that are the reasons for acting (Malle 1999). An intention is a representation of the action an agent believes will achieve a desired outcome; such intention can be expressed as a plan for the future. Performing the action intentionally (in other words, the intentionality of the action) depends not only on having the intention to act but also on having the skill required to perform the action and the awareness that one is performing it. Without skill and/or awareness, the action may be unintentional even though the intention is present. Thus, in some circumstances there may be intention without intentionality.

The distinction Malle and Knobe make between intention and intentionality allows us to explain how people intuitively understand the "twist" in what philosophers refer to as "deviant causal chains." In an often-quoted example (Chisholm 1966, cited in Searle 1983, p. 82), a man wanted to kill his uncle so that he would inherit a fortune. One day, while out driving, he got so worked up thinking how he could commit the murder that he carelessly drove over a pedestrian—who happened to be his uncle. For Searle, this is an unintentional killing because, although the man's action caused the outcome and the outcome matched the goal, the intention did not cause the action that brought about the outcome. However, such consideration of causal self-reference probably does not enter ordinary adults' reasoning, at least not explicitly. Consideration of skill and awareness (Malle and Knobe 1997a) is more intuitively appealing. Even though the man stood to gain from the pedestrian's death (that is, he had a reason to kill his uncle and indeed had intended to do so), we would not consider this road incident to be murder, because the man did not skillfully maneuver his car over the pedestrian and was indeed unaware that the pedestrian was his uncle. We might find the man guilty of driving without due care and attention, but we would not find him guilty of murder. Of course, we might try to prove that he really knew the pedestrian was his uncle but pretended not to and contrived to make the killing look like an accident—but even here, our judgment of intentionality depends on considerations of awareness and skill.

A fully developed concept of intention allows one to appreciate such subtleties. However, the inability to do so does not imply that one has no understanding of intention. A concept with this degree of complexity is most likely gradually acquired. This returns us to the paradox of intention. It is, on the one hand, the simplest and most obvious mental state. Yet, partly because of its causal self-reference, it is one of the most difficult to understand completely.

In this chapter I examine young children's developing concept of intention, focusing on their understanding of causal self-reference (that is, their understanding of intentional causation—that intentions cause the actions they represent). I argue that infants may detect intentions in action while having no explicit concept of intention. The concept begins to develop as language develops, but at first children understand intention just as a pro attitude intimately tied to acts and speech acts. Only later do they acquire a metarepresentational understanding and see intentions as representations, independent of actions in the world; that then allows them to understand intentional causation and to distinguish between intention and desire. Finally I argue that, although we cannot legislate everyday language use, in scientific discourse we can (and should) mark the distinction between early and full understanding of the concept of intention.

Infants' Detection of Intention

During the very first months of life, infants react to others, for example, by imitating their facial movements or participating in turn-taking exchanges of smiling and vocalizing. Trevarthen (1980) and some other researchers suggest that this sort of intersubjective social interaction implies that young infants attribute intentions to other people. Other researchers, while denying that these early interactions indicate any understanding of intention, claim that intention attribution is evident at 9 months, when infants begin to participate in triadic interactions involving self, adult, and object. For example, an infant will put an object into an adult's outstretched hand, will turn to look at an object the adult is looking at, and will respond to a strange object in accord with the adult's emotional expression of positive regard or revulsion. Tomasello (1999) argues that these behaviors come in around 9 months because of a change in infants' understanding of their own intentionality that is marked by the differentiation of means and ends. At this time, infants begin to see themselves as intentional agents. They already see other persons as "like me," as is evidenced in neonatal imitation (Meltzoff and Gopnik 1993; Meltzoff and Brooks, this volume), and they apply their new understanding of self as intentional agent to others, seeing intention in the other's behavior. Whether intention attribution is appropriately assigned to infants at the beginning or near the end of the first year, these perspectives focus on the intersubjective nature of intention attribution and its origin in interpersonal interaction.

From a quite different perspective, focused on the individual child's cognitive abilities, Premack (1990; see also Premack and Premack 1995) claims that infants' perception of intention is hard-wired. Infants are sensitive to changes in motion and categorize such changes as self-propelled or non-self-propelled. When the motion of a non-self-propelled object (e.g., a geometrical form in an animated video display) is changed by another object, the infant perceives causality. When the motion of a self-propelled object changes by itself, the infant perceives intention provided that the object engages in goal-directed movement. For example, when two self-propelled objects are seen together and one object stops, the other one touches it, and the first starts moving again, the infant perceives the second object as acting intentionally. Object movement is more likely to be seen as intentional and goal-directed if it exceeds base-line intensity—that is, Premack claims, infants have the ability to recognize "trying." This is important, as later I will argue that the concept of trying is a crucial early component of the child's concept of intention. It is only fair to say that, so far, data to support Premack's claims come only from 3–5-year-olds (Dasser, Ulbaek, and Premack 1989).[1]

Certainly, infants' ability to detect intentions in action is a currently lively research area. Several chapters in the present volume report recent work demonstrating such ability in infants, some as young as 6 months. Data from habituation studies show that infants perceive human movements as goal-directed actions; for example, 6-month-olds dishabituate to novel goals, not to novel movements (Wellman and Phillips, this volume; Woodward, Sommerville and Guajardo, this volume), and 10-month-olds dishabituate to interruptions in movement sequences when the interruption occurs before the goal is achieved but not when it occurs as the goal is achieved (Baird and Baldwin, this volume). Baird and Baldwin are cautious in the interpretation of their findings, suggesting that infants may have only low-level perceptual skills for detecting structure in the behavior stream and may not yet have the ability to infer intentions underlying behavior.

Early Understanding of Intention

Indeed, it is possible that none of the infant behaviors reported above—imitation, turn taking, joint attention, social referencing, differential responding to self-propelled and non-self-propelled objects, dishabituation to action interruption and to novel goals—imply any real understanding of intention on the infant's part, although they may appear to do so. It may be that they are just evolved social behaviors. Povinelli's "reinterpretation hypothesis" (this volume; see also Povinelli and Giambrone, in press) proposes, contra the argument from analogy, that similar social-cognitive behaviors in different species do not necessarily imply similar underlying cognitive processes. In comparative psychology, the argument from analogy, put forward by Darwin and Romanes, is that animals that produce the same external behaviors are motivated by the same internal states. Povinelli was disabused of this idea by his careful experimental work on chimpanzees' understanding of seeing and attention. He found that, despite possessing human-like gaze-following behaviors, chimpanzees really do not understand seeing and attention in the way that even very young children do. Povinelli (1999) extends his argument to infants and proposes that early gaze following is an evolved social behavior that implies no understanding of the other's attentional state.

Similarly, Povinelli (this volume) argues that infants' behaviors that appear to involve an understanding of intention really do not. Infants detect intention in behavior but have no conceptual understanding of it. Such detection may lead to an understanding of intention later on, perhaps through a mechanism of representational redescription (Karmiloff-Smith 1992) in which language development plays a part. It is interesting, in this regard, that researchers who are skeptical of 9-month-olds' capacity for intention understanding and attribution (e.g., Baldwin and Moses 1994) see the first clear signs of it around 18 months, when language is developing rapidly.

By 18 months, children can use the direction of a speaker's gaze to infer the referent of a novel word (Baldwin 1995). For example, in one condition an experimenter looked at and labeled a child's toy when the child's focus was on it, and in a second condition she looked at and labeled her own toy, again when the child's focus was on the child's toy. Children 18 months of age used the direction of the experimenter's gaze as an indication of her intention to refer to the child's toy in the first condition and to her own toy in the second condition, and they appropriately learned the two novel words. That is, children this age clearly attribute communicative intentions to another person. At this age, children also can infer intention in an adult's behavior (Meltzoff 1995). Eighteen-month-olds who had seen an adult try and fail to perform an action, when given the opportunity to imitate the adult, did not copy the movement they had witnessed but performed the action the adult was attempting to perform. Control conditions warrant the conclusion that the 18-month-olds were inferring the goal of the act and appropriately ascribing intention. Interestingly, if the adult made one attempt and failed, children did not imitate the intended action, but if the adult tried three times and failed, they did imitate it (Meltzoff, Gopnik, and Repacholi 1999). The ascription of intention seems to depend on a notion of "trying," in that it is the adult's repeated attempts that clue the child into the intention.

Baldwin and Meltzoff refer to toddlers' understanding of intention, whereas others refer to their understanding of desire. For example, Repacholi and Gopnik (1997) showed that 18-month-olds can attribute to another person a desire that is clearly different from their own desire. Wellman and his colleagues showed that 2-year-olds understand the connection between desires and outcomes and can recognize that an unsatisfied desire leads to further action (Wellman and Woolley 1990; Wellman and Phillips, this volume). However, although researchers talk differentially about toddlers' understanding of intention and desire, it is likely that the toddlers themselves do not make such a distinction. From the evidence reported, it seems clear that toddlers do have some understanding of intention and desire. They understand both as pro attitudes—motivational states that are intimately tied to acts and speech acts. There is as yet no evidence that they distinguish between intention and desire, or that they understand intentions and desires as representations, independent of act or speech act.

The Beginnings of Metarepresentational Understanding

Metarepresentational understanding is the understanding that people's beliefs, desires, and intentions are mental representations that mediate their actions in the world and their interactions with others in the world (Perner 1991). Children with this understanding think of beliefs, desires, and intentions as representations that are produced by the mind as a result of certain experiences and that effect actions in the world in certain specific ways. Once children understand this, they understand that the mind has a degree of autonomy from reality. They can then see that people do not have direct access to reality but construct the world in their mind, and this constructed world is the world in which people act, even when their representation is a misrepresentation of the way things really are.

The development of metarepresentational understanding has been the focus of intense research activity over the past 20 years. Spawned in part by the commentaries on Premack and Woodruff's 1978 article, from which I quoted at the beginning of this chapter, it has taken its moniker—children's theory of mind—from the title of that article. Premack and Woodruff (ibid., p. 515) defined theory of mind as follows: "An individual has a theory of mind if he imputes mental states to himself and others. A system of inferences of this kind is properly viewed as a theory because such states are not directly observable, and the system can be used to make predictions about the behavior of others." They claimed that the chimpanzee imputed the mental state of intention to a human actor faced with a problem, predicting his action on the basis of this attribution. Thus, they claimed that the animal had a theory of mind—a claim that did not pass undisputed. A number of commentators (Bennett 1978; Dennett 1978b; Harman 1978) described an experimental paradigm that would conclusively demonstrate whether the animal possessed a theory of mind as defined, which was taken up by two developmentalists (Wimmer and Perner 1983). Interestingly, although Premack and Woodruff had focused on the attribution of intention, the paradigm focused on the attribution of belief, perhaps because this provides the clearest case of mental-state attribution. Children who can attribute to another person a belief that is false from their point of view, and can predict the person's action based on that false belief, clearly have metarepresentational understanding. They understand that people act on the basis of their representation of the world, even when this is a misrepresentation of the actual situation.

False-belief understanding has been the central focus of research in children's theory of mind. Wellman, Cross, and Watson (in press) recently conducted a meta-analysis of 178 false-belief studies. In contrast, only a handful of studies have investigated metarepresentational understanding of intention. Nonetheless, because of the central importance of intention in social cognition generally and in moral judgment in particular, there is a huge body of research investigating children's understanding of intention, predating and concurrent with research on children's theory of mind. Many studies ask children to judge whether actions—real actions or ones depicted in stories or on film—are intended or accidental. However, in these scenarios children can think of intentions and desires as related to goal states without discriminating between intention and desire, and can succeed by matching goals and outcomes (Astington 1991). If the goal and the outcome match, they say that the action was intentional; if there is a mismatch, they say that it was accidental. Even 3-year-olds can respond appropriately in this way. The problem is that these studies do not allow for conclusions to be drawn regarding children's metarepresentational understanding of intention, which involves the ability to distinguish between desire and intention.

Why does metarepresentational understanding entail the ability to distinguish between desire and intention? Perner (1991) describes the 3-year-old as a "situation theorist" who can represent different situations, including hypothetical ones. However, the 3-year-old cannot metarepresent. That is, she cannot represent herself or another person representing the hypothetical situation. The 3-year-old ascribes desires and intentions to people by thinking of the desired or intended state (that is, the goal state) as a hypothetical situation and associating the person with that situation. She can then judge that the person will act to achieve the goal and will be happy if it is achieved (as shown by Wellman's experiments). However, in order to distinguish between desire and intention the child must represent herself or another person representing the hypothetical desired or intended situation. That is, the child has to understand that action to achieve the goal must be caused by some internal representation of it. In Perner's (1991, pp. 219–220) terms, in the situation theorist's view of goal-directed action there are only goals that people have and actions that they can take to achieve those goals. There is only the goal and the action, not the separate notion of the intention to act. The child who can metarepresent can separate these two notions; that is, the intention to act can be understood as a mental state representing that one will act. The representation of the action is not a hypothetical situation but part of the same world, albeit internal, as the action itself. Intention thus straddles the internal world of the mind and the external world of action, and the representational mental state can be understood as causally responsible for the action. Now it is possible to think separately of the desire for an outcome and the intention to act to achieve the outcome.

Assessing Metarepresentational Understanding of Intention

Developing awareness of the representational capacity of the mind brings about a change in the child's concept of intention because it allows the child to differentiate between desire and intention and to recognize cases, such as the deviant causal chain, in which intention is unfulfilled but desire is satisfied. Thus, the result of the child recognizing the mind's representational function is an appreciation of intentional causation. In order to assess metarepresentational understanding of intention, it is essential to ensure that desire and intention do not coincide, so that children cannot solve the task simply by considering desires. It is also essential to ensure that the task cannot be solved by simply matching goals and outcomes.

Phillips (1994; see also Phillips, Baron-Cohen, and Rutter 1998) adapted a goal-outcome matching task in order to separate intention and desire. In the original task (Shultz and Wells 1985), children shot at colored targets, judging shots intentional on the basis of a match between the color they chose to hit and the one they did hit. In Phillips's task, the targets were colored cans, some of which contained prizes. The apparatus was rigged undetectably so that, although children chose which color can they would aim for, the experimenter controlled which can actually fell and whether or not it contained a prize. The child's intention was to aim at a certain color; the desire was to get a prize. There were four conditions, in two of which intention and desire coincided (i.e., were both achieved or neither achieved), and in two of which intention and desire did not coincide—the latter are the conditions of interest. In one of the latter conditions (intention fulfilled/desire unsatisfied), the child hits the intended can but it does not contain a prize; in the other (intention unfulfilled/desire satisfied), the child hits the wrong can but it contains a prize, resulting in fortuitous success as in the deviant causal chain. Children were given four trials in each condition. At the end of each trial they were asked (where A or B—counterbalanced across trials—was the intended color) "Which color did you mean to shoot: the A one, or the B one?"

Two groups of children (one group with a mean age of 4 years, 6 months, the other with a mean age of 5 years, 7 months) were tested. The question of interest is how they responded in the discrepant conditions. Overall, 5-year-olds' responses were more accurate than those of 4-year-olds. However, the major difference between the two groups was in the intention-fulfilled/desire-unsatisfied condition. Here, 4-year-olds were more likely to say that they meant to shoot the other color. That is, the child said he was going to shoot (say) the red can, he did shoot the red can, and it was empty. When asked if he meant to shoot the red one or the green one, he said he meant to shoot the green one. However, in the other discrepant condition (intention-unfulfilled/desire-satisfied), the 4-year-old said he was going to shoot (say) the blue can, he shot the yellow can, and it contained a prize. When asked if he meant to shoot the blue can or the yellow one, he correctly said that he meant to shoot the blue one. Thus, it is not the case that 4-year-olds simply collapse the intention and the desire. In the fortuitous-success case, they recognize that they did not do what they meant to do even though they got what they wanted. Why then did they answer incorrectly in the other discrepant condition? It may be, as Phillips and her co-authors suggest, that the pragmatics of the situation encouraged children to say that they meant to shoot the other can as this might have prompted the experimenter to open it to see if it contained a prize.

One would anyway predict that 4-year-olds would succeed on this task, since by this age they are likely to have achieved an understanding of metarepresentation. Indeed, these 4-year-olds were also given two standard false-belief tests, on which they had an overall success rate of 77 percent. No child passed the intention task but failed false belief. We would like to know how 3-year-olds would perform on the task, but they were not included in the testing.

Schult (1996), however, did include 3-year-old participants in an adaptation of another Shultz task (Shultz and Shamash 1981). Children had to throw beanbags at colored buckets, some of which contained small pictures. They had to choose which bucket they were going to aim at. If the bucket they hit contained a picture, they stuck it on a scorecard, winning the game when their card was full. Similar to Phillips's task, the child's intention was to hit a particular bucket, and it was separate from the desire to get a picture. Thus, again, four conditions were possible. In two, intention and desire coincided; in the other two, they did not. Children were given three trials in each condition, and at the end of each trial they were asked "Which bucket were you trying to hit?" The participants were 3-, 4- and 5-year-olds (mean ages: 3 years, 6 months; 4 years, 6 months; 5 years, 4 months). There was no difference among the groups when the intention was fulfilled; that is, when the chosen bucket was hit most children reported that was the bucket they were trying to hit. However, when the intention was not fulfilled (that is, when a different bucket was hit), 3-year-olds performed significantly worse than 4- and 5-year-olds, particularly when the desire was satisfied (that is, when there was a picture in the bucket they did not choose but accidentally hit). In this last condition, only 27 percent of 3-year-olds correctly said that they were not trying to hit this bucket. This is what would be predicted by the matching-strategy hypothesis—the desire was satisfied and so the action was intended. One might argue that in a sense this was the bucket they were trying to hit (after all, it contained a picture), but 82 percent of 4-year-olds and 96 percent of 5-year-olds correctly reported that they were not trying to hit this bucket. It seems that 3-year-olds do not recognize that actions are intentional *under a description*.

Recall that in Phillips's task 4-year-olds' poor performance was in the intention-fulfilled/desire-unsatisfied condition where they were only 71 percent successful (chance is 50 percent), whereas in Schult's task 4-year-olds' responses were 93 percent correct in this condition (and chance is 33 percent here). It is difficult to make a direct comparison of children's performance across the two studies because there is no common task (e.g., a false-belief task). Nonetheless, both groups were the same mean age (4 years, 6 months), which gives some basis for comparison. In my view, the difference between performance in the two studies may be due to the verb used in the test question. Phillips asked "Did you *mean* to hit the A one or the B one?" Schult asked "Which one were you *trying* to hit?" Trying is associated with acting and may help young children make the link with intention (Astington 1999) boosting performance in the Schult task. However, there are other relevant differences between the two experiments, such as a forced choice versus an open-ended question. A more direct comparison is needed to assess the effect of the two verbs.

The tasks described so far assess children's ability to distinguish between their own desires and intentions in real situations. Researchers have also developed story tasks to assess children's metarepresentational understanding of intention from a third-person perspective. Again, the focus has been on children's ability to distinguish between desire and intention. Schult (1996) developed a set of stories that mirrored the four conditions in the first-person tasks just described—that is, in two types of story the protagonist's intention and desire are both satisfied or both unsatisfied, and in the other two types the protagonist's intention and desire do not coincide (one is satisfied and one is unsatisfied). There were two stories of each type, eight in all. At the end of each story, children were asked "Did [the protagonist] do what [he or she] planned to do?" and "Did [the protagonist] get what [he or she] wanted?"

Three groups of children, 4, 5, and 7 years old, were tested. No 3-year-olds were included here, but even the 4-year-olds (mean age 4 years, 7 months) had difficulty with this task in the discrepant conditions. In one fortuitous-success case (intention-unfulfilled/desire-satisfied), Andrew wanted soup and planned to make it for lunch, but when he came in his mother had already made lunch and gave him a bowl of soup. In the other, Becky wanted a doll she had seen at a toy store and saved up her money and planned to buy it, but before she went to the store her mother gave her the doll. Most 4-year-olds correctly said that the desire was satisfied (that is, the character got what he or she wanted), but only 50 percent of their responses (across the two stories) correctly said that the intention was not fulfilled (that is, the character did not do what he or she planned to do). In contrast, 83 percent of 5-year-olds' and 94 percent of 7-year-olds' responses correctly reported that the intention was not fulfilled. For the other discrepant stories (intention-fulfilled/desire-unsatisfied) 75 percent of 4-year-olds' responses correctly said that the characters didn't get what they wanted, but only 61 percent correctly said that the characters did what they planned to do. In all cases, the 4-year-olds understood and remembered the stories and reported the content of the characters' desires and intentions as accurately as the older children did.

One interesting aspect of both Phillips's and Schult's findings is that children's errors appear to indicate a primacy of desire over intention (Bertram Malle, personal communication, July 20, 1999). That is, in the cases where mistakes occur, children falsely claim an intention that is assimilated to the desire. Put differently, the desire content (e.g., getting the prize, having soup) is more salient than the intention content (hitting the can, making soup). The achievement of 5-year-olds, then, may lie in their appreciation of intention and action as important mediators between desire and outcome. In my view, it is the metarepresentational ability to see intentions as representational states causing actions that allows for an understanding of this mediation. However, the 4-year-olds in Schult's last study had difficulty recognizing whether an intention was fulfilled or not when it was discrepant from the satisfaction of desire. Despite being old enough to recognize false belief[2] (that is, to have achieved metarepresentational understanding of belief), they could not recognize the distinction between desire and intention. This suggests that something more than metarepresentional ability is required to distinguish intention from desire, unless the results are due to the particular story content and test questions Schult used. This is difficult to determine, because there are no other comparable studies.

One set of studies (Feinfield, Lee, Flavell, Green, and Flavell 1999) that aims to investigate 3- and 4-year-olds' ability to distinguish between intention and desire does not meet the requirements proposed above to ensure that children cannot succeed by simply matching goals and outcomes. The

first study by Feinfield et al. included four stories, in each of which the protagonist wants to go to a place (A) but decides to go to a place he dislikes
(B) because his mother wants him to go there; on the way to B, the bus driver gets lost, and the protagonist accidentally arrives at A. Children were
asked where the character was *trying* to go, where he *thought* he was going
to go, and where he *liked* to go. In this study, 4-year-olds but not 3-year-olds
were quite good at identifying that the character tried to go and thought he
was going to B although he liked to go to A. The second study included four
stories in which a mother tells a child to get an object (A), the child goes to
the anticipated location of A, and finds there a different, more desirable
object (B). Children were asked what the character was trying to get, what
he thought he was going to get, whether he got what he was looking for, and
which object (A or B) he liked better. The 4-year-olds performed well on all
four questions; 3-year-olds' performance was less good and was above
chance only on the questions that asked what the character was trying to
get and which object he liked better. Feinfield et al. conclude that their findings show that 4-year-olds understand intention and do not confuse intentions with desires or outcomes. The problem is that the stories of Feinfield
et al. (ibid.) do not depict situations in which the child has to distinguish
intentions as mental representations separate from the desires that motivate them and the actions they engender; that is, they do not require the
child to understand the causal chain whereby a desire may cause an intention which may cause an action which results in the desired outcome
(Astington 1993, pp. 94–96; Malle and Knobe, this volume). In Schult's
(1996) stories, described above, the propositional content of the desire and
the intention are connected in the right way in that the intention represents
the means to the desired end. In the intention-unfulfilled/desire-satisfied
condition (e.g., doesn't make soup but nevertheless gets soup), the desire is
fortuitously satisfied, as in the "rich uncle run over" deviant causal chain
story. One might argue that the stories used in the first study by Feinfield
et al. do represent the fortuitous fulfillment of desire in that the character
ends up at the location where he wanted to go. But here desire and intention
are not linked in a means-end relation. The character has changed his mind
about going to location A and decides to obey his mother and go to location
B. The lack of connection between desire and intention is even clearer in the
second study by Feinfield et al., in which the fortuitous satisfaction of desire

is absent. There are actually two desires: to have A (at the beginning of the story) and to have B (later on). One could say that there are also two intentions: a prior intention to get A and an intention-in-action to get B. The prior intention to get A is unfulfilled because A is not found. The intention-in-action to get B is fulfilled. There is no prior intention to get B because the character does not know that B exists until he sees it. Thus, one can answer the test questions about desire and intention by using the matching strategy that provides an inadequate test of children's ability to understand intention as a mental representation different from desire. The findings are consistent with previous findings in the literature. That is, 3-year-olds can recognize what someone is trying to do and can recognize the satisfaction or nonsatisfaction of desires. Presumably the 3-year-olds' performance was poorer than that of 4-year-olds because they found it harder to cope simultaneously with two situations (desiring A and B) that involved the use of matching strategies.

In sum, I have argued that metarepresentational understanding is required in order to recognize intentions as representations separate from the desires that motivate them and the actions they engender. However, there is little support for this claim in the data reported so far. Schult's target task provides some support, insofar as 4-year-olds were successful and 3-year-olds were not. But 4-year-olds were less successful on Phillips's target task. Further, 4-year-olds did not perform well on Schult's story tasks. They did better on the story tasks of Feinfield et al., but I argued that metarepresentational understanding was not required here. Most important, false-belief tasks, which provide a direct measure of metarepresentational ability, were generally not included. Only Phillips included false-belief tasks in her study; false-belief understanding appeared to be a necessary but not sufficient criterion for successful performance on the intention tasks.

Conclusion

In order to determine whether metarepresentational ability is required for intention understanding, we need to compare children's performance on intention tasks with their performance on false-belief tasks, where we know that metarepresentational ability is required for successful performance. We also need to design intention tasks that are no more linguistically demanding than false-belief tasks. Two decades ago, Shultz and his colleagues devised many tasks to investigate children's understanding of intention; these have provided a rich source for recent investigations, as we have seen. In one of their reports, Shultz, Wells, and Sarda (1980) showed that, although 3-year-olds could judge that mistakes were not intended, they nonetheless judged involuntary reflex movements as intended. A child was told to try not to move one leg; then the experimenter tapped that leg just below the knee, causing it to move (the knee-jerk reflex). The children could not distinguish this case from the one where they were told to move a leg; in both cases they said that they meant to do it. Perner (1991) argued that in order to understand that the reflex movement lacked intention the child needed a concept of intention as a representation in which the intention to move the leg causes the leg movement. Recently, Perner, Stummer, and Lang (1999) gave 3–5-year-olds a variety of tests, including the knee-reflex and false-belief tests. They found that, after controlling for age and verbal intelligence, scores on the knee-reflex test accounted for a further 30 percent of the variance in the false-belief test scores. These data support the argument that metarepresentational understanding is necessary and sufficient for understanding intention. However, this is the only evidence, and it places a lot of weight on a single test item.

There is still much work to be done. In particular, the metarepresentational hypothesis crucially lacks empirical support. Intention attribution appears to be more sensitive than belief attribution to the particular linguistic terms used (Astington 1999). In the standard change-in-location false-belief task (Wimmer and Perner 1983), it does not matter whether we ask the child where the protagonist will *look* for the relocated object or where he *thinks* that it is. Children's performance is the same in both cases (Wellman et al., in press) whether the focus is on action (*look for*) or mental state (*think*). However, children find it easier to attribute intention when they are asked whether the protagonist was *trying* to perform a certain action than they do when they are asked whether the character *meant* to perform that action (Astington 1999; Lee 1995). Here, children's performance is better when the focus is on action (*try*) than on mental state (*mean*). It is unlikely that this is because *mean* is a less familiar term than *try*; even 2-year-olds may say that they did not mean to do something (Astington 1999). However, it may be that because the early concept of intention is as a pro attitude, tied to action, the focus on action helps children when they are first acquiring a concept of intention as a representational state.

I have argued that infants' detection of intention in action entails no explicit concept of intention. The concept begins to develop during the toddler years, as language develops. At this stage, children understand intention as a pro attitude, not clearly distinguished from desire, and intimately tied to acts and speech acts. Then, at the age of 4 or 5 years, children come to see intentions as representations, independent of actions in the world, which allows them to understand intentional causation and to distinguish between intention and desire.

Povinelli (this volume) argues that the early system that allows for the detection of intention continues into childhood and adulthood, alongside the later-developing conceptual system. Likewise, Baird and Baldwin (this volume), who have shown that adults possess the same action-structure-detection skills as infants, argue that the low-level skills work in concert with a high-level intention-inferencing mechanism in the interpretation of behavior. One implication of these arguments is that it is possible that social behavior and social cognition are not necessarily closely correlated, at least at first. That is, social behavior may be based on the immediate detection of intention, and social cognition may depend on conceptual understanding. It may be some time before the two systems are integrated. Indeed, Thommen, Dumas, Erskine, and Reymond (1998) showed that 5-year-olds could see the difference between causal and intentional sequences involving geometrical forms in an animated video display but could not describe them differently, whereas 7-year-olds could. The younger children had the verbal skills needed to describe the sequences but did not differentiate between them. That is, although they could detect intention, they could not theorize about it.

It is important, in scientific discourse, to make a linguistic distinction between early and full understanding of the concept of intention. I have referred to the toddler's concept, which conflates desire and intention, as *desire-intention* (Astington 1993, p. 95). It is reminiscent of the toddler's concept that conflates pretense and belief, a concept to which Perner, Baker, and Hutton (1994) gave the name *prelief*. Perhaps we should coin an analogous term to refer to the conflated desire-intention concept: *destention*. However, we do not need such a neologism. A perfectly acceptable albeit archaic term exists in the literature: *conation*. That term was used in faculty psychology, along with *cognition* and *affection*, to refer to Plato's division of the soul into the appetitive, rational, and spirited faculties—that is, volition, intelligence, and sensibility. Let us say that toddlers have a concept of conation, a volitional state in which the concepts of desire and intention are not distinguished. These distinct concepts are acquired only later, perhaps with the advent of metarepresentational ability.

Acknowledgments

I am very grateful to Bertram Malle, Jodie Baird, and Terri Barriault for their helpful comments on this chapter, and to the Natural Sciences and Engineering Research Council of Canada for financial support.

Notes

1. But see Gergely, Nadasdy, Csibra, and Biro 1995 and Rochat, Morgan, and Carpenter 1997.

2. False-belief tasks were not given in this study.

5

Intentions as Emergent Products of Social Interactions

Raymond W. Gibbs Jr.

How does our recognition of other people's intentions shape our understanding of what they say and do? Consider a situation where you are talking with a friend and at one point that person smiles in response to something you said. An important question in our understanding of nonverbal acts is whether you, as a spectator, make any inference about your friend's putative intentions when he smiled. Under several accounts of nonverbal behavior, recognition of the individual's intentions is critical to making sense of his or her behavior (Gibbs 1999; Malle and Knobe 1997a). For instance, you may understand your friend's smile as being specifically intended to convey his emotional reaction to what you said (e.g., his surprise, joy, amusement, or even cynicism toward you or the topic of your utterance).

Understanding what another person intends is also critical to how we interpret language. Consider the following sentence describing New York Yankees pitcher David Cone's performance in a key game (Kahn 1996, p. 63):

Before the game, he had said that he would omit the split-finger, sparing his arm, but he threw an absolute Vermeer to Harold Baines in the fourth, and then struck out the next man, Robin Ventura, with another beauty.

How do we make sense of this odd sentence? The phrase *omit the split-finger* refers to a specific type of fastball pitch. The expression *threw an absolute Vermeer* certainly doesn't mean that Cone tossed a seventeenth-century Dutch painting by Johannes Vermeer at the batter. Readers easily recognize that the writer intended to communicate something about the beauty of Cone's pitch to Baines and that he uses *Vermeer* as a denominal verb to make this point. People don't react to this sentence by saying it is literally nonsensical, because they read it seeking the writer's intended meaning.

These examples of how we understand verbal and nonverbal behavior in terms of intentions assumes that intentions are a certain kind of mental state. Intentions are traditionally conceived of in individualistic and singular terms (Anscombe 1957; Bratman 1987). Philosophers, psychologists, and others tend to think of intentions as mental acts that precede the performance of behavioral acts. Intentions are psychological states, and we assume that the content of an intention must be mentally represented. A speaker or a writer, for example, must have in mind a representation of the set of assumptions which he or she intends to make manifest or more manifest to an audience. Thus, we assume that the writer's utterance about David Cone's pitch is preceded by a private mental act from which an intention to perform some behavior arises, namely to express in English some belief about the beauty of Cone's pitch.

My goal in this chapter is to argue that this view of intentions as determinate, private mental acts that precede human behaviors does not capture the complexity of all intentional actions in social situations. Many examples of intentional meaning, in particular, are inherently vague and indeterminate enough so that it makes little sense to claim that understanding what another person means rests solely on recovering his or her explicitly encoded intentions. I argue that this traditional account of intentions must be supplemented by the idea that intentions are, at least sometimes, emergent products of social interactions. Under this revised view, intentions are, in many cases, emergent products of interaction between individuals, and between individuals and the environment, and that therefore they exist in a distributed manner across individuals. This revised view has important implications for theories of intentionality and for current views of folk psychology within cognitive science.

The Traditional View of Intentions

A quick glance at how people talk about their own actions and those of others shows that appeals to what someone intends or intended to do are central to folk explanations of behavior. For instance, when questioned about their behavior, people often make statements like *I meant to arrive there at noon, but was delayed* or *I intend to go to law school when I graduate.* Many psychologists embrace the folk view that human action is intentional (in the psychological sense of "purposive"). Thus, Bruner (1981, pp. 41–42) once wrote: "What take for granted . . . is that most of what we speak of in common sense terms as human action is steered by intentions of the following kind and in the following way. An intention is present when an individual operates persistently toward achieving an end state, persists in developing means and corrects the development of means to get closer to the end state, and finally ceases the line of activity when specifiable features of the end state are achieved."

Many scholars, including Bruner, maintain that much goal-directed planning happens below the threshold of consciousness, and that the components of the resulting action will be organized in a hierarchical manner. For instance, a speaker's utterance often reflects a hierarchy of intentions, each level having a different relationship to consciousness (Dipert 1993; Gibbs 1999). *High-level intentions* refers to the beliefs, emotions, behavior, and so on that a person wishes to cause in someone else. Thus, I may utter *Eugene is a beautiful city to visit* with the high-level intention of getting you to adopt my belief about the wonders of visiting Eugene. *Middle-level intentions* are directed toward goals that are the planned means to achieve high-level intentions. In the case of my statement about visiting Eugene, my middle-level intention is for you to have a certain perceptual experience in which you recognize my statement as English language. Middle-level intentions, therefore, are directed toward chosen sense-experienceable features of the physical object of phenomena. Finally, a person must make decisions about how to produce certain sense experiences for others. These *low-level intentions* are directed toward the means of bringing about the middle-level intentions and the high-level intention in turn. Thus, I must make certain audible sounds that are recognized as English to get you to adopt my beliefs about the experience of visiting Eugene. Together, these three types of intentions constitute a hierarchy of different relations between means and ends. Understanding what any person intends depends on the ability to infer an individual's privately held high-level intentions from low-level and middle-level intentions.

One of the major proposals in the philosophy of mind is that understanding what speakers mean is clearly tied to recovering their original, private intentional thoughts (Grice 1957, 1968). Recall the statement describing David Cone's Vermeer pitch. Successful interpretation of this statement demands that the listener or the reader go beyond the literal meaning of the sentence and make an inference about what the speaker or the writer meant. Grice specifically argued that recognition of a person's intention is of a special kind, called a *meaning intention* (m-intention) (Grice 1968). An m-intention is a speaker's intention to produce an effect in the listener by means of the hearer's recognition of that intention. Thus, "communication is a complex kind of intention that is achieved or satisfied just by being recognized" (Levinson 1983, p. 16).

The Gricean perspective suggests, then, that speaker's meaning is one important type of intention. This linkage of meaning and intention is widely debated in the humanities and in cognitive science. (For an extended discussion, see Gibbs 1999.) Some scholars argue that linguistic communication is concerned only with recovery of speakers' intentions; others argue that what someone intends often has little to do with what that person means. Yet there is a tremendous body of evidence supporting the idea that people automatically seek out the m-intentions of others in understanding language, nonverbal gestures, and various kinds of human actions. (Again see Gibbs 1999.) These studies generally suggest that recovery of what another person intends to do significantly structures our understanding of people's actions. Moreover, interpretation of language, in particular, is focused on recognizing the communicative intentions another person expressed with the very intention to have us recognize that intention (H. Clark 1997), just in the way that Grice originally proposed. All this work still assumes a model of intentional behavior in which intentions are first private mental acts which get instantiated into language or action and which observers must then recover to understand what a person meant or is actually doing.

Problems with the Traditional View

The traditional view of intentions captures a significant element in meaningful experience of action. Yet the idea that intentions are solely private mental states in the minds of individuals misses the dynamic, interactive nature of intentional action. Most notably, the traditional view excludes the important role of others (listeners, readers, and observers) in intentional behavior and language use. The meaning of many communicative exchanges, for example, rests not just in the mind of a person, but emerges from the collaborative process of interaction between participants. Consider now several examples illustrating the necessity of looking at intentions as emergent products of social interactions.

An interesting complication for the traditional view is that speakers sometimes change their intentions about the particular meanings they wish their addressees to recognize. Speakers often deliberately offer their addressees a choice of construals, so when addressees make their choice, they help to determine what the speaker is taken to mean (H. Clark 1997). For instance, a speaker may present an utterance with one intention in mind, but where the addressee misconstrues it, the speaker then changes his or her mind and accepts the new construal. Here is an example once observed in a local bar (Gibbs 1999). The scene begins with my friend John spilling beer on the table:

John: I wonder if there is a towel behind the bar.

Nicole (goes over to the bar and grabs a towel):   Here you go.

John: Oh thanks! I wasn't actually asking you to get a towel for me. I just was thinking aloud about whether there might be a towel that I could get from the bartender. But thanks.

John intends his utterance with a particular meaning, but changes his mind and accepts Nicole's interpretation of what he said. Speakers often don't correct listeners' misunderstandings because they deem it too trivial, disruptive, embarrassing to correct, or because what listeners infer somehow works better in the situation (as in John's case). Still, once an interpretation is grounded, it is taken to be what the speaker meant. Listeners recognize that speakers can change their minds and leave part of the construal of utterances to them. All this points to the fact that linguistic interpretation does not consist solely of recovering a speaker's original thoughts or intentions. Instead, speaker's intentions can partly emerge from the process of negotiating meaning in conversational situations.

One may argue that Nicole's misunderstanding of John's first utterance only reflects the fact that listeners' interpretation of speaker meaning is different from their recovery of what a speaker originally intended. Yet Nicole's response here is based on her assumptions that what John meant was what he intended her to do as a result of understanding his utterance. In this way, once again, there appears to be a strong linkage of linguistic meaning with listeners' beliefs about what speakers intended to communicate. The fact that John altered what he believed to be his original intention shows that Nicole's interpretation of his intention actually shaped John's own conception of what that intention may be.

My claim that intentions arise from the interaction between speakers and listeners does not deny that individuals may have privately held, and explicitly represented, intentions motivating what they say. Yet the conversation between John and Nicole surely shows that recognition of John's original intention does not limit conversational interaction, and that a speaker's original intention can be indeterminate enough to be shaped by what others say and do.

Consider another example of how people modify original, private intentions during the course of conversation. This excerpt is from a telephone conversation between Gordon and Shawn in which Gordon talks about breaking up with a girlfriend (Hooper and Drummond 1990, p. 57):

Gordon: Oh actually, I'm glad she got the message because we had nothing in common . . and we would like talk on phone and we'd go

Shawn: Heh hh hh eh eh

Gordon: So *Shawn*: Ehh hh

Gordon: Ehh hh hh

Shawn: So you gave her to the big punt huh

Gordon: hhh. Thee old one two kick

Shawn: huh huh Drop kick huh huh

Gordon: huh hhhh No. I mean she's a nice girl and everything but

In the middle of the shared laughter, Shawn offers a characterization of what has just taken place between Gordon and his girlfriend: *So you gave her the big punt huh*. Gordon elaborates on this characterization by calling it *thee old one two kick*. Again, Shawn laughs and extends the metaphor by saying *Drop kick*. But Gordon now seems to reverse direction. As he laughs at Shawn's overbuilt rendering of *Drop kick*, he adds disagreement-relevant material to it. Even though Gordon introduced the topic of the breakup, and even though he has to this point encouraged Shawn to play with it, he shifts suddenly and resists Shawn's brusque characterization of his girlfriend. This instance displays how interpersonal goals, even after they have been accomplished, may continue to change shape as we recount their accomplishment to new recipients, and as these recipients react to the revelations.

The Gordon-Shawn conversation certainly demonstrates that what speakers say is in part determined by an individual's private, pre-conceived intentions. Thus, when Gordon comments *No. I mean she's a nice girl and everything*, he aims to correct what he believe may be Shawn's mistaken view of the girl. This statement, like many others, demonstrates that meaning intentions may still, at least in some cases, reside with individual speakers. Yet speakers' intentions also clearly shift as a result of conversation and may at times not be viewed as solely a product of an individual speaker's mind. Many face-to-face situations do not come with pre-specified intentional meanings that originate in the minds of speakers. Consider a situation where a parent attempts to get her son to do his homework by saying *We're going to Aunt Sarah's for dinner on Sunday. You'll have to plan around that in doing your homework*. Although the mother's primary goal may be to get her son to do his homework. she may also be concerned with other things, such as how to motivate her son to take responsibility for his behavior. In this case, getting the son to do his homework would be only a part of a broader goal.

Which intentions must we infer in order to adequately understand the mother's utterance to her son? This question assumes that intentions are directly linked to one individual—in this case, the mother. But, as Sperber and Wilson (1986, p. 201) argue, it is a fundamental mistake in the field of pragmatics (the study of utterance interpretation) to suppose that pragmatics "should be concerned purely with the recovery of an enumerable set of assumptions, some explicitly expressed, others implicitly conveyed, but all individually intended by the speaker." "There is," Sperber and Wilson continue, "a continuum of cases, from implicatures which the hearer was specifically intended to recover to implicatures which were merely intended to make manifest, and to further modification of the mutual cognitive environment of speaker and hearer that the speaker only intended in the sense that she intended her utterance to be relevant, and hence to have rich, and not entirely foreseeable cognitive effects." On this view, the mother did not only have one explicitly held communicative intention in mind when saying what she did. Thus, she may have had made her utterances to specifically make sure that her son's homework was done by the time the family went to Aunt Sarah's for dinner, but she may also have aimed to make manifest in a wide sense other meanings that she didn't explicitly have in mind when speaking to her son (e.g., that the son should take more responsibility in general for doing his school work before he engages in social activities, or that the son should be more responsible in general in meeting his various obligations, or that the son should take more responsibility for his actions in general). Thus, the mother might have in mind a "cognitive content" without explicitly having in mind everything that might be entailed by that cognitive content.

In many instances, a speaker will answer affirmatively when asked whether some interpretation of his or her utterance was appropriate even if this reading might not have been exactly what he or she had in mind when the utterance was first spoken. Thus, if the son questioned his mother as to her intentions in saying what she did, the mother could elaborate on her utterance by mentioning several possible meanings that she did not have firmly in mind when she first spoke. There is no reason not to expand the notion of an intended meaning in exactly this way so that speakers would, in fact, frequently accept as correct interpretations of their utterances various implicatures that they did not specifically have in mind when they originally framed the utterances. One may claim that the mother's utterance, despite its vagueness, is still in her mind in some manner. But saying that the mother had in her head some set of intentions that motivated her utterance does not explain how the mother's intention is refined and elaborated upon as a social product of her interaction with her son. Thus, the intentional meaning of the mother's utterance communication arises, at least in part, from the interaction between participants, and it does not necessarily, or directly, precede or causally generate what speakers say.

Although we sometimes talk of ourselves as the authors of our actions, we hardly ever act independently. When a second person responds to the act of a first, and thus acts in a way that depends on the first person's act, the activities of the second person cannot be counted as wholly his own. Important in all this is the idea that many individual actions are best characterized in collective, rather than purely individual, terms. When two people use language, it is, in its simplest forms, like shaking hands, playing a piano duet, or paddling a two-person canoe. Collective behavior is not just helpful behavior. Boxing is an example of collective behavior: The pugilists have agreed to cooperate, even though they are competing. Collective behavior is also not the same as a summation of individual actions, and the difference resides in the intentions of the actors. When engaged in collective activity, individuals are guided by collective *we-intentions* (Searle 1990).

Individual intentionality is not by itself sufficient to account for collective action, including conversation (Searle 1990). Collective actions are primitive and cannot be reduced to individual intentions supplemented with mutual beliefs. Instead, each person we-intends to achieve the collective goal by means of having an individual intention to do his or her part. Collective intentionality presupposes that each person assumes the existence of other agents as candidates for collaboration. Imagine, for instance, that you are ballroom dancing. As you dance, your moves are both continually affected by and an influence upon those of your partner. Your two sets of motion co-evolve in a highly interdetermined way.

One example of how individual and collective intentions differ is seen in the following (Velleman 1997). Imagine that a dean at a university asks the philosophy department how it intends to fill a faculty position. When the dean does this, she seems only to be asking the seventeen members of the department to form a single intention. She is certainly not envisioning that the various members of the department will arrive at seventeen individual intentions that will somehow converge. What rules out this possibility is not that convergence among the particular people is impossible; it is that none of them is in a position to have an individual intention about what the department should do. Each faculty member may have his or her own belief or desire as to what the department should do to fill the vacancy. Yet no individual can form an intention that speaks for the department as to what the department's plan should be. Filling the vacancy is up to the department, and so any intention on the subject must be formed and held by the group as a whole. This situation illustrates how intentions can be viewed as social products created through the interaction of mutual beliefs between relational participants. The ongoing context of interaction is not reducible to either the intentions or the actions of individuals. Thus, the department's collective intention is not the same as the sum of the faculty members' individual intentions. This does not imply that what individuals intend has no role in the construction of the department's collective intention. Yet the collective intention here is partly an emergent product of the interaction of the faculty and cannot be reduced to the individuals' intentions per se. When issues of intent arise, participants negotiate and construct a mutually shared social reality with individual and relational implications.

A final problem with the traditional view of intentions is seen in the work of some cultural anthropologists. Many researchers argue that the primary focus on an individual's intentions reflects a Western, and especially a white middle-class, bias about the nature of selfhood and meaning. For instance, the anthropologist Elinor Ochs (1984, p. 338) has argued that "the emphasis on personal intentions in Anglo society and scholarship is tied to a cultural ideology in which persons are viewed as individuals, i.e., coherent personalities, who have control over and are responsible for their utterances and actions." A culture's assumptions about how language works are likely to reflect local folk theories of human agency, personhood, and linguistic communication (Duranti 1988; Rosaldo 1982). The belief that a person can know what someone else is thinking, or have access to his or her mental processes, is not shared across cultures. Although many cultures appear to focus on individuals' subjective mental states (i.e., their thoughts, desires, beliefs, and intentions), other cultures focus on the consequences of a person's actions or talk, not on what a person did or intended to communicate.

In recent years, several anthropologists have claimed that the intentional view of mind vastly overemphasizes the psychological state of the person (or speaker) while giving inadequate attention to the social context in which action occurs (Duranti 1988). Students of Austonesian languages have been especially critical of the influence of personality theories of action on theories of language use. One of the most heavily studied cultures in this regard is that of Samoa. Samoans appear to conceive of the person not as an integral unit with a single, controlling will, but as an arena from which various behaviors, traits, and images manifest themselves. Samoans generally attribute responsibility for people's actions to interpersonal relationships and situations rather than to individual agents. For instance, problem children are seen as not being properly taught by their parents; a youth is viewed as stealing objects because he momentarily forgot about his relationship with his sisters; a son is seen as having been possessed by a ghost when he spoke harshly to his father. Individual behaviors are understood in interpersonal terms, not in light of what a person may have intended to do or say. Anthropologists argue that in many situations Samoans refuse to attribute particular mental states to individuals, especially when they explain another person's (or even their own) behavior. This does not imply that Samoans never attribute certain behaviors or dispositions to people, only that the causal basis for these behaviors are not linked to someone's putative internal mental states.

Linguistic anthropologists have examined how Samoans interpret linguistic meaning in various social contexts. These studies show that a speaker's own understanding of the event, and a speaker's personal motivations and intentions in saying what he said, are deemed irrelevant. What an utterance means depends on what others take it to mean. Consequently, a Samoan speaker will never reclaim the meaning of his words by saying *I didn't mean it*. The audience sometimes is more likely to be asked to say more about what something means than is the original speaker. Samoans ignore the orator's alleged intentions and concentrate on the social consequences of a speaker's words. Listeners do not speculate on what a speaker meant to say (a phrase that cannot be translated into Samoan); they rely on the dynamics between the speaker's words and the surrounding circumstances, which include the audience's responses, to assign interpretations. Furthermore, when talking about a speaker's messages, addressees do not provide interpretations based on their own interpretive intentions; rather, they focus on the relevance of what was said to the group or community as a whole. Samoans practice interpretation as a way of publicly controlling social relationships rather than as a way of figuring out what a given person meant to say. (For examples from other cultures, see Gibbs 1999.)

These problems with the traditional view of intentions suggest, as the philosopher Marcelo Dascal recently commented (1997, p. 62), that "intentional meanings are not fully defined complete entities before they get from the speaker's mind to her mouth." "Rather," Dascal continues, "once they materialize into utterances they enter a process of negotiation of meaning where the interlocutor's response plays a crucial role." In the same way, intentions, however they may be identified apart from communicative meanings, do not emerge full-blown from the minds of individuals. Instead, intentions are shaped by dynamic social processes, and in many cases they may best be viewed as one kind of distributed behavior, not just as private mental acts.

The Promise of an Emergent-Interactive View of Intentions

The social coordination needed to infer intentions suggests, once again, that we should at times conceive of intentions as the joint products of interaction between a speaker and a listener, between a writer and a reader, or between an actor and an observer rather than as purely individual, private mental acts. Rather than issue fully specified from people's heads or existing in some preregistered form "in there," intentions are said to be "constructed" or "negotiated" in interaction between persons and to be "constitutive" of their standard practices with artifacts and tools.

In the past several years, many cognitive scientists have advanced a view of mind according to which many aspects of action, thought, and meaning are accounted for by the process of *interactive emergence* (A. Clark 1997; Hendriks-Jansen 1996; Kelso 1995; Port and Van Gelder 1995; Thelen and Smith 1995). The essential idea of interactive emergence is that patterns of activity in which high-level structure cannot be reduced to specific sequences of movements may emerge from the interaction between simple reflexes and the particular environment to which they are adapted. My suggestion that intentions are emergent products of social interactions fits nicely with this idea of interactive emergence. This section offers several illustrations of how some aspects of intentional behavior are best characterized as examples of interactive emergence.

Hendriks-Jansen (1996) provides an interesting analogy to describe the idea of interactive emergence. Lorenz (1957), in his study of the behavior of mother ducks in the presence of their offspring, originally grouped the various activity patterns he observed under the general heading of "parenting behavior." Simply labeling the mother's behavior in this way makes sense for the purpose of descriptive classification. But labeling the mother's behavior in this way implied that there exists, somewhere in the mother duck, a common denominator for the different patterns of behavior (i.e., an internal representation of some kind corresponding to the duckling "out there"). Thus, a traditional interpretation of this explanation is that the mother duck possessed an internal representation about her ducklings and how she should act in regard to them. Yet, as Lorenz subsequently discovered, the various activities that together make up parenting behavior are all triggered by quite different processes. The only point at which these activities can be said to intersect is on the duckling "out there." The concept of parenting behavior is a helpful descriptive classification, as it focuses attention on certain activity patterns by supporting them with an evolutionary rationale. Nonetheless, the idea of parenting behavior as an internal representation in the mother is seriously misleading as a guide to the most fruitful natural kind from an explanation of the subtending mechanism (Hendriks-Jansen 1996). Parenting behavior is an emergent phenomenon that exists not in the mother or in the ducklings but in their interaction in various circumstances.

Earlier I mentioned how ballroom dancing may be characterized as an example of collective intention in which the intentional behavior emerges as a product of the individuals' joint actions. This same kind of complex intention is found in many person-environment interactions, such as between a windsurfer and his rig. The windsurfer continually affects and is affected by the set of the rig, so the behavioral intention to successfully windsurf emerges as a result of the interaction between the person and environment. Focusing on the agent alone, or on how the agent responds to the environment, fails to capture the complex nuances of windsurfing behavior. Just as it is important to understand the significance of paper and pencil when one does long division, where the cognition of doing long division is in part "offloaded" into the environment, the intentionality in windsurfing is best understood as a distributed cognitive behavior involving a person, a device, and the environment. It turns out that the operation of many mechanical devices can also best be explained in terms of complex, ongoing agent-environment interactions. Van Gelder (1995) demonstrated, for instance, that the Watt (centrifugal) governor is a device that maintains a steam engine at a steady speed by both affecting and being affected by the engine's speed. Thus, "the internal representation of a system interacting with an external world can be so subtle and complex as to defy description in representational terms" (ibid., p. 381). This conclusion mirrors the claim that the parenting behavior of mother ducks need not require positing an internal representation of the mother's intentional behavior.

A related example of interactive emergence is seen in recent work in robotics. Researchers constructing robots often aim, as part of their work, to demonstrate how intelligent behavior can arise without positing internal mental representations in the robot's mind (or program). Consider the case of a robot, developed by Mataric (1992), that was designed to follow the walls around a room. In Mataric's robot, low-level reflexes interact independently with the environment to produce the emergent behavior of wall following. Each of the robot's four sensor-feedback loops is in continuous operation, which affects the drive motor differently depending on the contingencies in the environment. There are no explicit instructions inside the robot that tell it to follow walls, nor are any formal definitions of walls necessary to produce the robot's behavior. The emergent behavior of the system as a whole is the result of various autonomous activities interacting with one another and with the environment, and not of a centralized system making decisions based on intrinsically represented courses of action or intentional goals. The robot is therefore unlikely to follow a particular wall in exactly the same way on different occasions, as its route will depend on its approach in a specific instance, or on noise in its sensory readings, and on the numerous unspecified contingencies of a dynamic environment. But the robot can be relied on to follow the wall every time. This robot shows how recognizable patterns of behavior may emerge from low-level interactions between an autonomous agent and the environment to which it has been adapted. In this sense, successful behavior requires no sense of internalized cognitive programs that plan or express intentions toward the environment. One may question the relevance of the robotics work for understanding human intentional behavior. Yet many scholars claim that behavior such as that of Mataric's robot provides an existence proof that at least some aspects of intelligent behavior need not stem from internalized cognitive programs or from explicitly encoded intentions.

The idea that intentional behavior is best understood as an emergent product of brains, bodies, and machines is nicely presented in Hutchins's (1995) account of ship navigation in the U.S. Navy. Each member of the ship's crew merely monitors and responds to specific simple environmental conditions. The individual actions of each crew member may perhaps be understood in terms of each person's individual intentions. But there is not a single collective intention that underlies the ship's appropriate movements. Rather, each person's responses alter a few aspects of the shared work space and thus promote and support similar forms of responsiveness among the other crew members. Overall, the whole process constitutes an environmentally extended process in which multiple agents, simple routines, and external devices (e.g., nautical slide rules) combine to solve the complex problem of navigating the ship. Yet the crew's collective behavior only emerges from the social interaction of people in combination with the environment, and not from any explicit agreement among the crew members as to how the ship will move.

A different example of interactive emergence is found in mother-infant interactions. Most explanations of mother-infant interaction are based on the idea that mothers behave as if their infants are intentional beings (see, e.g., Zeedyk 1996). As Bruner commented (1981, p. 317), "either the mother is a victim of common sense and does not really understand action . . . or she is behaving appropriately toward an immature member of the species who does in fact operate along the lines of intentional action originally proposed." Although mothers may indeed view their babies' behavior as intentional and as specifically directed toward the mothers, mothers may deceive themselves when they conclude that their infants engage in intentional acts (Hendriks-Jansen 1996). For instance, whenever the infant does anything that can be interpreted as a turn in the "conversation," the mother will treat it as such by filling in the gaps, pausing to allow the infant to respond, allowing herself to be paced by the infant, yet also leading the infant on in various ways. The mother could not do this without the belief that an actual dialogue is taking place, and that idea rests on her intentional explanation of the infant's activity patterns. Yet at this point it is the mother who contributes all the meaning. The mother-infant dialogue in the early months of the infant's life still has no specific content, as the infant's gaze is not about the mother (Johnson 1993). The "dialogue" cannot be conceptualized as a series of discrete intentional messages with specific meanings that are being passed back and forth.

Around 4 months, however, the infant begins to look away. The mother usually interprets this as an intentional act directed toward a specific object. But the infant does not appear to gaze at anything in particular and certainly is not trying to inform its mother of a newfound interest in objects (Collis 1979). Instead, the mother converts a particular object into the object of the infant's attention by interpreting its gaze as intentional. Under this view, an infant may perform a primitive reach-and-grasp gesture in the direction of a object; the mother may interpret this as an attempt to take hold of the object and may intervene to complete the infant's action. Overall, the observed movements of mother and infant are produced by interactive emergence, which arises from low-level responses of two continually active creatures, each of whose activities is adjusted from moment to moment to the position and movement of the other. The intentionality in the mother-infant interaction does not reside in any individual mind; it emerges as a product of their social interaction. Thus, what is intentional about the mother-infant interaction cannot be explained simply in terms of the mother's and the infant's intentions with respect to each other.

Are mothers (or any of us) simply ignorant when they (or we) assume intentionality in their infants' (or each other's) behavior? Why do we sometimes deceive ourselves about the intentionality of others' actions? Hendriks-Jansen (1996) argues that the mother's deception about her infant's intentions is essential for the infant's psychological development. The infant's pattern of activity and the mother's responses have been selected because they contribute to that deception. By treating their infants as intentional beings, the mother can "bootstrap" them into a cultural world that depends, in part, on the illusion of intentionality. With the aid of this dynamic scaffolding supplied by the mother, the infant then performs intentional acts (acts directed toward objects and about objects) and thus learn about the meanings and labels for different objects and actions. Eventually, the infant learns to attribute folk-psychological explanations to both its own and others' behaviors.

People's intentional descriptions of many behaviors can often be shown to be mistaken. These activities assume an "aboutness" for the behavior or activities that is not supported by the operations of an underlying, individually represented mechanism. The fixed action patterns and orienting mechanism that underlie a mother duck's behavior toward her ducklings requires no intentional representation of the duckling, the mechanism that control wall following by Mataric's robot do not refer to walls, and the focusing mechanisms that cause a young infant's gaze to center on its mother's face are not really about the mother (Hendriks-Jansen 1996). Many cognitive scientists now argue in a similar way that several aspects of mind, including attention (Desimone and Duncan 1995), consciousness (Freeman 1997), and emotion (Parkinson 1995), are best understood as emergent products of several person-person or person-environment interactions, so it makes little sense to characterize these properties of mind as solely private, internally represented mental entities. These developments suggest that some of our deeply felt assumptions about intentionality, at least as a property of individual minds alone, may be mistaken. The point here is that we researchers may grant that what a person (or an animal, or a mechanical object) does or learns is describable in a certain way without assuming that the person has, in some sense, internalized that (in this case intentional) description (Heil 1981).

Conclusion

The intentions constructed through the interactions between individuals and through those between individuals and the environment are not always hierarchical means-ends processes, as posited by the traditional view; at least sometimes, they are interactively emergent organizations of activity. A person's behavior does not have to be planned, starting out as an abstract internal representation in the person's head before it is executed. The complex structure can emerge from the dynamic coupling between organisms and between organisms and their environments. What we say and what we do are inextricably bound together. People assign meanings to their ongoing interactive activities as they occur. We may think that human actions are performed in accordance with certain rules which are founded in well-defined mental states, such as beliefs, desires, goals, or even intentions. Although this belief may be essential to the maintenance of social interaction (at least in some cultures), and although it clearly works on the level of folk psychology, it may be misleading if it is automatically used as a model of the underlying mental mechanism.

My argument has been that many aspects of intentional meaning and behavior are, at least partly, products of dynamic social interactions and not solely the result of privately held, internalized mental representations. The tight linkage of intentions with meaning and behavior is evident in the way both linguistic meanings and nonverbal behaviors are interpreted as intentional, even when the intentionality is best understood as distributed and not simply as subjective mental states. Nonetheless, the claim that intentions can in many cases be viewed as social products created through the interaction of between relational participants does not entirely reject the claim that some aspects of behavior can be attributed to intentional mental states which are indeed located in individual minds. Many features of meaningful action may be best characterized, both scientifically and in the folk view, in terms of private mental states that precede human action. Yet, in many cases, the meanings conveyed in interpersonal interaction are indeterminate, or vague, and can be explained only as emergent interactive phenomena. My plea is that we recognize the interactive emergent qualities of many "intentional" behaviors and not simply assume that intentions are best defined as private mental experiences.

II

Detecting Intentions and Intentionality

6

Developing Intentional Understandings

Henry M. Wellman and Ann T. Phillips

We assume that adults largely understand people in intentional terms, and ask: How do children come to these intentional understandings? Any answer to this question must be multi-level and developmental, because the notion of intention has several senses and children's construals of people demonstrably develop from infancy to older childhood. Our focus is intentional understandings in the first few years of life, and especially two informative developmental ages: the infant and the 2–3-year-old preschooler. By the time of their third birthday, children reveal an impressive, yet intermediate, understanding of intention useful for thinking about earlier and also later developments. Infants, we argue, reveal key competencies that lead to preschoolers' more developed conceptions.

Understanding Intentions

In everyday conception, people act intentionally, they have intentions, and they are intentional beings. This intentional construal of ourselves and others pervades our judgments about, talk about, and interactions with people. Intentionality matters: whether someone did something intentionally or accidentally matters; if intentional, whether the intention was good or bad matters. Sin, guilt, responsibility, and motives are all intentional constructs used by individuals and societies to understand, evaluate, and react to human behaviors. As is evident in these examples, intentional understandings and construals represent a collection of beliefs and distinctions rather than a single concept. Within this system of conceptions we emphasize three features that are central to an everyday understanding of people in intentional terms. We do not aim to advance a comprehensive definition but to provide a conceptual starting place for thinking about early yet genuine intentional understandings.

First, consider the everyday sense of intentional as doing something on purpose—because you meant to, or because you *wanted* to. Intentional actions are directed toward satisfying some desire or goal; an understanding of people in terms of their desires, including broad-based desires (e.g., wanting ice cream) and more specific goals (e.g., wanting to taste *that* ice cream cone) is thus crucial to characterizing intentional understanding. Of course, strictly speaking, intentions are different from and separable from desires (as discussed in the chapters in part I). Nonetheless, when we say that someone did something intentionally, we mean, at the least, that she meant to or wanted to.

A more important distinction than that between desires and intentions, for our purposes, is that between desires (or intentions) and actions. People act intentionally, but intentions are not actions, they are mental states. Of course, intentions and actions are linked in intimate ways. Actions (as opposed to movements) are typically intentional; certainly people's intentions are often expressed in their actions. We will consider intentional action more fully when we discuss infants. For now, however, note that in our everyday conception two persons could engage in the exact same behaviors, but from an intentional point of view we can construe those acts quite differently: for example, in one case as intended and in the other as accidental. Persons also can intend to do things but then fail to do so (unfulfilled intentions), and there are nonintentional human behaviors (such as reflexes). In short, critical differences exist between intention and actions, wanting versus doing. Our second emphasis, therefore, concerns when and how children understand desires as mental states that lie behind action but are not actions themselves.

A focus on mental states leads to our third emphasis. Intentions or desires take their place within a network of other related mental-state constructs, such as the actor's beliefs, emotions, and perceptions. On traditional philosophic accounts, it is the connection between desires and beliefs that is most important for intentional understanding. Certainly children's intentional understandings are reshaped as their conceptions of beliefs develop (Moses, this volume; Wellman 1990). But we argue that young children understand persons as intentional, as sensibly having desires for things and for actions, while understanding little if anything about beliefs. (See also Bartsch and Wellman 1995a.) Even this early intentional understanding, however, if genuine, must encompass some necessary connections between desires and other states and experiences. In particular, desires and intentions seem inextricably related to emotional and to perceptual experiences. If Jill wants to do X, and then fails, she'll be displeased, unhappy, even angry. If Bill wants a candy, but does not see one (even if one is there), he won't reach for it.

The connectedness of mental states is powerfully related to philosophers' characterization of all mental states as intentional in the broad sense of this term. In this sense, mental states are similarly intentional (Brentano 1874) in their "aboutness": a belief *about* candy, a desire *for* candy, and happiness *about* candy are all similarly about some object, proposition, or state of affairs. Importantly, when connected together in intentional understandings, various mental states are about or directed toward the *same* objects and goals. We ordinarily attribute to Jane, who is looking for candy in the cupboard, a desire for candy and a belief that candy is in the cupboard. We do not see Jane's intentional action in terms of a desire about dogs and a belief about Washington, DC. Similarly, we would not reason that any old desire explains Jane's happiness about finding candy, it is her desire for *candy* that provides this explanatory understanding. In reasoning about people, Jane's various states are connected by being "about" a focal object, event, or state of affairs, and this object is spotlighted by her desires or goals. In this way too, desires and intentions, as we consider them in this chapter, are focal for intentional understandings even in the broader sense.

In sum, we concentrate on an intentional construal of persons in terms of (1) desires or goals that are (2) internal psychological states that underlie and are separate from overt movements or from objective features of the world, and that (3) connect with other mental states and experiences.

Young Children's Intentional Understandings

Even 2-year-olds and 3-year-olds understand persons intentionally in these three senses. Consider a study with 2½-year-olds by Wellman and Woolley (1990). As shown on the left of figure 1, children made judgments about story characters in three situations. In the Finds-Wanted situation, a character wants something that might be in one of two locations; the character

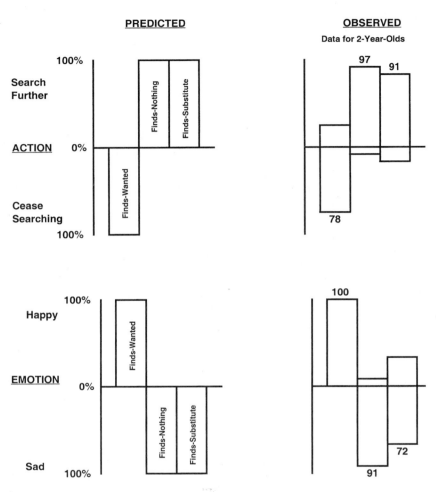

Figure 1
Left: A depiction of the predicted responses in the study by Wellman and Woolley (1990) if children understand persons in terms of their subjective desires. Right: Observed data from from 2-year-olds.

searches in one location and gets the object. The Finds-Nothing situation was identical to Finds-Wanted *except* that upon searching in the first location the character found that nothing was there. The Finds-Substitute situation was also identical to Finds-Wanted, except that upon searching in the first location the character found an attractive object but not the one said to be wanted.

In making Action judgments, children had to predict the character's subsequent action, that is whether he would go on to search in the second location or would stop searching after the first location. Suppose that children understand the character's desire, and thus understand the character's actions as intentional in the sense of attempting to fulfill his goal or desire. Then, to reiterate, the very same overt behavior could have very different construals. In this research, therefore, we carefully matched the Finds-Wanted and Finds-Substitute situations. In Finds-Wanted, Joe wants a bunny and finds it. In Finds-Substitute, Bill wants a dog but finds something else—in fact he finds the exact same bunny that Joe found. If we consider behavior at the level of movement and resulting objective outcome, Joe and Bill engage in the same behaviors. But at the level of intentions, these are very different actions because Joe got what he wanted and Bill did not. Intentional understanding should lead to a prediction of cessation of search in the case of Finds-Wanted, but continued searching in the very similar Finds-Substitute. Indeed, on an intentional understanding of these actions, the Finds-Substitute situation should be comparable to the Finds-Nothing situation instead. Consistent with these predictions, and as shown at the top right of figure 1, 2-year-olds' action judgments show an intentional understanding of these situations, that is, an understanding in terms of the actor's desires.

As shown at the bottom of this figure, children were also asked to make Emotion judgments, that is, to state whether the character would be happy or sad after opening the first door. As can be seen, 2-year-olds appropriately predict happiness for the Finds-Wanted situation but sadness for Finds-Nothing and Finds-Substitute characters. These judgments show that young children understand some of the connections between desires and other related mental states, in this case emotional states. (See also Wellman, Phillips, and Rodriguez 2000.) These emotion judgments also show ways in which 2-year-olds appreciate desires and intentions as internal mental states. Within an intentional understanding, whether some state of affairs is desirable is not an objective quality of the object or situation but is a *subjective* aspect of the person, determined by what he or she wants or likes. Consider again Joe (who wants a bunny and finds one) versus Bill (who wants a dog but finds the same cute, cuddly bunny that Joe found). Two-year-olds understood that this outcome was not objectively desirable and thus inevitably happy-making; happiness instead depended on the character's desires, consistent with a subjective understanding of desires.

The action and emotion judgments 2-year-olds made in this study are straightforward. But these judgments are straightforward only on the basis of the understanding that Joe's and Bill's actions and emotional reactions were shaped by their desires and that Joe and Bill had different desires or goals in spite of executing objectively identical actions.

These key aspects of young children's intentional understandings are also apparent in their everyday conversations. Children do not use such terms as *intend to*, *on purpose*, or *mean to* until about 3, 4, or 5 years, but as early as 1½ years they talk about persons' goals and desires, primarily with the term *want*. Bartsch and Wellman (1995a) examined talk about desires for 10 English-speaking children studied longitudinally from about 2 years to 5 years. Careful examination of more than 200,000 child utterances yielded more than 5000 instances that were judged to be genuine references to desire. By genuine references to desire we meant use of a term like *want* to refer to a person's internal state of wanting or longing to obtain an object, engage in action, or experience a state of affairs. Consider the first example in table 1. Ross's initial question might just have been a simple behavioral request: "Take it off." However, his follow-up question ("You want it on?") suggests more than just a behavioral request, because Ross did not simply take the button off or insist that his father do so. Instead, he continues to try to characterize his father's goal, his desire, in the absence, of or in advance of, instrumental actions. Genuine references to desire, like those in table 1, were frequent in children's conversations and were evident as early as the transcripts began, at right about the second birthday.

Beyond this general coding we looked for more exacting and precise uses that would further confirm children's understanding. Consider the distinction between desires in contrast to behavior or action. In their comments on *unfulfilled desires* (table 1) children often distinguished goals and desires from the behaviors that would enact those desires or the outcomes that would satisfy those desires. Equally intriguing, children often commented on their *future desires* (desires that would only be enacted later), thereby acknowledging that desires are separable from behavior (in this case, one as in the present and the other as in the future). Finally, young children revealed a subjective understanding of desire by explicitly contrasting two individuals' different desires for the very same thing (table 1). Taken together, everyday conversational references to people's desires illuminate an early intentional understanding of persons as having internal goals and wants that differ from person to person subjectively, that underlie intentional action, but that are also different from behavior in important ways.

If very young children are indeed understanding people intentionally, this might be especially revealed in their explanations of human activities and occurrences. Why do people do things? The most basic intentional explanation is "because they want to." Broader intentional explanations would also mention related mental states, such as the actor's beliefs, emotions, and perceptions. In an early series of studies, Bartsch and Wellman (1989) asked young children to explain everyday acts—for example: "Jane is looking for her kitten under the piano. Why is Jane doing that?" Overwhelmingly young 3-year-olds, as well as older children and adults, provided explanations that referred to the actors' mental states: "She thinks her kitty is there." "She saw her kitty under the piano." "She misses her kitty." And, they explained behavior in the narrower intentional sense of specifically citing the character's desires: "She wants her kitty." "She wants to find him." Desire explanations were the most frequent and typically the first explanation offered for an action.

Consider as well children's explanations of emotions. Wellman and Banerjee (1991) presented 3-year-olds and 4-year-olds with scenarios such as this: "Jane went to preschool and saw they were having apple juice for snack. She was very happy. Why was she so happy?" Notice that it would be extremely easy to resort to situational rather than mentalistic-intentional explanations for these sorts of stories and questions—"Apple juice is good." The stories themselves mention obvious external eliciting situations, and the child could respond just by citing those situations. In contrast, the stories themselves never mentioned the character's desires or beliefs. However, even 3-year-olds went beyond situationist explanations to provide mentalistic,

Table 1
References to desires in everyday conversation of 2–3-year-old children.

Genuine references to desires

Ross (2;6): You want it [a button] off?
Adult: No thank you.
Ross: You want it on?

Adam (2;7): Want spoon?
Adult: No thank you.
Adam: OK. You don't want spoon. Don't want a spoon.

Sarah (2;11): Eat; you eat water?
Adult: No, I don't want any water.
Sarah: I want some.

Ross (3;4): I wanted it to be a sunday but it didn't.
Adult: What? Sunday. You wanted it to be a Sunday, but it wasn't.
Ross: No, no. I wanted it to be a sun day, 'cause the sun didn't come out.
Adult: Oh you wanted it to be a sunny day.
Ross: I wanted to be sun.

Unfulfilled desires

Ross (3;2): Daddy I want to go to McDonald's and you didn't let me.

Peter (2;8): I wanna come out. I can't come out.

Sarah (3;10): Turtle. Turtle. I want a turtle, but I can't have one.

Future desires

Abe (2;6): Get a circle one for me [a kind of telephone].
Adult: No I won't get you a [telephone].
Abe: I want one. When I grow big I get one.

Ross (3;6): Are you going to die?
Adult: Not until you get to be an old man.
Ross: If you die, I want mommy to get another you.
Adult: Another me?
Ross: Yes, another Brian.

Sarah (2;9): I want to have one of those.
Adult: Tell Daddy.
Sarah: I want have one of those . . . for my birthday (several weeks away).

Subjective contrastives for desires

Adam (3;0): I don't like shaving cream. Daddy like shaving cream.

Abe (2;10): No.
Adult: You don't like it?
Abe: You like it?
Adult: Yes I do.
Abe: But I don't like it.

Sarah (3;11): You wanna take that off?
Adult: No, I don't want to take that one off.
Sarah: I did wanta take this one off.

Ross (2;9): That's kind of scary.
Adult: Well, but its neat. I like it.
Ross: But I don't like it.

---

intentional explanations: "She wants apple juice." "She thought there'd be apple juice." Some of the youngest 3-year-olds never mentioned beliefs, but all children frequently explained the character's emotions in terms of her desires, preferences, and goals.

Young children's judgments and explanations, thus, straightforwardly suggest that they see people in internal-state, intentional terms. However, young children's intentional understandings cannot be fully understood without also examining their judgments and explanations of *non*intentional behavior. For example, do young children understand that some human behaviors are *not* intentional?

Consider the types of actions and movements presented in table 2. Voluntary actions that actors perform because they want to are prototypic intentional actions (for example, a person pours milk on his cereal). As just noted, young children and adults alike typically explain such actions in intentional-psychological ways citing mental states generally ("He thinks cereal is tasty with milk") and citing desire-goal explanations specifically ("He wanted milk on his cereal"). Mistakes, biological movement, and physical object-like movements contrast with such straightforward intended actions. In one sense mistakes are unintended actions—something happens that is not a result of or encompassed by the subject's desires. However, for adults mistakes are still to be explained psychologically and intentionally: "He didn't know the pitcher had juice." "He thought it had milk." Or consider the explanation "He wanted to pour that pitcher, but he didn't want to pour juice." As Anscombe (1957) insists, actions are intentional "under a description." Mistaken actions are intentional under some description (pouring the pitcher) if not under others (pouring the juice rather than the milk).

Physical object-like movements, such as being drawn to the ground by gravity, however, require *non*intentional construal and explanation. The

Table 2
Example items for eliciting explanations from preschoolers (from Schult and Wellman 1997).

Intended action	Biological
It's time for breakfast, so Jimmy gets the cereal out of the cupboard. Now Jimmy has an idea. He wants to pour milk on his cereal. Jimmy takes a pitcher out of the refrigerator and pours it on his cereal. He pours milk on his cereal.	Robin is climbing a tree in her backyard. She's hanging from a branch, not touching the ground. Now she has an idea. She wants to hang on that branch forever, and never let go. Robin drops to the ground.
Mistake	**Physical**
It's time for breakfast, so Jimmy gets the cereal out of the cupboard. Now Jimmy has an idea. He wants to pour milk on his cereal. Jimmy takes a pitcher out of the refrigerator and pours it on his cereal. He pours orange juice on his cereal.	Bobby is playing in his bedroom. He climbs on top of this stool. Now he has an idea. He wants to step off the stool, and float in the air, up off the floor. Bobby steps off the stool, and comes right down to the floor.

explanations for object-like movements lie in the domain of physical understandings rather than intentional understandings. Similarly, the explanations for biological movements—such as fevers and muscle fatigue—lie in the domain of biological forces rather than intentions and reasons.

In several studies, Schult and Wellman (1997) presented 3-year-olds and 4-year-olds with scenarios of the sort depicted in table 2 and asked them to explain what happened—e.g., "Why did Jimmy pour orange juice on his cereal?" Far from regarding all human movements and acts as being due to the actors' desires, beliefs, and intentions, even 3-year-olds were appropriately selective as to the kinds of actions that deserved intentional explanation. The clearest contrast concerns Mistakes versus Object-like movements. Voluntary acts, but Mistakes as well, received psychological, intentional explanation. *Psychological explanations* referred to the character's mental states, such as desires, preferences, beliefs, and emotions: "He wanted to get down." "He just didn't know it was ketchup." "She thought it was milk." Unlike simple intended actions children rarely said that a character engaged in mistakes "because he wanted to." But, still, they explained these acts in terms of the character's psychological and intentional states—their knowledge and beliefs, as well as desires to do *some* things if not others: "He wanted to pour milk, but it was orange juice." In contrast, physical movements were explained quite differently; children gave them predominantly physical explanations. *Physical explanations* appealed to or implied physical forces, such as gravity or the wind, or declared the need for some other physical mechanism for the action to be carried out: "He's too heavy to float in the sky." "Gravity pulls him down." "Planes can fly and people can't, 'cause they don't have wings." In short, young children see much human behavior as intentional—caused by the actor's subjective desires—but they also appropriately understand other human behavior as nonintentional.

Examination of children's everyday conversations—in this case the explanations they offer and request in everyday situations with parents and peers—confirms these conclusions and extends them to 2-year-olds (Hickling and Wellman 2000; Wellman, Hickling, and Schult 1997). Thus, laboratory studies and natural language ones as well, and children's predictions and their explanations as well, converge to reveal an impressive intentional understanding that is apparent in children as young as 2 years. In this understanding, young children construe persons as having internal subjective desires that interconnect with other mental states, especially emotions, and that cause actors to do things. Intentional actions are desire-driven actions; people are desiring, acting beings. Even young children understand that desires are separate from actions, however, in that desires may never be enacted, may only be intended for future enactment, and may result in mistaken instead of intended outcomes. Furthermore, young children's intentional construals are appropriately limited in that they understand that some movements—e.g., object-like movements—can be unintended altogether.

Intentional understandings are not complete, or even largely developed, at the age of 2 or 3 years. As still older children come to understand more about person's beliefs, their larger psychological understanding of behavior changes (e.g., Gopnik and Wellman 1994); their understanding of intention itself also changes (Moses, this volume). And preschool children come to understand more clearly how desires can be distinguished from intentions (Astington and Lee 1991; Feinfield, Lee, Flavell, Green, and Flavell 1999; Schult 1999). Still, it is worth emphasizing how much 2-year-olds have come to understand. Their basic understanding, similar to our adult one, is that persons do things because they want to, that such wants are linked to related states such as emotion, that wants or goals differ from person to person, and that wants and actions are (crucially) separable. This understanding, apparent in 2-year-olds, is an impressive achievement that represents the culmination of earlier developments.

Infants

When infants first show genuine intentional understanding is not clear, but several recent studies demonstrate that by 18 months toddlers have achieved some important appreciations. For example, Repacholi and Gopnik (1997) had 18-month-old children taste two snacks: broccoli from one small bowl and goldfish crackers from another. Almost all children clearly preferred the crackers. Then an adult, facing the child across the table, tasted each snack, going "Mm" and smiling to one snack and "Eww" and displaying disgust to the other. In a Match condition, the adult liked the crackers and disliked the broccoli, matching the child's preference. In a Mismatch condition, she liked the broccoli instead. After displaying her reaction to each bowl, the adult held her hand halfway between the two bowls and said "I want some more, can you give me some more?" In *both* conditions 18-month-olds overwhelmingly gave the adult more of what the adult had liked. In the Mismatch condition, therefore, the children seemed to interpret the adult's unspecific request ("Give me some more") intentionally and subjectively, in terms of her previously displayed desires.

In Meltzoff's research (1995), 18-month-olds who watched an adult engage in an unsuccessful action imitated the model's actions, but in doing so they produced the intended, successful action—an action they had never actually observed—rather than the failed action that they had observed (Meltzoff and Brooks, this volume). Carpenter, Akhtar, and Tomasello (1998) similarly had 18-month-olds watch and imitate actions. When the adult performed one act, she emphatically said "Oops!" as if it were accidental; when performing another action, she emphatically said "There!" as if this was what she intended to do. Infants differentially produced the intentional action.

All three of these studies focused on older infants' understanding of behavior: their interpretation of an actor's behavioral request in terms of the actor's desires or goal; their imitation of a demonstrated behavior in its unobserved, intended form; their imitation of intentional not accidental actions although both were identical in form. Thus, by 18 months infants seem to understand human actions in some intriguingly intentional ways. What ways? And what understandings may appear still earlier? To address these questions requires characterizing intentional actions more clearly.

Intentional Actions

Philosophers (e.g., Dretske 1988) distinguish between movement (motion of the body regardless of intent) and intentional acts. In this sense, (1) below is a behavioral, movement description and (2) is an intentional action description.

(1) A hand moves out from a body and ends up in contact with a ball.

(2) A person reaches for and grasps a ball.

At the level of observation of behavior alone, (1) and (2) might look the same. At the level of intention, however, they can be quite different; an analysis of behavioral movements does not necessarily yield an analysis of intentional action. (See also Baird and Baldwin, this volume.)

However, the relation between behavior (at least intentional behavior) and intention is deep, intimate, and diagnostic. In fact, the relation between observable intentional actions and underlying intentions, we argue, parallels a relation familiar to cognitive scientists in the discussion of categorization, namely the relation between a concept's identifying features and its essential features. Figure 2 shows these parallel relations. In the case of categories, striped, meat-eating, ferocious, feline, and quadrupedal are all perceptual features of our everyday category of tigers. But these are not essential features of the category—even an albino (not striped), three-legged (not quadrupedal), infant (not ferocious), milk-drinking (not meat-eating) tiger cub is still a tiger. Yet stripes, meat eating, ferociousness, and quadrupedality remain typical manifestations of being a tiger. As typical manifestations of tigerhood, these perceptual features are critical to our

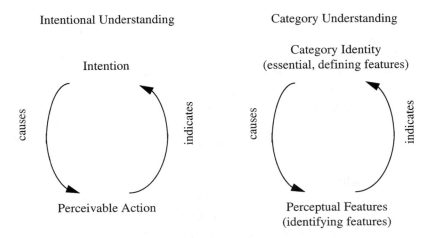

Figure 2
The parallel relationship between (right) essential versus identifying features of a category and (left) intentions versus behavioral features of intentional action.

everyday identification of tigers—recognizing a tiger in the wild depends on these identifying features, not on unobservable tiger essences. Thus, as captured in the figure, perceptual features allow one to identify tigers (sometimes erroneously) because these are the sorts of features that typically (though certainly not always) result when an item has the essential features of tigerhood (has underlying tiger DNA, perhaps).

A similar relationship exists, we argue, between perceptual features of intentional behavior and underlying intentions. Behaviors are not intentions, and behaviors may be mistakenly identified as intentional when they are not or mistakenly identified as nonintentional when they are. But often certain perceivable features identify a behavior as intentional, we propose. These features signal a behavior's underlying intentionality—that this behavior is an intentional action—and they can work to identify intentions, because intentions, when enacted, often (though not always) yield behaviors of a certain form.

This analysis assumes that there are some detectable, telltale, perceivable features of intentional behavior. It could be argued instead that there are no such features and that we humans only impose an intentional reading of behavior in our "minds' eyes." In defense, our assumption is a limited one: sometimes behavior observably manifests intention (sometimes it does not).

At the same time, we do not assume that intention is directly and necessarily perceivable in behavior, although others (e.g., Asch 1952; Premack 1990) have argued that humans are simply hard wired from birth to perceive self-caused behaviors as intentional. We assume, instead, a process of identification via perceivable features; intentionality is sometimes (not always) *identifiable* from behavior.

What features of perceivable behavior might plausibly indicate and manifest intentionality? We believe there are several candidates,[1] but we concentrate on two: *object directedness* and *action connectedness*.

Mandler (1992) suggests, using image-schema depictions, that infants can distinguish mechanical movements from biological self-propelled movements because of their differences on a number of perceivable movement features. Specifically, the mechanical movements of a physical object encompass contact with and transmission of force from one object to another and result in regular, linear trajectories of movement. Self-propelled motions, in contrast, arise on their own, without earlier contact, and result in irregular bio-mechanical movements and trajectories. These two movement types thus have different correlated perceptual features.

Intentional actions, we contend, require yet another image-schematic depiction and evidence yet other correlated perceptual features. Importantly, an intentional action is not merely self-propelled; it is oriented toward and moves toward an object or goal. The movement dynamics in this case thus encompass an orientation and a directedness. In simple action situations at least, the goal directedness of intentions can result in perceptually identifiable *object directedness* that is manifest in behavioral movements themselves as toward certain things and not others: a finger dialing a phone, a hand inserted into a glove, a person reaching for an ice cream cone, a hand pulling a cup toward a body.

Beyond directedness, intentional behaviors can manifest characteristic connections to other behaviors, expressions, and postures. Consider a reach for candy. Typically, such object-directed reaching requires perceptual guidance—manifest in head and eye orientations and trajectories. Furthermore, actually obtaining the goal object can result in distinctive facial expressions—those associated with happiness at success, or surprise at an unexpected result. Launching the reach and guiding it correctly might be manifest in a furrowed brow of concentration that is then relaxed as the target is grasped. Vocal accompaniments ("Oops," "There," "Yes," "Damn") are also typical. Intentional behaviors, therefore, also often manifest, and thus can be identified by, telltale *action connections*; the target action is connected to other behaviors and displays, especially to perceivable emotional displays and perceivable eye, head, and body orientations.

To be clear, the target action is not simply associated with or conjoined with other concomitant behaviors and displays. The connections are more functional. For example, intentional reaches often *require* visual guidance and hence certain visual orientations by the actor, and they *cause* certain emotional-cognitive reactions in the actor which are then, often, manifest in facial or verbal expressions. These functional connections are driven, often, by the object directedness of the action. The person reaches for *that* object and thus looks at *that* object and displays emotionally about *that* object. Thus object directedness and action connectedness are themselves linked, via the specific target object, in a particular fashion (similar to the way that mental-state connections are driven by the goal directedness of desires).

In sum, we propose that the object directedness and action connectedness of behaviors can often manifest and identify intentions. Consequently, one way to research infants' initial intentional understandings is to research infants' understanding of the object directedness and action connectedness of human action.

Infant Research

To understand actions as directed toward objects requires, at the least, appreciating certain associations between movable body parts and objects. Woodward (1998; see also Woodward, Sommerville, and Guajardo, this volume) has demonstrated that even 5-month-olds make such associations. Infants were habituated to a hand reaching to and grasping one of two toys. Then infants saw two test events, in which the locations of the objects were switched. In the *new object/old path* event, the hand reached to the old location and thus now grasped a different object. In the *old object/new path* event, the hand grasped the same object as in habituation, but it was now of course in the other location. If infants perceive or encode the habituation event simply in terms of the spatial movement of the hand, then the *new object/old path* event would seem familiar (because the arm and hand execute the same trajectory as habituation), and infants should look longer at the *old object/new path* event because it shows a novel arm movement. However, if the infants perceived or encoded the habituation movement in terms of the hand's association with the *target object*, then they should look longer at the *new object/old path* event, because there the hand is associated with a new object. Five-month-old and 9-month-old infants looked longer at the *new object/old path* event.

Perhaps infants not only understand some behaviors as associated with certain objects but also understand them as *directed toward* objects. Gergely and colleagues (Gergely et al. 1995; Csibra et al., in press) presented infants with computerized two-dimensional displays of circles involved in intentional-like motion. Specifically, infants were habituated to a circle moving up to and then over a wall-like barrier, then back down across the barrier to join up with a second circle. Thus, the first circle took an indirect route over the barrier to get to the second one. After habituation, infants saw two test events where the barrier was removed. In the *direct* test event, the first circle moved directly in a straight line to link up with the second circle (a path quite different from the indirect habituation event). In the *indirect* event, the circle moved in the same path as in habituation (although the barrier no longer intervened). Nine-month-olds and 12-month-olds, but not 6-month-olds, looked longer at the indirect test event. Gergely and his colleagues concluded that the infants perceived the moving circle as intentional, expected it to go directly for its object, and thus were surprised to see it taking the indirect route when it was no longer needed.

We have reservations about how to understand Gergely's rich interpretation of infants' understanding in terms of rationality; his claim is that the circle's indirect path is worthy of attention because it is seen as irrational.[2] But at the least these results suggest a budding understanding of object directedness. Our own recent studies with human actors and live behaviors provide further evidence.

In our research (Phillips and Wellman 2000), infants see a person reach over a barrier and grasp an object, as shown in figure 3. Once the infants are habituated, the barrier is removed and they are shown two test events. One test event shows a *direct* reach for the object; the other shows an *indirect* reach. These test events contrast two different construals of the person's actions, one in terms of object directedness and one in terms of physical motions of the arm. If in habituation the infant interprets the actor's action

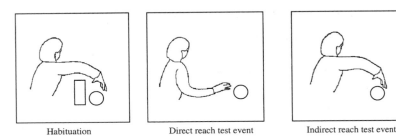

Habituation   Direct reach test event   Indirect reach test event

Figure 3
A depiction of the reaching events presented to infants in the study of Phillips and
Wellman (2000).

as object directed (as the actor going as directly as possible to get the object),
then when the barrier is removed the direct reach is the expected action and
the indirect reach would be more attention-worthy. In the indirect-reach test
event, although the actor's arm movement remains the same as during habituation, the actor is no longer going directly to get the object.

In fact, during tests, 12-month-olds look longer at the indirect reach.
They dishabituate to the indirect reach (even though it is showing the exact
same arm movement as in habituation) and do not dishabituate to the direct
reach (even though it actually shows a different physical arm movement).
This pattern is consistent with the hypothesis that infants construe the reach
as object directed.

Perhaps, however, infants just prefer to look at a curving arm motion. A
control condition tests for this possibility. For infants in the control condition, habituation and test were identical to those for infants in the experimental condition except that *no* object was ever present. In this case, since
there is no object, there is no presentation of an objected-directed action in
habituation. And in this case, appropriately, 12-month-olds do *not* prefer the
indirect-reach test event. So the experimental data do not just show a preference for looking at the curved arm motion. Instead, infant looking is sensitive to the object directedness of the action; in the context of *object-directed*
reaching (as depicted in the original habituation) then the indirect test event
becomes novel, unexpected, and worthy of attention. Data for 12-month-
olds in the experimental and control conditions are shown in figure 4.

Intriguingly, in this research 9-month-olds do not prefer the indirect reach
in the experimental condition. In habituation, experimental 9-month-olds

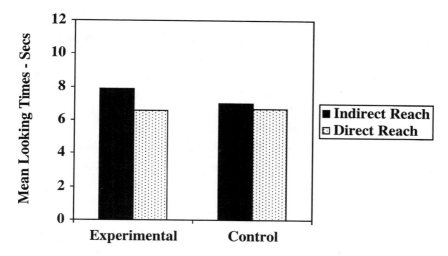

Figure 4
Twelve-months-olds' looking times to test events in the study of Phillips and Wellman (2000).

look for long times at the object-directed reach, and in test they look for long times at *both* experimental test events. Nine-month-olds look much longer at all these experimental events, where a goal-object is present, as compared to short looks at the control test events, where no object is present. An interpretation that we favor for these developmental findings is that 9-month-olds have some expectations that hands go with their target objects (as we know from Woodward's research). They are interested, therefore, in how people reach for objects, and thus they look longer at reaches directed toward objects (in our experimental condition) than they look at the exact same movements when no objects are involved (in our control condition).

If 12-month-olds, and perhaps even 9-month-olds, show a beginning awareness of object directedness, then they may also show beginning understandings of action connectedness. In other research, therefore, we are addressing infants' understanding of action connectedness.

In a series of studies, 12-month-olds and 14-month-olds saw an adult behind a table with two stuffed kittens, identical except for color (Phillips, Wellman, and Spelke 2000). During habituation trials, the infant saw a two-part event (figure 5). First, the adult exclaimed "Look at the kitty" while turning her head and looking to one of the stuffed animals with an expression of interest and joy. Then, a curtain was drawn to conceal both the adult and the animals. Second, the curtain was opened and the adult was shown looking down at and grasping one of the kittens. During the habituation trials, the second phase of the presentation always showed the adult holding the kitten at which she had looked and emoted earlier.

After habituation, two test events were presented. One event was, like habituation, *consistent* with the principle that actors' actions (e.g., the grasp of an object) are connected to where they look and express affect. In this test event, the experimenter first looked at the second toy (the one never regarded or held during habituation); then the screen closed, and upon its opening the adult was then holding *that* kitten. In the other, *inconsistent*, test event the adult looked at the first kitten (the one she had regarded and held during habituation), the screen closed, and when it opened she was then seen holding the second kitten. This event was inconsistent with the principle that people's acts are connected to their looking and emoting, because in this test event the experimenter first looked desiringly at one object but then was grasping a different object.

Note that in both the inconsistent and the consistent test events, after the screen was opened in each case the adult was holding the same object (the kitten not held in habituation). So, physical aspects of the target act itself—grasping the same stuffed kitten—were identical for the two test events.

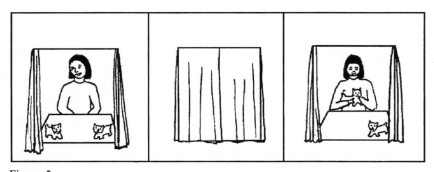

Figure 5
A depiction of the habituation events presented to infants in in the study of Phillips, Wellman, and Spelke (2000).

Twelve-month-olds, as well as 14-month-olds, looked reliably longer at the inconsistent test event. Thus, they seemed sensitive to how gaze and emotion connect to and signal the actors' grasp. This leads us to believe that at about 1 year infants are sensitive to action connectedness as well as to object directedness. We are working with several other paradigms to tackle this phenomenon. In one illustrative study (Phillips and Wellman, in preparation), 11-month-olds were habituated to a display that had two people and a single object within a three-part sequence. The adults were behind a partial screen so that only their faces were visible. For the first phases of the habituation event, one adult looked directly at and displayed neutral affect toward the object; the other adult looked at the object but displayed positive affect toward it. Then an anonymous hand reached through the center of the screen and grasped the object. Note that in these habituation trials the two persons were equidistant from the object, and both looked at the object, a single hand, but neither person was seen holding the object.

After habituation, the infants saw test events parallel to those seen during habituation, except with no screen between people and object. In the initial phase of the test events, the infant observed each person express the same affect expressed during habituation, but since the screen was not present the infant was then able to witness which adult grasped the object. In one test event (the *consistent* event), the infant saw the adult who expressed positive affect grasp the object, consistent with the principle that positive perceptual/emotional regard is connected to approach-like action directedness. In the other test event (the *inconsistent* event), the infant saw the adult who expressed neutral affect grasp the object.

If infants connect object directedness to the type of emotion displayed, then during habituation the infants in our study could have understood or encoded the positive adult as grasping the object, even though the identity of the person holding the object could not be seen. If so, then the inconsistent event should have seemed more novel and elicited greater recovery of looking. And indeed, sixteen 11-month-olds looked longer at the inconsistent test event, in which the neutral person grasped the object. In a contrasting control condition, 11-month-olds otherwise showed an expected preference for looking at the positive face. In view of our earlier data on infants' understanding of object directedness, we expect that in future research 6-month-olds and 9-month-olds will have difficulty with this new task whereas 12-month-olds will succeed, just as they succeed on the "kittens" task.

Conclusions

Our chapter encompasses conceptual analyses and empirical data. For preschoolers, the data demonstrate that they appreciate three conceptually important aspects of human intentionality by the age of 2 years: an understanding of intentions or goals in terms of a person's desires for things, an understanding of desires as a mental state intimately related to but independent of action itself, and a beginning understanding of several ways in which desires coherently connect to other mental states (especially emotion and perception). For infants, we have offered a general analysis of the relation between observable behavior and underlying intentions (figure 2, left), a claim that two action features (object directedness and action connectedness) are often crucial to identifying intentions, and evidence that infants between 9 and 12 months are beginning to recognize human actions in terms of (first) object directedness and then action connectedness.

We want to emphasize that the findings with infants are consistent with two quite different interpretations. (See also Baird and Baldwin, this volume; Povinelli, this volume.) Under one interpretation, early appreciations of object directedness and action connectedness would be manifestations of an infantile intentional understanding of human action. On this account, infants expect these action regularities to obtain because they construe persons intentionally. Under an intentional construal, these action features are the expected, identifying features of people's actions, and so a failure of these intentional action features to appear is novel and thus worthy of attention. Thus, on this interpretation, infants in our studies are displaying their intentional understandings. Their appreciation of perceivable behavioral regularities is based on their construal of those behavioral regularities in a top-down way, via intentional understandings.

Alternatively, in the first year of life infants may be learning about behavior in a more bottom-up fashion. Because parents, siblings, and strangers in the child's life act in intentional fashions, the actions that infants observe are saturated with object directedness and action connectedness. Thus infants come to expect these behavioral regularities. When they are present, behavior seems familiar; when they are not present, behavior seems unfamiliar and puzzling. On this interpretation, infants operate solely in terms of the behavioral regularity, without any intentional understanding.

These possibilities are part of a larger debate in the literature between lean and rich interpretations of infant behaviors. For example, both social referencing and gaze following (along with early words and gestures) could be seen as indexing infant intentional understandings or not (Moore and Corkum 1994; Baldwin and Moses 1996; Wellman 1993). Our data cannot decide between these two possibilities. But on either account, the sorts of action understanding we have been investigating must be central to developing intentional understandings. Suppose, on the one hand, that infants early in life construe persons as having intentional states. If so, they still must come to understand how those states manifest themselves in various human behaviors; they must come to understand intentional *action* in its various forms and connections. Thus, action understandings (and especially understandings of object directedness and action connectedness, we would claim) are needed to "flesh out" and employ intentional understanding in everyday interaction and social cognition.

Suppose, on the other hand, that infants do not at first understand humans in such intentional terms. How do they come to do so? Analyses of overt observable human behaviors would constitute an important source, perhaps the critical source, for the development of intentional understandings. On this alternative possibility, infants use observations of behavior to infer or abstract conceptions of intentions. But not just any observations of behavior would do. Only some sorts of behavioral features would be correlated with and hence informative of *intentional* understandings. Object directedness and action connectedness, we contend, are the sorts of features that could informatively help to do this job. In particular, the object directedness of behavior foreshadows the goal directedness of desires and goals. The action connectedness of actions, gazes, and emotional expressions foreshadows the intentional connections of desires, perceptions, and emotions.

On either interpretation, therefore, infants' understandings of action are crucial for developing intentional understandings. That infants as young as 12 months display appreciations of object directedness and action connectedness reveals and helps shape their developing intentional understandings.

Acknowledgment

Preparation of this chapter was supported by NICHD grant HD 34004.

Notes

1. For more on this, see Baldwin and Baird 1999 and Baird and Baldwin, this volume.

2. In addition, findings for the needed control condition were not straightforward. In the control condition of Gergely et al. (1995), infants were again habituated to a circle taking the same indirect path as in the experimental condition described in the text, but in this case even in habituation there was *no* barrier to circumvent. The control condition test events compared direct and indirect paths with *no* barriers just as in the experimental condition. In the control condition, 12-month-olds dishabituated to *both* the direct and indirect test events. Dishabituation to the indirect test event in both the experimental and control conditions raises the suspicion that the indirect test event was somehow just generally attention-eliciting.

7

How Infants Make Sense of Intentional Action

Amanda L. Woodward, Jessica A. Sommerville, and José J. Guajardo

A glance out the window reveals a scene populated by two kinds of entities: inanimate objects (such as cars, trees, and fire hydrants) and animate beings (in particular, people). Adults discriminate these two kinds of entities readily and have very different expectations about how members of each class will behave. Adults understand not only the physical regularities that govern the motions of inanimate objects but also the psychological underpinnings of human action. This "folk psychology" allows us to make sense of human behavior in terms of the goals and plans that drive it, the beliefs that inform it, and the emotions that color it, among other things. At the core of this folk theory is the idea that human action, unlike object motion, is driven by intentions. Adult understanding of intentions is embedded in rich knowledge about mental states and behavior. This enables adults to detect intentional actions on the basis of behavioral evidence and to reason about the particular intention behind an action.

One of the most enduring questions in developmental psychology is how children come to understand the distinction between inanimate objects and animate beings. A key part of this distinction is how children come to understand intentional action. How do children first detect intentional actions, and how does their understanding of intentions develop? Folk physics has roots in infancy (Baillargeon 1995; Spelke, Breinlinger, Macomber, and Jacobson 1992). In our work, we ask whether folk psychology also has roots this early in life. That is, do infants have ways of making sense of intentional action that are continuous with adult understandings?

A number of theorists have considered this question in recent years. There have been two major, and conflicting, views of the development of intentional understanding. One set of theorists has focused on the social abilities that appear during the toddler years. At about 12 months, babies make impressive strides as interactors. They begin to produce and respond to communicative gestures such as points, to actively follow other people's gaze, to engage in social referencing, to play games such as peek-a-boo, to imitate the goal-directed behavior of others, and to understand words. (For a review, see Tomasello 1995.) Several theorists have proposed that the onset of these abilities signals an understanding of other people as intentional agents (Bretherton 1991; Carpenter, Nagell, and Tomasello 1998; Tomasello 1995). Because these behaviors are absent in infants younger than 9–12 months, it is sometimes further concluded that "there is no joint attention or any other indication that infants at this age understand others as intentional agents" (Tomasello 1995, p. 108). Thus, under these accounts, the birth of intentional understanding occurs at around 12 months. Other theorists have interpreted infants' naturally occurring social behaviors as evidence that the birth of intentional understanding occurs still later, at 18–24 months (Barresi and Moore 1996).

At the other extreme, several theorists have proposed that infants are innately endowed with abstract and elaborate systems for interpreting intentional action, including notions of goal-directedness, perceptual contact, affinity, reciprocity, the ability to learn, enduring preferences, and rationality (Baron-Cohen 1995; Gergely, Nadasdy, Csibra, and Biro 1995; Premack 1990). These notions would be activated by the presence of perceptual cues, such as self-propelled or biological motion. To illustrate, Premack (1990) suggests that when infants see that an object is self-propelled they then infer that it moves intentionally. Premack also hypothesizes that, as a part of understanding the intentions of the object, infants may also infer that it will prefer its own kind and seek to reciprocate the actions of other objects. While proposed to be different from full-fledged adult systems of reasoning, these innate systems would provide a critical substrate for further development, on analogy with proposals for innate core knowledge in other domains, such as physics (see, e.g., Spelke et al. 1992; Spelke and Newport 1998). The existence of early abstract expectations about intentional action has not generally been evaluated by direct empirical tests (but see Gergely et al. 1995). Instead, theorists have argued that the concept of intentional action is so complex and so important for survival that strong innate constraints are required to explain its ontogeny.

In our work, we question both of these accounts. First, we take seriously the possibility that infants, before they acquire the communicative tool box of the 12–24-month-old, understand some aspects of intentional action. Second, we take seriously the possibility that intentional understanding develops a piece at a time based on experience with particular actions and actors, rather than being innately specified in some abstract form.

Action as Goal-Directed

Mature conceptions of intentional action are multi-faceted. Adult folk psychology explains behavior in terms of an actor's goals, perceptions, emotions, beliefs, knowledge, preferences, and personality traits, among other factors (Heider 1958; Wellman 1990). In investigating the potential infant precursors to this mature system of knowledge, therefore, the first decision we faced was where to start. We began by exploring a foundational component of folk psychology: the assumption that human action is goal-directed. Both adults and preschoolers understand human behavior not as an undifferentiated series of motions through space but rather as actions directed toward goals (Heider 1958; Lillard and Flavell 1990). This insight provides one important basis for understanding intentional action.

Recent research indicates that an understanding of goal-directed action is present very early in childhood, as young as 14 months. Fourteen-month-olds are more likely to imitate actions that appear to be purposeful than behaviors that seem to be accidental (Carpenter, Akhtar, and Tomasello 1998), and older toddlers show similar attention to goal-directed actions over other kinds of behaviors in word learning (Tomasello and Barton 1994). When 18-month-olds see a person slip and fail to complete an intended action, they imitate the intended action and not the actual movements that the actor made (Meltzoff 1995). Thus, toddlers selectively attend to and remember the elements of an event that are relevant to the actor's goals.

Our first question, then, was whether infants share this propensity to pay attention to the goals of an actor. We began with the familiar goal-directed action depicted in figure 1. Infants saw a person reach into a curtained stage, move her arm through a distinctive path, and grasp one of two toys that were mounted on the stage. There were at least two aspects of this event

Habituation Event

New Path Test Event   New Goal Test Event

Figure 1
Sample habituation and test events for the human grasp (based on Woodward 1998).

that infants could attend to and remember: the salient path taken by the actor's arm and the relation between the actor and the object that was her goal. Adults would likely describe the event in terms of the latter ("She grasped the bear") rather than the former ("She moved her arm through 10 inches of space from the bottom right corner of the stage to the far left side"). Adults can notice either aspect of the event, but because reaching is understood as goal-directed, the goal-related features seem more central than others.

To assess infants' construal of the event, we used the visual-habituation paradigm. A well-established finding is that once infants habituate to one stimulus they will look longer at another stimulus that seems new to them. We drew on this response in tapping infants' representations of the grasp event. To determine which aspect of the event infants weighted most heavily in their representations, we measured the strength of the novelty response to a change in each aspect. After the infant habituated to one event, we reversed the positions of the toys and presented test events in which there was a change in either the relation between the actor and the goal (new-goal trials) or the path of reach (new-path trials). Figure 1 provides an example of these events.[1] Six-month-olds and 9-month-olds showed a stronger novelty response (i.e., looked longer) on new-goal trials than on new-path trials (Woodward 1998). That is, like toddlers, young infants selectively attended to and remembered the features of the event that were relevant to the actor's goal.

As is the case for toddlers (Meltzoff 1995; Meltzoff and Brooks, this volume), infants' propensity to attend to goals seems to be specific to human actors. Infants did not selectively attend to the relation between actor and object for events involving a range of inanimate "actors" (Woodward 1998). For example, when 6-month-olds saw a mechanical claw grasp the toy (figure 2), they showed somewhat greater recovery on new-path trials than on new-goal trials. The claw events were similar on several dimensions to the hand events: there was motion through space ending in contact with the toy, the claw was covered in cloth that matched the actor's sleeve and hand, and the claw grabbed hold of the toy. Nevertheless, infants construed the hand events and the claw events differently.

Subsequent analyses revealed that this pattern of findings was not a by-product of infants' interest in hands as compared to their interest in claws and other inanimate actors. Infants across studies and conditions had their attention drawn to the toy that was contacted, whether it was contacted by a hand or by an inanimate object. However, infants who saw a hand differed from those who saw an inanimate actor in the features they weighted most heavily in their representation of the event.

This set of findings is the first to indicate that infants under a year of age understand certain human actions as goal-directed, in that they construe these actions primarily in terms of the relation between the actor and the goal. (For further evidence, see Wellman and Phillips, this volume.) By themselves, these findings leave open the question of exactly how infants understand this relation. Infants' understanding of action as goal-directed is likely quite different from adults'. Adults understand goals as mentally represented

Habituation Event

New Path Test Event   New Goal Test Event

Figure 2
Sample habituation and test events for the inanimate grasp (based on Woodward 1998).

entities that are embedded in the rest of a person's mental life. A person's goals relate to that person's beliefs about the world, beliefs about his or her abilities, desires, and preferences. In view of the literature on theory of mind in preschoolers, it is very unlikely that infants have a full-fledged understanding of this sort. However, infants may understand agent-object relations in other ways that are continuous with adult understandings.

One possibility is that, in addition to understanding that certain actions imply a relation between a person and an object, infants understand these actions as being "directed at" the object. This possibility, considered by Wellman and Phillips in the present volume, is also consistent with our data. There are at least two ways in which infants could understand action as directed toward objects. For one, infants might understand this aspect of action at a purely behavioral level. Csibra and Gergely (1998) have developed an account of such a system of knowledge that could serve as a precursor to later mentalistic understandings of goals. In addition, infants may understand something about the internal aspects of the relation between an actor and the actor's goal—for example, that the phenomenological experience of wanting something accompanies the actions that are deployed to get it. Infants could understand this aspect of goal-directed action without yet understanding very much about mental life. Further empirical work is required to explore these possibilities.

These issues aside, our findings indicate that infants are on the right track, in that they are attending to just those aspects of actions that are relevant to goals in the adult sense. These findings have implications for the theories we outlined earlier. They weigh against the claim that infants younger than 12–24 months lack any understanding of intentional action or of relations between agents and objects (Meltzoff 1995; Tomasello 1995). Six-month-olds construe one intentional action, grasping, in terms of the relation between the actor and the goal. In addition, 6-month-olds have begun to draw the line between animate and inanimate entities, interpreting motions of the former, but not the latter in terms of the relation between agent and object. Therefore, by the time they are 6 months old, infants can detect certain instances of intentional action, and they attend to the aspects of the action that are critical for understanding the specific intention behind it.

Our subsequent studies revealed important limitations on infants' early propensity to attend to human goals. These limitations are relevant to theories at the other extreme, that is, theories that posit infants to be endowed with rich and abstract notions of intentional action.

The Specificity of Infants' Understanding of Goal-Directed Action

As we mentioned earlier, some theorists (Baron-Cohen 1995; Gergely et al. 1995; Premack 1990) have proposed that the ability to understand action as intentional is rooted in rich, innately specified systems of reasoning, rather than being acquired through experience. Because they are not rooted in knowledge about particular actions, these systems of reasoning are argued to be very general, potentially applying to any event the infant sees.

To limit the cases in which infants interpret an event as intentional, theorists further propose that there is a perceptual "trigger" that activates these innate systems of knowledge. For example, Premack (1990) has proposed that infants are born with a system for interpreting action as intentional, and that it is triggered whenever they see self-propelled motion. (See also Baron-Cohen 1995.) Other triggers that have been proposed are the biological patterns of motion associated with animals and people (Baron-Cohen 1995) and apparently rational motion toward a goal (Gergely et al. 1995).

These features would generally serve to identify the actions of people. However, they will always be at best an approximate cue. Many apparently self-propelled motions are not intentional, even those produced by people. On Premack's theory, infants would over-attribute intentionality to inanimate objects that move with no apparent external force (such as drifting leaves) and to human behaviors that are not purposeful (such as sneezes or stumbles). In our later studies, we evaluated these predictions. Our findings indicate that, contrary to these proposals, infants' initial understandings of agents and actions are rooted in their knowledge about specific agents and specific actions.

How Do Infants Identify Agents?

Do babies attribute the potential for goal-directed action to anything that presents the right perceptual trigger? In all theories that posit a trigger, the trigger is argued to be a characteristic pattern of motion—most often, self-propelled motion.[2] Baron-Cohen (1995, p. 34) proposes that even though "the visual input might look as shapeless as an amoeba, as weird as a giraffe, or as minimal as a stick insect," nevertheless "because of their self-propelled motion, all these are instantly interpretable as agents with goals and desires."

There are two levels at which this proposal can be evaluated. First, is it really the case that properties of motion are the sole basis for infants' judgments of agency? Second, regardless of the particular features infants use, is the idea of a hard-wired trigger accurate? Our findings address each of these questions.

On the one hand, this emphasis on patterns of motion seems intuitively correct. After all, one critical feature of animate entities is that they can move on their own. On the other hand, it seems equally intuitive that other features bear on whether an object is identified as animate. Imagine you are walking through the woods and see a long thin object lying motionless across the path. If the object has the texture of snakeskin, you will likely react quite differently than if it has the texture of tree bark. Similarly, imagine you enter a room to find a blue plastic disk moving through the air, apparently without an external source of energy and in an irregular "biological" manner. You would likely be much less surprised to discover that the disk was attached to a mobile by means of a thin wire than to discover that it was a kind of flying animal.

Our earlier findings indicate that by 6 months infants distinguish between people and inanimate objects such as mechanical claws, but they leave open the issue of the means by which infants make this distinction. With respect to self-propelled motion, the hand and claw events were equally ambiguous. From only the information in the display, it was not clear whether either the hand or the claw was self-propelled, because the infant could only see the end of the arm or claw. The display did not specify whether the hand and claw started up on their own or were made to move by another object. The claw clearly differed from the hand on several other dimensions, including patterns of motion (biological versus mechanical), parts (e.g., fingers), overall shape, and texture (skin versus plastic).

In an ongoing set of studies (Guajardo and Woodward, in progress), we are testing infants' sensitivity to texture. Will infants differentiate between objects that have identical motion properties but different textures? The set-up and the procedure of the study are similar to those depicted in figure 1. However, the grasping action is performed by an actor wearing a metallic-gold-colored evening glove. The glove covers all traces of skin but preserves the characteristic patterns of motion, parts, and overall shape of the actor's hand. In the first study, the actor reached in through a curtain so that infants could only see her arm (clothed in a magenta sleeve) and her hand (in the gold glove). We tested infants at two ages: 7 months and 12 months. Control groups of 7-month-olds and 12-month-olds watched the events performed by an ungloved hand, just as in earlier studies. The control groups at both ages showed the same patterns seen in previous work: they responded strongly to a change in the relation between actor and goal, and less strongly to a change in the path taken by the actor's arm. In contrast, infants at both ages who saw the gloved hand did not show this pattern. The younger group looked marginally longer on new-path test trials; the older group looked about equally as long on the two kinds of test trials. At both ages, infants' overall level of attention did not vary as a function of whether they saw the glove. That is, the difference between the findings in the two conditions does not seem to be due to infants' finding the glove either extremely interesting or extremely aversive. Infants were equally attentive to the gloved hand, but they did not seem to treat it as an agent. Contrary to the predictions of several theories, then, texture is an important cue in infants' determination that an entity is capable of goal-directed action. This finding concurs with work by Smith and Heise (1992), who found that texture is a powerful source of information for young children in categorization tasks involving animals and artifacts.

One possible conclusion from these findings is that the idea of a hard-wired trigger is correct, but the trigger is textural rather than motion based. Perhaps infants consider an entity to be an agent so long as it has skin. However, our later findings argue against this conclusion. For one thing, as we will discuss below, infants do not treat all motions of a naked human hand as goal-directed. In addition, we found we could alter babies' interpretation of the gloved hand by giving them more information about it. We reasoned that the original events gave infants very little evidence that the hand was a part of a person. Most of the actor (including her face) was hidden from view, and the actor never spoke or interacted with the infant. Thus, the actor in the display lacked many of the features that infants probably associate with people. This fact, coupled with the absence of skin texture, might have undermined infants' understanding that the hand was a part of a person. In the next study, we again showed 12-month-olds the gloved hand grasping the toy, but this time accompanied by other cues that the hand was a part of a person. We showed infants the actor from the waist up. At the start of each trial, she made eye contact with the baby, said "Hi," and then said "Look" as she turned to look at and grasp one of the toys. After habituation, as in previous studies, the toys' positions were reversed, and infants saw the actor reach for the same toy, now on the other side of the stage (new-path test events), or for the other toy (new-toy test events). The actor wore the same gold gloves and sweater as before. This time, however, 12-month-olds interpreted the movement of the golden hand as goal-directed, looking reliably longer on new-goal trials than on new-path trials.

These findings run counter to the idea that infants rely on the presence or absence of a single trigger feature in determining whether they are seeing an agent. The patterns of motion associated with humans were not sufficient to convince infants that the gloved hand was an agent. Texture is also important. However, texture is not the only feature that matters for infants. When given more information about the gloved hand (that is, when they could see it attached to a person), infants readily interpreted its motions as goal-directed. More generally, babies do not seem to focus on only one feature, but instead respond to several different kinds of cues to agency. These findings suggest that, rather than attributing agency to an overly broad class of items that share a single feature, infants begin by focusing on one specific kind of entity, the person, which has many typical features.

How Do Infants Identify Goal-Directed Actions?
Nativist theories predict overgenerality not only in the entities identified as agents but also in the actions identified as intentional. On Premack's (1990) account, any movement of a self-propelled agent would be considered as intentional, including "bumps between people, as well as falls or tumbles" (p. 13). On the account of Gergely et al. (1995), infants would consider as intentional any motion through an apparently rational path toward a potential goal. On these accounts, because infants would initially identify an overly broad set of behaviors as intentional, development would be a process of paring down the range of events considered as intentional.

We tested this possibility using the same paradigm as in earlier work with a normal, ungloved human hand, this time varying the type of contact between the hand and the object (Woodward 1999). In one condition, the actor reached toward and grasped one of two toys. In the other, the actor lowered her arm toward the toy, letting her hand fall the last few inches so that it landed, palm up, on top of it (figure 3). Aside from this difference, the two events were similar on several dimensions. In both events, the actor's arm moved through the same paths and the actor's hand hid roughly the same portion of the toy from view. The two events took the same amount of time and were equally effective at drawing infants' attention to the toy that was contacted by the hand. Critically, each event involved self-propelled, biological motion toward the object, and each involved a human actor.

Grasp Condition   Back-of-Hand Condition

Figure 3
Sample habituation events for different kinds of contact between actor and object (based on Woodward 1999).

As in previous studies, infants were habituated to one event and were then shown test events that altered either the path of motion taken by the actor's arm or the identity of the object that was contacted. We first tested 9-month-olds. Despite the similarities between the grasp and back-of-hand events, infants encoded the two events differently. For grasps, infants responded more strongly to a change in goal object than to a change in path, as in earlier studies. That is, infants represented this event primarily in terms of the relation between the actor and the goal. The infants who saw the actor touch the toy with the back of her hand did not do this; they looked equally at the two kinds of test events. This difference was not due to infants' finding the back-of-hand events much more interesting or much less interesting than the grasp events. The overall amount of looking in the two conditions was the same. In a follow-up study, 5-month-olds showed similar though somewhat weaker patterns. As early as we have seen evidence that infants construe grasping in terms of the relation between actor and object, therefore, we have also seen evidence that infants distinguish between grasping and other manual actions. Counter to the predictions of several nativist theories, infants do not construe all self-propelled motions or even all human motions as goal-directed.

These findings argue against the conclusion that infants initially identify an overly broad set of behaviors as goal-directed. They further suggest two possible means by which infants might identify particular actions as goal-directed. One possibility is that infants understand some features of action (for example, smooth movements, articulated motion with respect to an object, and palm orientation) as evidence of goal-directedness. The grasp and back-of-hand events differed on each of these dimensions. By 18 months, babies use this kind of evidence to interpret novel behaviors (Meltzoff 1995; Tomasello and Barton 1994). A second possibility is that infants' ability to determine whether behaviors are goal-directed initially derives from their familiarity with particular actions. Grasping is ubiquitous in infants' environments and is also an action they have experienced from the agent's point of view. On the basis of these experiences, infants may have learned about the goal-directed nature of grasping. Since they are unlikely to have encountered the back-of-hand event before, they may not have a ready way to make sense of it.

Another finding from our lab is consistent with the second of these possibilities. In an ongoing series of studies, we are testing infants' understanding of pointing. Like grasping, pointing involves smooth, coordinated motion toward an object and (in the events for this study) contact with the object. In addition, like grasping, pointing indicates a relation between an actor and an object for adults. Adults understand a good deal about the specific nature of the relations between objects and people who grasp them or point at them. Grasps are understood as indicating a desire on the part of an actor, whereas points indicate an attentional state and perhaps the intention to communicate with someone about the object. Even if infants did not understand the exact nature of these actor-object relations, in order to understand the point gesture in even a rudimentary way they would have to know that there is some relation between the actor and the object of her point.

We used the same methodology as in previous work to study whether 9-month-olds and 12-month-olds represent pointing in terms of the relation between the person who points and the referent object (Woodward and Guajardo, in progress). We showed infants events similar to the grasp events in our first studies, except that now the actor pointed to and touched the toy instead of grasping it. Some infants saw only a pointing hand; others saw the actor's upper body and face too. In this case, the actor began each trial by making eye contact with the infant, saying "Hi," and then saying "Look" as she looked at and pointed to the object. We thought that these behaviors might provide further evidence that the point was directed toward the object. However, we found that the results in the two conditions did not differ. As in previous studies, infants, having been habituated to a single event, then saw test events in which either the path taken by the actor's arm or the identity of the referent object had changed. Despite the presence of behavioral cues that the point was directed at the object, 9-month-olds did not seem to construe it in this way. They looked equally long at the new-referent and the new-path test events. In contrast, 12-month-olds showed a greater novelty response on new-referent trials than on new-path trials. These findings are noteworthy because it is between 9 and 12 months that babies begin to follow other people's points (Butterworth and Grover 1988; Schaffer 1984) and to use the point gesture to direct other people's attention (Bates et al. 1979).

There are several reasons why infants may have a harder time discovering the relation between a person who points and the referent of the point than discovering the relation between a person who grasps and the object of the grasp. As has already been noted, grasping and pointing are manifestations of different kinds of underlying intentions, and these may more easily be understood for grasping than for pointing. Moreover, in everyday life grasping is accompanied by concrete cues to the actor's intentions. Grasping often involves physical consequences for the object (e.g., it might be moved closer to the actor), which could help infants to understand the actor's goals (e.g., obtaining the object). In contrast, pointing may not have clear physical consequences for the referent object. In addition, outside the laboratory pointing most often occurs at a distance from the object. The demands posed by relating entities separated in space may make it difficult for infants to learn about points.

In summary, our findings indicate that the early development of intentional understanding is not a process of paring down initially overgeneral notions but instead a process of building up initially undergeneral ones. Infants begin by understanding particular actions as goal-directed, and with time the range of actions they understand in this way increases. Just as infants' notions of actors seem to focus on people in particular, rather than on the broad class of anything that moves on its own, so infants' notions of goal-directed action seem to focus on particular actions.

A Developmental Challenge: How Are Early, Specific Notions Enriched?

The above conclusions raise this question: How do infants move beyond these early, specific beginnings to a more general understanding of intentional action? In recent work (Woodward and Sommerville 2000), we have investigated one means by which infants' understanding of intentional action may be enriched.

Adults are not limited to understanding just a few actions, or even to understanding only actions with certain behavioral features, as intentional. Instead, adults can interpret action in context, and thus can understand completely novel actions as intentional. At the heart of this ability is the understanding that distinct actions can often be related to the same overarching goal (Schank and Abelson 1977; Searle 1983). For example, on observing someone grasp a refrigerator door handle, pull open the door, grasp a gallon jug of milk, and carry the jug to a waiting glass, adults readily interpret the sequence as "getting a drink of milk" and understand the separate actions as relating to this overarching goal. This ability to interpret actions in sequence provides adults with a way to infer the intention behind novel or ambiguous actions. Running a thumbnail around the top of the milk jug might not in itself have a clear goal, but in an informative behavioral context it can be understood it as a means to opening the jug and thus as related to the goal of getting a drink of milk.

If infants could link actions to an overarching goal, therefore, this would provide them with one way to interpret novel actions. (For a discussion of this problem and another approach to it, see Baird and Baldwin, this volume.) To test this possibility, we created a simple analogue of the above situation for 12-month-olds. First, we devised an action that we hoped would be ambiguous to babies (figure 4). On a stage sat two clear boxes, each a different color of translucent plastic and each containing a different toy. Infants saw an actor reach into the stage area, rest her hand on top of one of the boxes, and hook her thumb under the lid. For reasons that will become clear, we called this the *single-action* condition. This action could be construed as being directed at the toy inside the box or at the box itself. In order to determine how infants construed it, we tested whether they showed a greater novelty response to a change in the relation between the

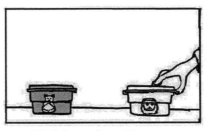

Habituation Event

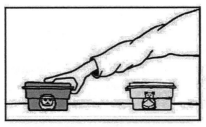

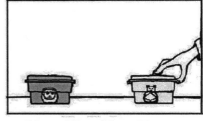

New Box Test Event   New Toy Test Event

Figure 4
Sample habituation and test events for the single-action condition (based on Woodward and Sommerville 2000)

actor and the box or to a change in the relation between the actor and the toy. After habituation we switched the positions of the toys and then showed infants two kinds of test trials in alternation. On new-box trials, infants saw the actor perform the same action on the other box, which contained the toy associated with the reach during habituation. On new-toy trials, infants saw the actor perform the action on the same box as in habituation, which now contained the other toy. Twelve-month-olds looked equally long at the two test events, indicating that the goal of this action was ambiguous to them.

For a second group of infants, we embedded this ambiguous action in a sequence that culminated in an action infants understand as goal-directed—namely, grasping. We called this the *embedded-action* condition. After touching the box lid, the actor opened the box and grasped the toy within it. Infants saw this event during habituation. After habituation, we showed infants the same two test events as in the single-action condition. The actor touched the top of the box but did not open it, and there was either a change in the relation between the actor and the box or a change in the relation between the actor and the toy. In this condition, infants looked longer on new-toy trials than on new-box trials. That is, infants now interpreted touching the lid as being directed at the toy within the box. In sum, infants used the second action (grasping the toy) to interpret the first (touching the lid).

From the results so far, it is not clear how infants related the two actions. One simple strategy would be to assume that any actions that occur in sequence are related to the same goal. Young infants have the wherewithal to employ this strategy, since they are adept at detecting temporal patterns (Saffran, Aslin, and Newport 1996). However, this strategy runs the risk of relating actions that co-occur serendipitously. Imagine someone reaching into a cookie jar and pausing in mid-reach to pick up a ringing phone. Adults would not think that the reach to the phone and the reach to the cookie were directed toward the same goal. If infants relied solely on co-occurrence, they would make this error. In relating actions to overarching goals, adults draw on their knowledge of the constraints in a situation, including physical constraints (e.g., whether an action is a possible means to obtaining the goal), psychological constraints (e.g., what the actor knows), and social constraints (e.g., conventionally appropriate behaviors). In our study, there was a physical relation between the two actions that could have led infants to relate them. In order to obtain the toy, the actor had to first touch (and remove) the box lid. The question was whether infants used this relation to link the actions.

To address this question, in the next study we showed infants events in which the temporal relation between opening the box and grasping the toy was identical to that in the embedded-action condition, but in which the causal relation between these two actions was disrupted. Rather than sitting inside the boxes, the toys sat outside and in front of them. During habituation, infants saw the same event sequence as in the previous study. The actor opened the lid and grasped the toy that now stood in front of the box. The test events were like those in the first study. The toys' positions were reversed, the boxes remained closed, and the actor either reached to a new box or to the box behind a new toy. If infants relate actions based only on temporal sequencing, we would expect the same findings as in the previous study. What we found was almost the opposite. There was a marginal trend toward looking longer on the new-box trials than on new-toy trials. Thus, disrupting the causal connection between the two actions interfered with infants' propensity to relate them. Like adults, therefore, infants draw on their knowledge of the causal constraints in a situation in relating actions to overarching goals.

These findings indicate a mechanism that would allow infants to move beyond highly specific ideas about goal-directed action. The ability to use familiar actions to interpret ambiguous actions would enable infants to understand a much greater proportion of the actions that they witness in day-to-day life than they would if they understood only the goals behind certain isolated actions. Importantly, the ability to consider the causal constraints in a situation in relating actions would enable infants to determine which components of an event sequence are relevant to a particular goal. When considering which actions are related to a goal, infants can limit their search to actions that appear to be causally related to obtaining the goal (for example, opening a box when the goal object is inside it) and exclude those that are not causally related to obtaining the goal (for example, opening a box when the goal object is not inside it). One important question for future research concerns the range of causal constraints that infants can use in this way. Children may initially be limited to understanding some of the physical constraints in a context, and only later come to understand the role of psychological and social constraints.

These findings also point to a potential general advance in infants' understanding of intentional action. They indicate that 12-month-olds understand actions as means to an end. When seeking evidence for the onset of intentional control of infants' own behavior, Piaget (1952) focused on means-end problem solving. He reasoned that when infants produce a clearly independent means to obtain a goal (for example, pulling a cloth in order to grasp a toy placed at one end of it) this is evidence that the intention of getting the toy is represented independent of the particular actions that are commonly associated with the toy. Carpenter, Nagell, and Tomasello (1998) have drawn on Piaget's account to propose that a critical step in infants' developing understanding of intentional action is the realization that actions are means to an end. Our findings suggest that this element of intentional understanding is in place by 12 months.

We do not yet know whether infants younger than 12 months understand this aspect of intentional action. Some researchers (e.g., Carpenter, Nagell, and Tomasello) have interpreted Piaget's observations about the development of means-ends problem solving as evidence that they do not. On the other hand, Baillargeon, Graber, DeVos, and Black (1990) report that 5½-month-olds apparently understand means-ends relations when this understanding is measured by visual attention rather than action. It is possible, therefore, that infants younger than 12 months can draw on this knowledge in interpreting goal-directed actions.

Interpreting actions as means to an end is an important advance because it suggests that infants understand goals as separable from the particular actions that they drive. For example, the act of touching the box lid does not express a single, unvarying intention. It could be driven by any one of several underlying goals, such as obtaining the box, exploring the texture of the box, indicating the box to a conversation partner, or opening the box to obtain its contents. The infants in our study seemed to understand this fact: They interpreted the action differently depending on the context in which it occurred. Similarly, the goal of obtaining a toy inside a box could be attained by a number of means, such as opening the box oneself, enlisting the aid of one's mother, or holding the box upside down so that the lid opens. Any one of these actions will work toward obtaining the toy in some situations, but not in others. The understanding that goals and actions exist independently may be a step toward understanding goals as mentally represented entities—that is, understanding that goals exist in people's minds, not in their hands.

Conclusion

We began with two accounts of how early intentional understanding might arise. On one account, the seeds of intentional understanding appear at the end of the first year and are tied to acts of communication and social life. On a second account, the seeds of intentional understanding are present from birth, by virtue of an innate system for interpreting self-propelled motion. Our findings suggest a third alternative: that early in life infants come to understand certain actions as goal-directed, and this early, specific knowledge provides a foundation for later developments in intentional understanding. This knowledge is evident several months before infants begin to engage in the joint attention behaviors taken to be critical evidence by the first account, and is tied to the specifics of actors and actions in a way that is not predicted by the second.

Premack and others suggest that the earliest notions of intentionality have their origins in the infant's inherited starting equipment. Our findings indicate, in contrast, that initial understandings of intentional action may well derive from experience, because infants' notions of agents and actions seem to be grounded in the particular details of their experience. Infants' notion of agent seems to focus on the person, the type of agent that they most commonly encounter. In addition, the first action that we find infants to understand as goal-directed—grasping—is frequent in everyday life and is an action with which infants literally have firsthand experience. There is circumstantial evidence for a relation between infants' experience as graspers and their understanding of grasping in others as goal-directed. Six-month-olds show strong attention to the goal-related properties of reaches (Woodward 1998), 5-month-olds show this pattern more weakly (Woodward 1998 1999), and, in pilot work, 3-month-olds have not shown this pattern at all. This period, between 3 and 6 months, is the period in which infants become expert reachers.

The ability to understand certain isolated actions as goal-directed is an important initial foothold for infants, but this ability alone would leave much of human behavior uninterpretable. Moreover, to the extent that young infants are limited in this way, their understanding of intentions would be quite different from the mature concept of intentions as independent of particular actions. By 12 months, infants are breaking free of these limitations. They have widened the range of actions understood as goal-directed, can relate distinct actions to overarching goals, and can interpret new actions on the basis of the context in which they occur. Here there are points of contact between our findings and descriptions of burgeoning social competence in 12-month-olds. First, as would be expected from these descriptions, we find that infants begin to understand pointing in terms of the actor-object relation between 9 and 12 months. Second, the finding that 12-month-olds can relate actions to overarching goals could help to explain the onset of behaviors such as imitation of novel goal-directed actions, social referencing, and word learning, since these all require relating distinct actions to the same goal (e.g., gaze, pointing, emotional expressions, and utterances).

Our findings have just begun to sketch an outline of early intentional understanding. They leave many critical questions unanswered, but nevertheless they give a strong indication of the kind of account that will best address them. Infants' first attempts to make sense of intentional action seem not to be driven by abstract, innate expectations, but rather by what they have learned and by the development of general abilities such as means-end reasoning. In this way, our account dovetails with those of Baird and Baldwin and those of Wellman and Phillips (this volume). There is good reason to believe that infants' understanding of intentional action emerges in large part from general properties of learning and early experience. In the case of intentional action, the information available to infants is rich from the beginning, including countless hours of observing the actions of others as well as the firsthand experience of gaining control over their own actions. These experiences could well provide the initial basis for making sense of intentional action.

Acknowledgments

The research described in this chapter was supported by grants from the John Merck Fund, the Robert R. McCormick Tribune Foundation, and the National Institutes of Health (FIRST grant No. HD35707-01) to the first author. We are grateful to Catharine Seibold and Anneliese Hahn for their assistance in completing the studies, and to the parents and infants who participated. We thank Dare Baldwin and Bertram Malle for insightful comments on an earlier version.

Notes

1. In all our studies, the side of the stage to which the actor reaches during habituation and the type of test trial given first are counterbalanced.

2. The proposal that motion provides the basis for the agent/nonagent distinction is a common starting point for a range of theories, which vary in the extent to which they posit elaborate innate structure (e.g., Gergely et al. 1995; Leslie 1995; Mandler 1992).

8

"Like Me" as a Building Block for Understanding Other Minds: Bodily Acts, Attention, and Intention

Andrew N. Meltzoff and Rechele Brooks

Wayne Gretzky was a genius. He could do things on the ice that seemed magical. When asked his secret to scoring goals, he said: "Hockey is simple. You just see the game, and then you skate to where the puck will be." Other hockey players often struggle over this advice and ask: "But how do you know where it *will* be?" Gretzky just shrugs at this. He doesn't have other help to give: "You just see it. It's obvious before it happens." He can't imagine a hockey player being restricted to seeing where the puck actually is. He thinks everyone ought to be able to see what the players will do next. What a disadvantage only to see the actual, and not the future movements of other players! He might call it hockeyblindness.

Children with autism are sometimes described as having a kind of mindblindness. They can't predict what others will do. They can see what another person is doing, but it doesn't provide enough purchase to predict what will happen next. Through rote memorization and laborious learning they can participate in repetitive social routines, but it is never quite right. Even high-functioning people with autism are a step behind in the game of social interaction, having to think through what comes naturally to us.

The normal baby, on the other hand, is facile at skating to where the social puck will be. Part of the joy, the exhilaration of interacting with normal babies is that they get the gist of what you are doing. They can meet you where the interaction is leading, without your laboriously pulling them along. You can make mistakes, and they can read what you meant to do. This simplifies things. It "slows down" the interaction for them, just as the hockey game is running in slow motion for Wayne Gretzky. The typically developing child is to a child with autism as Gretzky is to the rest of us with

respect to hockey. Typically developing children are geniuses of social cognition in comparison to children with autism.

How do young children so readily understand our behaviors, interpret
our intentions, and skate to where the interactive puck will be? You could
say it is "natural" for them. But we think this can be analyzed further. What
seems to come naturally to normal children is actually the product of innate
foundations and much development. In this chapter we will analyze the
contributions from both.

Origins of Understanding Others—God Only Knows?

If we take Piaget's (1952) starting state, the newborn is in a condition of
"normal autism." The neonate has only a few reflexes to work with (e.g.,
sucking and grasping), and the behaviors of others are registered meaning-
fully only to the extent that they can be assimilated to these schemes. The
child battles its way out of normal autism by 18 months. This is a very long
road to understanding other minds. If we take Skinner's starting state, . . .
well, never mind.

We now know there is a much richer innate state than Piaget, Skinner,
and all previous learning theorists ever dreamed. In this sense the nativists
have won the battle over the newborn's mind. But some of us think that
there are also developmental changes that occur as a result of infants' using
this innate state to interpret input from the rich social environment. We call
this "starting-state nativism," as opposed to "final-state nativism" (e.g.,
Gopnik and Meltzoff 1997; Meltzoff and Gopnik 1993). On this view, evolution has provided the human newborn with "discovery procedures" for
developing adult common-sense psychology, but the final state is not specified at birth or through maturation alone. Starting-state nativism is different from Piaget's and Skinner's views, but it is also different from Fodor's.

Chapter 1 of Fodor's (1987) rather slim guide to human development
says:

Here is what I would have done if I had been faced with this problem in designing
Homo sapiens. I would have made a knowledge of commonsense *Homo sapiens*
psychology *innate;* that way nobody would have to spend time learning it. . . . The
empirical evidence that God did it the way I would have isn't, in fact, unimpressive.
. . . Suffice it that: (1) Acceptance of some form of intentional explanation appears
to be culturally universal. . . . (2) At least in our culture, much of the apparatus of

mentalistic explanation is apparently operative quite early. . . . (3) I take the lack of a rival hypothesis [to nativism] to be a kind of empirical evidence; and there are, thus far, precisely no suggestions about how a child might acquire the apparatus of intentional explanation "from experience."

Fodor is not alone in invoking God. Galileo (1613) reasoned that God would have taken exactly the opposite approach regarding worldly experience:

And who wants to set bounds to the human mind? . . . I do not think it is necessary to believe that the same God who has given us our senses, reason, and intelligence wished us to abandon their use, giving us by some other means the information that we could gain through them.

For Galileo, God would set few bounds and would maximize learning from experience. For Fodor, God would set many bounds and would not waste our time with learning. Does it all come down to who has God on his side? Developmental psychologists are not immune to such religious wars, but we take a different approach. We consult the newborns. It's our job to do the dirty (sometimes quite literally) work. We have learned quite a bit.

From Shared Acts to Shared Minds: A Developmental Hypothesis

Newborns do not do much in the way of intentional interaction, but one surprisingly "sophisticated" thing they can do is imitate bodily acts of other people (Meltzoff and Moore 1977, 1983, 1989). This sensitivity to human acts and ability to map equivalences between self and other provides leverage for understanding the beginnings of social cognition.

For newborns, *human acts* provide the most elementary parsing of the world into entities that bear on self-other relations and those that do not. Human acts are especially relevant to infants because they are visual manifestations of how the infant feels itself to be and because they are movements infants can intend. Of all the sights in a room—a stethoscope, clothes, a bed, a shimmering light—the human act is something interpretable: "That (seen) event is like this (felt) event." There is a cross-modal match between the acts seen in others and the acts done by the self. It is not simply the static features of the adults—eyes, hair, smell—that are special for infants; it is also the way the adult's body moves and its relation to the self. The fact that infants can re-create the acts with their own bodies allows infants to give them special meaning.

Infants' attention to and imitation of human acts has interesting developmental sequelae:

- The world of material objects is then divisible into those that perform human acts (people) and those that do not (things).

- Because human acts are seen in others and performed by the self, the infant can represent the other as "like me": I can act like the other and reciprocally the other acts like me. Persons are special entities, the only entities in the world with whom I can share behavioral states. *The cross-modal knowledge of what it feels like to perform observed acts provides a privileged access to people not afforded by things.* This sets the child down the pathway of ascribing psychological properties to people.

Three things give infants a jump start on common-sense psychology:

innate equipment Infants can recognize equivalences between perceived and executed acts. This is a starting state, as documented by imitation in newborns (Meltzoff and Moore 1997).

intra-personal experience When infants perform bodily acts themselves (when lying in their crib, in social interaction, etc.) they have certain mental experiences. For example, emotional expressions or effortful strivings considered merely bodily acts are systematically related to certain mental states.

inter-personal inference When infants see others acting "like me," they project that others have the same mental experience that goes with those behavioral states in the self. This gives infants some purchase on understanding others, establishing a kind of toehold until spoken language can be used.

Infants do not need to have adult common-sense psychology "preloaded" into the mind. It could develop, at least in a very elementary and schematic form, on the basis of the similarities between self and other at the level of acts. This is not Piagetian "natural autism." Nor is it Skinnerian learning by shaping and reinforcement. Fodor's claim that these are nonstarters for the growth of common-sense psychology may be correct. Starting-state nativism embraces innate imitation and cross-modal mapping between self and other and suggests that infants can elaborate their understanding of others by processing them as "like me." Infants learn about others by analogy to the self, but this "analogy" is not based on years of thinking things through; it is, rather, the starting point.[1]

Infants' Earliest Construal of Bodily Acts

Twenty years of research has established that early facial imitation is innate and also goal directed and purposeful. This particular starting state was not imagined in the armchair. The empirical work takes some patience to get through but is worth the trouble; the data give teeth to the notion of an innately based "like me" mechanism.

Innateness

According to classical theory, young infants were incapable of imitating facial gestures. The problem was as follows: Although infants can see another person move, they have no visual access to their own faces. Similarly, they can feel their own faces, but have no access to the "feeling of movement" (an internal state) of the other. There seems to be a gulf between self and other. Self and other seem to be known in fundamentally different ways.

How can the infant connect the visible others with nonvisible aspects of self? Such links were thought to be forged through postnatal learning. To eliminate such learning we tested imitation in newborn babies, the youngest only 42 minutes old (Meltzoff and Moore 1983, 1989). The results demonstrated successful facial imitation. Apparently, facial imitation is innate.

Flexibility and Purposefulness

Some form of nativism is called for, but this by no means ends the discussion. The spectrum of choices now ranges from reflexive, wholly stimulus-driven behavior to a more goal-directed cross-modal matching of human acts. It makes a difference to our theories of mind to determine whether the newborn is simply a collection of reflexes or is capable of acting intentionally.

One relevant finding concerns the range of gestures that can be imitated—the generativity of the phenomenon. Numerous independent studies report tongue-protrusion and mouth-opening imitation in infants less than 2 months old. Early imitation has also been reported for components of emotional expressions and for a variety of other gestures, including head movements, brow and cheek movements, and hand gestures. (For a review, see Meltzoff and Moore 1997.)

Other research explored whether early imitation is rigidly time-bound and stimulus-driven in the manner of the classic reflexes. The evidence shows it is not. In one study infants were shown gestures while they had a pacifier in their mouths which engaged the sucking reflex. There was no attempt to imitate during the display. The adult then assumed a neutral face and removed the pacifier. Infants initiated imitation over the next several minutes while looking at the neutral face (Meltzoff and Moore 1977). In a more dramatic example, 6-week-olds imitated across a 24-hour delay. Infants saw a gesture on one day and returned the next day to see the adult with a neutral-face pose. Infants stared at the face and then imitated yesterday's act from long-term memory (Meltzoff and Moore 1994). It makes little sense to say that infants have a "reflex" that fires 24 hours after the target act has disappeared! They were imitating on the basis of their remembrance of things past. (See also Meltzoff and Moore 1992.)

Goal Directedness

A characteristic of goal-directed action is that it converges toward the goal along flexible routes (Heider 1958). Such goal directedness has been demonstrated in early imitation. Infants gradually correct their imitative attempts in order to achieve a more accurate match to the target. This systematic error correction occurs even when the adult gives no feedback to the child (Meltzoff and Moore 1994).

Infants also respond in "creative" ways. One study showed infants the novel gesture (not seen in their base-line activity) of poking out the tongue at 45° off midline (from the side of the mouth). Infants responded by doing straight tongue protrusions and simultaneously turning their heads to the side, which results in their own version of a kind of sideward tongue protrusion (Meltzoff and Moore 1997). Although the literal muscle movements differed, the *goal* of the act is similar. Tongue protrusion + head turn is a creative error.

Correction of imitative responses and creative errors suggest a common story. In the former, infants make repeated attempts, and their intention is not satisfied by the initial motor performance stemming from it. This suggests that there is a differentiation between the representation of the target act that was derived from the external world and the representation of the infant's own body acts. The goal is apparently to bring these two into congruence. Creative errors suggest that the response is not simply "released" in the manner of a classic reflex but is actively constructed.

Mechanism of Self-Other Mapping

Taken as a whole, the findings suggest that early imitation is based on active cross-modal mapping (Meltzoff and Moore 1994, 1995, 1997). Figure 1 provides a schematic of this hypothesis. The central notion is that imitation, even early imitation, is a matching-to-target process. The goal or behavioral target is specified visually. Infants' self-produced movements provide tactile-kinesthetic feedback that can be compared to the visually specified target. Meltzoff and Moore propose that such comparison is possible because both perceived and performed human acts are represented

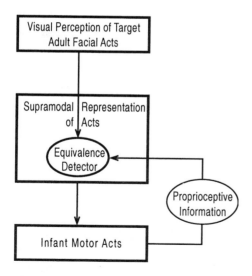

Figure 1
Facial imitation is based on cross-modal matching between self and other (reprinted from Meltzoff and Moore 1997).

within a common, "supramodal" framework. On this view, the infant's representation of bodily acts is not restricted to modality-specific terms. The bodily acts of self and other can be related by making visual-kinesthetic cross-modal comparisons. Other research has provided converging evidence for cross-modal equivalences of form (not simply timing) using both tactile-visual (Meltzoff and Borton 1979) and auditory-visual (Kuhl and Meltzoff 1982, 1984) tests; therefore, infants' matching of the *form* of the bodily acts fits with a larger body of research. A more detailed analysis of the cross-modal "metric of equivalence" thought to be used in facial imitation can be found in Meltzoff and Moore 1997.

We conclude that young infants engage in comparisons between themselves and others. This is a starting point for social cognition, not an endpoint reached after months of postnatal learning. Our intention for the remainder of the chapter is to show that further developments in social cognition may be grounded in the cross-modal equivalences between self and other that are first manifest in early imitation.

Infants' Construal of Shared Games

Let us assume a starting state of innate cross-modal mapping and imitation. What happens when we add social interaction and culture to the mix? Instead of thinking that social interaction molds a blank slate, we immediately see that the rich starting state allows the child to interpret interpersonal exchanges in special ways.

Adults across cultures play reciprocal imitative games with their babies. The social literature emphasizes the temporal turn taking of these games (Brazelton and Tronick 1980; Bruner 1975, 1983; Stern 1985). Timing and contingency detection are important, but we think these games are uniquely valuable because of the structural congruence between self and other. Physical objects may come under temporal control. Only people who are paying attention to you and acting intentionally can match the form of your acts in a generative fashion. Only people can act "like me."

Meltzoff tested whether infants recognize when another acts "like me" and the emotional consequences of this experience. A broad range of ages was used, from 6 weeks to 14 months. One experiment involved 14-month-olds and two adults. One of the adults imitated everything the baby did; the other adult imitated what the previous baby had done. Although both adults were acting in perfectly infantile ways, and thus were good controls for one another, infants reacted differentially. Infants selectively looked longer at the person who was imitating them and also smiled more often at that person (Meltzoff 1990).

This selective looking and affect could be based on temporal contingency detection. We examined this in the next study by having both adults act at the same time. When the infant happened to produce a behavior from a predetermined list, both adults sprang into action. One of the adults matched the infant; the other performed a mismatching response. Thus, both of the adults acted contingently on the infant. Infants looked significantly longer and smiled more at the imitator. Evidently, infants recognize a deeper commonality between self and other than timing alone—they recognize an adult acting "just like me," not "just when I act."

Infants also exhibited "testing behavior," which indicated that they were interested in working out the causal relations. When infants performed these tests, they made sudden and unexpected movements while staring at the adult, as if to check whether the adult was intentionally copying them. For example, the infant might slide the toy across the table as it stared at the adult's face, then modulate its act by going faster and faster as if to check if the experimenter was shadowing . . . or suddenly freeze all actions to see if the experimenter froze. (Infants acted much like Groucho Marx in front of a "mirror" in *Duck Soup* when he is trying to determine whether he is seeing a reflection of himself or merely someone acting like him.) Infants selectively directed this testing behavior to the adult who was acting "like me."

We found this pattern of behavior at all the ages we tested down to about 9 months. However, this is not an innate reaction. Infants in the first months of life are attentive to being imitated, but they don't switch to mismatching gestures to test if they will be copied. For example, if an adult systematically matches a young infant's mouth opening and closing, the infant's attention is attracted, and it generates more of this behavior, but it doesn't switch to tongue protrusion to test this relationship. Older infants go beyond this and treat the interaction as a generative matching game. Older, but not younger, infants seem to abstract the notion that the game is "you do as I do," where the particular behaviors are infinitely substitutable. Older infants do not simply register behavior-to-behavior links, as neonates do, but the abstraction of a "matching game" generalized across particular instances.

"Like Me" + Social Interaction as an Engine for Developing Intentionality

Once the social interaction is construed at this abstract level, it provides an occasion for infants to go beyond surface behaviors to the intentions that underlie them. Here are four things infants can abstract from mutual-imitation games:

- The adult's behavior matches the infant's.

- It is not a chance congruence but a systematic following of the infant's acts.

- The specific behaviors don't matter, because the game is "to match."

- From the infant's viewpoint, its own novel behaviors are intended acts.

Taken together, these four points provide the grounds for infants' enriching their construal of others on the basis of an analogy to the self: the infant purposely produces and systematically varies its own acts, the other systematically performs matching acts, perhaps the other also is acting purposively. This new construal would expand interpersonal understanding beyond that of the neonate. On the one hand, the infant now ascribes more to the other; the adult is a purposive other. On the other hand, the infant is construing self and other as equivalent agents—bearers of commensurate psychological properties, not just common body movements.

Infants' Construal of Intentional Acts

In adult common-sense psychology, people are agents just like me who have intentions like my own. What do we know about the infant's understanding of the intentions of others?

Gergely, Nádasdy, Csibra, and Bíró (1995), Wellman and Phillips (this volume), Woodward, Sommerville, and Guajardo (this volume), and other researchers have developed preferential-looking procedures to help get at this question. Meltzoff (1995) developed a more active procedure: a nonverbal procedure called the "behavioral reenactment technique." The procedure capitalizes on imitation, but it uses this proclivity in a new, more abstract way. It investigates infants' ability to read below the visible surface behavior to the underlying goals of the actor.

One study involved showing 18-month-olds an unsuccessful act, a failed effort (Meltzoff 1995). For example, the adult "accidentally" under- or overshot his target, or he tried to perform a behavior but his hand slipped several times; thus the goal state was not achieved. To an adult, it was easy to read the actor's intention even though he did not fulfill it. The experimental question was whether infants also read through the literal body movements to the underlying goal of the act. The measure of how they interpreted the event was what they chose to re-enact. In this case the "correct answer" was not to copy the literal movement that was actually seen, but to copy the actor's goal, which remained unfulfilled.

The study compared infants' tendency to perform the target act in several situations: after they saw the full target act demonstrated, after they saw the unsuccessful attempt to perform the act, and after it was neither shown nor attempted. The results showed that 18-month-olds can infer the unseen goals implied by unsuccessful attempts. Infants who saw the unsuccessful attempt and infants who saw the full target act both produced target acts at a significantly higher rate than controls. Evidently, young toddlers can understand our goals even if we fail to fulfill them.

In a recent extension, Meltzoff (1999) sought the earliest age at which infants inferred absent goals. The results suggest it is first manifest between 9 and 15 months. Fifteen-month-olds behaved much like the 18-month-olds in the original study. Nine-month-olds, however, did not respond above base-line levels to the "failed-attempt" demonstrations, although they could succeed if the adult demonstrated successful acts.

In further work, 18-month-olds were shown the standard failed attempt display, but they were handed a trick toy. The toy had been surreptitiously glued shut before the study began (Meltzoff 1996). When infants picked it up and attempted to pull it apart, their hands slipped off the ends of the cubes. This, of course, matched the surface behavior of the adult. The question was whether this imitation of the adults' behavior satisfied the infants. It did not. When infants matched the surface behavior of the adult, they did not terminate their behavior. They repeatedly grabbed the toy, yanked on it in different ways, and appealed to their mothers and the adult (cf.

Baldwin, Markman, and Melartin 1993). Interestingly, 90 percent of the infants looked up at an adult immediately after failing to pull the trick toy apart. They did so with a mean latency of less than 2 seconds, and they vocalized while staring directly at the adult. Why were they appealing for help? They had matched the adult's surface behavior, but evidently they were striving toward something else: the adult's goals, not his literal behavior. This eliminates the possibility that infants in the original study had merely tried to imitate the surface behavior of the adult (hands slipping off the cubes) and had pulled the toy apart by mistake.

If infants are picking up the underlying goal or intention of the human act they should be able to achieve the act using a variety of means. This was tested in a study using a dumbbell-shaped object that was too big for the infants' hands (Meltzoff 1996). The infants did not attempt to imitate the surface behavior of the adult. Instead they used novel ways to struggle to get the gigantic toy apart. They might put one end of the dumbbell between their knees and use both hands to pull it upward, or put their hands on inside faces of the cubes and push outward, and so on. They used *different means* than the experimenter, but toward the *same end*. This fits with Meltzoff's (1995) hypothesis that infants had inferred the goal of the act, differentiating it from the literal surface behavior that was observed.

Another study investigated how 18-month-olds responded to a mechanical device that mimicked the movements made by the actor in the failed-attempt condition. A device was constructed that had poles for arms and mechanical pincers for hands. It did not look human, but it traced the same spatiotemporal path that the human actor traced and manipulated the object much as the human actor did. The results showed that infants did not attribute a goal or an intention to the movements of the inanimate device when its pincers slipped off the ends of the dumbbell just as the actor's hands did. Although infants looked at it as long as at the human display, they simply did not see the sequence of actions as implying a goal. Infants were no more (or less) likely to pull the toy apart after seeing the failed attempt of the inanimate device than they were in base-line levels when they saw nothing.

In a final study (Meltzoff 1996), the inanimate device succeeded in pulling the dumbbell apart. After witnessing this display, infants were given the dumbbell. They too pulled it apart. Evidently, infants can pick up certain information from the inanimate device, but not other information: They can understand successes, but not failures. This makes sense because successes lead to a change in the object, whereas failures leave the object intact and therefore must be interpreted at a deeper level.

In summary, the infants distinguished between what the adult meant to do and what he actually did. They ascribed goals to human acts; indeed, they inferred the goal of a sequence of behaviors even when the goal was not attained. This differentiation lies at the core of our common-sense psychology. It underlies fluid communication as well as our moral judgments (Baldwin and Moses 1994; Bruner 1999; Chandler, Sokol, and Hallett, this volume; Kaplan, this volume; Tomasello and Barton 1994). The infants in these experiments already exhibit a fundamental aspect of our common-sense psychology: the acts of persons (but not the motions of unambiguously mechanical devices) are understood within a framework involving goals and intentions.

Infants' Construal of Attentional Acts

Other people not only intentionally manipulate objects; they also attend to objects from afar. They direct their perceptual systems toward objects and thereby pick up information about them despite the spatial gap. In common-sense adult psychology, we ascribe intentionality to the gazer. How do infants interpret the bodily act of an adult turning her head and eyes to look at an object? When do they begin to interpret this act as indicating that the adult is psychologically connected to the object of their gaze?

A great deal of research has been aimed at dissecting what is going on when an infant follows the gaze of another person (Baron-Cohen 1995; Baldwin and Moses 1994; Butterworth 1991; Moore 1999; Moore and Dunham 1995; Scaife and Bruner 1975). One debate concerns whether gaze following indicates anything more than the infants' being attracted to the spatial hemi-field toward which the adult's head is turning. At the most elementary level, a young infant might simply track the adult's head movement and thereby swing its own head to the correct half of space, without any notion of the adult's "attention to an object" or even the object directedness of the adult's gaze (Butterworth and Cochran 1980; Corkum and Moore

1998; Hood, Willen, and Driver 1998; Moore and Corkum 1994). This kind of lean interpretation has garnered support from experiments showing various types of errors infants make before about 18 months (Butterworth and Jarrett 1991; Corkum and Moore 1995, 1998; Morissette, Ricard, and Décarie 1995; Moore and Corkum 1998).

We recently reexamined gaze following by infants. We began by investigating a specific question: whether infants are restricted to using gross cues such as head movements. We set up a standard gaze-following test in which an adult looked at one of two objects. The infants were 12, 14, and 18 months of age. Two identical objects were used, so toy preferences were controlled, and the adult turned in silence with no verbal or emotional cues. The interesting manipulation was that the adult turned to the target object with eyes *open* for half the infants and with eyes *closed* for the other half (Brooks and Meltzoff 2000). In both cases infants saw a person who had been interacting contingently and talking with the infant before the trial. If infants relied on gross head motions, they should turn indiscriminately. If they relied on a general top-down rule and looked in the same direction as a "contingent interactant with a face," they should also look whether the adult's eyes were open or closed.[2]

The findings were that both 14-month-olds and 18-month-olds turned selectively—they turned significantly more often toward the target object in the eyes-open condition than in the eyes-closed condition ($p < 0.01$). The 12-month-olds showed a trend toward this selectivity, and we are currently conducting further tests to clarify the effects at this transitional age. One interpretation of these findings is that 14-month-olds have begun to realize that attending/looking is not a fixed property of animate agents. The same person may either be a perceiver/looker or not, depending on the status of his or her perceptual systems.

Taken in isolation, studies of gaze following are open to several interpretations. (See, e.g., Baldwin 1993a, 1995; Baldwin and Moses 1994; Carpenter, Nagell, and Tomasello 1998; Flavell 1999; Johnson 2000; Moore and Corkum 1994; Taylor 1996.) Therefore, Brooks and colleagues used converging methods (Brooks 1999; Brooks, Caron, and Butler 1998). They modified Woodward's (1998, 1999) procedure for investigating goal-directed reaching and used it to examine whether infants coded the link between the adult and the physical target of the adult's gaze.

In the Brooks work, 15-month-olds and 18-month-olds saw a videotape of a person who silently turned and oriented toward one of two toys (figure 2). After familiarization with this scene, the toy positions were laterally switched and infants saw two test events. In one, the person made the same head motion to the same location as in the familiarization trials. Thus, the head motions remained identical, but the adult was now oriented toward a new toy (new target/old side). In the other test event, the person made a head movement in a new direction; thus, she was oriented toward the old toy (old target/new side). The importance of eyes was tested in both conditions, with half of the infants presented with head turns with the adult's eyes-open and half with the adult's eyes closed.

If infants are coding the familiarization event in terms of the person-object link, they should look longer at the new target/old side event (figure 2, left panel). It does not maintain the original link between the person and the toy. If infants are coding the familiarization event in terms of the physical movements of the head, they should look longer at the old target/new side event. The person makes a novel head movement (figure 2, right panel). This logic

Familiarization

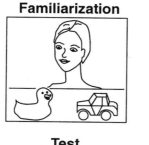

Test

New Target/Old Side   Old Target/New Side

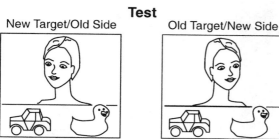

Figure 2
Preferential-looking procedure used to test infants' construal of adult gaze toward objects (adapted from Brooks 1999).

is identical to Woodward's studies of manual grasping movements.[3] The study extends the work on manual grasping in that the adult is not physically interacting with the toy but has a distal relation to it and in that the adult's eyes are either open or closed. The eye open–eyes closed manipulation allows for a stringent test of whether infants are coding the link between the gazer and the target. If so, they should look longer when the adult orients to the new object *only* when the adult's eyes are open and not when they are closed.

The results (figure 3) fit with this prediction. In the eyes-open condition, infants looked longer when the adult turned to look at the new toy (new target/old side) than when she turned to look at the old toy (old target/new side event), $F(1, 23) = 7.26$, $p < 0.05$. In the closed-eyes condition, they did the reverse and responded purely on the basis of the gross physical movements involved. Infants looked longer when the adult turned to the new side ($F(1, 23) = 4.68$, $p < 0.05$). This distinction between closed and open eyes remained significant at each age.

We thus have two studies that manipulated eyes open versus eyes closed using different techniques. The results suggest the same story—a comforting situation when comparing preferential-looking measures and action measures (and one that does not always obtain; see Meltzoff and Moore 1998). The findings do not prove that infants ascribe to the adult an "internal experience of attending," but they certainly move beyond the

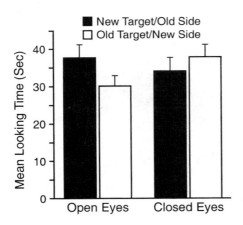

Figure 3
Mean looking time for infants ($n = 25$ per condition) viewing the stimuli portrayed in figure 2.

leanest interpretations of gaze following. Taken together they suggest that 14–15-month-olds represent the "object directedness" of adult gaze. (See also Wellman and Phillips, this volume.) In the adult framework, it is not enough to face the right way; you have to be looking in order to see. Not all people are visual perceivers; only those with open eyes are. As every parent of a teenager knows, "Face me" is not the same as "Look at me!" Fourteen-month-olds are beginning to make this critical distinction in common-sense psychology.

Conclusions: The "Like Me" Analogy

The foregoing research invites speculation about infants' construal of human acts as goal directed and about the "like me" analogy as a foundation for social cognition.

Goal Directedness of Acts

In Piagetian theory, infants acting in goal-directed ways and interpreting the goal directedness of others were slow to emerge (e.g., means-ends development, Piaget 1952, 1954). The research discussed in this chapter and elsewhere (e.g., Baird and Baldwin, this volume; Meltzoff and Moore 1995, 1997; Woodward et al., this volume) indicates that seeing human acts as goal directed is far more basic.

Three examples suffice to make this point:

- Woodward's (1998, 1999) work shows that young infants construe a reach-and-grasp event in a goal-directed manner.

- Experiments on infant understanding of adult gaze by Brooks and Meltzoff and many others (e.g., Wellman and Phillips, this volume; Woodward 2000) indicate that infants understand the object directedness of an adult act even when the adult has only a distal relationship with the object. The perceptual act is directed toward an external target or goal.

- Meltzoff's (1995, 1996) studies demonstrate that toddlers can infer unseen goals on the basis of an adult's failed attempts. They attribute invisible goals to human acts.

Evidently, infants construe human acts in goal-directed ways. But when does this start? We favor the hypothesis that it begins at birth. The relevant data come from the studies of how neonates code and imitate human acts. Of course, neonates are focused on elementary problems. They are concerned with understanding human acts themselves, not adults' physical manipulations of objects or adults' attention to distal objects. However, the available data show that infants first parse human acts in terms of goals rather than physical motions in space, specific muscle movements, and the like.

Consider, for example, the neonates' reaction to seeing the novel gesture of sideward tongue protrusion. Their responses provide critical clues to their representation of human acts. Infants produced a straight tongue protrusion coupled with a simultaneous head turn. It is only at the level of *goals* that the infant's head turn is relevant to the adult's act. Although the literal muscle movements were very different, the *goal* of the perceived act and the executed act was the same.[4]

The hypothesis is *not* that neonates represent goal directedness in the same way that adults do. In fact, neonates probably begin by coding the goals of pure body acts and only later enrich the notion of goals to encompass object-directed acts. The claim here is simply that infants begin by interpreting human behavior in terms of acts and goals, not muscle movements or physical motions. This seems to be the starting state.

The "Like Me" Analogy as Foundational

Let us return to the religious wars mentioned at the beginning of this chapter. There are two chief worldviews concerning the roots of common-sense psychology. Fodor's is that infants innately assign adult common-sense psychology to people, without having to waste time learning it. Variants of this view propose that the assignment may first be made to a broader class than people—to "self-propelled objects" (Premack 1990) or "entities with eye-spots" (Baron-Cohen 1995)—but the core idea is the same. The opposing school of thought (advocated by those too numerous to cite) is that newborns are devoid of common-sense psychological attributions. Advocates of this school begrudgingly grant that newborns may be attracted to faced-ness and biological movement, but these are seen simply as perceptual attractors. Infants learn the adult common-sense psychology through social interaction with adults.

Starting-state nativism offers the beginnings of a third way—which means it can be attacked by both factions! It grants far more to the newborn than the second view, while stopping short of the first. In particular, we suggest that coding the "like me" analogy between self and other is a starting point of social cognition. The "like me" analogy is a discovery procedure infants use to learn about people, but it is not itself a product of learning. Newborns bring it to their very first interactions with people, and it provides an interpretive framework for understanding the behavior they see.

It has long been appealing to think that "like me" is involved in our common-sense psychology (Goldman, this volume). Empathy, role taking, and all manner of putting oneself in someone else's shoes emotionally and cognitively seem to rest on the equivalence between self and other. The problem was that the self-other equivalence was thought to be late developing and therefore could not be playing a formative role.

Twenty years of research on infant imitation revises the time frame. It indicates that young infants can represent the acts of others and their own acts in commensurate terms (Meltzoff and Moore 1995, 1997). They can recognize cross-modal equivalences between the acts they see others perform and their own tactile-kinesthetic sense of self. Moreover, the cross-modal comparisons run in both directions—infants can imitate (mapping from other to self) and can recognize being imitated (mapping from self to other).

In view of this facile self-other mapping, input from social encounters is more interpretable than is supposed by "blank-slate" theories. Infants have a storehouse of knowledge on which to draw: they can use the self as a framework for understanding of the other. Having performed an act, the infant has subjective, experiential knowledge of that act.

Armed with a cross-modal representational system, the infant can interpret a seen act in terms of its own subjective experience. For example, the infant knows that when it wants something it reaches out and grasps it. It experiences its own internal desires and its bodily hand extension and finger curling. When it sees another person reaching for an object, it sees the person extending his hand in the same way, complete with finger curlings and facial expressions matching the infant's own. We know that infants can detect the similarity between their own manual movements and those they see adults perform—for example, they imitate manual movements (Meltzoff and Moore 1977, 1997; Piaget 1962). The experience of grasping to satisfy desires gives infants leverage for making sense of the grasping behavior of others. Thus, a basic "like me" analogy may underlie the behavior that Woodward (1998, 1999) reports.

A similar argument applies to the goal-directed "striving" and "try and try again" behavior used in Meltzoff's (1995, 1996) studies. Infants have experienced their own desires and acts of "try and try again." When an infant sees another act in this same way, the infant's self-experience could suggest that there is a goal beyond the surface behavior itself; the surface behavior would be seen as a familiar "type" indicating effortfulness or striving, rather an end in itself.[5]

Finally, even making sense of others' visual perception could benefit from experience of oneself as a looker/perceiver. Infants in the first year of life can imitate head movements and eye blinking (Meltzoff 1988; Meltzoff and Moore 1989; Piaget 1962). As unlikely as it seems at first blush, these data indicate that infants can map between the head movements they see others perform and their own head movements, and between adults' eyelid closures and their own eye closures. Infants' subjective experiences gained from "turning in order to see" could be used to make sense of the head movements of others who are orienting toward an object. Moreover, the infant's experience is that "closed eyes" cuts off the infant's own perceptual access. If an infant can map the eye closures of others onto its own eye closures (something infants manifest in imitating blinking), these mappings may provide data for developing inferences about perception in others.[6]

Starting-state nativism does not deny development; it embraces it. The innate equipment undergirds development through interaction with others who are perceived as "like me." What an infant learns about itself is used to interpret others, and what it learns from watching others changes the infant. Normal infants are Wayne Gretzkys of common-sense psychology: they have innate gifts not possessed by everyone (autistic children? nonhuman animals?), and they exercise these gifts all day long, for years on end, as long as they can find friends to play with. This results in an adult who seems to understand the game naturally and effortlessly.

Without an initial grasp of others as "like me," common-sense psychology would never get off the ground; however, without social interaction, common-sense psychology would not take the form it does.

Acknowledgments

Preparation of this chapter was supported by a research grant to ANM (HD-22514) and by postdoctoral training support to RB (HD-07391). We thank Keith Moore and Alison Gopnik for helpful discussions, Bertram Malle and Dare Baldwin for insightful editorial comments, and Craig Harris for assistance in preparing the chapter.

Notes

1. The onset of language provides a more efficient means of probing others' mental states (but even language is not fail-safe: my "red" may not be the same as your "red"). The claim is not that language is unimportant. The idea is that the "like me" analogy plays a powerful role in understanding others during the first two years before linguistic exchanges are of use. Two caveats: (1) "Like me" is more useful in interpreting emotions, desires, and purposiveness, rather than beliefs, because the former have relatively more visible indicators. (2) "Like me" more easily contributes to understanding congruences than it contributes to divergences in the mental states of self and other. Adults and older children have clearly outgrown such limitations, but they fit well with the empirical findings from preverbal infants (Gopnik, Meltzoff, and Kuhl 1999; Meltzoff, Gopnik, and Repacholi 1999; Repacholi and Gopnik 1997).

2. The results of Johnson, Slaughter, and Carey (1998) raise the latter possibility.

3. Woodward (2000) also recently tested looking.

4. For further discussions of the coding of humans acts in terms of goals, see Meltzoff and Moore 1997 and Gleissner, Meltzoff, and Bekkering 2000.

5. The similarity between self and other does not specify the content of the adult's goal unless that goal is familiar to the child. In cases of novel goals, "like me" simply indicates to the child that there is a goal beyond the surface behavior. It indicates effortfulness—that the adult is striving for something beyond what they are doing. An additional inferential process comes into play to determine the nature of the invisible goal. Thus, the "like me" analogy is supplemented by an inferential system (Gopnik and Meltzoff 1997).

6. In the case of understanding others' visual experiences, there is an obvious need for an additional inferential process beyond the basic self-other mappings. Multitiered systems of this sort have been suggested in social cognition and other domains (Baird and Baldwin, this volume; Gopnik and Meltzoff 1997; Meltzoff and Moore 1998; Povinelli, this volume).

9

Making Sense of Human Behavior: Action Parsing and Intentional Inference

Jodie A. Baird and Dare A. Baldwin

Human behavior is sufficiently complex to render the task of interpretation formidable. Behavior tends to flow continuously, lacking pauses to identify boundaries between distinct actions. Despite this complexity, adults and even preschoolers readily make sense of human behavior, identifying actions within the behavior stream and interpreting them in terms of intentions and what they reflect about other mental states (Malle and Knobe 1997a; Schult and Wellman 1997). How is this achieved? We will explore the possibility that a basic ability to detect structure in human behavior supports the system of intentional understanding. In particular, we will suggest that there may be physical and temporal features of action that correlate with the initiation and completion of intentions. Sensitivity to this structure would enable observers to extract the portions of behavior that are meaningful for understanding an actor's intentions. Moreover, infants as well as adults may possess these structure-detection skills, laying the groundwork for the subsequent development of genuine intentional understanding.

In the first section, we present new research documenting adults' and infants' sensitivity to structure inherent in intentional action. We follow this with a discussion of the kinds of mechanisms that might subserve these structure-detection skills and to what extent such mechanisms might be domain-general or domain-specific.

Adults' Action Parsing

Previous research on action parsing has concentrated on adults' ability to identify units within the behavior stream when asked to do so deliberately. In Newtson's (1973, 1976) unit-marking procedure, for example, observers watch a sequence of behavior (for example, a man repairing a motorcycle) and press a button on an event recorder when they determine that one meaningful action has ended and another has begun. This technique has revealed strong agreement among adult observers regarding action-unit boundaries: Their judgments reliably cluster within intervals of behavior ranging from 1 second to 5 seconds (Newtson 1976).

Despite consistent evidence of adults' capacity to detect units in the behavior stream, the question of precisely what defines these units remains controversial (see, e.g., Wyer and Srull 1989). Newtson and his colleagues have suggested that unit boundaries correspond with distinctive changes in the stimulus array, such as bodily shifts in the actor's position (Newtson and Engquist 1976; Newtson, Engquist, and Bois 1977). Avrahami and Kareev (1994) have argued instead that a sequence of behavior becomes perceptible as a unit only after it has been observed many times across varying contexts. However, neither of these proposals addresses how the units achieved in parsing relate to a conceptual-level interpretation of action. At the conceptual level, it seems clear that the structure derived from observing others in action tends to be framed in terms of ideas about the actors' goals and intentions. In explaining the actions of others, adults refer to psychological explanations, citing beliefs, desires, and intentions as the primary factors underlying human behavior (Heider 1958; Malle 1999, this volume). The central role of intentions in adults' folk theories of mind and behavior hints at the possibility that observers spontaneously segment the behavior stream into units that coincide with its intentional structure.

Both the problem we are outlining and our proposal for its solution are reminiscent of issues that have emerged in the domain of speech processing. Much like human behavior, speech proceeds as a continuous flow, lacking pauses to indicate appropriate segmentation. Fodor and Bever (1965) hypothesized that adults parse speech by perceiving it according to the constituent structure defined by underlying syntactic principles. To test this idea, Fodor and Bever (p. 415) capitalized on "the tendency of a perceptual unit to preserve its integrity by resisting interruptions." Adult participants in their study listened to tape recordings of sentences in which a "click" (a burst of white noise) was heard somewhere in each sentence. Their task was to recall the precise placement of the click within the sentence. Fodor and Bever reasoned that if grammatical constituents operate as units in adults' processing of the speech stream, then participants' subjective placement of the clicks should cluster at the boundaries of such constituents. This is precisely what they found. When clicks occurred at major constituent boundaries, participants' judgments were quite accurate. In contrast, when clicks occurred elsewhere in the sentence, participants' judgments erred in the direction of major constituent boundaries. These findings support Fodor and Bever's suggestion that speech is processed with respect to its underlying constituent structure.

To test the analogous question in the action domain—whether observers' spontaneous organization of behavior coincides with an analysis of the actor's intentions—we applied a variant of Fodor and Bever's click methodology to the study of action parsing (Baird, Baldwin, and Malle 2000). We first videotaped everyday action sequences, such as a woman cleaning her kitchen. She washes a dish, hangs a fallen towel, puts ice cream in the freezer, and so on. The movement in these action sequences flows continuously, with no physical pauses to identify boundaries between intentions. We digitized the action sequences and then artificially inserted tones in two different kinds of locations: *endpoint* tones coincided with the completion points of intentional action, whereas *midpoint* tones interrupted the ongoing action just before the completion of intentions (figures 9.1 and 9.2). Our logic was as follows: If the boundaries between intentions coincide with psychologically salient portions of the behavior stream, then adults should demonstrate greater success at recalling the location of endpoint tones (which highlight these boundaries) than at recalling the location of midpoint tones (which bear no relation to these boundaries).

Rather than rely on our own intuitions to select the locations of endpoint and midpoint tones, we presented the action sequences to a group of adult coders. Their first task was to select the portions of action that were meaningful in terms of understanding the actor's intentions. Next, they were asked to identify the point at which each of these action units was completed; that is, the point at which the intention was fulfilled. We instructed the coders to identify intentions at two levels of analysis. At the first level of analysis, coders identified intentions such as hanging a towel and putting ice cream in the freezer. We called these *tasks*. At the second level of analysis, coders identified intentions such as picking up the ice cream and grasping the freezer door. We called these *smaller actions*. In our instructions, we described these

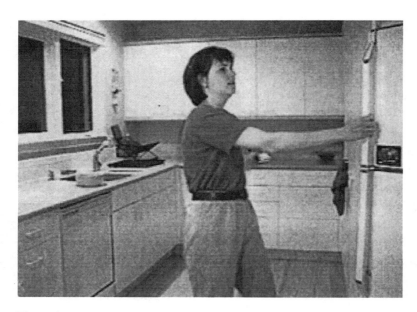

Figure 1
A frame in which an endpoint tone occurred.

Figure 2
A frame in which a midpoint tone occurred.

two levels to the coders using examples from a different, unrelated action scenario to avoid influencing their judgments. Coders' judgments turned out to show remarkable agreement. At both levels of analysis, coders tended to identify the same intentions, and their judgments of completion points were tightly clustered. On the basis of these judgments, we determined the differential placement of endpoint and midpoint tones in two kinds of stimulus action sequences: long action sequences (with tones at the task level) and short action sequences (with tones at the smaller-action level).

After constructing the stimuli, we presented a new group of adults with four different action sequences, two of each length. Each action sequence had two endpoint tones and two midpoint tones in alternating, counterbalanced order. To eliminate auditory interference with the presentation of the tones, action sequences were presented with their original soundtracks turned off. In the presentation phase of the procedure, adults viewed an action sequence once, with the instruction to pay close attention to the locations of the four tones. In the test phase, they watched the same action sequence again, this time without any tones, and were asked to click a computer mouse at the precise points at which they remembered the tones having previously occurred.

There are at least two reasons to predict that adults' subjective placement of endpoint tones should be more accurate than their placement of midpoint tones. First, tones located at endpoint locations correspond to boundaries between intentions. Thus, if intention boundaries coincide with psychologically salient junctures in behavior, adults should demonstrate greater accuracy in recalling endpoint locations relative to midpoint locations. Second, processing demands are lower at endpoint locations. When a tone occurs at an endpoint, adults should have completed their processing of the intention and thus should be able to concentrate solely on the task of processing the tone's location. When a tone occurs at a midpoint, however, adults should be in the midst of processing the intention in addition to the tone's location. Under these dual task conditions, their placement of midpoint tones should suffer relative to their placement of endpoint tones.

To examine the degree of error adults displayed in judging the locations of endpoint and midpoint tones, we first analyzed their absolute error scores in response to the two types of tones.[1] These scores were substantially smaller for endpoints (M = 430 milliseconds, SD = 173) than for midpoints (M = 643 milliseconds, SD = 261), confirming that adults were more accurate in their placement of endpoint tones than in their placement of midpoint tones. To investigate the direction of adults' error (for example, anticipation vs. delay), we next calculated their signed error scores in response to endpoint and midpoint tones. On average, adults reported endpoint tones to have occurred a mere 7 milliseconds (SD = 306) after their actual locations. In contrast, they demonstrated significant delay in their placement of midpoints: Adults judged midpoint tones to have occurred, on average, 379 milliseconds (SD = 393) after they actually did. Hence, adults misremembered the midpoint tones as having occurred much closer to the actual endpoint locations. This considerable delay in the placement of midpoint tones supports the idea that intention boundaries define units in adults' parsing of the behavior stream.

A potential concern with our methodology is that factors other than the meaningful placement of endpoint and midpoint tones within the action sequence—for instance, the timing of the tones relative to each other rather than the relation between the tones and the action—may have driven the pattern of errors adults displayed. In fact, a similar issue was raised in response to Fodor and Bever's original study. Reber and Anderson (1970) were concerned that nonlinguistic factors could have been responsible for adults' placement of the clicks at constituent boundaries. To test this, Reber and Anderson conducted a study in which they replaced linguistic sentences with streams of broad-band white noise. The patterns of errors adults displayed in response to these meaningless messages were similar to the error patterns evidenced in response to grammatical sentences, suggesting that nonlinguistic mechanisms could have been responsible for Fodor and Bever's findings.

To control for a similar possibility in our own research, we conducted a follow-up study in which we replaced the human action sequences with sequences of colored images. These new sequences preserved the precise timing of the tones, yet lacked meaningful action information. Despite identical tone information, the predicted performance pattern demonstrated in response to the human action sequences disappeared in response to the color sequences, indicating that the systematic performance differences evident in the first study were due to the meaningful placement of endpoint and midpoint tones within the action sequence, and not to other factors such as the rhythmic timing of the tones. Taken together, the findings from these two studies suggest that adults do indeed parse human behavior along intention boundaries. Moreover, this research provides the first demonstration of a link between adults' parsing of the behavior stream and their conceptual interpretation of intentional action.

Infants' Action Parsing

The relation between adults' organization of behavior and their reasoning about behavior raises the possibility that action parsing abilities, if possessed by young infants, might critically subserve the ontogeny of genuine intentional understanding. To investigate whether infants possess skills for parsing action, we tested the ability of 10–11-month-olds to detect disruptions to the structure inherent in intentional action (Baldwin, Baird, Saylor, and Clark, in press). Using a variant of the habituation/dishabituation paradigm, we presented infants with digitized video sequences of everyday action; for example, one sequence depicted a woman reaching to grasp a towel and hang it on a rack. In a familiarization phase, infants viewed the same action sequence repeatedly across several trials. In a subsequent test phase, infants viewed two different versions of the original action sequence, this time with still-frame pauses inserted at certain points in the course of action. The *intention-completing* test version, like the endpoint tones in the adult work, highlighted the boundaries between intentions with a still-frame pause occurring just as the actor completed an intention. In contrast, the *intention-interrupting* test version disrupted the intentional structure of the action sequence with a still-frame pause occurring midstream as the actor pursued an intention. In both versions, the pauses suspended the ongoing action for 1.5 second without deleting any information. Moreover, in an effort to eliminate any auditory differences between the intention-completing and the intention-interrupting videos, the still-frame pauses interrupted the original soundtrack of the actor's movements and vocalizations equally often in the two versions.

Infants viewed four familiarization trials in which the unjunctured action sequence was presented. This familiarization phase gave infants adequate opportunity to go beyond superficial characteristics in their processing of the action information. They then viewed two trials each of the intention-completing and intention-interrupting test videos in alternating, counterbalanced order. If infants parse behavior according to the structure inherent in intentional action, they should look longer at the intention-interrupting test videos (which violate this structure) than at the intention-completing test videos (which preserve this structure).

Infants' looking decreased from the first to the last familiarization trial, indicating that they indeed processed the unjunctured action sequence. When subsequently presented with the two types of test videos, infants demonstrated renewed interest—that is, longer looking times relative to the last familiarization trial—only in response to the intention-interrupting video, indicating that this video, but not the intention-completing video, violated their expectations. These findings demonstrate that infants, at least by 10–11 months, readily parse ongoing behavior along intention boundaries.

However, these results leave open the possibility that infants had a starting preference for the intention-interrupting test videos over the intention-completing test videos due to basic salience differences between the two types of test videos. To test for this possibility, we showed a new group of 10–11-month-olds just the intention-completing and intention-interrupting test videos without first familiarizing them with the unjunctured action sequence. Infants in this study looked equally long at the two types of test videos, clarifying that the longer looking at the intention-interrupting video in the first study was due to infants' sensitivity to violations of the structure of intentional action and not to any starting preference for that test video.

Possible Mechanisms

Our data provide clear evidence that infants as well as adults detect structure in action that coincides with the initiation and completion of intentions. At the same time, we cannot yet provide a complete account of *how* such structure is detected. At present, all our findings are consistent with both high-level and low-level explanations. On the high-level account, a conceptual understanding of the actor's intentions and goals may have driven structure detection in a top-down fashion. For example, knowledge of typical kitchen activity may have facilitated parsing of the action sequence. Alternatively, parsing may have been driven by low-level perceptual skills for recovering physical and temporal structure in the behavior stream that coincides with its intentional structure. For instance, as actors initiate intentions in the physical world, they first locate relevant objects with their sensors (typically the eyes), then move toward those objects, contact and manipulate them, and ultimately release contact as intentions are completed. This highly typical sequence is accompanied by a characteristic temporal dynamic: Movements in the sequence have a ballistic quality once initiated and follow one after another in rapid succession. A basic sensitivity to such predictable sequences of movement within the behavior stream could enable observers to extract just the right units of action for drawing inferences about the actor's intentions.

In the case of adults, we suspect that both mechanisms—a top-down understanding of the particular intentions involved and a bottom-up skill for identifying structure in action—likely operated to generate our findings. The action sequences adults viewed in these studies depicted well-known, everyday activities about which adults unquestionably possess sophisticated knowledge and expectations. This makes it likely that high-level mechanisms played some role in adults' processing of the action sequences. However, there are at least two theoretical reasons to suspect the additional involvement of low-level mechanisms. First, to the extent that there are indeed physical and temporal correlates of intentional action, it could only facilitate adults' action parsing to be sensitive to such structure. Second, a basic capacity to detect structure in action may be useful in the face of novel action sequences for which preset expectancies about the relations between actions and intentions will not suffice. Though it may in fact be rare for adults to observe extended novel action sequences, we suspect that there are novel elements in many of the action sequences that adults observe. When such novelty is encountered, adults must generate new action-intention relations. Doing so relies on an ability to organize the action itself in the absence of conceptual interpretation, and to use such action analysis as a basis for inferences about intentions.

In the case of infants, once again both the high-level and the low-level mechanisms postulated could account for the action-processing abilities recently documented in our own laboratory and in several others (Wellman and Phillips, this volume; Woodward, Sommerville, and Guajardo, this volume; see Povinelli, this volume, for a similar point). No existing data clarify this issue. It is quite possible that both high-level and low-level mechanisms are operative in infants' action processing. However, we strongly suspect that a low-level mechanism plays an especially important role in the structure-detection ability infants have displayed in our own research. For one, infants younger than 10 or 11 months are known to be capable of sequence learning (Clohessy, Posner, and Rothbart 1992; Haith, Hazan, and Goodman 1988) and statistical covariation detection (Aslin, Saffran, and Newport 1998; Saffran, Aslin, and Newport 1996), skills akin to those we are proposing here. Moreover, a low-level skill for detecting meaningful structure in the behavior stream seems to be a prerequisite for infants' emerging sophistication in the realm of intentional understanding. Each day, infants confront a host of novel action sequences for which they lack the world knowledge needed to understand the relevant intentions. A basic sensitivity to physical and temporal regularities in the behavior stream that coincide with intentions would enable infants to identify the meaningful portions of an action sequence even when they do not yet understand the particular intentions involved. Armed with the appropriate units, infants would then be well positioned to engage in further processing, ultimately yielding the discovery of those intentions. Thus, a low-level mechanism of the kind we are proposing would be a critical prerequisite for the developmental emergence of genuine intentional understanding.

Intentional Understanding: A Two-Tier System

Intentional understanding is the ability to draw inferences about psychological motivations guiding human action. In our view, at least two mechanisms are crucially involved in the development of intentional understanding. First, as we have already suggested, a low-level mechanism for detecting statistical structure in human action enables observers to identify relevant units in the behavior stream. For the achievement of genuine intentional understanding, however, a higher-level mechanism is still required to make sense of the resulting units in terms of psychological motivations. In what follows, we will address some basic questions one might ask regarding the nature and functioning of this two-tier system.

Are These Systems General or Specific?
Both of the mechanisms we are proposing could well operate in a domain-general fashion, supporting structure detection and inferential reasoning in

any arena with similar processing demands. With respect to the low-level mechanism, the language domain is the arena in which infants' structure-detection skills have been documented most clearly. Specifically, the detection of statistical regularities seems to enable infants to extract word-like units within the speech stream (Aslin et al. 1998; Saffran et al. 1996). This kind of statistical recovery has been modeled successfully by associative networks, clarifying the low-level nature of these structure-detection skills (McClelland and Plaut 1999). As we have suggested, low-level structure-detection skills of this same kind may have generated infants' parsing of intentional human action in our studies. Moreover, these skills could help infants to recognize important structural *differences* among various forms of movement in the physical world. For example, infants need to acquire the ability to distinguish between intentional action and inanimate motion. Furthermore, intentional action must be distinguished from behavior that is accidental or inadvertent. As it turns out, there is evidence suggesting that young infants appreciate some basic differences between human action and inanimate motion, although the mechanism underlying this ability is not yet clear. For example, 7-month-olds recognize that humans, but not inanimate blocks, can cause one another to move in the absence of direct physical contact (Woodward, Phillips, and Spelke 1993). Infants might even be able to make the important distinction between intentional action and unintentional behavior on a structural basis. As an illustration of the structural differences between these two classes of human movement, consider a clumsy mistake such as dropping a towel while reaching to place it on a rack. In this unintended scenario, the initial trajectory of motion involving the towel is interrupted; additionally, eye gaze is directed toward the floor belatedly, following (rather than preceding) the towel's fall.

Regarding the high-level mechanism, we believe inductive reasoning plays a crucial role across a variety of domains in assigning functional significance to units extracted via low-level structure detection. In the language domain, for example, a low-level mechanism may enable the detection of word-like units within the speech stream, but an inferential mechanism is necessary to assign semantic content to those units once identified. Likewise, units of action extracted by means of structure detection are not conceptually meaningful until the intentions motivating them are inferred. Explicit models of domain-general inductive mechanisms such as those we are proposing have been constructed to account for a range of relevant phenomena in adult reasoning; see, e.g., Gentner and Markman 1997 and Holland, Holyoak, Nisbett, and Thagard 1986.

In suggesting that intentional understanding may be driven at least in part by domain-general mechanisms, our proposal is notably different from others currently available in the literature. For example, both Premack (1990) and Baron-Cohen (1995) credit infants with biologically prepared, fully specified "intention detection" systems. In Premack's account, this system not only detects that an intention is occurring but also recognizes the content of at least some specific intentions (Premack and Premack 1995). In contrast, we are proposing that early in infancy *structure* can be detected in action, not necessarily the content of intentions per se. An interpretation of action in genuinely intentional terms requires the operation of a higher-level inferential mechanism.

How Do These Systems Interact?

In adults, we suspect that these two mechanisms—low-level structure detection and high-level inferencing—work in close concert, operating in a highly interactive and parallel fashion to guide people's rapid processing and interpretation of others' action. For example, when adults encounter novel actions in a foreign culture, the low-level mechanism operates to derive meaningful portions of action while the high-level mechanism simultaneously strives to interpret those units in intentional terms.

Both high-level and low-level mechanisms are likely operative in infancy. However, unlike adults, young infants presumably know little of the diverse objects cluttering our physical world. Such knowledge plays a central role in driving appropriate, high-level inferences about intentions in any given context. For example, to fully understand intentions such as those underlying the kitchen-cleanup scenario we presented, one must grasp the relevance of water to dirty dishes, that of freezers to melting ice cream, and indeed that of a clean kitchen to an orderly life. Without such world knowledge, infants' processing of action cannot be driven by the kinds of specific inferences about intentions that likely aid adults' action processing. Hence the benefit of a low-level structure-detection mechanism.

A low-level mechanism of the kind we are proposing would provide infants with an initial organization of the behavior stream in the absence of sophisticated understanding of specific intentions. Specifically, low-level structure-detection abilities yield relevant units of behavior from which the high-level inferential mechanism can begin to generate intentional inferences. We are not denying that infants possess domain-general inferential abilities; in fact, there is evidence to suggest that they do by at least 9 months (Baldwin, Markman, and Melartin 1993). We are simply arguing that in order for their inferential skills to produce the appropriate inferences about intentions in the domain of action interpretation, the low-level mechanism must first provide the relevant units on which to base such inferences. Thus, the low-level mechanism likely plays a more crucial role for infants than adults.

Questions for the Future and Concluding Remarks

Our two-tier account of the system for intentional understanding raises a number of questions for future investigation. First, with respect to the low-level mechanism, precisely what characterizes the structure of intentional action? It will be important to identify, for example, the physical and temporal properties of action that covary with transitions between intentions. Also, in what ways does the structure of intentional action differ from the structure inherent in other forms of physical movement, such as unintentional behavior and inanimate motion? When observing any kind of movement, are adults, and perhaps even infants, biased to extract intention-relevant structure in preference to other kinds of available structure? Are there individuals with specific deficits in detecting structure within action?

Regarding the high-level inferencing mechanism, how do observers resolve which intention is relevant on any given occasion? Each and every action can be interpreted in many ways; how do observers constrain the field of possibilities to an appropriate set of specific intentions? Finally, who is capable of drawing inferences about intentions? Perhaps some individuals suffer disruptions in this ability. Sabbagh (1999) has recently argued that those with autism and right-hemisphere damage have impairments that specifically undercut their ability to draw inferences about intentions. Moreover, there may be important species differences in inferential reasoning that yield corresponding differences in intentional understanding.

Along these lines, Povinelli (this volume) argues convincingly that chimpanzees and other higher primates are skilled at detecting structure in action but lack the inferential ability necessary to interpret this structure in genuinely intentional terms. If so, then divining the intentional significance of one another's actions may be a uniquely human preoccupation. We join with Povinelli in hoping to focus future inquiry on the precise nature of the relation—in both evolution and development—between skills for low-level behavior analysis and inferences about intentions.

Such questions aside, our findings clarify that infants as well as adults readily detect structure in action that is relevant for drawing inferences about intentions. In our view, low-level action analysis skills likely enable such structure detection. These basic parsing abilities gain infants access to appropriate units within complex, continuous behavior, and help adults similarly process novel action sequences for which they lack a ready motivational explanation. In this sense, structure-detection skills play a crucial role in potentiating our lifelong pursuit of interpersonal understanding.

Acknowledgments

This work was supported by a National Science Foundation Graduate Research Fellowship to the first author and by a NSF New Young Investigator award (No. 9458339) and a John Merck Scholars Award to the second author. Our thanks to Janet Astington, Rebecca Brand, Diego Fernandez-Duque, Bertram Malle, Lou Moses, Daniel Povinelli, and Mark Sabbagh for helpful comments.

Note

1. The same pattern of results was found for both long and short action sequences. For clarity, only the findings from the short action sequences are presented here.

10

Desire, Intention, and the Simulation Theory

Alvin I. Goldman

A common goal of philosophy of mind and psychology is to understand how people acquire, represent, and deploy such mentalistic concepts as desire, intention, and belief. Developmental psychologists call this subject *theory of mind*. Although this label may not commit them to the so-called *theory-theory*, almost all developmentalists (with the major exception of Paul Harris) in fact favor the theory-theory approach to the subject. A greater division of opinion prevails among philosophers, with a dedicated coterie advocating a competing approach known as the *simulation theory* (Gordon 1986; Heal 1986; Goldman 1989; Currie 1995). In this chapter I argue that the vaunted theory-theory (TT) is not on very secure ground, that it suffers from serious weaknesses not adequately appreciated by many of its advocates, and that the simulation theory (ST)—at least, its "introspectionist" variant —promises to be a cure for many of these ills. I discuss these issues with special attention to desires and intentions.

Theory-Theory and Conceptual Change

The standard version of TT is a combination of two theses: (1) that common-sense psychological concepts are theoretical concepts, similar in all relevant respects to the theoretical concepts of physical science, and (2) that people detect psychological states in themselves and in others by making theoretical inferences. In trying to defend these two theses, developmentalists typically appeal to multiple stages in children's grasp of mentalistic concepts. First, they find evidence of performance changes in mental-state attributions. Second, they interpret these performance changes as changes in children's conceptual repertoire concerning mentalistic states. Third, they infer from these supposed changes in conceptual repertoire that the concepts in question must be theoretical ones.

The orthodox position is that children move from a nonrepresentational understanding of mind to a representational understanding. This orthodoxy, however, has two variants. On one view, children's grasp of the very same mentalistic term changes over time. For example, they initially understand *belief* in a nonrepresentational fashion, but later (e.g., by age 4) they understand *belief* representationally (Gopnik 1993). On the other view, there may be no single mentalistic term that is conceptualized differently at different times. Rather, before a certain early age only nonrepresentational concepts are acquired, and representational concepts are mastered later. Bartsch and Wellman (1995a) deny that belief is first grasped nonrepresentationally and later grasped representationally. Nonetheless, they retain allegiance to the basic progression from nonrepresentational to representational concepts in claiming that only nonrepresentational concepts (such as the "simple," nonrepresentational concept of desire) are grasped before age 3, and the representational concept of belief is acquired thereafter. Similarly, Perner (1991) appears to hold that no truly representational concept is acquired before age 4, and up to that age children do not really understand any concept of belief. I shall examine these two variants of the orthodox TT position separately, identifying difficulties for each.

The first view is supposedly supported by a change in children's competence at false-belief tasks. It is assumed that this change can be attributed to a change in the *conceptual grasp* of belief, from a nonrepresentational to a representational understanding. The tenability of this assumption, however, has been undercut by accumulating evidence that young children's poor performance on false-belief tasks is not a *conceptual* deficit. A number of studies suggest that 3-year-olds' fragile memories for narratives are central to their poor performance on the traditional false-belief tasks. Three-year-olds do succeed on these tasks when they receive an aid to memory, or when they consolidate the required information in memory by hearing a story line twice (Mitchell and Lacohee 1991; Lewis, Freeman, Hagestadt, and Douglas 1994; Freeman and Lacohee 1995). Clements and Perner (1994) find evidence of an implicit grasp of false belief even when explicit answers to false-belief questions do not reveal understanding.

Three-year-olds also demonstrate an ability to recognize false beliefs associated with unfulfilled intentions (Moses 1993).

Another alternative to the conceptual deficit explanation of 3-year-olds' poor performance on false-belief tasks is the executive-control explanation offered by Russell. In the "windows task," Russell, Mauthner, Sharpe, and Tidswell (1991) found that in 3-year-olds and in autistic children salient knowledge of physical reality overwrote knowledge of mental reality. These children could not help pointing to a box that visibly contained a chocolate rather than to an empty box, even though they knew that it was in their interest to point to the empty box. Their failure to point to the empty box perseverated over 20 trials. This failure of 3-year-olds and autistics, in contrast with normal 4-year-olds, was associated with comparable performances on false-belief tasks, suggesting that the latter task is also difficult because it requires subjects to inhibit reference to a salient object.

Finally, Bartsch and Wellman's (1995a) extensive data provide no evidence that 3-year-olds have only a nonrepresentational construal of belief. They write (ibid., p. 57):

... our data provide no evidence that a representational understanding of beliefs is a significantly later achievement, following only on the heels of an earlier "connections" misconstrual of beliefs. Instead, the data suggest that very soon after children begin to talk about thoughts at all, they discuss a variety of distinctions among mental contents and states of the world, including some that seem to presuppose a representational understanding of mental contents as separate from but about the world.

Let us turn, then, to the second variant of the orthodox TT position, which holds that during an early period only nonrepresentational mentalistic concepts are grasped. This view is defended in detail by Wellman and collaborators (Wellman 1990; Wellman and Woolley 1990; Bartsch and Wellman 1995a), who argue that the concept of desire is acquired much earlier than that of belief—roughly at 2 years—but is a nonrepresentational concept. Like Flavell (1988) and Perner (1991), Wellman and collaborators say that 2-year-olds have only a simple "connectionist" grasp of wanting, involving a relation between the target person's mind and some object or state of affairs *in the world*.[1] Wanting is not construed as involving a mental representation of objects or states of affairs. As Wellman puts it (1990, p. 211), "the conceiver can simply think of the target person as having an internal longing for an external object."

Let us examine more closely this story about desire, which I shall call *the world-related story*.[2] Two-year-olds, say Bartsch and Wellman, do not attribute any mental content to the target agent to whom the desire is imputed. "Whatever contents are involved are out there, in the world, rather than in the person's mind." (Bartsch and Wellman 1995a, p. 151) Can this account of a simple form of intentionality work? Bartsch and Wellman acknowledge that, even for 2-year-olds, desires are not restricted to physical items such as apples or toys. Objects of desire include actions and states of affairs (even states of affairs that do not currently obtain). A 2-year-old might construe someone as wanting a future state of affairs, such as a full cup of milk being before her.

To assess the prospects of the world-related story, it behooves us to begin with the type/token distinction. As applied to actions, it should be drawn as follows. Actions can be considered either as types or as tokens. *Winning a race* is a generic *type* of action, which different people can instantiate (realize, token) on different occasions. The general type, winning a race, is something like a universal (in the philosopher's sense), and therefore it is not something in the world. But different *tokens* or realizations of this type *are* in the world: Sergio's winning the race in Italy last Sunday, Kristin's winning the Boston marathon last summer, a certain thoroughbred's winning the fourth race at Hialeah. Of course, action tokens are in the world only if they are actual, not merely possible or potential (though their actuality might reside in the future). The same points apply to states of affairs.

Now, under the world-related story about desire, what token is the object or "relatum" of an action desire when that desire goes unsatisfied or unfulfilled? Suppose Sammy wants to win the 50-yard dash at school today, but actually he loses. What action token *in the world* is Sammy's desire related to, according to the world-related story? Since there is no actual token of Sammy's winning that race, it is far from obvious what a plausible candidate might be. It wouldn't be Sammy's winning the 50-yard dash last week, since Sammy's desire of today is not directed at last week's victory. Nor would it be somebody else's winning a 50-yard dash today; Sammy did not desire anybody else's victory, only his own. There seems to be no good candidate for an action token in the world that is the relatum of Sammy's desire. This is precisely why philosophers of intentionality have argued that intentional mental states, like desires, wishes, or intentions, are relations to some sort of mental contents or representations.

Bartsch and Wellman (1995a, pp. 152–153) try to address this issue, using an example of a target person wanting a cup of milk when there is no visible cup of milk in the wanter's neighborhood:

> . . . since the milk is not visible, where does the child's construal of the target person's desire for it come from? On this proposal, it comes from the 2-year-old's knowledge of the world. The child simply knows . . . that there are such things in the world (even if none are currently visible), and he attributes to the target person a simple desire for those real-world contents. The 2-year-old's knowledge of the world fills in certain gaps, but what the 2-year-old attributes to people is a desire for real objects, actions, and events in the world.

This does not resolve the problem. Suppose the 2-year-old attributes to the target a desire to drink a cup of milk. It does not help to be told that the attributer knows that there have been various milk drinkings in the past. The question remains: Which actual milk drinking in the world does the attributor take the target's desire to be related to? (Assume, as before, that the desire does not get fulfilled.) No answer seems to be forthcoming.[3]

The drift of my argument is that no good sense can be made of desire without positing something like mental representations as the relata of desire.[4] Of course, this does not mean that mental representations are *what* people want in the sense that the existence of such a representation automatically fulfills or realizes their desire.[5] Rather, mental representations express or constitute the *contents* of their desires—contents that may or may not be realized. Real-world entities cannot cover the relata of desire in all cases, including cases understood by 2-year-old attributers.

It may be responded that, even if no coherent, comprehensive, world-related story can be told about desire, that does not prove that 2-year-olds do not have such a conception. Maybe they are confused; they just haven't thought the matter through very clearly. I agree that this is possible. On the other hand, what evidence convicts 2-year-olds of such confusion? We *could* ascribe a confused model of desire to them; but what compels us to withhold from them a representational model, and what forces us to ascribe to them a confused, world-related model?[6]

Indeed, there seems to be every reason to ascribe a representational model to 2-year-olds. It is universally agreed that an understanding of false belief is a sufficient indicator of a representational concept of belief. Unfulfilled desire (or intention) is precisely analogous to false belief; the only difference is "direction of fit" between mind and world (Searle 1983). Since Bartsch and Wellman grant that 2-year-olds understand that desires can go unfulfilled, the parallel conclusion to draw is that 2-year-olds have a representational concept of desire. True, desires do not represent in exactly the same way that beliefs do. Desires do not depict the way the world *is*; they only represent how the world *should be* (as judged by the agent's preference). But this simply is the direction-of-fit difference between desire and belief. It is not a reason for a theorist to withhold representational status from desire, unless the theorist confuses the generic idea of representation with a particular subspecies of it (viz., *depictive* representation).[7]

An additional problem with the second version of the orthodox TT approach arises from the doctrine of *meaning holism* that is usually associated with TT. TT standardly includes the idea that mentalistic terms, being theoretical terms, are defined or understood in terms of the theory in which they are embedded. This view is inherited from traditional philosophy of science. When the theory changes, the meanings of the terms change—at least when there are changes in the laws or explanations in which those very terms appear. Even with the mere expansion of a theory (as opposed to its revision), the terms of the expanded theory will express different concepts than those of the predecessor theory. Let us apply this to the story about desires and beliefs that Bartsch and Wellman (among others) tell. When the child has a concept of desire without any accompanying concept of belief (between ages 2 and 3, according to Bartsch and Wellman), the concept of desire will be defined in one way. When the child then acquires a concept of belief (at age 3, roughly), the concept of desire will have to undergo some sort of change, because it will no longer be embedded in the same theory. The theory will at least be expanded, if it is not revised. So the 3-year-old cannot have the same concept of desire as the 2-year-old, according to TT. What is the evidence, however, that such a change occurs? I do not know of any such evidence. This raises doubts about the conceptual doctrine of TT, in comparison with alternative doctrines which would not require old concepts to change merely because new ones are added. Such an alternative would go naturally with introspectionist versions of ST unwedded to meaning holism.[8]

It is instructive to appreciate the counterintuitiveness of meaning holism when applied to conceptual expansions. Suppose a child already has the concept of paper. She has drawn on paper with pencils and crayons, she has glued things to paper, and so forth. One day she is introduced to pen and ink, and shown how to use them on paper. Her paper concept can now be deployed in new types of explanations and predictions: ones involving pen and ink. Does the child's old concept of paper necessarily change in virtue of this, simply because the range of explanations and predictions she can make with the paper concept has expanded? Surely not.

I have been pointing out counterintuitive consequences of the TT approach in virtue of its association with meaning holism. But now let me return to the core thesis of developmental TT: that the incidence of mentalistic conceptual change in childhood—assuming it can be established—would prove the occurrence of theoretical change. This contention is also problematic, because additional arguments would be needed to demonstrate theoretical change. Not all *conceptual* changes are *theoretical* changes. A person might change his concept of a "message," for example, from a communication written on a slip of paper to a communication conveyed by any kind of medium. This would be a change in how a term is conceptualized, but not obviously a change in theory. Of course, much depends here on what is meant by *theory*. But if a theory is construed as a set of law-like generalizations (a common construal by developmental theory-theorists), then not all concepts are theoretical concepts. So conceptual change per se does not suffice to establish theoretical change.

Proponents of TT often argue that ST is unable to explain the chronology of mentalization in young children. For example, can ST account for the fact that the desire concept is acquired earlier than the belief concept? Bartsch and Wellman (1995a, pp. 178–179) claim that ST has no satisfactory account of this. One possible answer is suggested by Harris (1996): that there is a social premium on the communication of desire as compared with the communication of belief. A great deal of child-adult activity involves collaborative action, the success of which depends on the communication of the desires of each. This premium on desires, with beliefs left unspoken, might explain the child's greater preoccupation with desire and consequent earlier mastery of the language of desire. Another possible explanation of the early emergence of desire talk is a more salient phenomenology. Desires may recruit comparatively greater attention, directed at finding means to their fulfillment. The phenomenological explanation is admittedly tenuous, because, as Bartsch and Wellman indicate (1995a, pp. 180–181), the phenomenology of knowledge also has salient dimensions.

But what is TT's *own* explanation for the comparatively early emergence of desire talk? Bartsch and Wellman's explanation is that the desire concept (at least the 2-year-old's desire concept) is nonrepresentational, and therefore easier to grasp than belief. This explanation works as long as the following two claims hold: (1) The (early) desire concept is nonrepresentational. (2) The belief concept is (always) representational. But both of these assumptions are open to challenge. My previous discussion challenges claim 1. Claim 2 is challenged by other theory-theorists, who deny that belief is always understood representationally. So the alleged asymmetry in representational status between desire and belief is tenuous.

In contrast with developmentalists, philosophers usually regard beliefs and desires as symmetrical in representational status, for reasons similar to those reviewed above. To make a convincing case for a representation-based explanation of the earlier emergence of desire talk, TT proponents need more compelling evidence of representational asymmetry. Now suppose, for the sake of argument, that solid evidence for such an asymmetry were forthcoming. Why couldn't ST then invoke this same asymmetry to explain the earlier emergence of desire talk? It is not clear why such an asymmetry would not be usable by ST. Thus, I see no reason why ST is at a comparative disadvantage in trying to explain the chronology of mentalization.

First-Person Attribution of Mental States

People detect and report mental states of self and of others. How is it done in each type of case? Do they use the same processes and heuristics for self-attribution as for other-attribution? Or are the processes fundamentally different?

The standard TT view, clearly enunciated by Gopnik (1993), is that the processes are exactly the same. We adults believe that our knowledge of our own mental states is substantially different from our knowledge of other people's mental states (much more "direct" and error-free), but this is just an illusion. To support this view, Gopnik cites evidence that 3-year-olds make certain consistent mistakes about their own immediately past mental states, and these mistakes parallel mistakes they make about others (Gopnik and Astingon 1988; Gopnik and Slaughter 1991; Wimmer and Hartl 1991). Gopnik takes this as evidence that we have no "privileged access" to our own mental states and that the processes used to detect our own states are the same as those used for others.

Defenders of privileged access maintain that it applies only to current mental states. Gopnik's evidence concerns past mental states—not long past, but nonetheless past. Moreover, in surveying the evidence Gopnik overlooks the fact that the very experimenters she cites, herself included, routinely rely on the *accuracy* of children's reports of their own current states. This point is well emphasized by Harris (1992, 1993). Gopnik and Slaughter (1991) showed 3-year-olds a familiar crayon box, asked what they thought was inside, then showed them the actual contents (candles), and finally asked them what they had earlier thought was inside. All 3-year-olds were accurate in response to the first question, about their then-current thoughts, at least as far as could be judged. The experimenters themselves assumed that the children answered this question accurately, an assumption on which they relied in concluding that the children's later reports were mistaken. So if we focus attention on *current* self-reports (the nub of the issue), the evidence does not favor TT. Instead, privileged access seems better supported.

In any case, Gopnik has told us next to nothing about exactly how one manages to detect one's own current states. Does one proceed by theoretical inference from observation of one's own behavior or of environmental circumstances that are potential causes of one's mental states? I have previously dramatized the implausibility of this approach by an example of waking up with a morning headache (Goldman 1993). One can immediately detect and classify such a headache without any previous information about its observable causes or effects. Here let me elaborate the point with a different example: a current intention. I now have an intention to snap my fingers in the next 10 seconds. How do I know that I have this intention? I have not detected any observable environmental cause of the intention, nor have I performed any overt behavior that might provide some clues. It is hard to resist the explanation that I have some sort of direct access to my intending state. Other advocates of TT, including Nichols and Stich (2000), are now coming around to this traditional and compelling approach. The details of privileged access are exceptionally controversial, and this is not the place to address them. But so long as TT rejects all forms of privileged access, it will face serious difficulties.[9]

Critics of an introspectionist or direct detectionist approach sometimes suggest that it is incompatible with conceptual change. According to Gopnik and Wellman (1992), simulationism conjoined with introspectionism implies that "the child (or adult) doesn't need and doesn't appeal to a theory of mind, a conceptual understanding of mental states, to predict behavior or understand others. Instead she simply runs a perfect working model of a mind, her own mind. . . . Moreover, access to [her] own states requires no inference or interpretation, no conceptual intermediaries, no theorizing, you simply read them off." (ibid., pp. 159–160) Similarly, Bartsch and Wellman (1995a, p. 175) say this: ". . . when reasoning about minds [according to ST], we do not resort to concepts but rather more simply to our firsthand experience of mental life." These passages wrongly suggest that introspectionist ST excludes conceptual intermediaries and conceptual understanding. Introspectionist ST does not claim that concepts are unnecessary or dispensable in the tasks of detecting one's own states or detecting the states of others. The main point to emphasize is that detection or attribution of a mental state, whether in oneself or in another, is a conceptual act: it consists in classifying the target state as of one type or another. In the case of propositional-attitude states, the type is always complex, including both an attitude type and a specific content. The attributor must decide whether the target state is a belief, a desire, a wish, or a fear, and what its specific content is. All these classifications require concepts. Perhaps a type just *is* a concept. Of course, introspectionist ST may depart widely from TT in its specific account of mental types or concepts—in other words, in its account of how ordinary attributers conceptualize desires, beliefs, and fears. Introspectionists might wish to link these conceptualizations (partly or wholly) to phenomenological materials rather than to causal-functional relations (Goldman 1993), but this does not mean that proponents of introspectionist ST hold that concepts are irrelevant. Moreover, various types of conceptualizations may figure critically in the simulation heuristic involved in third-person attribution. For example, to execute a successful simulation of another person's thought one may have to "quarantine" or "overwrite" one's own knowledge. And it may be necessary to "flag" the simulated states of another person *as* simulated, pretend, or make-believe (Harris 1991, 1995; Harris and Kavanaugh 1993). These activities require conceptualization of some sort, though not necessarily theoretical conceptualization. Children lacking the appropriate conceptualizations will not succeed at folk-psychologizing tasks.

Simulation, Re-Creation, and Pretense

The fundamental idea of TT is that a mental-state attributor arrives at an attribution to a target person by reasoning theoretically from observed behavior of the target and/or from environmental conditions that might influence his or her mental state. Or, if the attributor has previous knowledge of some of the target's mental states, he or she might reason from these previously known mental states to others. The crucial point is that theoretical reasoning is the fundamental method or heuristic that attributers deploy.[10]

The prime example of theoretical reasoning, though not the only possible one, is reasoning in accordance with (believed) laws—specifically, *psychological* laws that relate mental states to one another and to inputs and outputs.

The process of simulation posited by ST stands in sharp contrast to this story. In using the simulation heuristic to detect a target's mental state (for example, a future decision), an attributor begins by taking the target's "perspective." That is, he *pretends* to be in certain states the target is in, as suggested by his previous information about the target (gleaned, perhaps, from previous simulations). He feeds these "pretend" starting states into an appropriate cognitive mechanism of his own (for example, a decision-making mechanism) and lets it operate on them. This mechanism outputs a new state (e.g., a decision), and the attributor then attributes that decision to the target. In other words, the attributor tries to make his own mind "emulate" the mental sequence the target will go through (or, in the case of attributing a past state, did go through). The heart of this procedure is that the attributor tries to *reproduce* or *match* what transpires in the target—something not featured in the TT approach at all. The process of mental reproduction or matching substitutes for theoretical reasoning in accordance with psychological laws, which are unnecessary under the simulation heuristic. This is not to say that simulation never involves reasoning. On the contrary, if an attributor simulates a process of practical reasoning, he himself engages in practical reasoning. But it is not an instance of theoretical reasoning, which is what TT always requires. There are special cases in which simulation even involves theoretical reasoning, as when an attributor simulates a physicist, an engineer, or any other target person engaged in theoretical reasoning. A simulation of theoretical reasoning may even feature beliefs in laws of some sort. But when the target reasoning involves physical subject matter, the simulator will only appeal to (possibly "pretend") beliefs in *physical* laws, not to beliefs in *psychological* laws. Notice that ST need not claim that *all* mentalizing takes the form of simulation; it need only claim that mentalizing often takes that form, or that simulation lies at the roots of mentalizing.[11]

The popularity of TT as an account of folk psychology probably stems in part from the fact that the "dominant explanatory strategy" in cognitive science, as Stich and Nichols (1992) put it, is to view cognition as the acquisition and application of internally represented knowledge structures. These same authors regard ST as potentially "an insidious threat to traditional theories in cognitive science" (Nichols, Stich, Leslie, and Klein 1996, p. 40). However, I believe that the use of simulation in mentalizing tasks would not be an island in a sea of theorizing, and its postulation is certainly no threat to cognitive science. Simulation is an intensively deployed type of heuristic in many sectors of human cognition. Once this fact is appreciated, its plausibility as a hypothesis about folk psychology will have a better ring in the ears of cognitive scientists.

The first point to emphasize here is that human cognition is a large collection of heterogeneous mechanisms that evolution has found useful. The visual system alone incorporates an assortment of heuristics. Even depth perception, just one task of vision, is subserved by a bundle of disparate heuristics. So we should not be surprised to find an eclectic bag of tricks in nature's repertoire, rather than one homogeneous mode of cognizing. Furthermore, the device of mimicry or synchrony is present in a wide range of physical, physiological, and mental dimensions of human life. (For a review, see Levenson and Ruef 1997.) Young children and adults revel in mimicry, whether it involves postures, vocalizations, or facial expressions.

The generic trick I wish to highlight, however, has an epistemic, or information-gathering, theme. I shall call it *investigation through re-creation*.

Human beings engage in a variety of behaviors, both overt and purely mental, in which they try to "re-create" scenarios either previously observed or anticipated as possibilities. I conjecture that the function of such behaviors is to investigate, study, or explore the actual or possible scenarios that they model. In other words, to gain information about target scenarios, people create models that can disclose some of their properties. I do not say that these re-creative activities are always executed with this conscious aim. Rather, nature has given us propensities to engage in such re-creative activities because they have, as a frequent by-product, the disclosure or discovery of useful information. Mental simulation, I conjecture, is one specimen of this generic type of heuristic.

I start with direct behavioral imitation. Meltzoff and Moore (1977, 1983) discovered that newborn infants have an innate ability to imitate facial expressions. Imitation remains an important proclivity among older infants and young children (Meltzoff 1995; Meltzoff and Gopnik 1993). Clearly, direct behavioral imitation re-creates an observed scenario. Another trait of all normal children is pretend play, in either solo or cooperative variants. Pretend play is not direct imitation, but it is quasi-imitation of a genre of activity. When a child pretends to talk on a telephone by using a banana as a prop (Leslie 1987), he is not precisely imitating normal telephone usage, but the (overt) pretense does re-create selected aspects of the modeled activity. Similarly, the entire idiom of drama is a medium in which people imitate or impersonate individuals—typically not actual individuals or events but persons and scenarios that might exist or occur. The apparent cross-cultural universality of the dramatic idiom throughout recorded time strongly suggests an innate basis for this kind of activity.

I turn now to purely mental re-creation. Visual imaging is a form of mental re-creation. If I visually imagine the rooms in my house, I re-create (to some approximation) the visual perceptions associated with being in those rooms and looking around. Prospective re-creation occurs when one engages in planning activity. A person in the process of climbing a tree or a cliff may imagine how he would be positioned if, in his next move, he were to place his left foot onto a particular branch or ledge.

My general idea is that these forms of re-creation are valuable because they characteristically yield useful information. Visually imagining the rooms in one's house can yield information about the layout of the rooms, or about how many windows are in the house. Imagining the result of a prospective climbing maneuver can yield information about the effectiveness or ineffectiveness, the riskiness or nonriskiness, of that move.[12] Attempts at behavioral imitation can yield other types of information. They can help the imitator learn what is required, in motor terms, to reproduce the target action. And they can help the actor discover the physical and social consequences associated with that type of behavior, including responses from other members of the actor's community. These are all valuable pieces of information, for children especially. Pretense has similar epistemic payoffs, at least in many cases. A child who practices talking on the telephone in "pretend" situations will be more skilled at doing the real thing and will make fewer mistakes when it "counts." She may learn the expected elements and proprieties that govern and facilitate telephonic conversation. Impersonation and drama help people learn how circumstances and situations different from their own will be experienced.

I do not claim that every act of behavioral imitation, pretense, or imagination yields useful informational bounty. Nor do I claim that the *only* benefits of re-creative acts are epistemic ones. My conjecture is that, in the main, these kinds of re-creative activities disclose useful information for creatures who need to chart a course through a physical and social environment. This is why these types of activity proved adaptive and why evolution wired us up with these propensities, though we make little or no conscious calculation of their epistemic benefits. Gopnik and Meltzoff (1997) make a convincing case for the thesis that infants and children are inquiry-driven creatures, a characteristic that surely has a genetic basis. I am suggesting that children's dispositions to engage in a variety of re-creative activities are specimens of this trait of inquiry-drivenness. My next suggestion, obviously, is that mental simulation has similar roots. If mental simulation enables us (often if not always) to make correct mental-state attributions to others, this epistemic payoff will be useful enough to have been favored by evolution.

Mirror Neurons and the Simulation Theory

Is there more specific evidence for evolutionary origins of mental simulation? A plausible case can be made for this in the discovery of *mirror neurons* in macaque monkeys. Certain neurons in the monkey's premotor cortex discharge not only when a monkey initiates specific goal-oriented acts but also when it observes another monkey (or a human) initiating the very same acts (Rizzolatti, Fadiga, Gallese, and Fogassi 1996). All mirror neurons discharge during specific goal-related motor acts, such as grasping, manipulating, or holding an object. The discharge of a specific group of mirror neurons is correlated with having a particular motor goal or intention. But the very same mirror neurons discharge when a monkey does not act but merely observes another monkey (or a human) engaged in that type of goal-related action. Vittorio Gallese and I conjecture that mirror neurons are a primitive version of, or a precursor to, mental simulation (Gallese and Goldman 1998), insofar as they are a vehicle by which an observer *mimics, resonates with*, or *re-creates* the mental life of a target. (In the observer's case, the motor plan is not executed. It seems to be taken "off line," which resembles the hypothesized pattern of mental simulation.)

There is evidence of a similar mirror system in humans. When people observe the actions of others, such as the grasping of an object, there is a marked increase in motor evoked potentials from the same hand muscles that are recruited when those actions are performed (Fadiga, Fogassi, Pavesi, and Rizzolatti 1995). Clinical evidence of such a phenomenon is found in so-called *imitation behavior* (Lhermitte, Pilon, and Serdaru 1986). Patients with prefrontal lesions compulsively imitate gestures or even complex actions performed in front of them by an experimenter. This behavior is explained as arising from an impairment of inhibitory control that normally governs motor plans. Apparently, when observing someone else perform an action, a normal human generates a plan to do the same action, or an image of doing it himself. This plan is inhibited—and thereby taken "off line," as simulationists like to say—so that it does not yield motor output; but such inhibition is impaired in the relevant patient population. This is further evidence of the mental "re-creation" of a target's action plans, of the very type ST postulates.

Nothing I have said here constitutes conclusive evidence for simulation as the core mechanism of interpersonal mind reading. Nonetheless, there is converging evidence of its inherent plausibility as such a mechanism. We have seen, moreover, that the vaunted advantages of TT and the putative weaknesses of ST do not withstand scrutiny. Thus, ST deserves to be treated, by psychologists as well as philosophers, as a very serious contender for the key to the mystery of folk psychology.

Acknowledgments

This chapter has benefited greatly from the extremely helpful commentary, both critical and constructive, of two of the volume's editors: Lou Moses and Bertram Malle. I also thank Henry Wellman and other conferees in Eugene for their patient attempts to help me understand things their way. I can only hope that my stubbornness in the pursuit of my own vision may ultimately have a community-wide epistemic payoff.

Notes

1. Perner (1991, pp. 115–116) does not restrict the objects of desire to *actual* objects or states of affairs, but he does agree with Wellman in not importing *representations* into early conceptions of desire.

2. I introduce *world-related* to replace *connectionist*, which has a distracting, irrelevant association with parallel distributed processing.

3. The problem can be applied to cases involving intentions drawn from Meltzoff's (1995) study of 18-month-olds. Children saw an adult try and fail to execute some novel action. They proceeded to "re-enact" the action that the adult presumably intended. Meltzoff's findings strongly suggest that these children ascribed this intention to the adult. According to the world-related story, what is the token action that is conceived of as the relatum of the adult's intention? Could it be the *child*'s own action? But the adult's intention is for *him* to do the action, not the child; so why would the child's performance be the relatum of the adult's intention?

4. I say "something like" because I don't wish to be committed, or to commit 2-year-olds, to a view of mental representations like, e.g., Fodor's (1981) language of thought. In fact, I am not happy with the putative exhaustiveness of the two conceptions of desire offered by Bartsch and Wellman: the world-related conception and the representational conception. However, since a full discussion of these issues would take us far afield, I restrict my discussion to these two options.

5. Thanks to Josef Perner for calling attention to the need to avoid this confusion.

6. In the past, when false-belief errors seemed to show that young children lack a representational model of belief, it was reasonably natural to infer that they would also lack a representational model of desire (at the same and earlier stages). But in the wake of the recent evidence about false-belief tasks, cited above, we must reassess earlier assumptions about young children's models of belief. The same should be done for their models of desire.

7. Schwitzgebel (1999) presents evidence that some theorists—though not Bartsch and Wellman—*have* confused these matters.

8. For general doubts about the tenability of meaning holism, see Fodor and LePore 1992. Moses and Chandler (1992) also appeal to holism to criticize some aspects of orthodox TT, but their point alleges that an asynchrony between an early understanding of desires and a later understanding of beliefs would be *nonsensical* under the TT approach. My criticism does not make quite so strong a claim. At the same time, I find it very puzzling how the 3- or 4-year-old is supposed to work with a theory of mental states in which *some* mental states (desires) have *real-world* relata whereas other mental states (beliefs) have *representational* relata. It is radically unclear how these two families of relata can readily be coordinated with one another.

9. It is standard among theory-theorists to regard intentional states as "unobservables." For example, Leslie (1994a, p. 211) writes: "How is the preschool child able to learn about mental states when these are unobservable, theoretical constructs? Or put another way: how is the young brain able to attend to mental states when they can be neither seen, heard nor felt?" On other occasions, theory-theorists take a softer position. In one place, for example, Gopnik and Wellman (1994, p. 290) say that their preference for TT over ST "does not mean that we completely reject a role for first person knowledge in the formation and application of a theory of mind. Our own first-person psychological experience provides a body of data that strongly informs and shapes our concepts of mind." It is not clear to me, however, how this last passage fits with Gopnik's (1993) explicit denial of privileged access. Perhaps Gopnik and Wellman mean that phenomenological experience plays a role in (mental) concept *formation* but offers no noninferential method for *classifying* one's own current states. If this interpretation is right, then privileged access is still denied.

10. Theory-theorists occasionally concede that simulation can play *some* role in mental-state determination. For example, Gopnik and Wellman (1994, p. 280) write: ". . . we do not wish to deny an important role for the simulation of others' states of mind. A theory of mind must confront the problem of inferring the mental states of others in particular cases. Several devices can be used to aid in this process. but imagining what your own mental states would be rates high among them. We contend, however, that such simulations are theory-driven." If this point were made systematically, it might constitute an important dimension of compromise with ST. However, the suggestion that simulation is "theory driven" presents simulation in a somewhat different light than orthodox ST proposes. Simulation theorists draw a distinction between "theory driven" and "process driven" simulation, and advance the hypothesis that *process driven* simulation lies at the core of third-person mind-reading (Goldman 1989, p. 173). Some erstwhile theory-theorists have recently adopted an even more qualified position than the quoted passage from Gopnik and Wellman suggests. For example, Perner (1996) describes himself as advocating a "simulation-theory mix."

11. ST's willingness to admit that not *all* mentalization involves simulation may be a partial compromise with TT, but it is not a capitulation or "collapse" into it. Mentalizers may construct generalizations or schemata based on earlier instances of

simulation, and then use those schemata for new acts of mentalizing without simulation (Goldman 1989, p. 176). But under this scenario, the roots of mentalizing are still anchored firmly in simulation.

12. The value of strategy testing has been offered by Currie (1995) as an evolutionary explanation of imagination and of (mental) pretense. Currie credits Dennett (1978a). Neither of these authors generalizes this sort of explanation, as I am doing, to all varieties of re-creative activity.

11

On the Possibilities of Detecting Intentions Prior to Understanding Them

Daniel J. Povinelli

Most authors in this volume are united in the opinion that the ability to conceive of intentions is a fundamental and universal aspect of how our species thinks about the social world. The question of how and when human infants and children develop this ability, however, inspires a good deal less harmony.

What scientific techniques can be brought to bear on this question? There are many, of course, but perhaps the most interesting—and most controversial—involves use of visual habituation-dishabituation procedures and related techniques. In such research, infants are allowed to repeatedly observe a stimulus that embodies some conceptual principle (e.g., that unsupported objects fall) until their visual attention to the stimulus wanes. Generally, it is assumed that this decline in visual attention signals infant's habituation to both their own visual experience of the stimulus and whatever conceptual interpretation of the stimulus they may possess. Once habituated (as measured by their viewing time), the infants are typically divided into an experimental group and a control group. These groups observe slightly different stimuli. The experimental group is typically presented with a stimulus that violates the conceptual principle embodied in the original stimulus but, significantly, is designed to be visually quite similar to the original stimulus. The control group is presented with a stimulus that is perceptually different from the original stimulus but which embodies the same conceptual principle. If the experimental group exhibits a greater rebound in visual attention than the control group, many researchers feel comfortable arguing that the infants are sensitive to the particular concept instantiated by the original stimulus. Although the general reasoning behind such procedures (offering pre-linguistic infants the opportunity to express what they know through their nonverbal behavior) is clear, in practice these techniques have elicited considerable controversy—see, for example, the debate between Haith (1998) and Spelke (1998).

In this chapter, I address the controversy over how to interpret the results of such research as it applies to the development of intentional understanding. (In this volume, see the chapter by Baird and Baldwin, that by Wellman and Phillips, and that by Woodward, Sommerville, and Guajardo.) In particular, I explore the possible ways in which the kinds of knowledge or "sensitivities" revealed through visual habituation-dishabituation procedures (and related techniques) can be interpreted. To begin, I identify three distinct possibilities for any given dishabituation effect:

- The visual dishabituation effect may be evidence that infants possess second-order mental states (i.e., that they reason about intentions).

- Although the dishabituation effect is not unequivocal evidence that infants reason about intentions, it is good evidence that infants have begun the process of constructing the system that will ultimately be capable of reasoning about intentions. (There are several ways in which these early abilities could be causal precursors to the ability to explicitly reason about intentions, and I shall flesh these out later in the chapter.)

- The dishabituation effect may be evidence that infants possess a system for detecting the intentional structure of action, but this system may be separate (both developmentally and evolutionarily) from a later-developing system for understanding of intention as a mental state.[1] These early dishabituation effects may reflect the operation of ancient, low-level mechanisms that evolved separately from a psychological system, unique to humans, that interprets the structure of behavior in mentalistic terms.

In the remainder of the chapter, I present my reasons for believing that the third possibility must be taken just as seriously as the first and the second. I begin by briefly describing a theory that my colleagues and I have developed concerning the evolution of second-order mental states (Povinelli and Prince 1998; Povinelli and Giambrone 1999; Povinelli, Bering, and Giambrone 2000). This theory argues that long before the ability to sustain second-order mental states evolved, the sensory and brain systems of many species evolved the ability to detect and process the statistical regularities of the behaviors of others. In other words, psychological mechanisms unrelated to reasoning about intentions may have evolved to detect the same kinds of regularities in behavior that adult human folk psychology now explains in terms of intentions. Our theory directly establishes credibility for the alternative described above in that it raises the specter that the abilities revealed by habituation-dishabituation studies in human infants and in non-human primates may not play a direct causal role in fostering the development or evolution of the psychological system that reasons about intentions (or any other mental states, for that matter).[2]

Although the purpose of this chapter is to grapple with the development of human intentional understanding, I begin (for reasons that will become obvious) by considering a different question: whether other species develop such an understanding.

Do Other Species Reason about Intentions?

Because they are our nearest relatives, chimpanzees may be the species most likely to share with us an explicit understanding of intention. Indeed, Premack and Woodruff (1978) argued that chimpanzees are capable of reasoning about the intentions of others. In their study, an adult female chimpanzee observed videotaped sequences of a human struggling to solve a staged problem. She was then presented with photographs, some of which depicted the solution to the problem and others of which were distracters. Premack and Woodruff argued that the chimpanzee's ability to select the photograph that depicted the solution to problem demonstrated that she was capable of inferring the intention of the actor from the sequence of video images, and thus she understood that only one of the test options represented the fulfillment of the actor's intentions. They concluded that chimpanzees possess the ability to reason about the unobservable mental states of others—an ability they dubbed a *theory of mind*. "A system of inferences of this kind," they observed (ibid., p. 515), "may be properly viewed as a theory because such [mental] states are not directly observable, and the system can be used to make predictions about the behavior of others."

In the late 1980s, inspired by this and by related work concerning the ability of many great apes (but not other nonhuman primates) to recognize themselves in mirrors (Gallup 1970, 1982), my colleagues and I designed a series of comparative experimental studies to explore whether chimpanzees were somehow special among nonhuman primates with respect to the ability to reason about mental states.[3] Rather than providing strong support for a difference between great apes and other nonhuman primates, a critical analysis of these and other results led many researchers to question whether even chimpanzees are capable of reasoning about mental states (Povinelli 1993, 1994; Tomasello, Kruger, and Ratner 1993; Heyes 1993). However, much of this early work had been designed to probe for the existence of quite advanced second-order mental states—at least from the perspective of human development. For example, several of our early studies explored the ability of chimpanzees and other nonhuman primates to reason about the knowledge states of others.[4] Thus, it stood to reason that chimpanzees and other nonhuman primates might exhibit stronger evidence for understanding mental states if we were to question them about their ability to reason about the perceptions, desires, or intentions of others.

In 1991, to address these and other problems, my colleagues and I launched a long-term project to follow the cognitive development of seven 2–3-year-old chimpanzees. We have conducted dozens of experiments in an effort to explore what, if anything, these chimpanzees know about the mental states of others.[5] Some of the questions we have addressed relate quite directly to whether chimpanzees understand that others possess intentions and goals, whereas other studies have focused on their ability to reason about the attentional, belief, and perceptual states of others, as well as of themselves.[6] The combined results of this research have led us to conclude that, although chimpanzees are quite sophisticated at reasoning about the behavior of others, they do not conceptualize this behavior within a framework of folk psychology. In short, chimpanzees seem to reason about the behavior, not the mental states, of others.

Let me be bit more clear about the distinction between thinking about behavior and thinking about mental states. Consider some rather extensive research we have conducted on the question of what chimpanzees know about seeing. We began by asking a very simple question: Do chimpanzees appreciate that others see? This seemed like an excellent place to begin because it appeared intuitively obvious from their spontaneous behavior that they must have a pretty solid grasp on the fact that both they and their fellow chimpanzees can see things.

If you ever have a chance to spend an hour or two playing with a group of young chimpanzees, you will notice right away that they seek to make eye contact with you at crucial junctures in their play routines—apparently checking to make sure that you have seen their latest move or gesture. Or, if you happen to find yourself enjoying a cool soda on a summer afternoon in New Iberia, Louisiana, it is very likely that you will spy a chimpanzee reaching out a hand in your direction, palm up, looking into your eyes. These are communicative acts that chimpanzees exhibit no matter where you encounter them, and their meaning seems at once familiar and obvious. For example, the chimpanzee looks up into your eyes after gesturing at your soda, is obviously doing so in order to be sure that you have seen him. Likewise, the chimpanzee who takes a toy bucket, covers her head, and frolics around her enclosure until she bumps into something must surely know something about seeing—and about *not* seeing.

Another behavior that chimpanzees naturally exhibit similarly tempts the interpretation that they know something about seeing: They follow each other's gaze. If you make eye contact with a chimpanzee, and then look behind him, he will immediately turn and glance in the same direction. Since our first controlled experimental demonstration of this fact (Povinelli and Eddy 1996a, experiment 14), this finding has been replicated and extended on a number of different occasions, and certain aspects of the ability have been extended to other primate species (Itakura 1996; Povinelli and Eddy 1996b, 1997; Povinelli, Bierschwale, and Cech 1999; Tomasello, Call, and Hare 1998; Call, Hare, and Tomasello 1998; Emery, Lorincz, Perret, Oran, and Baker 1997). Indeed, the sophistication of gaze following in chimpanzees appears comparable to the abilities found in 18–24-month-old human infants (table 1). In any event, when a chimpanzee turns to look where you are looking, and then looks back into your eyes, it is difficult to avoid thinking that he is trying to figure out what you are looking at.

On the basis of such observations, there was a time when I felt sure that chimpanzees must understand that other beings have visual experiences. But could this issue be addressed more rigorously? Let me begin with the first idea that occurred to us. We reasoned that if we offered our chimpanzees

Table 1
Evidence that humans and chimpanzees possess a homologous psychological system controlling gaze-following. Sources: Povinelli and Eddy 1996a, 1996b, 1997; Povinelli et al. 1999; Tomasello et al. 1998; Call et al. 1998.

	18–24-month-old human infants	Juvenile and adult chimpanzees
Respond to whole head movement	Yes	Yes
Respond to eye movement alone	Yes	Yes
Left/right specificity	Yes	Yes
Follow gaze outside immediate visual field	Yes	Yes
Scan past distracter targets	Yes	Yes
Account for opaque barriers	?	Yes

the opportunity to use their natural begging gestures to request food from one familiar caretaker at a time, and then at a later stage gave them the option of choosing between two caretakers, one of whom could seem them and one of whom could not, then surely they would gesture to the caretaker who could see them. Figure 1 shows the general setting of the test; figure 2 shows several of the initial "seeing" and "not seeing" conditions we came up with to test our simple prediction. In fact, we were so confident that our apes would gesture to the caretaker who could see them that we began to think up additional questions that we could ask them about seeing. As it turned out, we had gotten ahead of ourselves. Something far more interesting occurred in the interim: Despite our interpretation of their spontaneous behavior, our apes seemed to insist that they did not grasp that one caretaker could see them whereas the other could not.

Elsewhere, my colleagues and I have published detailed reviews of the procedures and results of these studies (Povinelli 1999; Povinelli and Giambrone 1999). In brief, this research consistently revealed that our apes did not appear to possess an understanding of seeing. In virtually every case, they were initially just as likely to gesture to the caretaker who could see them as to the caretaker who could not. We did not simply test our apes on each of these conditions and accept the results at face value—mainly because we had such a difficult time believing, for example, that our apes did not realize that a blindfolded person could not see them. As a consequence, we designed and

Figure 1
Mindy approaches Roxanne and uses her species-typical begging gesture to request a food reward.

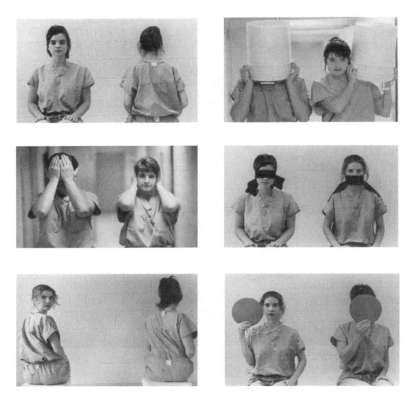

Figure 2
Conditions used to determine if chimpanzees would selectively gesture to the person who could see them.

conducted more than 20 experiments using variations of this procedure, offering our apes every opportunity to show us that our initial results were mistaken. We even went as far as conducting longitudinal assessments of their understanding of this kind of situation as they matured from juveniles to adolescents and finally to full adults (Reaux, Theall, and Povinelli 1999). However, the results continued to suggest that our apes did not appreciate that only one of these caretakers could see them.

It is not that our apes were unable to *learn* in these situations. After enough experiences of gesturing to someone with a bucket over her head and then not being handed a banana, our apes learned to select the other option. Did this mean that they were learning something about 'seeing' per se? Quite to the contrary. Our results suggested that the apes were not focusing on the *psychological* attributes of the two individuals ("Gesture to the human who can see me"), but rather that they had learned rules related to the *physical postures* of the persons involved (i.e., "Gesture to the person who is facing me" or "Gesture to the person whose face is visible"). Even as full adults, our chimpanzees appeared to be relying on these kinds of procedural rules, even in situations that they had experienced on dozens of previous occasions. (See especially Reaux, Theall, and Povinelli 1999, experiment 4.)

Of course, one's conclusions should never rest on a single experimental procedure, no matter how extensively it is elaborated. Recognizing this, we developed several other techniques for asking our apes about seeing. (See, e.g., Povinelli, Bierschwale, and Cech 1999; Theall and Povinelli 1999.) However, these studies too supported the idea that our chimpanzees failed to grasp that others see. Furthermore, other aspects of our research suggest an even broader conclusion: Chimpanzees may not reason about mental states at all. To date, we have asked our apes about their understanding of pointing, the distinction between accidental and intentional actions, their understanding of cooperation, and their understanding of the referential aspect of emotional outbursts. Consistently, the results have supported the idea that, although chimpanzees are adept at learning about the behavior of others, and about its relationship to the world, they do not think (as we do) that behavior is prompted by unobservable mental states or processes. Research by Michael Tomasello and his colleagues has suggested a similar conclusion (Tomasello, Call, and Gluckman 1997; Call, and Tomasello 1999; Nagell, Olguin, and Tomasello 1993). To put it simply, we have concluded that, although chimpanzees (and many other animals) are experts at understanding behavioral propensities, they do not appear to reason about mental states.[7]

The Reinterpretation Hypothesis

Many researchers have found our experimental results difficult to believe. For one thing, they fly in the face of common sense. One common reaction goes something like this: "But chimpanzees *must* have a theory of mind. After all, it would be very useful. Anyhow, in view of what you say they do naturally, how could they not have one?" I understand this reaction; before undertaking the bulk of the studies to which I have just alluded, my experiences with chimpanzees had convinced me that this was an animal that understood more about me than just my behavior—an animal that was in contact with my mind Thus, for a while I experienced an uncomfortable tension between the extensive set of experimental results that we (and others) were obtaining and what my common sense was telling me. It was not possible to simply shrug off the similarities between our chimpanzees' behavior and my own as the results of dumb learning or mindless imitation on their part. No, the detailed patterns of behavioral similarities implied deep, psychological similarities as well. And because I believed that I could identify the psychological states that caused the behaviors in me, it was difficult to deny that the same psychological states were not also at work in chimpanzees. Indeed, from the British philosopher David Hume to the founder of modern biology, Charles Darwin, there was a long and distinguished history of using this approach to infer the likely mental states of animals. Hume (1739) had even once quipped that only the "most stupid and ignorant" of individuals could attempt to deny this "evident truth."

Gradually, however, this tension was released as I began to see the behavioral similarities between chimpanzees and humans in a different light. Soon the following idea took shape: What if the ability to reason about mental states was not only a unique specialization of the human species but one whose initial function was to give us the ability to understand ancient behaviors in novel ways—not one that endowed our species with a whole set of novel behaviors? In short, what if human evolution had been characterized by the emergence of a qualitatively new psychological system for reasoning about mental states—one that was initially selected for because it increased flexibility in the planning and execution of useful, but already-existing, ancient behavioral abilities? If so, then the initial advantage of having a theory of mind was not the generation of a large set of fundamentally new behaviors but the ability to put old behavioral patterns to slightly new uses. The significance of this framework is that it leads one to *expect* chimpanzees and humans to share numerous, nearly identical behavioral patterns, and yet to interpret them in different ways (chimpanzees reasoning strictly about the behavioral propensities of others, and humans reasoning about both behavioral propensities and underlying mental states). Because this idea envisioned that humans had evolved a cognitive specialization that allowed the species to interpret existing behaviors in new ways, we labeled it the *reinterpretation hypothesis* (Povinelli 1996; Povinelli and Prince 1998; Povinelli 1999; Povinelli and Giambrone 1999).

Implications for Chimpanzee Cognition

The reinterpretation hypothesis has at least two broad implications, one for chimpanzees and the other for humans. For chimpanzees (and many other species), it implies that when we see them engage in gaze following, deception, or other social behaviors that look remarkably like our own, we should resist the reflexive urge to assume that psychological states like the ones that would be present in us are likewise present in them. Indeed, the reinterpretation hypothesis leads us to expect that the spontaneous behavioral patterns of humans and chimpanzees will structurally resemble each other, precisely because, in an evolutionary sense, they are the same behaviors. Thus, the model leads us to expect humans and chimpanzees to differ in the high-level psychological systems that interpret the behaviors, not in the low-level systems that produce and respond to them.

An example concerning the attention-getting behaviors of humans and chimpanzees may help to clarify this point: Chimpanzees know how to get your attention. For example, if you are passing out juice to chimpanzees, the ones who are waiting will tug on your shirt, tap on the mesh fence, slap the floor, or even make distinctive vocalizations. Chimpanzees display these attention-getting behaviors in much the same way that children do—indeed, many visitors to our chimpanzee colony remark that these actions remind them of the behavior of their 2-year-olds (or even their teenagers). But what about the psychological states underpinning these behaviors? Are the apes reasoning strictly about your behavior ("Hurry up and give me some juice!"), or are they reasoning about both your behavior and your internal attentional state ("Look at me! Now, hurry up and give me some juice!")?

Despite the structural similarity between these kinds of attention-getting behaviors in humans and chimpanzees, our experimental research suggests that the two species differ dramatically in their understanding of what these gestures are for. In one experiment, we confronted our chimpanzees with a familiar human who was sometimes attentive to them and sometimes not (Theall and Povinelli 1999). On most trials, the chimpanzee approached the person, gestured, and was handed a food reward. However, on certain trials, as soon as the chimpanzee gestured, the person activated a 20-second timer hidden in her ear. For 20 seconds, the person engaged in one of four behaviors: (1) She stared directly at the ape and attempted to maintain direct eye contact. (2) She made direct eye contact with the ape while engaging in slight back-and-forth movements of the head (a signal of 'attention' in chimpanzees). (3) She closed her eyes and waited. (4) She looked above and behind the ape. The first two of these conditions were "attentive" cases (after all, the person maintained a state of visual attention with the ape during the 20-second period). The latter two conditions were "inattentive" cases (the person was visually inattentive to the ape during the waiting period). If the apes appreciated this difference, they should have displayed more nonvisual attention-getting behaviors (i.e., touching or slapping at the person, banging on the fence, or vocalizing) in the inattentive conditions, and displayed them sooner than in the attentive cases. On the other hand, if the apes were reasoning strictly about the relevant behavioral states and outcomes (e.g., "She hasn't handed me any food yet"), there should have been no difference in the overall level or in the temporal patterning of gestures during the waiting periods of the attentive and inattentive cases.

What did the apes actually do? First, they readily engaged in the relevant attention-getting behaviors—in fact, they displayed at least one such behavior on more than 70 percent of the trials (figure 3). However, they did not exhibit more of them, longer episodes of them, or display them any sooner in the inattentive cases as compared to the attentive ones (figure 4). Thus, although the apes exhibited actions that were structurally identical to actions exhibited by humans, they did not seem to understand their behavior as an appeal to an inner, psychological state of attention. This finding illustrates our broader point: Chimpanzees and humans share attention-getting behaviors because they inherited the same psychological systems for generating such behavior from a common ancestor. We humans, however, understand the behaviors in light of a cognitive specialization that evolved some time after our lineage split off from that of chimpanzees. If the ability to reason about mental states evolved in the manner we have suggested, this qualitative difference between humans and

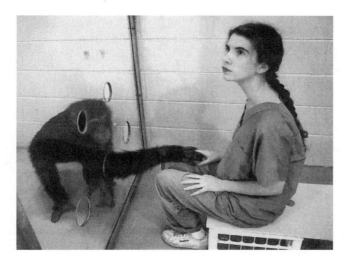

Figure 3
Apollo displays a typical attention-getting gesture during the 20-second waiting period.

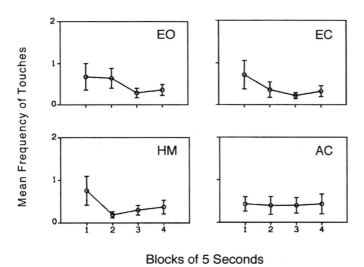

Blocks of 5 Seconds

Figure 4
The temporal structure, overall frequency, and (not shown here) mean duration of the chimpanzees' attention-getting gestures do not vary with the attentional state of the person. EO: experimenter with eyes open. HM: experimenter displaying attentive head movement. EC: experimenter with eyes closed. AC: experimenter gazing above chimp (condition shown in figure 3).

apes will be very difficult to detect by observing their *spontaneous* behavioral interactions. Rather, experiments will always be needed to reveal the differing ways in which the two species interpret the same basic behavioral patterns (Povinelli and Giambrone 1999).

It follows from the above considerations that chimpanzees should be very good at detecting and responding to the behavioral manifestations of intentions, and hence should display sensitivities very similar to those of human infants on habituation-dishabituation tasks. And yet, if our view is correct, they do so in the absence of an understanding of intentions.

Implications for Human Cognition

At this point, one might be puzzled: If a particular behavior is homologous between humans and chimpanzees, doesn't it stand to reason that there is a homologous psychological system involved in controlling the behavior? The answer to this question leads directly to the implication of our theory for human cognition. The reinterpretation hypothesis argues that humans have a unique psychological system that now resides alongside lower-level systems that we share in common with chimpanzees. In this sense, for any particular behavior that chimpanzees and humans share, there are likely to be at least two systems at work: a low-level one (which both species possess) and a high-level one (found only in humans). Human introspection, however, may only have access to the more recently evolved, higher-level system. Thus, one implication for human cognition is that our private acts of introspection may simply be unsuited to diagnose which system (the ancient or the new) has caused a particular behavior.[8]

So what causal role do second-order mental states play in generating human behavior? The reinterpretation hypothesis suggests that there is no single, simple answer to this question. Indeed, I suspect that most of the *possible* causal relationships between second-order mental states and behavior are, in fact, realized. Here are just a few of them:

• In some cases, our second-order mental states may be rapid, after-the-fact "redescriptions" (Karmiloff-Smith 1992) of behaviors that are actually prompted by psychological systems that are impenetrable to our higher-order cognitive systems.

• In other cases, our second-order mental states may be generated before the execution of a particular behavior but still play no direct causal role in launching it. However, the fact that the second-order mental state occurs before the act may create a cognitive illusion that it has caused the behavior. For example, in many cases, relevant external stimuli may initiate two parallel psychological operations: one related to the generation of second-order mental-state descriptors of the stimuli and one that generates the neurophysiological activities that ultimately launch the behavior. The relationship between these parallel operations may be quite complicated. In some cases, the two systems may function independent of each other; in other cases, the two systems may begin independently but the higher-level system may later inhibit (or excite) the lower-level system.

• In some instances in which second-order mental states are generated before the execution of the behavior, the second-order mental state may indeed play a necessary causal role in launching the behavior.

If the first two sets of possibilities do in fact occur frequently, then many complex social behaviors that, in our species, are *accompanied* by second-order mental states may also be found in other species that do not possess second-order mental states at all. Furthermore, because the reinterpretation model postulates that the human specialization in reasoning about mental states was woven into our neural circuitry right alongside ancestral psychological systems, our introspections may often misdiagnose the causes of our behaviors (Povinelli and Giambrone 1999).

Implications for the Development of Human Intentional Understanding

At this point, I can return to the problem I addressed at the outset of this chapter: What are the alternative ways of interpreting the results of recent research using habituation-dishabituation (and related) procedures? As we shall now see, the reinterpretation hypothesis bolsters the plausibility of at least one of the alternatives. Briefly, let me recall and elaborate on the three alternatives.

First, the visual dishabituation effect may, by itself, be evidence for the infant's understanding of intention. This is the position adopted by strong nativists such as Premack (1990) and Gergely, Nádasdy, Csibra, and Bíró (1995) and one consistent with the theoretical speculations of strong modularity theorists such as Fodor (1983, 1992).

Second, it is possible that such studies do not offer evidence that infants are reasoning about intentions, but that they do reveal an early stage in infants' ongoing construction of a system that will ultimately be capable of reasoning about intentions. This seems to be the cautious view favored by at least two of the research teams contributing to this volume (Woodward, Sommerville, and Guajardo; Wellman and Phillips). Wellman and Phillips argue that their findings indicate that infants possess "key competencies that lead to preschoolers' later more developed conceptions" and that such competencies "must be central to developing intentional understandings." They conclude by suggesting that the infant's ability to analyze the observable aspects of human behavior "would constitute an important source, perhaps the critical source, for the development of intentional understandings." Similarly, Woodward, Sommerville, and Guajardo argue that our adult folk psychology has its "roots" in infancy, and ask "do infants have ways of making sense of intentional action that are continuous with adult understandings?" Woodward et al. acknowledge that infants may first understand the actions of others in purely behavioral terms, but they maintain that their results reveal that infants are "on the right track, in that they are attending to just those aspects of actions that are relevant to goals in the adult sense." Perhaps because it is not their central concern, these authors have left a certain ambiguity about what they mean by claiming that the infants are "on the right track" toward the development of an understanding of intentions. Nonetheless, the idea that the early detection of the structural regularities of behavior is the first step in the construction of the psychological system for reasoning about the intentions of other beings would seem to be common to these viewpoints.

The third alternative, however, posits that the abilities revealed by habituation-dishabituation research (and related research) reflect the operation of only one of several psychological systems which are developing concurrently in human infancy—systems that are both evolutionarily and developmentally dissociable. This alternative highlights the possibility that the early detection of the structural regularities of behavior are not, strictly speaking, the early manifestation of the uniquely human system for reasoning about intentions. To be sure, this early system will become intimately linked with the system that generates the representation of intentions, but the third alternative specifies that these two systems have separate evolutionary and developmental origins. If so, then infants do not construct an understanding of intention from an overt analysis of behavior. Rather, these two systems are envisioned as maturing independently and only later becoming intertwined.

The reinterpretation hypothesis provides theoretical grounding for the third alternative just described. Recall that the key idea behind the reinterpretation model is that, although the capacity to generate second-order mental states is a unique attribute of the human species, its initial appearance was not associated with the emergence of myriad new behavioral elements. Rather, the model argues that it was initially selected for because it offered more flexibility in organizing and deploying existing behavioral elements, thus putting old behaviors to new uses.

One assumption of this model is that long before second-order mental states evolved, many species already possessed complex nervous systems that could detect the various statistical regularities in the behavior of others. To understand the broad implications of this simple fact, we must consider the evolutionary history of the central nervous system. The initial brain organ was quite limited in comparison to the more elaborate structures found in many modern descendant species. Indeed, in many conservative living species the central nervous system is no more than a small cluster of nerve cells at the anterior portion of the organism (Bullock, Orkand, and Grinnell 1977). However, as the central nervous system diversified and enlarged in certain lineages, an intimate coevolution occurred between the sensory and brain systems. Indeed, the sensory systems of organisms can be thought of as gateways that control the flow of information into the brain organ. In other words, the sensory systems act as initial filters on the kinds of external stimuli that can be detected. Clearly, natural selection favored sensory and brain systems that could detect and process the important temporal regularities in the world of a particular species. Indeed, this must be the very process that gave rise to the brain's first psychological functions: habituation and associative learning (MacPhail 1987).

What regularities in the world were among the first to be discovered? The answer undoubtedly depends on the ecology of the species in question.

However, for many social species one of the most important temporal regularities was the behavior of other conspecifics. In solitary living species, of course, the behavior of other organisms may have been largely irrelevant, hardly demanding the evolution of brain systems specifically designed for reasoning about social events. However, as some lineages evolved increasingly complicated social interactions, brain systems dedicated to detecting and processing information about the regularities of the behavior of others must have begun to emerge as well. In many sexually reproducing organisms, for example, the act of mating requires attention to the posture, motion, and communicative signals of the potential mate (Tinbergen 1951). More generally, however, most vertebrates have a range of communicative postures and actions that must be detected and correctly processed not just during mating displays but also during aggression encounters over scarce resources (figure 5). Our general point is that for hundreds of millions of years the sensory and brain systems (and the visual systems in particular) of vertebrates and other taxa have been detecting, filtering, and processing information about the regularities in the behavior of others that is important to their reproductive fitness. The reinterpretation hypothesis, however, argues that it was not until the advent of humans that these abilities were accompanied by an understanding that these behaviors are grounded in mental states such as intentions.

Let me develop the implications of this argument for infancy research using habituation-dishabituation techniques (and related techniques). In view of the evolutionary dissociation between the ability to detect the behavioral expression of intentions and the ability to conceive of intentions, it is possible that the origins of the two systems are not intimately linked in human development either. Rather than interpreting the early detection of behavioral regularities as an early (perhaps the first) manifestation of a system that is slowly and seamlessly constructing an explicit understanding of intention, it is possible to imagine that the two systems have separate ontogenetic histories. The early competencies revealed through habituation-dishabituation and related procedures may reflect the operation of ancient evolutionary forces that selected for the ability to monitor the behavior of others and keep track of the statistical regularities embedded therein. In contrast, the later-emerging understanding of intentions may be the result of initially unrelated cognitive systems that were added during human evolution. Thus, the ability to explicitly conceive of

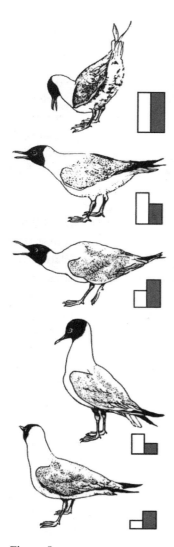

Figure 5
Threat postures of the black-headed gull (after Moynihan 1955; reprinted from McFarland 1993). Such communicative postures are widespread in animals, as they function to mediate social interactions. Clearly, such signals are effective only insofar as they are appropriately produced by the sender and detected and processed by the receiver. However, nothing about such communicative interactions forces us to conclude that the recipient understands the intentions (qua mental states) underlying the sender's behavior. Many of the sensitivities displayed by human infants in studies using visual dishabituation and related techniques are open to the same interpretive ambiguities.

intentions (and other mental states) may have its own evolutionary history—a history that may be closely linked to the emergence of the representational structures that support human language.

Consider the elegant research of Woodward and her colleagues (this volume), which has shown that infants display kinds of sensitivity to hand-object relations and rod-object relations. Woodward et al. interpret their findings as evidence of an early part of a developmental process that will ultimately lead to the construction of an ability to reason about intentions. However, it is a simple fact about the way in which the primate hand has evolved that there are visually obvious and important regularities in how the hand approaches objects, in the posture that the hand typically adopts once it has grasped an object, and in the ensuing spatial and temporal association between the hand and the object as they move off together in space. Rather than interpreting the infant's sensitivity to these specific relations as causal precursors to the development of an understanding of intention, it is possible to see these abilities as direct expressions of a primate visual system that evolved to detect certain statistical regularities in the motions of hands—a detection unrelated to an understanding of the intentions underlying the reaching hand.[9] Indeed, I suspect that for each species in which the reaching hand is involved in important social interactions (whether in the context of ritualized gestures, foraging, or aggressive acts) a distinct set of sensitivities will be uncovered through the application of habituation-dishabituation and related research techniques.

By now, the "bottom line" of the third alternative should be clear. The sensitivity to the behavioral regularities surrounding the expression of intentions is an ancient psychological phenomenon, one rooted in the very nature of the brain systems that receive and filter sensory information about the external world and ultimately use this information to direct the behavior of the organism in whose body those brain systems reside. In contrast, the ability to reason about the intentions underlying a particular behavior (in the case of the research by Woodward et al., the reaching hand) is a recent cognitive capacity that may be present in only a single living species—our own.

Our reinterpretation model, in some important ways, may be the evolutionary analogue of Karmiloff-Smith's (1992) developmental model of representational redescription. Karmiloff-Smith argues that, within certain domains, cognitive development is largely a process of processing information at increasing levels of explicitness, so that information that is initially available *in* the mind becomes increasingly available *to* the mind. Implicit knowledge is redescribed in increasingly explicit ways as the infant or child constructs its understanding of the physical and social world. Our model adds to this developmental account by putting an evolutionary face on it, thereby helping to reveal exactly why results from habituation-dishabituation research are so ambiguous with respect to the emergence of intentional understanding.

Pursuing the Third Alternative

The third alternative I have explored in this chapter argues that at least two separate psychological systems related to detection and interpretation of intentions are operating in parallel in human infancy. One is purported to be involved in detecting the statistical regularities of behavior, the other in interpreting it in psychological terms. From the developmental perspective, the third alternative bears strong similarities to the model offered by Baird and Baldwin in this volume. Indeed, after some extended discussion of the models, Dare Baldwin and I have concluded that perhaps the most notable differences between our proposals may lie in their emphases. Our proposal emphasizes an explanation for why the low-level system exists in the first place and highlights the possibility that core aspects of it evolved thousands (or perhaps hundreds) of millions of years ago. Thus, because of its evolutionary focus, our proposal sees nothing remarkable about the fact that human infants are sensitive to precisely those aspects of behavior that correspond to the initiation, execution, and/or termination of intentions. After all, these are abilities that have been honed by natural selection over untold generations in many social species, and perhaps especially so in social birds and mammals. By way of contrasting emphases, Baird and Baldwin highlight the importance of this low-level system as the input to the high-level psychological system which will, at some point, draw inferences about intentions. In doing so, they seek to emphasize the connection that must emerge between the low-level system (action-parsing mechanism) and the system for reasoning about intentions (inferential mechanism).

In emphasizing the evolutionary aspects of the problem, I am not attempting to downplay the role of the low-level mechanisms in providing input to the uniquely human systems for making intentional inferences. Indeed, the proposal I have outlined here and the one outlined by Baird and Baldwin are united in the idea that the high-level and low-level systems become linked at some point in human development. In this respect, if these proposals turn out to have empirical merit, researchers interested in the development of intentional understanding should still be interested in the early-developing sensitivities displayed by infants. Nonetheless, this does not alter the central premise of the third alternative that I have outlined: Many (perhaps most) of the early abilities detected through habituation-dishabituation and related techniques in very young infants are not evidence that the uniquely human system for reasoning about intentions is under construction.

Some might follow the general line of reasoning that I have outlined in this chapter but point out that there are many possible ways of thinking about the causal relations that might exist between the low-level and high-level systems. On the one hand, they might agree that the low-level system need not inevitably generate a system that can explicitly conceive of intentions (witness chimpanzees). On the other hand, they might note that it is nonetheless possible that the human system for explicitly understanding intentions is built on the foundation of lower-level systems—thus arguing that there is a weaker sense in which the earlier system could be a causal precursor to the later one. Fair enough. But the third alternative draws direct attention to the more specific possibility that the ability to conceive of intentions may not be fostered by early action-parsing systems, or by the object-directedness and action-connectedness sensitivities described by Woodward et al. and by Wellman and Phillips. Rather, the system for generating intentional understanding may have evolved long after—and may begin to develop independent of, although in parallel to—the more ancient systems for detecting behavioral regularities. For example, if selection had favored a different low-level system—one sensitive to slightly different intentional joints in the action stream—the evolution of intentional understanding would have mapped onto *those* regularities instead. In short, it may be that the development of intentional understanding is an independent system that proceeds without respect to specific behavioral sensitivities that happen to be in place. In this chapter I have stressed the possibility (not contradicted by any empirical findings) that representational systems unique to humans (ones that may be related to language) may generate the notion of intention quite broadly, and that these concepts may then be mapped onto the structure of action that is most salient in the culture in which the infant develops.

But what about the broader claim that at least *some* kind of psychological system for detecting the statistical regularities in behavior is necessary (though not sufficient, as the chimpanzee case demonstrates) for the construction of an ability to reason about intentions? To some extent, of course, this must be true. Intentional descriptions of actions require, by definition, the demarcation of a set of distinct actions. What we really want to know is whether the kind of fine detection of the structural regularities of behavior play a critical role in the infant's and the young child's development of intentional understanding, or whether they serve as a kind of given, passive backdrop onto which such understanding is mapped. One useful way of approaching this question might be to explore cases of traumatic brain injury in humans in order to determine how the neural systems for detecting fine behavioral regularities can be dissociated from intentional understanding. The possible patterns of breakdown between these systems might ultimately help us to understand the exact nature of the causal relation between the systems that are dedicated to detecting behavioral regularities and those that generated intentional representations of actions, as well as to determine whether there are unique behavioral detectors specifically associated with intentional understanding.[10]

Conclusion

I have sought to clarify the possible causal relations that might exist between infants' detection of behavioral regularities and the development of intentional understanding. In particular, I have tried to highlight the inherent ambiguity in the claim that human infants' early sensitivities to the intentional structure of action indicates that they are "on the right track" toward developing an understanding of intentions—an ambiguity that reflects the mosaic nature of the evolution of the relevant psychological systems. Indeed, some ambiguity of this sort will always be present when we are dealing with complexly evolved systems. As an example, consider the similarity between the above claim and the claim that because infants are born into the world with two legs they are "on the right track" to walking bipedally. There is, of course, a trivial sense in which both of these statements are true and important. But there is also a deeper sense in which both may be misleading: In both cases we run the risk of focusing on abilities or structures that may have evolved in isolation from of the uniquely human abilities that captured our interests and imagination in the first place.

Acknowledgments

The research and the writing were supported by NSF Young Investigator Award SBR-8458111, by the UL Lafayette Foundation, and by a Centennial Fellowship from the James S. McDonnell Foundation. I thank Bertram Malle and Lou Moses for comments on an earlier version, and Dare Baldwin for extensive and intriguing discussions. The photographs are by Donna Bierschwale and Corey Porché.

Notes

1. For a related proposal, see the chapter by Baird and Baldwin.

2. In this chapter, I focus on this implications of our theory for visual habituation-dishabituation studies related to intentional understanding. However, the same line of reasoning applies to interpreting the results of similar investigations concerning infants' understanding of folk physics (see Povinelli, in press, chapter 12).

3. For a review of these early studies, see Povinelli 1993.

4. For other early research on this topic in nonhuman primates, see Premack 1988 and Cheney and Seyfarth 1990a.

5. For an overview of this research, see Povinelli and Prince 1998.

6. For an overview, see Povinelli, in press.

7. For similar conclusions see Tomasello, Kruger and Ratner 1993 and Cheney and Seyfarth 1990b.

8. For a detailed treatment of this issue, see Povinelli and Giambrone, in press.

9. With respect to the question of whether these abilities are constructed through experience or whether they are under tighter epigenetic control, our theory has no direct predictions. Clearly, this is an empirical issue that cannot be settled theoretically.

10. Although the idea may be disfavored for reasons of parsimony, it does not seem completely improbable that the human system for generating inferences about intentions has evolved its own set of capacities for detecting the structural regularities in behaviors. If so, then it is possible that the early abilities detected by habituation-dishabituation research may be completely unrelated to the human system for reasoning about intentions.

III

Intentionality and Behavior Explanations

12

Action Explanations: Causes and Purposes

G. F. Schueler

Two undeniable facts about the explanation of human behavior, when considered together, generate a dilemma sharp enough to be called a paradox. Human beings are obviously animals, physical organisms, parts of nature whose movements and internal states are as much governed by the laws of physics and chemistry as are those of any other part of nature. To figure out why someone's arm or leg moved in a certain way, we look at the person's muscles, nerves, and so on, in the end typically tracing the relevant causal chains back to various chemical or electrical changes in the brain. At the same time, in ordinary life, when we explain our intentional actions to ourselves and others, we do so (standardly at least) in terms of our reasons for doing what we did—reasons that either are given in terms of or obviously presuppose mental states such as beliefs, desires, hopes, and fears (Malle, this volume). It was my desire to catch the 5:15 bus, together with my belief that I could do so but only if I ran, that caused me to sprint by you yesterday without stopping. Such explanations in terms of the agent's reasons (which I will call *reason explanations* for short) are ubiquitous in everyday life and seem to be, often at least, perfectly successful.

But although each of these facts seems quite obvious in itself, the two are very hard to put together. Taken at face value they say that all human action is amenable to two distinct, adequate explanations—that is they say that all human action is overdetermined. This seems astounding. Cases of overdetermination in the rest of nature, though not unknown, are quite rare, the surprising results of an unlikely coincidence of distinct sets of causal factors. Yet the two facts just mentioned seem to entail that, unlike in the rest of nature, absolutely every intentional human action is overdetermined. The strangeness of such a view is easiest to see for dualist positions, where this overdeterminism would involve two different kinds of causal chains—one physical and one mental—behind all human actions. But it is hardly less strange for nondualist positions, where the overdeterminism would involve two distinct explanatory schemata or theories for the same set of events.

That is one horn of the dilemma. The other horn is this: If one wanted to deny that every human action is overdetermined, one would seemingly have to hold that one or the other of the two explanations is a fake, not a real explanation at all. Since it seems utterly impossible that physics, chemistry, physiology, and neurophysiology could be mistaken in their application to human behavior, we seem to be left with the thought that reason explanations in terms of the agent's beliefs, hopes, desires, and so on are not genuine explanations.

For dualists this would be "epiphenomenalism"—the idea that the choices, desires, etc. that figure in reason explanations and seem to us to explain our actions are not really parts of the explanation at all. They would involve the sort of illusion of causality that comes in movies or cartoons, where the events we observe may seem causally connected but in fact are not, because they are in reality caused by the unseen, background operation of the projection equipment. For materialists this horn of the dilemma would involve either "eliminativism" (the idea that reason explanations should simply be dropped as confused relics of outdated folk-psychological theories) or some version of the view that, although mental properties supervene on physical states or properties, it is only in terms of the underlying physical states that we can understand the relevant causal interactions.[1] Even if we set dualism aside (as I am going to), neither horn of this dilemma, which for convenience I will call *overdeterminism* and *epiphenomenalism*, seems at all attractive. Although strictly speaking, I suppose, neither is impossible, each is profoundly counterintuitive. Choosing either horn of this dilemma would leave one defending what on its face is a deeply implausible position.[2] Thus, it looks as if we need to rethink things, and the only way I can see to avoid ending up on one or the other horn of the dilemma is to reconsider some of the presuppositions that have led to it. I am going to suggest here that two presuppositions are central to keeping this dilemma in play. First, we have to hold that the two sorts of explanation distinguished above are genuinely distinct—i.e., that the explanatory force of neither one reduces to or can be explained in terms of the other. And second, we have to hold that both sorts of explanation are causal—i.e., that the explanatory force of each kind of explanation depends at bottom on the idea of one event causing another. Reject either of these presuppositions and the dilemma disappears.

It seems clear enough that if the two sorts of explanation were not distinct—if, for instance (to take the clearest case), one were simply reducible to the other—it would not be true that actions were overdetermined. If there were not two genuine explanations but only one, no problem of overdeterminism would arise in holding that both sorts of explanation really work, so there would be no dilemma.

It is perhaps not quite so clear that the dilemma also depends on both sorts of explanation being causal, but I am going to argue that that presupposition is also essential. And since I think that the two sorts of explanation really are distinct, I will argue that the only way to resolve this dilemma is to abandon the thought that reason explanations are purely causal explanations. In essence, then, I will argue that the factors that show that the two sorts of explanation really are distinct are the very ones that show that reason explanations are not purely causal.[3]

We can begin by looking at "causalism"[4] about reason explanations— the claim that such explanations are at bottom causal. The version of this thesis that generates the dilemma is the claim that the explanatory force of ordinary reason explanations of actions is to be *completely* accounted for by reference to the causal connections between the various mental states of the agent and the action that the agent performs. (Thus, functionalism, as it is usually explained, seems to be a version of this form of causalism.) This is a strong claim, but it is also the most interesting version of causalism; any weaker version leaves something in the explanatory force of reason explanations unaccounted for.

Clearly causalists think that reason explanations of actions are genuine explanations, since they are trying to *account for* the explanatory force of reason explanations. The epiphenomenalism horn of the dilemma is thus avoided by them. Thus, if the strong causalist thesis were true, its defenders would have to hold that the two sorts of explanation are not distinct, on pain of being caught on the overdeterminism horn of the dilemma. Hence, showing that the two sorts of explanation really are distinct also shows this strong causalism to be false (at least if one assumes that ubiquitous overdeterminism is too much to swallow). I will give two arguments for thinking that the two sorts of explanation are distinct, one at least suggestive and the other, I think, conclusive.

The issue is whether reason explanations of actions are somehow reducible to, or explicable in terms of, explanations of the same set of states or events that use only the concepts available to physiology and neurophysiology. The suggestive reason for thinking that the answer is No here is that reason explanations, unlike physiological explanations of relevant muscle contractions and the like, always make essential use of the representational content[5] of the mental states of the agent. The content of my belief that *if I run I can still catch the 5:15 bus*, along with the content of my desire *to catch the 5:15 bus*, plays an essential role in the reason explanation of why I am running toward the bus stop. This belief and this desire work in this explanation only because they have the content they do.

Thus, holding that these two sorts of explanation are not distinct entails holding, in this case and in every other such case, not only that some explanation of the representational content of my mental states can be given in terms of the physiology of my brain (or the like) but also, as a part of this, that the explanatory force of the reason explanation of my action will also get accounted for once this explanation of representational content is set out in full. It entails, in short, explaining the representational content of mental states, and the accompanying explanatory force of reason explanations, in terms of elements that are utterly without representational content, such as muscle contractions or the action of neurotransmitters between nerve cells. In view of the horrendous difficulties philosophers have had trying to explain how it could be possible to do this, I suggest that perhaps we ought to consider the possibility that it can't be done.[6] If it can't, then there is an essential feature of reason explanations—their use of the representational content of mental states—that can't be accounted for in physiological terms.

The second (and, I think, the ultimately conclusive) argument for holding that the two sorts of explanation are genuinely distinct is simply that reason explanations of intentional actions are inherently normative, in a way I will explain in a moment, whereas physiological explanations involve no normative element at all.[7] There is just no way of explaining this normative element of reason explanations in non-normative terms.

Suppose you decide that my reason for running toward the bus stop is that I want to catch the 5:15 bus and think that only by running can I do so. Here you have offered an explanation of what I am doing, running toward the bus stop, in terms of two of my mental states: my desire to catch the 5:15 bus and my belief that only by running (in this direction, etc.) can I do so.

This explanation is open to criticism of two quite different kinds. First, there are various ways in which it might just fail to be the correct explanation of what I did. It might be, for instance, that I don't actually have one or both of these mental states, in which case, of course, they can't be part of the explanation of my running toward the bus stop. Perhaps I don't care at all about catching the bus but simply decided to break into a sprint out of my natural high spirits and exuberance. Exactly the same action, sprinting in a northeasterly direction, could result from this.

Or, even if I do indeed have both these mental states (a desire to catch the 5:15 bus and the belief that only by running in this direction can I do it), and am indeed running toward the bus stop, citing these mental states might still not explain what I am doing. I may not be running toward the bus stop *because* I want to catch the 5:15 bus. Perhaps, just as I realized that I would need to run to catch the 5:15 bus, I noticed an irate student bearing down on me from the southwest. Thoughts of bus schedules were at once overwhelmed by incipient panic, and to avoid the student I immediately sprinted off in the opposite direction—that is, toward the bus stop. If that is what happened, then even though I did indeed want to catch the 5:15 bus, and I did indeed think that only by running toward the bus stop could I do so, this was not *my reason* for running toward the bus stop. I was running toward the bus stop in order to avoid the irate student. Thus, this first sort of criticism contests the claim that the reason explanation offered actually does explain what I am doing.

More important for our purposes, though, is a second sort of criticism. Though I was indeed running toward the bus stop because I wanted to catch the 5:15 bus and I thought that only by running could I do so, it could still be that these are absolutely terrible reasons for running toward the bus stop—even, one might say, not reasons at all. It could be that the bus stop is actually several miles away, and so my belief that I could catch the 5:15 bus by running toward the bus stop is completely unfounded, since I have only 5 minutes before it arrives. Or it could be that my desire to catch the 5:15 bus is itself unwarranted. Perhaps I want to catch it because I know that that is the bus my wife usually takes home, but have forgotten that the reason I need to take the bus at all is that she has our car today.

The important thing to notice is that this second kind of criticism is aimed not at the reason explanation itself, really, but at the person whose action is being explained. The first sort of criticism shows, if successful, that the purported explanation is not really the correct explanation of why I was running toward the bus stop. The second sort of criticism, however, *presupposes* that this *is indeed* the correct explanation. It argues not that there is something wrong with the purported reason explanation of what I did but that there is something wrong with me, the person who did it *for those reasons*. I was confused about whether my wife would be on that 5:15 bus, perhaps, or I was wildly unrealistic about my running ability. In more complex or more interesting cases, the sorts of criticism might be correspondingly more complex and interesting. My reasons might, for instance, reveal some character flaw on my part. Some such flaw, perhaps cowardice or irresponsibility, might even be indicated in this case if my reason for running toward the bus stop was really to escape an irate student.

None of this is at all surprising; we use this sort of reason explanation all the time. But the upshot for the dilemma we started out with is interesting. If, as I think, this second, normative feature of reason explanations is actually essential to them, then we have found a feature of this sort of explanation that could not possibly be reducible to, or explicable in, physiological (or other physical) terms. That feature is normativity, being open to the second sort of criticism just described. (The "normativity" here is just that when we explain an action in terms of an agent's reasons, *those very reasons* are automatically and necessarily open to evaluation as being—or not being—real reasons, "good" reasons.)

It follows that the two sorts of explanation I distinguished above, physiological explanations and reason explanations, must be distinct. And from that it follows that the strong causalism about reason explanations described above must be false; that is, that there must be *some* aspects of the explanatory force of reason explanations that are not causal (unless one is willing to accept the ubiquitous, explanatory overdeterminism that constitutes the first horn of the dilemma with which we started). To put this another way, since the two sorts of explanation are really distinct, the only possible way to avoid the dilemma between overdeterminism and epiphenomenalism would seem to be to reject the strong causalism required to get the dilemma started. That will leave us with the question, which I will take up in a moment, of how we can understand reason explanations if not in purely causal terms.

First, though, we must think for a moment about why the normativity of reasons that grounded the second kind of criticism I just described is really an essential feature of reason explanations. One possible source of confusion to be set aside here is that there is a sense of the term *reason* that is in fact not at all normative. This is a sense that just overlaps *because*. We say, for instance, things like "*The reason* the grass is brown is that it hasn't rained in a couple of weeks." But this is not the sense of this term that I have been using in referring to "reason explanations of actions." We could just as well say "The grass is brown *because* it hasn't rained in a couple of weeks." And that is clearly a different matter than when we speak of *someone's reason for doing something*, which implies an agent and which opens the agent whose reason it is to normative criticism. (That is why it couldn't be other than a joke to speak of the grass's reason for turning brown, as if that were something the grass deliberated about and decided to do.[8])

That reason explanations contain an ineliminable normative element, and thus cannot be completely understood in causal terms, can be seen by looking at how such explanations work. Actions are essentially purposive, in the sense of *purpose* in which something can have a purpose only if someone has a purpose for it. There is another sense of the term *purpose*, a sense that I would rather mark by the use of a different term such as *function*, in which something can have a function even though no one had any purpose for it, for instance because of its evolutionary history. This is the sort of thing we refer to when we say the function of the heart is to pump blood. That is different from the sense of *purpose* in which something such as an action has a purpose. For something such as an action to have a purpose, someone must have had a purpose for it.[9]

To explain an action by citing the agent's reason or reasons for doing what she did is to explain it by reference to what it was the agent was trying to do—that is, by reference to whatever purpose she had in doing what she did. *That* is why reason explanations always include some reference to what the agent "wanted" in acting as she did. To explain an action in terms of what the agent wanted is to explain it in terms of the purpose or point she had in mind for it. At the same time, to explain something someone did in terms of her reasons for doing it necessarily involves "looking into her mind," that is, attributing some thoughts to her. This is because the purpose *that something has*, whether it is someone's action or just, say, a nail in the wall in her house, is there only because *she* (or someone) *has a purpose for it*. That is, it has a purpose only because *she thinks of it* as figuring into some plan or project of hers in some way. There is nothing about the thing itself (or about its causal history, say) that gives it this purpose. Her purpose for that nail in the wall might be to hold up a certain painting even though, unbeknownst to her, the painting is far too heavy to be held by such a small nail. And when she realizes this, perhaps days later and miles away, she might change the purpose of that nail simply by rethinking the purpose she wants it to serve (say, to hold up a little plastic thermometer instead), without the nail (or its causal history) changing at all.

Thus, a reason explanation of an action necessarily involves attributing a thought, which gives the purpose of the action, to the agent whose action we are trying to explain. But reason explanations *account for* this purpose in a way that always contains an essentially normative element of the sort just described in the second kind of criticism above. Attributing to others thoughts about what their reasons for their actions are requires that we regard the others as having and acting on thoughts about what gives them reason to do what they do.[10]

Thus, our explanations of actions in terms of the agents' reasons will necessarily involve normativity. The argument for this involves two steps. First, explaining actions in terms of the agents' reasons means regarding those agents as being capable of weighing what seem to them the various considerations that speak for and against doing whatever they are thinking of doing and then, at least sometimes, acting accordingly. That is, when we give the agent's reasons for doing whatever she does, we don't simply cite some goal or purpose she has in mind. We regard her as thinking that *there is something to be said for* doing whatever she did (perhaps even that there is more to be said for it than for anything else she could think of doing). We regard her as thinking that what she did is, at least to some degree, worth doing. Thus, the *content* of the thought we attribute to her must be normative in this way.

We can put this same point in terms of practical reasoning. Of course, not all actions (perhaps, in fact, relatively few) are preceded by actual psychological episodes of practical reasoning or deliberation. But to say that someone acted for a reason is to say that we can "reconstruct" what she had in mind in terms of the practical reasoning that she could have offered in support of her action. And practical reasoning, in order to have any chance at validity, must always include a normative or evaluative premise, since it always purports to support a conclusion about what the agent *should* do.[11] Roughly speaking, practical reasoning must always include a premise to the effect that some considerations are more important or more worth acting on than some other considerations.

It is easy to get confused about this because some philosophers have pictured practical reasoning as just a sort of interplay of desires leading to an action and because a very common account of practical reasoning, the so-called practical syllogism, typically focuses on just one desire and the reasoning about how to satisfy it. But these accounts can't be correct: If practical reasoning were just a matter of listing one's desires, or figuring out how to satisfy one (or some) of one's desires, all practical reasoning would commit the fallacy of *ignoratio elenchi*.[12] The conclusion about what one *should* do would not even be addressed, let alone supported. The premise that I have a particular desire will support the conclusion that I *should* act so as to satisfy it only if we add a premise to the effect that it is important (or valuable, or worthwhile, or the like) that this desire be satisfied. Thus, unless we want to say that the reason or reasons on which people act (that is, the reasons that would be made fully explicit in a piece of practical reasoning) never even get close to actually giving any real reasons for their actions, we have to attribute to them the thought that the considerations on which they act make performing the action somehow worthwhile, i.e., are things that *should* be acted on. And this is a normative thought.

It might be claimed that this is not enough to show that reason *explanations* are necessarily normative. I have been arguing that reason explanations necessarily involve attributing to the person whose action is being explained a normative or evaluative thought—roughly, the thought that what she is doing *has something to be said for it*, that it is worth doing in some way. That is, I have been arguing that the content of the thought we attribute to the person must be normative. But of course the attribution of a normative thought to someone is not itself a normative thought. If I think it important or worthwhile to sprint toward the bus stop, then I have a normative thought, a thought about the value of my sprinting toward the bus stop. But you, who are trying to explain my action, don't have a normative thought when you explain my action by attributing to me the thought that it is important to sprint toward the bus stop. Thus, someone might argue that, even if I am right in saying that an agent's reasons always involve normative thoughts (i.e., that they always have a normative or evaluative content), that still does not show that *explanations* in terms of reasons are normative, since these explanations make use, not of the normative thoughts themselves, but of attributions of these thoughts to the agent in question.

This is right as far as it goes, but there is a further point here: the second step in the argument referred to a few paragraphs above. I have argued that to explain someone's action in terms of her reasons we must attribute to her a normative thought, namely, as a minimum, the thought that her action is in some way worth doing, that there is something to be said for it. I have been arguing that it is important to see, first, that we *have to do this*, at least implicitly, in order to give a reason explanation. The second point, though, is that in doing this we are already opening the person whose action we are explaining to just the sort of normative criticism I am claiming is an essential feature of reason explanations.

That we have to attribute to the person whose action is being explained the thought that her action has something to be said for it can, perhaps, be fully supported only by working through some attempts to do without such an attribution and seeing that they fail. But perhaps it will help to point out that this is a consequence of what is sometimes called *the principle of charity*, the idea that it is a requirement for understanding a person that we understand her to be as rational as it is possible to be. (See, e.g., Davidson 1980a, essay 11.) Trying to make it a *general feature* of reason explanations that they involve no thought on the part of the agent that there is anything to be said in favor of her action would have the effect, as

I said above, of leaving all practical reasoning automatically fallacious. That would be incredible, hardly a charitable way of understanding human practical rationality.

The second feature is also important. If reason explanations of actions always involve attributing to the agent a normative thought of the sort I have described, then explaining someone's action in this way automatically opens her to normative or rational criticism of a sort that has no analogue in other sorts of explanation. Philosophers have often pointed out that means-ends criticism is appropriate to reason explanations, as in the earlier example if I could not possibly make it to the bus stop in 5 minutes no matter how fast I ran. But if, as I am claiming, one's reasons for doing something must always involve the thought that this action has something to be said for it, then to offer a reason explanation of someone's action is always and automatically to open that person to the full array of normative considerations, including moral ones.

If I am running toward the bus stop because I want to catch the 5:15 bus, then I must judge that my desire to catch that bus is more important (i.e., gives me more reason to act so as to satisfy it) than any of the considerations I am aware of that argue for doing something else. If, for instance, I am supposed to give a class at 5:15, and I haven't called it off or forgotten it, then I must have judged that my desire to catch the 5:15 bus (or whatever is behind this desire) is more important—more worth satisfying—than my holding that class. Of course, I might have good reason to think this (and I might not). But the point is that, if an explanation of my action in terms of my reasons really does apply to me, then I am by that very fact automatically open to the question of whether these normative judgments being attributed to me are correct. That is, I am put, *by such an explanation*, into the "game" of making and defending normative claims.[13]

This is not a feature of reason explanations that can be explained in terms of the physiology of muscles, brain cells, and so on.[14] That leaves us with the question of how we can make sense of this feature of reason explanations. In the remainder of the chapter, I will sketch very briefly an account (which will be at least partly noncausal if my earlier argument was correct) of how reason explanations work. If it is successful, it will have the virtue of showing why such explanations have the normative feature I have been discussing.

The trick, I think, is to focus on the first-person case and on the situation where one is actually doing something, performing some action. To simplify, it helps to use a case where the reasoning is explicit. In such a situation, I first try to figure out what there is to be said for and against the alternative actions that I think are open to me, decide as best I can which action has the most to recommend it, and then (if all goes well) perform that action. Nothing about this *process* pins down what is to count as telling in favor or against any action, but the process itself requires *that I hold* that, at the very least, something does count.

By the same token, such a process of deliberation includes the possibility that I can foul it up in various ways. I might, for instance, not notice some action that I could perform, or I might think there was something I could do which in fact I could not. Likewise, I might give too much or too little weight to something that I think argues for or against performing some action. But in the end (if all goes well) I will come to some conclusion about what I have most reason to do, and I will do it, *on the basis of this reasoning.*

If this is correct, then I think we have at least the essential elements of the answer to the general question of how reason explanations work. This is because when I explain my action to myself in terms of my reasons for performing it, this will be the kind of story I tell myself. Since this story includes "trying to figure out which action has the most to be said for it," it automatically includes the possibility of my going wrong in this attempt—that is, it opens me to the possibility of criticism about what really does count for or against this action. And of course there is nothing about such criticism that restricts it to being made by me, the person performing the action. I may know what considerations I weighed, and how much weight I gave them, better than you do, or I may not, but the issue of the reasonableness of these considerations (whatever they are) is necessarily an objective one and hence is at least potentially open to public discussion. It is necessarily objective because what I am trying to figure out is not what I *think* speaks for or against the action I am considering but what *really does* speak for or against it. The process requires that.

Thus, my suggestion is that, when you explain my action in terms of my reasons, what you are doing is trying to figure out this same story about my reasoning—the one that, in the best circumstances at least, I am typically in a good position to know just from the fact that I was the one doing the reasoning in the first place.

Acknowledgments

This chapter benefited greatly from the comments and suggestions of Barbara Hannan, Amy Lund, Bertram Malle, Jennifer Nagel, John Taber, Sergio Tenenbaum, and Aladdin Yaqub.

Notes

1. For a somewhat different statement of the issues here, not put in terms of a dilemma, see Dretske 1988. In contemporary philosophy, the classic attempt to resolve this dilemma without accepting either horn is Donald Davidson's 1963 paper "Actions, reasons, and causes" (reprinted in Davidson 1980a).

2. Saying that these two different schemata "answer two different questions" or "are on different levels" or the like merely points at, or labels, the difficulty here without solving it. Why are there two levels or questions? And (the tough one) what is the relation between them?

3. This same view, more or less, has been supported in recent philosophy by some famously bad reasoning, much of which is demolished in Davidson 1980a. I hope the reasoning here is better.

4. The term comes from George Wilson (1989), via Alfred Mele (1997b, p. 3).

5. In accordance with the conventions of this book, *representational content* will be used here to refer to the content of the beliefs, or other mental states, under discussion. (This is what, following Brentano, is often called their *intentional content.*) The representational content of my hope that this book is worth what you paid for it is "This book is worth what you paid for it."

6. The most serious, sustained attempt to provide such a reductive explanation of intentionality is that of Dretske (1988). Kim (1993) argues that the dilemma explained here can be solved only by a return to the idea that mental states must be reduced to physical ones. Part of Dretske's argument is criticized in chapter 4 of Schueler 1995. This general problem is one of the central issues discussed in Searle 1992.

7. For a defense of a similar conclusion, see Darwall 1983. Antony (1989) argues that Davidson's attempted solution of what is in essence this dilemma founders on his commitment to the normativity of reason explanations.

8. For a fuller account of the senses of the term *reason,* see chapter 2 of Schueler 1995.

9. With this distinction between function and purpose, I am taking a stand, spelled out in the next few paragraphs, on the question of whether genuinely normative elements are included in what I am calling the function of something. (They are not.) In a volume such as this, space is too limited to argue for this answer in any detail. For a good discussion of the possible uses of the term *function*, see chapter 1 of Godfrey-Smith 1996.

10. In fact, I want to say, intentional actions just are things done for reasons. Calling something an intentional action is just the same thing as saying that it is open to an explanation in terms of the agent's reasons for doing it.

11. It is important not to confuse what a piece of practical reasoning is about or refers to (typically, some possible action or course of action) with what judgment it supports (which will be the judgment that this action is what the agent should do—i.e., has most reason to do). For a good explanation of the structure of practical reasoning, see essay 2 in Davidson 1980a or chapter 3 of Schueler 1995.

12. For those for whom "Intro Logic," with its cute Latin names for fallacies, is only a distant memory: This is the fallacy more prosaically known as *irrelevant conclusion*.

13. Of course, just by existing I am open to some sorts of normative criticism. Some might criticize my propensity to break into tears during sappy movies, for instance, and that doesn't seem to have anything to do with any intentional actions I perform. The point here, however, is that to attribute to me thoughts about the worth of what I am doing is to regard me as committed to some normative claims. And that normative feature does not derive just from existing.

14. Nor, for that matter, can it be explained in terms of the causal history of the organism, as is argued by, e.g., Dretske (1988). Fully defending my claim here involves the same considerations that are involved in the purpose/function distinction explained above and would take more space than is available.

13

Folk Explanations of Intentional Action

Bertram F. Malle

How much easier it is to do psychology than philosophy! If I had to provide philosophical arguments for the unique modes of explanation that intentional action demands, I would swiftly be trapped in the hoary thicket of causality, free will, and the mind-body problem. As a social psychologist, I face a lighter task: I merely need to demonstrate that people explain intentional actions differently from how they explain other events. Such a demonstration, however, goes against a firmly established thesis in social psychology: that people explain all behavior (whether intentional or unintentional) by citing causes that are either internal or external to the agent. Even though this thesis is, on a basic level, correct (behavior explanations do provide, among other things, causal information), it grossly simplifies the conceptual structure and social functions of folk explanations of behavior. In particular, it fails to acknowledge the central role that people's concept of intentionality plays in shaping their explanations of behavior.

In this chapter I try to describe in detail how people explain intentional behavior, spelling out the unique conceptual, linguistic, and social features of these explanations. I argue that people explain intentional actions primarily with reasons (the explanation mode traditionally associated with intentionality) but also with two other modes that are conceptually and functionally distinct. I then compare the resulting model of folk explanation of behavior to classic attribution theory and recent developmental work on explanations. Finally, I apply the model to the debate between simulation theorists and theory-theorists, seeking an integration between the two approaches.

Intentionality and the Three Modes of Explaining Action

The social practice of behavior explanation is embedded in the folk theory of mind and behavior (Bruner 1990; Gopnik 1998; Heider 1958). Explanations both rely on and reveal this framework's central concepts—first and foremost, the concept of intentionality (Malle 1999; Malle and Knobe 1997b). Therefore, an account of how people explain behavior naturally begins with an analysis of the folk concept of intentionality.

The Folk Concept of Intentionality

Intentionality is a complex folk concept that specifies under what conditions people judge a behavior to be intentional (Malle and Knobe 1997a). A behavior is judged intentional when the agent has, at least, a desire for an outcome, a belief that the action leads to that outcome, an intention to perform the action, the skill to perform the action, and awareness of fulfilling the intention while performing the action. These are the minimal conditions for folk judgments of intentionality, but they do not yet tell us how people *explain* intentional behavior. To identify actual modes of explanation, we must separate the components of intentionality into three domains of intentional action that people find worthy of explanation (figure 1).

The first domain refers to factors that enabled the action to come about as the agent intended it (Malle 1999). Without such enabling factors, the intention would merely lead to an attempt, not to a completed action. The folk concept of intentionality specifies only one necessary enabling factor: the agent's skill.[1] That is, if a behavior is performed and fulfills an intention, the agent must have brought about that behavior with skill (rather than luck) for the action to count as intentional (Malle and Knobe 1997a; Mele, this volume). There are other enabling factors (among them effort,

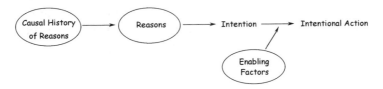

Figure 1
Domains of explanation (circled) within the folk concept of intentionality.

persistence, opportunities, and removed obstacles) that are not necessary for an action to count as intentional but are necessary for the action to be performed in the first place (McClure and Hilton 1997; Turnbull 1986). What all enabling factors have in common is that they explain how it was possible that the agent turned her intention into the intended action.[2] For example, "She hit her free-throws because she had practiced them all week." For many social actions, a "How possible?" question does not even come up; however, when it does come up (under conditions that will be discussed later), *enabling factor* explanations are the mode of choice to answer this question.

The second domain worthy of explanation refers to the reasons the agent had for acting (Audi 1993; Buss 1978; Davidson 1963; Locke and Pennington 1978; Malle 1999; Read 1987). Reasons are seen as representational mental states (desires, beliefs, valuings) that the agent combines in a (sometimes rudimentary) process of reasoning that leads to an intention and, if all goes well, to the intended action. The concept of intentionality specifies two minimal reasons for an action to be intentional: that the agent have a desire for an outcome and that the agent have a belief that the intended action leads to that outcome. These minimal reasons are sometimes explicitly mentioned in explanations of intentional action. For example, a student explained why she chose psychology as her major by saying "I want to go to graduate school in counseling psychology; I think psychology is the right major to have as background for counseling psychology." In many naturally occurring explanations, however, other reasons are mentioned, such as desires for avoiding alternative outcomes, beliefs about the context, beliefs about consequences, and valuings of the action itself.[3]

The intention underlying an action seldom serves an explanatory function by itself because the propositional content of an intention to A is the action A itself, which is then still left to be explained: "Why are you going shopping now?" "Because I intend to go shopping." Some scholars' claims about the explanatory function of intentions typically rely on a confounding of desires and intentions (Malle and Knobe, this volume; Moses, this volume). Intentions do answer an important question, namely, *what* the agent is doing ("She is trying to fix the computer"). But in answering this question, the intention describes the action at the right level (from the agent's perspective) without actually explaining it (Malle 1999, note 1).

The third domain of explanation refers to factors that lie in the causal history of reasons and thus clarify what led up to these reasons in the first place. The folk concept of intentionality is silent on the causal history of reasons. No matter how an agent's reasons originated, what counts toward intentionality is whether the reasons include a desire for an outcome and a belief that the action leads to that outcome. But under some conditions folk explainers are interested in this causal history, and I will discuss these conditions for *causal history of reason* explanations in more detail later.

The concept of intentionality thus allows us to locate three domains of explanation and their corresponding modes of explanation: how it was possible that a given action occurred (enabling factor explanations), why the agent intended to act that way (reason explanations), and what lay in the background of these reasons (causal history of reason explanations). For research purposes it is important to note that these three explanations can be reliably distinguished from one another when coding naturally occurring folk explanations of behavior ($\kappa = 0.72$–0.88).[4]

I will now discuss each of these explanatory modes in detail, beginning with reason explanations. They are the most frequently used explanation mode; they also have unique conceptual and linguistic features that differentiate them from all other explanations.

Reason Explanations

Reasons are mental states that help produce an intentional action. In this sense, they are considered to have "causal power." However, they are quite distinct from mere causes, because they perform a very specific function in bringing about intentional behavior. Mental states count as reasons only if they played a role in the agent's reasoning toward forming an intention to act, and this role is characterized by two essential features: *agent subjectivity* and *rationality*.

Two Essential Features of Reason Explanations
Agent Subjectivity
When providing reason explanations, folk explainers cite those mental states in light of which, to their best knowledge, the agent formed an intention to act. They try to reconstruct the decisive deliberations that the agent

underwent when forming her intention and thus take the agent's subjective viewpoint in explaining her action. There may be other good reasons for acting the way the agent did, but what counts as an explanation must refer to her own subjective reasons in deciding to so act. Because of the agent subjectivity of reason explanations, and because of the assumption that an agent undergoes some sort of reasoning process, folk explainers assume that the agent had at least minimal awareness of (the content of) her reasons; otherwise they would not be *her* reasons.

Consider the explanation "Shanna ignored her brother's arguments because they were irrelevant." If folk explainers consider this a reason explanation, they should assume that the agent was aware of the explanation's content and consequently should reject as senseless the added claim "even though she was not aware of the fact that they were irrelevant." We designed a study that would test this prediction across different behaviors and explanations (Malle, Knobe, O'Laughlin, Pearce, and Nelson 2000).

We first constructed several behaviors and, for each, various explanations that contained no obvious linguistic markers of reasons. Thus, we removed mental state markers such as "he wanted" or "she thought," and we excluded all desire reasons (because they have a characteristic linguistic structure of "so (that) . . ." or "(in order) to . . ."). Then we presented these behavior-explanation pairs to undergraduate students and selected seven pairs that were clearly judged to be reason explanations by a majority of the students (ranging from 78 percent to 98 percent per explanation). We had also included explanations of the same actions that were not reasons but causal histories of reasons, which provided a judgmental and statistical contrast to the reasons. Each of the seven reason explanations was then paired with a statement that negated awareness, of the form "even though [agent] was not aware that/of [explanation content]"—for example, "Carey watered her plants because the leaves were wilting (even though she was not aware that the leaves were wilting)." These statements were presented to a second group of students, and when asked whether these reason explanations made sense or not, an average of 77 percent said they did not make sense (versus 28 percent for causal history of reason explanations). A follow-up study clarified why 23 percent of students claimed that a reason explanation could still make sense even though the agent's awareness was negated. Virtually all of them assumed that the offered explanation described some preceding cause, not a reason: when given an opportunity to clarify their judgments, they spontaneously offered alternative reasons for which the agent in fact acted (Malle et al. 2000, study 2).

Rationality

Besides agent subjectivity, folk explainers assume a second essential feature of reason explanations: a rational link between the reasons and the intended action. They try to cite only mental states that would make it appear rational for the actor to form her intention. The constraint of rationality excludes beliefs and desires that bring about an intentional behavior in a merely causal way and are therefore not the agent's reasons for acting that way (e.g., "She came to the party 'cause she didn't know that her ex was gonna be there"). The rationality assumption also explains why one reason typically implies a host of other reasons. For example, the explanation "Anne was driving above the speed limit because she knew the store closed at 6 o'clock" cites a belief reason that readily entails the desire reason "and she wanted to get to the store." Similarly, the explanation "Anne was driving above the speed limit because she wanted to get to the store before 6 o'clock" cites a desire reason that readily entails the belief reason "and she thought that only by driving fast could she be there by 6 o'clock." Nothing in the desire (as stated) entails the belief, and nothing in the belief (as stated) entails the desire. Only under rationality constraints—the assumption that reasons combine rationally in the formation of an intention—do these implications follow.

Of course, folk explainers need not share or approve of the agent's reasons; they need only acknowledge that, given those reasons, it is rational (reasonable, intelligible) for the agent to form her intention. That also implies that an agent who avows her behavior as intentional subjects herself to the scrutiny of rational criticism (Schueler, this volume). Conversely, if the agent tries to appear rational, she will portray her behaviors as intentional and, in particular, explain it with reasons (Malle et al. 2000).

It is still a matter of debate what the rationality assumption exactly entails (cf. Føllesdal 1982). Some scholars (e.g., Davidson 1980c) require logical consistency within the agent's reasoning chain; others (e.g., Collingwood 1946) require only intelligibility for the explainer. Yet others invoke a more general normativity rather than a specific rationality norm (Schueler, this volume). Clearly there is a need for empirical work on the exact features of rationality that ordinary people assume when they ascribe reasons to an agent.

The Grammar of Reasons

Reason explanations are often expressed in natural language, either when the agent gives an account of her own action or when an observer gives an account of another's action. To understand the function of reasons in social interaction, we must identify the "grammar" of reasons—the conceptual and linguistic parameters that differentiate reasons from each other. I will focus on three such parameters: what type of mental state constitutes the reason, whether that type is linguistically marked, and what the mental state represents in its content.

Reason Types: Desires, Beliefs, Valuings

Consider the following reason explanations for why the agent teased another person:

(1) because she wanted to make the other kids laugh

(2) because she disliked the way the person looked

(3) because she thought that the boy was too feminine.

All three of these reasons are clearly marked as subjective mental states (of wanting, disliking, thinking), and each implies a larger network of mental states that were involved in the agent's reasoning (e.g., the belief that the boy was too feminine implies in this context that the agent didn't like that and wanted to make fun of it). Reasons such as these can usually be classified as desires (1), valuings (2), or beliefs (3).

Desire reasons reveal the action's desired outcome, which is often called the action's goal, aim, end, or purpose. Consequently, desire reasons are answers to the question "For what purpose?" or "What for?" An unfulfilled desire is the paradigmatic instigator of action, as it represents something the agent lacks and tries to get through acting. Mentioning a desire reason thus portrays the agent as deficient (i.e., "wanting") in some respect and as driven toward removing the deficiency. Moreover, mentioning a desire as a reason for acting (not just as a description of a mental state) portrays the agent as endorsing the desire as worth pursuing (Schueler, this volume). Thus, merely by placing an outcome in the content of a desire reason, the explainer can indicate the outcome's worthiness, at least from the agent's subjective perspective: "Why did she turn up the volume?" "To make her brother mad."

Valuings, like desires, indicate positive or negative affect toward the representational object. This affect can be absolute (liking, hating, missing something) or relative (preferring one thing over another). Valuings are primarily used to indicate the inherent desirability of an action (e.g., "Why did she go dancing?" "She loves dancing"), whereas desires typically indicate the desirability of an outcome (Malle and Knobe, this volume). Like desires, valuings ascribe to the agent an evaluative attitude toward an object (or the action itself); however, unlike desires, valuings do so explicitly and without highlighting the agent's deficiency.

Belief reasons encompass a broad range of knowledge, hunches, and assessments that the agent has about the outcome, the action, their causal relation, and relevant circumstances. Beliefs are aimed at representing reality and thus are not, by themselves, apt to instigate action. But they are essential in choosing worthwhile outcomes to pursue and actions to select as means. They help the agent track feasible paths of action, consider the consequences of those actions, and navigate around obstacles, and they can represent other people's wishes and reactions. The latter is crucial in coordinating one's actions with others.

My co-workers and I have recently begun to explore the determinants and functions of explainers' choice of reason type. Across thousands of free-response behavior explanations, we are finding a base rate distribution of roughly 50 percent desires, 10 percent valuings, and 40 percent beliefs. We are also finding systematic variations in the use of reason types. For example, when people explain their own behavior, they use belief reasons to present themselves as rational (Malle et al. 2000). Furthermore, there is a reliable actor-observer difference: Observers tend to use more desire reasons and fewer belief reasons than actors (Malle, Knobe, Nelson, and Stevens, in preparation), presumably because desire reasons are more generic and easier to guess whereas belief reasons require situated information that may be idiosyncratic to the agent.

Mental State Markers

The nature of reasons as subjective mental states can be linguistically highlighted with verbs such as "I thought," "he wanted," and "she likes." If no such mental state markers are used, only the reason's propositional content is cited in the explanation. For example, when explaining why Anne waters her plants with vitamin B, we may cite a desire reason that is marked ("because she wants them to grow faster") or unmarked ("so they will grow faster"). Similarly, we may cite a belief reason that is marked ("because she thinks they will grow faster") or unmarked ("because they will grow faster").

The linguistic device of mental state markers has a number of interesting implications for reason explanations. First, unmarked beliefs downplay their nature as mental states. For example, "Joan canceled the party because it was raining" looks, on the surface, identical to "Joan got wet because it was raining." But of course in the first explanation the rain did not directly cause Joan's behavior—she decided to cancel the party in light of her belief that it was raining. In accordance with the subjectivity assumption for reasons, the explanation is shorthand for "Joan decided to cancel the party because *she thought* it was raining." However, omission of the marker and direct reference to the content make the action seem to be more rational and a "natural" response to the situation. Indeed, actors who attempt to appear rational do so primarily by increasing their use of unmarked belief reasons (Malle et al. 2000). Second, by marking a belief reason with a mental state verb, social perceivers can emphasize that this was the *agent's* belief and was not necessarily shared by the perceiver: "She's quitting her job because she thinks her pay sucks." Thus, explainers can distance themselves from an agent's reasoning by using mental state markers or can embrace this reasoning by omitting them. With this subtle linguistic tool, they communicate to their audience how reasonable or justified they feel the agent's action was (Malle et al. 2000). Third, when desire reasons are expressed without mental state markers, they still indicate their nature as subjective reasons. Grammatically, unmarked desires are always expressed in the form of "(in order) to," "so (that) . . . ," or "for . . . (sake)," each citing the agent's purpose for acting. Thus, even in their unmarked form they express the reason's subjectivity. The marked form, however, can highlight the agent's deficiency (e.g., "He went to the store because he *needed* more milk") or self-centeredness (e.g., "We had to stop because he *wanted* to have some coffee").

Reason Contents
Reasons, as representational states, always have a content: the object, action, or state of affairs that is desired, valued, or believed. The content of reasons is what the agent considers in forming an intention (e.g., "They say it will rain tomorrow [belief content]; having the party in the rain wouldn't be fun [valuing content]; I'd better cancel it [intention]"). Thus, the content of reasons is what renders actions intelligible. Whereas the general folk model of reason explanation specifies that actions are to be explained by *some* beliefs, desires, and valuings, the actual explanation of a concrete action requires one to know which particular reasons the agent had, and this particularity is given by the content of reasons.

Even though reason contents are essential for explanations of intentional action, their psychological study is marred by difficulties. For one thing, a given reason content can be represented in various ways on the linguistic surface. For example, I might say "I wish I were rich" or "I want to be rich" to express exactly the same desire content of being richer; however, the first expression mentions the agent (*I were rich*), whereas the second does not (*to be rich*), following a simple grammatical operation of "equi-subject deletion" (Givon 1993). Research that classifies behavior explanations according to their mentioning of the agent versus the situation (e.g., McGill 1989; Nisbett, Caputo, Legant, and Marecek 1973) is therefore oversensitive to surface variations and grammatical rules rather than to the actual mental content represented in the reason.

But even refined classifications of reason content that take grammatical rules into account (and, for example, code "I want to be rich" as referring to agent content) quickly run into difficulties. For example, how should one classify "I cried because I received a farewell letter from her"? Is the receiving agent in the foreground, or should we code for the implicit sender of the letter? My co-workers and I have tried to be inclusive and permit a variety of interaction codes for these complex cases (e.g., interactions between the agent and the situation, the agent and other people, other people and the situation, etc.; see Malle 1998). However, even with coding that is sensitive to grammar and to complex contents, we have not yet found reason content to be reliably predictive of other psychological variables. For example, the classic thesis that people explain their own actions more with reference to the situation and others' actions more with reference to them as agents (Jones and Nisbett 1972) does not hold up to scrutiny (Malle 1999; Malle et al., in preparation).

It is conceivable that reason content is so action specific that it defies general psychological regularities. Because reason content provides the rational connection among beliefs and desires in leading up to an intention, it may not have to serve any further psychological function. But before we accept this conclusion, other classification schemes might be tested. Instead of classifying reason content into agent, situation, and various interactions, perhaps we should code the content for its social desirability. We might examine whether reasons with desirable content are more accepted by audiences than those with undesirable content, whether explainers are more likely to lie when the true content of their reasons is undesirable in the eyes of a given audience, and whether desirable content is sought when excusing an agent and undesirable content is sought when accusing an agent.

Clearly, much research is needed on the psychological functions of the three parameters of reasons (and on other parameters not discovered so far). Another topic of research, which already has some findings to report, concerns the question "Under what conditions are reason explanations used in the first place?" The answer is simple: In about 80 percent of cases, people explain intentional actions by means of reasons, because reasons answer directly what a why-question inquires about (namely, what motivated the agent to perform the given action—what was the *reason*-ing behind it). The more complex question is "When and why do people *not* use reason explanations and instead use causal history of reason explanations or enabling factor explanations?" I now turn to the conditions under which people do use these alternative modes of explanation.

When People Use Causal History of Reason Explanations

One alternative to providing reasons when explaining intentional behavior is to cite factors that lay in the causal history of the agent's reasons (Malle 1994; Malle 1999; see also Hirschberg 1978; Locke and Pennington 1982). Consider the following examples:

Anne invited Ben for dinner because she is friendly.

Carey watered the plants because she stayed at home in the morning.

Even though these explanations clarify intentional behavior, they do not mention what reasons the agent considered when forming her intention; rather, they mention the causal history of those reasons. Causal history of reason (CHR) explanations describe the context, background, or origin of reasons, so they are not constrained by the agent-subjectivity or rationality rules that apply to reasons themselves. Anne did not consider "I am friendly, I better invite Ben for dinner." Rather, her friendly disposition triggered some of her reasons, such as a desire for talking to Ben or doing something nice for him. Similarly, Carey probably did not consider "I stayed at home in the morning; therefore I will water my plants." More likely, her being at home triggered her desire to care for her plants or made her realize that they needed water.

CHR explanations account for only about 20 percent of intentional-behavior explanations; thus, when explainers offer CHR explanations, they deviate from the standard of giving reasons. Under what conditions do explainers do that? O'Laughlin and Malle (2000) suggest two conditions; I add a third.

Knowledge

If the explainer does not know the exact reason for an intentional behavior but nevertheless wants to offer an explanation, he may offer a causal history explanation. Consider the following transcript: "Then why would Tanya come up and talk to us out of her own free will?"—"Well . . . weird people do these kinds of things." As can be inferred from the explainer's hedging, he does not actually know the reason why Tanya decided to talk to them. Instead of admitting his ignorance, however, he offers an explanation citing a personality trait that presumably caused whatever specific reason Tanya had for her action.

The knowledge condition predicts an actor-observer asymmetry of using CHR explanations (relative to reason explanations). Actors typically know the reasons for their own actions and should therefore offer mostly reason explanations, whereas observers often do not know others' reasons and should therefore offer relatively more CHR explanations. Indeed, we found this asymmetry across a wide variety of contexts, including conversations, memory protocols, questionnaires, and interviews (Malle et al., in preparation).

Conversational Relevance

Explanations in conversation are subject to rules of relevance (Grice 1975; Hilton 1990; Sperber and Wilson 1986; Turnbull 1986). Reasons typically provide the most relevant and informative answers to why-questions; sometimes, however, they are cumbersome or obvious, and in these cases explainers may prefer to use CHR explanations. I will describe these cases in turn.

When a series or trend of intentional behaviors is explained, the reasons for each specific action may vary, while the "historic" determinants of this set of reasons may be constant. Thus, a causal history explanation can offer a parsimonious account of the whole class of possible reasons that the actor may have for each respective action. For example, in "I go to the supermarket almost every day because I have three kids," the fact of having three kids is not the agent's conscious reason for going to the supermarket. Rather, on each separate occasion, the fact of having three kids brings about a reason to go to the supermarket: one time a child is sick and needs cough drops, another time a child stains the carpet and there is no stain remover in the house, and so on. Across these occasions (and their corresponding reasons), the single fact of having three kids explains why the actor repeatedly goes to the supermarket, and it does so more parsimoniously than a string of individual reasons would. The same logic of parsimony applies to the explanation of aggregate behaviors, which describe behavior trends across people rather than behavior trends of one person across time. When a whole group of people act in similar ways but each individual has different reasons to so act, a CHR explanation is a parsimonious account of the entire group's behavior, setting aside the variety of individual reasons (O'Laughlin and Malle 2000).

A second case in which conversational relevance favors CHR explanations is when an agent's reasons are obvious and the explainer seeks to provide an answer that goes beyond the obvious: "Why is she planning to get pregnant?" "I guess her biological clock is ticking." In this example, the explainer probably assumed that the questioner already knew the woman's reason for getting pregnant (her desire for a child). What the questioner may wonder is why she has this desire in the first place. A CHR explanation that clarifies the origin of her desire provides an informative answer to this question.

Strategic Presentation
Finally, causal history explanations can be used strategically to downplay the agent's reasoning process (which is normally highlighted by offering reason explanations, especially belief reasons). For example, a suitor may want to downplay the degree of deliberation behind his actions: "Why did you come all the way to bring me the book?" "Oh, because I was in the area, and I happened to have the book with me." Moreover, CHR explanations are occasionally used to downplay intentionality and responsibility and thus mitigate blame or punishment (Wilson 1997). For example, Nelson and Malle (2000) found that people's use of causal histories is greater when explaining undesirable actions than when explaining desirable actions.

To summarize: People use causal history factors to complement reason explanations or to substitute them for reasons that are not known or would not achieve a particular communicative goal. Because some CHR explanations refer to traits, the concept of causal history explanations also helps clarify the relationship between traits and mental states in explanations of intentional behavior (Rosati, Knowles, Kalish, Gopnik, Ames, and Morris, this volume). Traits can be used instead of mental state explanations when the agent's reasons are unknown or do not fulfill the speaker's conversational goals. Moreover, traits can elucidate the background and origin of the agent's specific reasons. Finally, because traits are temporally stable, they aide in predicting the agent's future behavior in different contexts regardless of the agent's context-specific reasons.

When People Use Enabling Factor Explanations

The second alternative to using reasons when explaining intentional behavior is to cite enabling factors. Enabling factor explanations do not answer a motivational question (as do reason and CHR explanations); rather, they answer a performance question. Consider these examples:

How come John aced the exam?—He's a stats whiz.

Phoebe got all her work done because she had a lot of coffee.

Enabling factor explanations exist because of the imperfect link between intention and action. An agent might have reasons to act a certain way and so might form an intention. But whether this intention is turned into a successfully performed action often depends on factors beyond the agent's intention and reasons—factors that *enable* the action. Because enabling factor explanations clarify performance rather than motivation, they should increase in response to the question "How was this possible?" relative to the motivational question "Why?" or "What for?" Indeed we found that enabling factor explanations occurred 4–12 times more frequently in response to a "How possible?" question than in response to any other explanatory question (Malle et al. 2000).

A second condition under which enabling factor explanations increased in frequency was when the behavior in question was difficult (as is the case with artistic, athletic, or complex actions). In such cases it may often seem surprising that the behavior was successfully performed, and surprise demands explanation. Accordingly, we found that enabling factors occurred 7–8 times more frequently with difficult behaviors than with easy behaviors. (See also McClure and Hilton 1997.)

Competing Models of Folk Explanation

Two models of folk explanation have received generous support and attention in the psychological literature: social psychology's attribution theory and developmental psychology's study of children's explanations within their theory of mind.

Attribution Theory

Attribution theory has been the favored psychological model of folk explanations of behavior for more than 40 years. Its history began when Heider (1958) offered insights into folk explanations by considering them part of people's "naive theory of action." However, the models developed later by Jones and Davis (1965) and Kelley (1967) left the central aspect of this naive theory—the concepts of intention and intentionality—behind. Heider repeatedly emphasized the importance of intentionality, but he used the terms *personal causality* and *impersonal causality* to refer to folk conceptions of intentional versus unintentional behavior (Heider 1958, pp. 100–101). This choice of terms and the occasional ambiguities in Heider's writing (Malle and Ickes 2000) led to a major recasting (and misunderstanding) of his distinction into one between "person causes" and "situation causes." Soon after Kelley's (1967) landmark paper, attribution researchers classified all folk explanations of behavior into those that cite person causes and those that cite situation causes, irrespective of the behavior's intentionality.

The person/situation dichotomy may appear simple, elegant, and predictively useful. Its major flaw is, however, that people don't think about behavior solely in terms of person causes and situation causes. In fact, no direct evidence has ever been provided that people's theory of behavior assigns a significant role to the person/situation dichotomy. All evidence comes from reactive measures that forced people to express their explanations in terms of person/situation ratings or from content codings that classified only the linguistic surface of explanations (Malle et al. 2000). In contrast, there is evidence that people alter their explanations depending on the behavior's intentionality, and that they explain intentional behavior primarily with the agent's reasons whereas they explain unintentional behavior with mere causes (Malle 1999). Attribution theory provides a good account of how people explain such unintentional behavior using "cause explanations." However, a causal attribution model is insufficient as an account of how people explain behavior in general and intentional behavior in particular.

For example, attributional analyses of reason explanations have ignored the complex grammar of reasons and drawn misleading conclusions from reasons' linguistic surface (Malle 1999; Malle et al. 2000). In particular, when reasons lack a mental state marker and their content mentions something about the situation, researchers have mistakenly classified them as "situation causes" (e.g., "She didn't go because her ex was there"). But in such unmarked reasons explainers are not referring to situational causes that somehow made the agent act; rather, they are expressing the content of a belief that the agent considered before acting. The mistake of treating reason contents as causes is most obvious when that content speaks about future or hypothetical states, as in "He doesn't let his daughters go out after midnight because something could happen." No doubt the explainer is referring here to hypothetical dangers that function not as mere causes but as contents of the agent's belief.

Developmental Work on Explanations

The last 10 years have seen a surge of interest in children's theory of mind. Even though explanations are considered a hallmark of this developing theory (Gopnik 1998), researchers have only recently turned to examining children's explanatory reasoning in detail (Bartsch and Wellman 1995b; Kalish 1998; Schult and Wellman 1997; Wellman, Hickling, and Schult 1997). Two assumptions have guided much of this research. The first is that children develop three distinct explanatory models: a folk psychology, a folk physics, and a folk biology. The second is that folk-psychological explanations construe human behavior in terms of internal states, particularly beliefs and desires. Unfortunately, this classification system blurs the critical distinction between reason explanations and other modes of behavior explanation by treating beliefs and desires broadly as mental states and not functionally as either reasons, causes, or causal history factors.

For example, Schult and Wellman (1997) group under "psychological explanations" those statements that refer to the agent's mental states, including desires and beliefs, but also moods and lack of knowledge. (See also Bartsch and Wellman 1995b, chapter 6.) The examples cited by Schult and Wellman show that the class of "psychological explanations" includes both reason explanations of intentional behavior ("Why did Jimmy pour milk in his cereal bowl?" "Because he likes it") and cause explanations of unintentional behavior (e.g., "Why did Sarah squeeze ketchup on her ice cream?" "Because she didn't know it was ketchup.").[5] Moreover, Hickling and Wellman (2000) seem to classify some reason explanations as nonpsychological explanations when the content of the reason refers to biological or physical states—for example, "The reason I ask for so much juice is because I get thirsty."

Wellman and colleagues have demonstrated that children as young as 3 years systematically use mental state explanations for human behavior, but these findings leave open the question whether children differentiate between mental states as reasons and mental states as mere causes. Perhaps children first apply mental state explanations broadly to human behaviors and learn to distinguish between reasons and other mental causes only after acquiring the concept of intentionality, around the age of 5 years (Shultz and Wells 1985). Command over this concept would probably involve an understanding of the scope and limits of choice, also acquired around age 5 (Kalish 1998). One test for whether children understand the reason-cause distinction might involve asking them to differentiate belief/desire explanations that function as reasons from belief/desire explanations that function as causes (or as causal histories of reasons, in which case the explanations are equated in terms of accounting for intentional behaviors).

Explanations as Cognitive Process: Theoretical Inference, or Simulation?

Much research and thinking regarding explanations has been devoted to the question of what cognitive processes underlie the forming of explanations. The dominant answer within social psychology has been that all explaining—regardless of the object of explanation—relies on domain-general (tacit) cognitive mechanisms, such as covariance analysis, evidence updating, or connectionist nets. (See, e.g., Cheng and Novick 1990; Kelley 1967; Kruglanski 1989; Read and Marcus-Newhall 1993; van Overwalle 1998.) However, it is hard to see how these models would account for the distinction between reasons and other modes of explanation. After all, explanatory reasoning would only consist of correlating causes and effects, no matter whether those causes are reasons and the effects are intentional actions. What makes a reason explanation plausible and acceptable, however, is not just the assumption that the hypothesized mental state probably caused the action in question but also the assumption that it was a *rational reason* for acting that way, and such considerations involve domain-specific semantic analyses rather than domain-general syntactic analyses.

The literature offers two main candidates for such domain-specific structures. One is theory-theory, which postulates that people use distinct concepts (e.g., intention) and rules (e.g., that intentional behavior always has a point or purpose) when explaining human behavior, and these concepts and rules together make up a folk theory of mind and behavior. An alternate candidate is simulation theory, which postulates that perceivers simulate others' putative mind states, using their own faculties of perceiving, reasoning, and feeling as models that deliver (off-line) predictions or explanations (Gordon 1986; Goldman 1989).

Without reconsidering the entire debate between simulation theory and theory-theory (Carruthers and Smith 1996; Davies and Stone 1995), I would like to explore briefly how simulation and theory-theory might account for the four modes of folk explanation of behavior identified earlier: reasons, causal histories of reasons, enabling factors, and mere causes. I am not assuming that simulation theorists would necessarily claim to account for all four modes of explanation (as theory-theorists would). In fact, most simulationists might claim to account only for explanations involving mental state ascriptions, others perhaps only for reason explanations. Even so, we must ask what theoretical apparatus researchers have to adopt in order to account for all four modes of explanation.

Enabling factor explanations present the most clear-cut case. In describing what made it possible that a given action was accomplished, these explanations concern the process that allowed an intention to "come into the world," which is something that perceivers cannot simulate experientially but can only think through theoretically. Over time, they will acquire generalizations about the kinds of factors that enable certain types of actions. Thus, theory-theory provides an adequate account for enabling factor explanations, but simulation theory does not.

When discussing cause explanations of unintentional behavior, we must distinguish between two major types of unintentional behavioral events. The first includes events that are "biological" or "physical" in nature, such as sweating after exercise or tripping over a root. An adult perceiver does not simulate exercising to know why someone in athletic clothes looks sweaty and exhausted, and it is unlikely that children would first have to exercise and sweat themselves before they can learn the empirical generalization in question. Cause explanations of physical or biological behavior thus seem to be based on learned knowledge structures, hence on some version of a theory.

The second type of unintentional behavior includes "psychological" events, such as sadness after losing a game or pain from an injection. These phenomena are clearly open to simulation. In fact, some psychological behaviors automatically trigger empathic simulation (which is why people cry in movie theaters and look away when somebody receives an injection). Empirical research on emotional contagion and empathy (see, e.g., Levenson and Ruef 1997) supports the claim that feelings and emotions are suitable and frequent objects of imitation and simulation. Occasional knowledge-based prediction or explanation is not ruled out, but the prevalence of emotional imitation and contagion in children suggests that the simulative approach may come first in this domain (Goldman, this volume). Thus, a full account of cause explanations requires both theory-theory (to account for biological and physical events) and simulation theory (to account for psychological events).

In the case of reason explanations, the challenge is to account for the normative and rational "glue" that connects reasons to intentions and actions. Theory-theory would postulate that social perceivers assume a rationality principle (e.g., "People act to get what they want, given what they believe about how to get it" (Ripstein 1987, p. 468)), and a version of this rule is indeed part of the adult concept of intentionality (Malle and Knobe 1997a). However, it seems highly implausible that 3-year-olds have such an abstract insight into rationality. At the same time, 3-year-olds seem to be quite adept at offering reason explanations (Bartsch and Wellman 1995b). The simulation approach does not postulate anything special in the child perceiver (even in one only 3 years old) that we don't already attribute to the child agent, namely a practical reasoning faculty that *itself* rationally progresses from beliefs and desires to intentions and actions. However, such simulations would be hard to get started without general rules that guide the search for possible explanations—rules such as "If the behavior looks intentional, search for beliefs and desires and plug them into the deliberation mechanism." On the other hand, it is not clear how perceivers who according to theory-theory follow a general rationality rule "fill in" the concrete beliefs and desires that might be the agent's reasons. Inferring on the basis of a rationality rule that the agent had *some* beliefs and desires is one thing;

inferring the specific ones in this context is quite another. Thus, perceivers may well project their own perceptions of the situation onto the agent and may occasionally complement them with beliefs and desires that they regard as idiosyncratic to the agent. This input could then be fed into the perceiver's own practical reasoning faculty or, once sufficiently developed, into a more abstract inference heuristic. For reason explanations, then, as for cause explanations, both simulation theory and theory-theory are needed.

CHR explanations, too, may require a mixed account. CHR explanations referring to abstract cultural and personality factors are difficult if not impossible to simulate experientially, whereas those that refer to specific situational or internal triggers invite an act of pretending to be in the agent's shoes. Once the perceiver simulates the agent's situation or internal state, it may become apparent why the agent acted in this particular way. As an example, Ripstein (1987) offers Orwell's explanation for why he did not shoot an enemy soldier: the man was running across the trenches, holding up his trousers. In this case, simulation rather than general rules seems to lead to explanation and understanding of the agent's action. The specific image of a man holding up his trousers seems to trigger in anybody the desire to not shoot him, and once one experiences that image and the consequent desire the decision not to shoot the person is wholly intelligible (and much more so than if one merely cited the obvious desire "he didn't want to shoot him"). Not surprisingly, good writers, filmmakers, and defense lawyers lead their audiences to simulate a character's situation in such detail that the agent's subsequent reasons and actions seem to follow with utter necessity.

Stich and Nichols (1995) argued that "it may well turn out that some of our folk-psychological skills are indeed subserved by simulation processes, while others are subserved by processes that exploit a tacit theory." Similarly, the full range of folk explanations of behavior appears to require both the capacity to simulate and the capacity to use generalized knowledge structures.

Summary

I have tried to demonstrate that the concept of intentionality is a key to understanding folk explanations of behavior. The structure of intentionality defines three domains of intentional action that people find worth explaining: the factors that enable an action's successful performance, the reasons for acting, and the causal history of those reasons. In contrast, behaviors not considered intentional are straightforwardly explained by antecedent causes. Among these four modes of explanation, reason explanations are unique in that they must meet the constraints of agent subjectivity and rationality, thus capturing agents' own reasoning toward their intentions to act. Future research should focus on the social functions of behavior explanations and the cognitive processes, such as inference and simulation, that underlie folk explanations of behavior.

Acknowledgments

Preparation of this chapter was supported by NSF CAREER award SBR-9703315. I am grateful to Alvin Goldman, Joshua Knobe, Sarah Nelson, and Fred Schueler for their comments on an earlier draft.

Notes

1. Awareness is not actually an enabling factor; it only ensures that the agent monitors her action and executes it in such a way as to fulfill the intention she has. Awareness therefore has no explanatory function for intentional actions. "Why did he leave the room?" is not answered by "He was aware of doing it." However, lack of awareness can be used to explain why an intended action remained unsuccessful.

2. Throughout this chapter I use female pronouns for agents and male pronouns for explainers.

3. The question of how people select the reasons they cite from these many possibilities has not been studied in great detail (Hesslow 1988). General parameters include the explainer's knowledge (e.g., O'Laughlin and Malle 2000) and his assumptions about the audience's knowledge (e.g., Hilton 1990; Turnbull and Slugoski 1988). Another parameter is the motive to present an image of the agent as, say, rational or moral (Malle, Knobe, O'Laughlin, Pearce, and Nelson 2000).

4. For detailed coding rules, see Malle 1998.

5. Compare "Why did the gun accidentally go off?" "John was trying to clean it." (Wellman 1990, p. 99)

14

The Rocky Road from Acts to Dispositions: Insights for Attribution Theory from Developmental Research on Theories of Mind

Andrea D. Rosati, Eric D. Knowles, Charles W. Kalish, Alison Gopnik, Daniel R. Ames, and Michael W. Morris

In a famous paper, "The rocky road from acts to dispositions," Edward Jones (1979) reviewed several decades of research on how people attribute the observable acts of others to causes such as personality traits, attitudes, and other unobservable dispositions. Social psychologists since Heider (1958) had focused on the attribution of dispositions because the attribution of enduring properties to persons is thought to strongly shape social interaction. The dispositions that actors in a given context tend to attribute to one another, for example, elucidate many important dynamics of social interaction (Morris, Larrick, and Su 1999; Morris and Leung 1999; Morris and Su 1999). By pointing to "rocks" in the road to dispositions, Jones acknowledged that social-psychological models of the process of dispositional attribution had not fully captured complexities surrounding people's inferences regarding the proximal motives and intentions behind an act that pave the way for ascribing a personal disposition. Since attribution theories emerged from an interest in the behaviors that follow from dispositional inferences—rather than from an intrinsic interest in the inferences leading up to them—it is not surprising that attribution theory left stones unturned in the inferential process. In this chapter, we argue that attribution theory can be enriched by drawing on concepts from the developmental-psychology literature on children's theories of mind.

Before suggesting ways to add nuance to social-psychological models of the process of dispositional attribution, it is worth reviewing how the complexity of these models has changed throughout their history. In the descriptions of Heider (1958), the social perceiver is a "naive scientist" relying on a complex combination of folk beliefs and perceptual data to proceed through a chain of inferences about an actor's intentions, desires, beliefs, feelings, and traits. Over time, more parsimonious models emerged. Theorists have portrayed a shorter, more direct cognitive path from observable actions to trait attributions (Kelley 1967; Trope 1986; Winter and Uleman 1984). Notwithstanding this trend, countervailing theorists have questioned whether the "naive scientist" could really be as naive as portrayed in attributing dispositions. Important inferential steps similar to those described by Heider have been proposed as complications to more minimal models (Buss 1978; Fein 1996; Jones and Davis 1975; Kruglanski 1975; Malle, this volume). A barrier to progress in this regard, however, has been that critics have not agreed on the steps they have emphasized, or on the conceptual distinctions driving their arguments. On a deeper level, social psychologists seem to have lacked a shared language about the perceiver's mental representations of the target's mental representations that would allow a more complex model of attribution.

Interestingly, while social-psychological debate about trait attribution has suffered from the lack of a model of how perceivers represent the mental states of others, developmental-psychological research on children's theories of mind has refined such a model, drawing on frameworks honed over the centuries in the area of philosophical scholarship known as *theory of mind*. Over the past 20 years, the development of a theory of mind in children has become a major research focus for developmental psychologists. Premack and Woodruff (1978) noted that the human concept of mind is theory-like in that mental states are unobservable entities used to predict and explain behavior. Since then, many insights into how young children conceptualize others' mental states and how they use this knowledge to predict and explain behavior have emerged. (See Wellman and Phillips, this volume.) For example, infants under a year old react more positively to displays in which objects move in a manner suggestive of animacy than to displays that do not suggest animacy (Leslie 1982). At a year and a half, they begin using expressed emotions to predict another person's desires (Repacholi and Gopnik 1997). Two-year-olds use information about desires to predict a person's actions and reactions to situations (Wellman and Woolley 1990). By age 4, children are more like adults in that they understand that actions are constrained by the extent to which a person's beliefs about reality correspond to actual situations (Perner 1991).

Intentionality is central both to developmental research on theory of mind and to research on adult attribution processes. An understanding that mental states cause actions necessarily entails perception of others' intentionality, in that an understanding of mental states requires an understanding of how people act on and react to an external, shared reality (Malle 1999). Thus, although the road from acts to dispositions is rocky, it is paved with ascriptions of intentionality. In this chapter, we will explore how the wealth of information about intentionality and mental-state ascription from the theory-of-mind research tradition can inform social-psychological models of trait attribution.

Views of the Road from Acts to Dispositions

Before we address the relationship between mental states and traits, let us review several ways social psychologists have portrayed the cognitive path from observations of another's acts to an attribution. Some models have portrayed social perceivers as fairly *data driven* in that they assign acts to causes on the basis of bottom-up perceptual data about how observable events covary. In their correspondence inference model, Jones and Davis (1965) postulated that an analysis of "noncommon" effects of an action underlies the attribution of a particular intent, and of the particular disposition reflected in that intent, to the actor. In considering why an individual has performed a socially desirable action, for example, a perceiver considers whether the act was constrained by social norms or role requirements, which would favor a "situational attribution." If not, then the act will be attributed to the intent of helping, and ultimately to a disposition of helpfulness. Thus, although Jones and Davis acknowledged that perceivers take an actor's intentions into account, this process was considered by their model to be only a step toward the attribution of dispositions. According to Kelley's (1967) covariation model, perceivers assess the covariation of a behavioral effect with potential causes by checking whether an actor's behavior is distinctive to the particular situation, whether it is consistent across time in that situation, and whether there is a consensus for acting that way in the situation. Other social-psychological models have emphasized ways in which social perceivers are *theory driven* in that they assign acts to causes on the basis of prior knowledge structures. A first wave posited implicit theories or causal schemata to account for why attribution patterns differ depending on the domain of behavior under explanation. Implicit theories that guide attributions in domains such as achievement and wrongdoing were proposed (Kelley 1972; Reeder and Brewer 1979; Weiner 1985). Researchers have also explored the role of knowledge structures such as scripts and goals in person perception and causal understanding (Schank and Abelson 1977). Read and colleagues (Read 1987; Miller and Read 1991), for example, have suggested that perceivers construct scenarios from social and physical knowledge to explain the relations between actions and outcomes. The extended sequences of behavior encoded by these scenarios allow perceivers to make inferences about actors' underlying plans and goals.

A more recent wave has posited individual differences in implicit theories to account for individual differences in attribution. Some have accounted for fine-grained attributional patterns by measuring subjects' causal schemata or theories about specific causal mechanisms (Morris and Larrick 1995; Roese and Morris 1999). Dweck and her associates (Chiu, Hong, and Dweck 1997; Dweck, Chiu, and Hong 1995) postulate a very general difference between individuals who conceptualize others as stable entities or as processes undergoing incremental change. Thus, entity theorists, believing that an individual's personality consists of static, fixed traits, are more likely to use dispositions to predict and explain behavior than are incremental theorists, who view personality as consisting of dynamic qualities that can be changed or developed. In a series of experiments, Chiu, Hong, and Dweck (1997) investigated whether entity and incremental theorists differed in inferential practices thought to be associated with *lay dispositionism* (i.e., the tendency of perceivers to explain behavior in terms of traits; Ross and Nisbett 1991), including viewing behavior as a reflection of an underlying disposition, predicting behavior in a particular situation from knowledge of a relevant trait, and expecting behavior to be consistent across situations. As predicted, they found that entity theorists were much more likely than incremental theorists to engage in all three processes.

A third wave of proposals about implicit theories have accounted for cultural differences in attributional patterns. The prevalent theories in individualist cultures, such as the United States, stress the personal autonomy of individuals and are likely lead to trait attributions for an actor's behavior. In collectivist cultures, such as East Asian Confucian societies, implicit theories stress the role of social structures, such as groups and role relationships, in determining the causes of an actor's behavior. Morris and Peng (1994), for example, found that American and Chinese subjects differed in their explanations for various crimes in that American subjects focused on internal dispositions of the actor whereas Chinese subjects were more likely to point out the social context in which the crime had occurred. The greater tendency of Americans to focus on internal dispositions was specific to their explanations of individuals involved in social as opposed to mechanical causation (Morris, Nisbett, and Peng 1995) and specific to explanations of individuals as actors as opposed to social groups as actors (Menon, Morris, Chiu, and Hong 1999). Further evidence that the differences reflect an implicit theory are findings that cultural differences are magnified under conditions known to accentuate theory-based processing, such as cognitive busyness (Knowles, Morris, Hong, and Chiu 2000), need for closure (Chiu, Morris, Hong, and Menon 2000), and priming (Hong, Morris, Chiu, and Benet-Martínez 2000). An emerging body of findings weighs conclusively in favor of the position that implicit theories, rather than more sweeping differences in motivation or worldview, explain many cultural differences in psychological tendencies. (For reviews, see Menon, Ames and Morris 2001; Morris and Fu, in press; Su, Chiu, Hong, Leung, Peng, and Morris 1999.)

These cultural differences seem likely to be due to differences in implicit theories construed at a cultural level—that is, to learned differences in behavioral norms and the corresponding intentions that are supposed to underlie them. Miller's (1986) research provides empirical support for this notion in that these attributional differences emerge relatively late in development, perhaps as knowledge of norms accrues. Norms, once acquired, are understood as causes of actions and may be used to predict and explain behavior in a variety of settings.

The Role of Intention in the Architecture of Traits

Dimensions of Traits

To ascribe a mental trait to someone, or to explain someone's behavior as resulting from a mental trait, is to make reference to some enduring influence on intentions. However, it is important to point out that this characterization holds true for all uses and senses of the term *trait*. When we attempt to locate the notion of trait within the framework of a theory of mind, it becomes apparent that there are many kinds of traits; put another way, *trait* does not refer to a single kind of entity or process. One of the virtues of recasting traits within a broader framework of theories of mental causation is that it is possible to make some finer-grained distinctions among different types of trait-like behaviors and explanations.

Viewed as a relatively global term, the central significance of a trait seems to be something like an indication of a stable, enduring quality of a person. Whereas trait explanations of behavior place the locus of causation in the individual, situational explanations place the locus of causation in the transitory, specific collection of circumstances obtaining at the moment. In our usage, the situational influences on a person's behavior may be both internal and external. Though situational factors are usually thought of as external, transitory mental states (e.g., passing fancies or momentary urges) may also be thought of as situational in that these mental states arise in specific, transitory contexts. The term *situational*, then, does not in and of itself distinguish between mentalistic causes (such as temporary beliefs and desires) and other kinds of causes (such as physical or biological influences on behavior). Similarly, in a basic sense, the term *trait* is silent about the nature of the causal process involved in some outcome. People talk about biological traits (e.g., blond hair) that may explain outcomes that have no connection to mental states or psychological events; similarly, some researchers (e.g., Buss and Craik 1983; Yuill 1997; Yuill and Pearson 1998) have pointed out that it is possible to conceive of traits solely as summaries of behavioral regularities. On this view, a trait ascription or explanation provides no information about underlying causal processes. In providing an account of trait reasoning based in theories of mind and psychological causation, it is crucial to distinguish psychological senses of *trait* from nonpsychological (or noncausal) senses. Below we discuss research exploring both the development of children's understanding of traits as part of a conception of psychological causation and work aimed as distinguishing psychological traits from nonpsychological traits.

Before considering how theory of mind might explicate the notion of traits, we want to consider another distinction among types of traits. Within those traits identified as involving psychological causation, some trait explanations and ascriptions refer to intentional or voluntary causal sequences; other traits seem to be parts of an involuntary cascade of mental events. Fearfulness, for example, is a trait that operates outside of intentional control; if you are fearful, the appropriate stimuli automatically generate fear. Generosity (or stinginess) is a trait that enters into a chain of voluntary action; no matter how strong the trait of generosity is within an individual, we still credit them with an intentional decision for each act of altruism. One implication is that trait attributions may put the locus of causation within the individual and indicate in this way that the individual was responsible for the action (Weiner, this volume). In a richer, moral sense, however, trait ascriptions differ in their implications for responsibility. A more general point is that the term *trait* might be a rough indicator of a stable influence, but there will have to be further refinements to explicate different sorts of influence.

The notion of traits within theory of mind seems to be "the element or aspect of the mind that biases people toward certain mental states." All sorts of questions about trait attributions (e.g., Why do some people make many trait attributions and other people make few?) will likely require us to understand something more about how people conceive of traits as well as about their role in producing mental states. Most work in theory of mind has focused on conceptions of the mental states that are the efficient causes of behaviors (Astington, this volume; Moses, this volume). To the extent that research has explored conceptions of the distal causes of mental states, the focus has been on perception and inference as sources of belief. The origin of desires, however, seems to lead most directly to the social-psychological notion of traits (Yuill and Pearson 1998), although traits such as "gullible" do seem related to belief. Research is just beginning to explore the ways in which traits might be represented within theories of mind. Later we will review some of that research as an illustration of the application of theory of mind to an important construct within social psychology. As notions of traits are reconstrued in terms of theory of mind, it becomes apparent that *trait* is not a "natural kind" term, as different traits work differently and function in different ways to produce mental states. Only by refining our understanding of theory of mind will we be able to arrive at a typology of traits.

Mental vs. Behavioral Traits

Perception and comprehension of intentions is common ground for theory-of-mind research and for the study of attribution in social psychology in that both disciplines are concerned with how people associate specific behaviors with the internal states of actors. However, it would be rash to suppose that *all* traits are equally mentalistic. Certainly, although "helpful" may dispose one to a desire to help, the belief that one can help, and the intention to help, it does not follow that "clumsy" must also consist of an analogous cluster of mental states. We believe that some traits (e.g., "clumsy") may specify predominantly behavioral, rather than mentalistic, tendencies.

We propose that there are two important classes of traits: *behavioral* and *mental*. Behavioral traits, such as "clumsy" and "nervous," are those underlying unintentional behavior, such as tripping or fidgeting. In contrast, mental traits, such as "generous" and "aggressive," describe dispositions toward certain kinds of behavior guided by particular mental states (such as beliefs and desires) that generate intentional action. In this chapter, we focus our discussion mainly on mental traits as a venue for integrating theory of mind and adult person perception. We adopt a stance of mental traits as theory-like in that these traits, mediated as they are by mental states, function as knowledge structures that encode stable, underlying patterns of mental states and the intentional actions that result from them. Mental-trait ascription, then, is the imputation of stable configurations of the beliefs, desires, plans, and emotions that explain regularities in social behavior.

A model of traits as mediated by mental states such as beliefs and desires is not incompatible with other theory-based or knowledge-structure-based views of traits. One possible explanation of the difference between entity and incremental theorists may be simply that entity theorists are more likely to rely on traits as both a cognitive and a conversational shorthand for intentions, whereas incremental theorists think and speak more directly about the more basic mental states that underlie them. In fact, Chiu, Hong, and Dweck (1997) found empirical evidence for this notion: Incremental theorists were more likely than entity theorists to explain characters' behaviors by referring to "internal psychological states"—e.g., to explain that a character stole "because he was hungry or desperate" (ibid., p. 28). Entity theorists, then, may view individuals as independent, stable beings whose behavior always tends toward the same intentional tendencies; incremental theorists may view the self as more flexible in terms of mental states and behaviors.

Traits and Theories of Mind: Empirical Evidence

Insights from Developmental Psychology

The developmental literature suggests an interesting account of the genesis of trait attributions. Why do children attribute traits in the first place? If we think of traits as theory-of-mind terms, then they may well arise from the same explanatory pressures as other theoretical terms. They may be motivated by what Gopnik (1998) and Schwitzgebel (1997) have called "the explanatory drive." Understanding the mind in terms of occurrent intentional states such as beliefs and desires leaves out an important regularity: Individual actors tend to have recurring beliefs and desires, and these tend to be different from those of other actors. If we want to explain this consistency and variance, simply talking about occurrent beliefs and desires will not do. The theoretical attribution of traits does have some explanatory power, even if we may sometimes overestimate that power (as in other cases of theoretical attribution). Just as we think that children develop a notion of representational belief (and indeed perhaps of belief, tout court) in order to explain regularities in intentional action, so they may later develop a notion of traits as a way of explaining these regularities in individual actors.

An interesting fact in this context is that trait attribution in children seems to blossom in the school-age period, after belief-desire psychology has been established. An important ecological difference between preschoolers and school-age children is a new concern for peers and for peer-group relations (even in cultures without formal schooling). In the context of a family, individual differences may best be explained by roles: Mom does this; big brothers do something else. But members of a peer group typically share similar socially defined roles: We are all third graders together. Explaining consistent individual differences in beliefs and desires among peers requires something more like a trait concept. One might hypothesize that this helps drive the development of trait concepts in this age range.

A theory of personality traits is likely a refinement of a more rudimentary theory of mind that associates the causal relationship between simple mental states, such as beliefs, desires, plans, and emotions, with simple behaviors. Later in development, as children work out the basics about minds in general, they can begin to perceive the finer distinctions between individual minds that lead to unique and complex behavior patterns for different individuals. A coherent understanding of personality is thus likely to follow a coherent understanding of how intentions commonly function in people.

If the use of traits to predict and explain behavior stems from a theory we have of ourselves and others, we may expect to see changes in how traits are used as that theory is enriched through experience with the causal relationship between intentions and behaviors. We may expect a period in development, for example, before a theory of traits has been established, during which traits either are not used or are used infrequently for attributions of behavior. With increasing abilities to abstract information, children's uses of traits might also be predicted to shift from a focus on more concrete features of persons (such as height) to more abstract features of persons (such as shyness) over the course of development. Certain trait terms, such as good/bad and smart/not smart, may be more likely to appear earlier in children's lexicon simply because of salience or transparency of meaning. Finally, if trait understanding is based on a theory of minds and persons, we may expect cultural differences in those theories and thus in how traits are used to explain behavior. In this section, we review evidence addressing these points, with particular emphasis on mental traits and the mediation of these traits by mental states such as beliefs and desires.

Increasing Dispositionism over the Course of Development

If mental traits presuppose knowledge of how intentional actions are mediated by beliefs and desires, we may expect a period in development during which this knowledge is impeded by a lack of experience with integration of intentions and behaviors. During this period, a theory of traits may be not yet established or may be under active construction. In accordance with this view, developmental research suggests that an understanding of underlying dispositions does not begin to emerge until around age 7 (Ruble and Dweck 1995).

One method that has been used to study trait understanding asks children to predict a character's behavior in a novel situation on the basis of the character's behavior in a past situation. If children believe that information about a person's traits or dispositions can be used to predict behavior, they will use that information to predict the behavior in a new scenario. Gnepp and Chilamkurti (1988) presented kindergarten, second-grade, fourth-grade, and college students with a series of stories that described three examples of a character's past behavior from which a personality trait could be inferred. In addition to predicting the character's future behavior, subjects were also asked to predict and explain the character's emotional reaction to a new event. They found an increase with age in the use of personality attributions to predict and explain behavior, and an increasing tendency to use trait information to predict emotional responses. Similarly, Rholes and Ruble (1984) found an increase with age between 5 and 9 years in consistent behavior predictions: Although younger children recognize and use the appropriate trait term for a given behavior, they are less likely to generalize the behavior to new situations. Thus, although trait terms may be used at an early age to label behavior, this does not seem to suggest an understanding of traits in terms of stable, underlying mental states.

A study by Aloise (1993) using a *confirmability paradigm*, in which subjects were asked how many instances of a particular behavior they would require before attributing a trait to an actor, suggests that adults use traits to explain behavior more quickly and with more facility than do children. She found that younger subjects (grades 3–5) set higher attribution criteria than did college-age subjects along trait dimensions such as *smart–dumb*, *polite–rude*, *gentle–rough*, and *messy–neat*. Aloise (1993) concluded that the developmental decrease in the number of instances of behavior required for trait ascription is due to the fact that younger children have not had as much experience in noting the behavioral consistencies of individuals.

Young children may simply lack experience at noting any kinds of consistency. Ongoing research by Kalish (1999) suggests that reluctance to make dispositional attributions is not a global feature of children's causal reasoning but is rather a reflection of children's beliefs about the ways human behavior is caused. Young children do predict consistent outcomes for nonpsychological events; for example, they expect that a person will have the same sensory capacities from occasion to occasion. However, consistent with the results described above, not until about age 7 do children predict consistency in people's voluntary behaviors (e.g., choices), such as expecting that a person who chose a blue toy in the past will choose a blue one again in the future. Moreover, the younger children are not simply random in their responses. They show a marked tendency to predict that a person will behave differently on different occasions; that is, they ascribe complementarity rather than consistency. Kalish (1999) argues this "anti-dispositional" responding is consistent with a causal model in which people act intentionally and are wont to change their minds. Importantly for our argument, the development of trait attributions does not seem to be accounted for by general changes in causal reasoning. Rather, it is children's changing appreciation of the causes of human behavior that underlies changes in trait ascription.

Criteria for Trait Ascription Shift over Time

Changes in how children use traits to predict and explain behavior verify that traits exist as theory-like structures subject to updating and to revision in light of new data. As children become more concerned with underlying mental states and intentional actions and less concerned with physical appearance and overt behavior, we may expect an "update" to a theory of personality traits in that traits become differentiated into the two classes of traits proposed by our model: those determined by behavior alone (which lead to unintentional action) and those mediated by mental states (which lead to intentional action). Support for this notion comes from a study by Livesley and Bromley (1973), who found that before age 8 children are much more likely to refer to *peripheral*, perceptually salient features of appearance and behavior when asked for open-ended descriptions of themselves, whereas after age 8 children are more likely to focus on *central* features such as personality traits, motives, and needs. Before age 7 or 8, then, it may be that children have yet to perceive stabilities in individuals' mental states and intentional actions.

An ongoing study by Rosati (2000) provides further evidence that the criteria for trait ascription appear to shift over the course of development from a focus on overt behavior to a focus on underlying mental states. When subjects are presented with a story character whose behavior conflicts with their desires, 5-year-olds and 6-year-olds ascribe to that character a personality trait that is based on the character's overt behavior. Younger subjects thus ascribe the trait "nice" to a character who perform good deeds even if the character harbors mean thoughts. By age 9 or 10, subjects more often cite underlying mental states in their ascriptions of personality traits to characters (Rosati 2000).

Domain Specificity in Trait Understanding Increases with Age

Ruble and Dweck (1995) review evidence suggesting that when children younger than 7 use dispositions to explain behavior, those dispositions tend to be characterized by domain-general goodness or badness. Five-year-olds and 6-year-olds who receive criticism for failure at a task, for example, are likely to conclude that they are bad, rather than that they are not smart (as older children conclude) (ibid.). Early trait concepts thus appear to consist of only a few general categories that are likely very familiar or salient to children. One explanation of these findings, suggested by Rholes, Newman, and Ruble (1990), is that young children's trait terms do not imply the same internal, causal structure that the same trait terms imply for older children and adults but rather exist as a global, evaluative category system based on general valence and on whether the terms have a positive or negative impact on the child.

Cultural Divergence in Trait Ascription Occurs at a Specific Point in Development

If traits are governed by knowledge structures that develop through increasing experience with intention and behavior, we would expect differences in the use of those structures to predict and explain behaviors in cultures that provide very different experiences of associations of intention and behavior. Miller's (1986) research provides support for a theory model of traits in that American and Hindu Indian subjects became differentiated in attributional patterns over the course of development. In her study, 8-, 11-, and 15-year-old American and Indian subjects were asked to provide examples of pro-social and socially deviant behavior. She found that, when asked to explain an agent's behavior, the youngest subjects in both cultures preferred concrete, instance-oriented social concepts that required minimal abstraction and inference as the causes of behavior. Over time, American subjects became more oriented toward dispositions as causes of behavior; Indian subjects became more likely to refer to situations (often social contexts) as the sources of an agent's behavior. The fact that children in very different cultures appear to reason similarly about the causes of behavior, and to diverge with respect to their preferred stated causes only in later childhood, provides further support for a notion of theory-like traits that govern, and are in turn governed by, specific social and cultural interactions.

In sum, though even young preschoolers demonstrate an understanding of how mental states such as desires and beliefs can cause a person to act and behave in specific ways (Wellman and Woolley 1990), children do not seem to infer dispositions toward particular mental states and their subsequent behaviors before they are about 8 years old. We may posit, then, that understanding of mental states and intentional action in early childhood is limited to general tendencies of persons and to singular cause-and-effect relations between particular mental states and particular behaviors. Increasing use of personality traits to explain behavior and increasing abstraction provide support for the notion of a change in theory of mind in later childhood. This theoretical shift encompasses the understanding that individual minds tend to have particular patterns of mental states and that these patterns of mental states, as encoded by personality traits, affect and govern a wide range of behaviors.

Adult Folk Theories of Personality Traits

Having charted the development of mentalistic trait conceptions in children, we now turn to evidence from the "endpoint" of development. Specifically, we review social-psychological evidence that adults' trait ascriptions constitute ascriptions of constellations of mental states and thus reflect the application of a theory of mind.

Some Traits Are Consensually Mentalistic in Meaning

Despite the enormous amount of social-psychological research exploring the conditions under which individuals explain the behavior of others in terms of traits, few researchers have examined what traits actually mean to people. If our present thesis is correct—if some traits encode underlying patterns of mental states—then the onus is on us to "unpack" adults' traits conceptions and show that they are mentalistic after all. Although to show that adults construe at least some traits as having mental, intentional content is crucial to our present aims, we may also consider a diversity of trait conceptions in which not every trait is mentalistic. If traits are theory-like, and thus defeasible and domain specific, it is natural to expect that not all traits will be equally mentalistic in content.

In ongoing work, Knowles and Ames (2000b) have uncovered suggestive evidence that some frequently used folk traits are heavily mentalistic, and that most are at least partly mentalistic. These researchers began by collecting a sample of the most-used trait terms among various populations, including college-age students and adults. Another group of participants rated the extent to which knowing that a target had each trait would allow two kinds of predictions: the individuals' future actions (behavioral predictions), and future thoughts (mentalistic predictions). Results suggested that certain traits (e.g., "rude") support predominantly behavioral predictions and other traits (e.g., "honest") support predominantly mentalistic predictions. Moreover, there was substantial interjudge agreement as to which kind of predictions a given trait supported.

Some Perceivers Have a Proclivity for Mentalistic Construal of Traits

In addition to discovering diversity among trait terms, such that some are more mentalistic in character than others, Knowles and Ames (ibid.) found reliable differences in perceivers' proclivities for these different modes of construal. The researchers administered an individual difference measure of the tendency toward mentalistic vs. behavioral interpretation of behavior. Items measured both mentalism (e.g., "When I try to figure people out, I try to learn what they think, not just what they do") and behavioralism (e.g., "I care more about what someone does than what they think"). This measure was found to predict subjects' ratings concerning the degree to which given traits supported predictions of behavior vs. predictions of mental states.

Trait Ascription Reflects the Mentalistic Content of Traits

As Knowles and Ames (ibid.) have shown, the nature of many trait terms is at least partly mentalistic. This and other developmental theory-of-mind work (e.g., Rosati 2000) suggests that mental-state inferences must play an important role in impression formation. Ames (2000b) has shown that the route from observed behaviors to trait inference is often mediated by judgments about a target's mental states.

Ames (ibid.) found that mental-state inferences mediate the "road" from acts to disposition inferences in a range of cases. In one set of studies, perceivers reviewed a variety of ambiguous events (e.g., a student helping a professor with a broken bicycle, an office worker being singled out for credit after explaining his work team's ideas to his superior) and imputed wide-ranging belief, desire, and emotion states to actors. These behaviors were varied slightly between participants (e.g., a "helping" student repeatedly reminding his professor of his name versus not mentioning it at all), and the resulting mental-state inferences mediated the impact of behaviors on global impressions. The same pattern of mediation emerged in actual interaction in pairs of participants. When two strangers got to know each other, the effect of one partner's perceptions of the other partner's behaviors on his or her general impressions of the partner was entirely mediated by judgments of the partner's beliefs and desires. In another study, in which videos of real-life blind dates were used, and female participants formed impressions of the men on the dates. In various cases, some of the men's socially desirable behaviors (e.g., joking, self-disclosure, listening intently) were omitted; in other cases, socially undesirable behaviors (e.g., taking the date to a strip club) were omitted. These behaviors had a dramatic effect on impressions and trait ascriptions, but this effect was entirely mediated by judgments about the mental states of the actor. In sum, as developmental theory-of-mind scholarship would predict, adult impression formation relies heavily on inferences about actors' mental states.

Conclusions

We have attempted to show that personality-trait inference, one of the areas of greatest interest in social psychology, can be enriched by one of the most fruitful research traditions in developmental psychology: theory of mind. The link, we have argued, stems from the fact that the everyday trait conceptions studied by social psychologists encode the underlying mental states and intentional actions that have long been the focus of theory-of-mind research. In terms of Jones's metaphor, intentions pave "the rocky road from acts to dispositions." That is, perceiving good intentions or bad intentions is a key step in attributing a positive or negative personality trait. We have reviewed developmental and social-psychological evidence that suggests that the development of personality-trait conceptions appears to parallel the development of theory-of-mind abilities, and that children's use of traits exhibits properties (i.e., defeasibility, cultural variation, and domain specificity) that one would expect if, indeed, trait conceptions are theory-like. In the social-psychological sphere, we have presented preliminary but suggestive evidence that folk trait conceptions have mentalistic content, and that the process of trait ascription reflects this content. We believe that this fundamental continuity between theory of mind and folk conceptions of traits, largely unacknowledged by both research traditions, is a rich resource for all future studies of person perception, regardless of the age of our subjects.

Acknowledgments

We would like to thank Bertram Malle for many helpful comments on previous drafts. Chuck Kalish's work on this manuscript was supported by a grant from the Spencer Foundation.

IV
Intentionality and Responsibility In Social Context

15

The Social Folk Theorist: Insights from Social and Cultural Psychology on the Contents and Contexts of Folk Theorizing

Daniel R. Ames, Eric D. Knowles, Michael W. Morris,
Charles W. Kalish, Andrea D. Rosati, and Alison Gopnik

The question of how a person makes sense of others' behavior—how a perceiver of action judges such things as intentionality, causality, and responsibility—is central to many areas of study. Much work in social and developmental psychology addresses such questions of perception and judgment, as does scholarship in various parts of philosophy, jurisprudence, organizational behavior, and game theory. In most cases, the perceiver is portrayed as something of a lone, semi-rational folk scientist drawing conclusions in a fairly deliberate fashion from everyday theories and from the data of an isolated actor's observable behavior. This perceiver-as-scientist metaphor has been invoked in models of how observers assess one another's personalities, how negotiators consider strategic moves, how jurors decide guilt, how managers appraise employees, and a host of other forms of social inference.

Although such a description of ordinary social judgment is certainly fruitful, and perhaps necessary in some sense, it has tended to leave several important aspects of everyday perception unexplored. Notably, its seems clear that folk scientists are themselves enmeshed in social contexts that shape their thinking. Status demands, for instance, affect who pays attention to whom and for what reason. Likewise, conversational audiences affect what judgments are produced and how they are framed. Yet not only are folk scientists themselves enmeshed in social contexts; their ordinary theories reflect such social phenomena. Perceivers make use of information on group membership in judging actors, and they understand behavior in light of obligations attached to social roles. Further, perceivers often make important judgments about groups as social entities, assigning praise to a team or responsibility to a corporation. Thus, the image of a lone folk scientist laboring to make sense of a single agent's behavior is helpful but incomplete in its recognition of social context as it surrounds the perceiver and as it is reflected in the perceiver's folk theories.

In this chapter, we review insights from social and cultural psychology that both confirm and expand the perceiver-as-scientist view. First, we discuss how folk theories reflect social contexts as perceivers use them to understand groups, acknowledge norms, and perform other feats of inference that reflect a social world beyond a single target of perception. The implication is that scholars of social judgment should be inclined to ascribe such social theories—a folk sociology, or a folk social psychology—to ordinary perceivers. Second, we address how folk scientists perform in social contexts, examining important interpersonal factors (including roles and interaction goals) and the intrapersonal mechanisms they affect. Here, we portray the folk scientist as concerned not only with truth but also with adaptive, pragmatic action in the social world. In the third section, we explore the role of culture as it relates to both of the other themes. Perceivers are members of cultures, and cultures shape folk theories and folk theorizing. The image that emerges from these three related collections of observations is that of the *social* folk theorist—the perceiver as a folk scientist embedded in social context and invoking folk theories of the social world.

Before we review selected research, though, let us briefly clarify our perspective. In chapter 14, we tried to bring insights from developmental theory of mind[1] to social psychology. This chapter is an effort to bring relevant social-psychological observations to developmental psychology and other traditions. We recognize, though, that other disciplines have aims that differ from those of social psychology, and we don't propose abandoning them. Instead, we suggest that a variety of fields concerned with social judgment can benefit in their own aims from the insights described here into how folk theories reflect, and are put to work in, social context.

We also note that the literature of social psychology is extremely pluralist, perhaps too much so, in its approach to social inference. Various scholars study attribution, trait ascription, stereotyping, impression formation, assessments of responsibility, blaming, account giving, explanations, and a variety of other kinds of social judgments. These literatures are often isolated from one another, and for the most part they do not treat these phenomena from the perspective of theory of mind or intentionality. Still, ideas and findings can be culled from all these areas that bear on questions of folk theorizing and the perception of intentionality. At the heart of all these judgments are inferences about the mental properties of others: explaining, forming impressions, and assigning responsibility are all close cousins, connected by the ability of perceivers to make inferences about others' minds. Thus, this chapter borrows from a wide range of research traditions, but it does so in the service of examining the contents of folk theories of mind and the contexts in which those theories are put to use.

Folk Theories Reflect Social Contexts: The Role of Groups and Norms in Social Inference

One way social psychology can inform theory-of-mind research is by extending the range of explanatory entities scholars ascribe to folk perceivers in social sense making. Theory-of-mind scholarship has focused almost entirely on folk-psychological conceptions of the minds of *individuals*. Moreover, it has focused on a particular set of such abstract entities, particularly beliefs, desires, perceptions, and emotions. These individual mental states, however, do not exhaust the concepts perceivers use in explaining human action.

The literatures of social and cultural psychology point to other explanatory concepts that are equally abstract but very different from the usual apparatus of belief-desire psychology. In particular, they suggest that people often explain behavior in terms of *groups* rather than individuals—that is, people give explanations that rely on groups as agents and also explain the actions of individuals in light of their group memberships. Perceivers have a folk sociology or a folk social psychology in addition to a folk cognitive psychology, a folk motivational psychology, and a folk affective psychology. Social-psychological work also suggests that perceivers often explain action in terms of deontic concepts such as rules and norms. In explaining why a person commits some action, perceivers may say "She was obliged to" or "He promised he would." Such explanations clearly rely on theory of mind, but they may reveal a distinct mode of inference that should not be reduced to individualistic belief-desire psychology. In the following sections, we take up this issue of deontic concepts and also

examine how folk theorists deal with groups and with the social contexts
of targets.

Groups, Group Members, and Construal of the Agent

A notion like group identity is described by developmental-theory-of-mind
scholars, and some trace it to the very beginning of development. Various
scholars have suggested that an infant's first conception of minds may be
supra-individual (Gopnik and Meltzoff 1997). At the start, infants may
have a notion of group mental states, although the group may only be the
dyad of "me and the one I love." Psychologists point to a variety of fine-
grained communicative interactions and conversational dances that take
place between infants and caregivers as evidence for such a supra-individual conception. Gopnik and Meltzoff (1997) have argued, in particular, that
the phenomenon of early imitation is both evidence for such an early social
conception of the mind and a mechanism in establishing it.

Nevertheless, the progress in theory of mind in the developmental literature has largely been conceived of as a move away from these early, more
nearly all-embracing views to views that recognize individual variation and
difference. Meanwhile, the perception of groups has stood out as a major
topic of active study in social psychology for the discipline's entire history.
This tradition has featured considerable research examining the role of stereotypes and social-category information in social inference; judgments about
groups themselves as agents have also been an important focus of study.

Stereotyping and Social Categories

A schoolboy walks down a crowded hall and clips another young man
with his shoulder, sending him lurching forward. An accident, a playful
bump, or a menacing shove? The question turns on perceived intention.
As a long tradition of experiments from the classic work of Floyd Allport
to the more recent research of Sagar and Schofield (1980) has shown, perceivers use social-category information in answering it. Acts such as
ambiguous shoves are interpreted as substantially more threatening when
they are performed, all else equal, by blacks rather than whites—an effect,
Sagar and Schofield demonstrate, that holds for both black and white perceivers. Even though these authors don't frame the findings in theory-of-
mind terms, it can sensibly be concluded that the inference of intentions

underlying such ambiguous behaviors is at least partly driven by the group membership of agents. Perceivers' stereotypes shape their inferences of an agent's mental states.

A number of social psychologists offer models of person perception that highlight the role of social-category information in inference. Many of these models are cast as theories of stereotyping. (For a recent review, see Fiske 1998.) Taylor's (1981) categorization theory, for instance, argues that information tagged by distinctions such as race and gender guides stereotypic interpretation of behaviors, ultimately leading to exaggeration of between-group differences and minimization of differences within the in-group. Brewer (1988) proposed a dual-process model in which perceivers rely initially on category information in judging persons and later, if time and resources permit, revise that impression with individuating information. However, stereotypes are involved in more than just general impressions (such as "he is aggressive"). Many studies (e.g., von Hippel, Sekaquaptewa, and Vargas 1995) have shown that stereotypes guide basic attention, perception, and encoding early on in the interpretation of behavior. Surely such stereotype-driven (i.e., theory-driven) construals have consequences for inferences of intentional states. The perceiver's journey from witnessing ordinary behaviors to inferring underlying intentions may often be routed, perhaps implicitly and automatically, through social-category stereotypes.

Judgments about Groups

The targets of social judgments are not always individuals. Perceivers often make inferences at the group level—for instance, that a family is happy, or that a comedy troupe is perverse. A person may judge that a team of company executives is liable, or that a group of bystanders bears some responsibility for the outcome of an accident. People may even ascribe mental qualities to groups, saying that a collection of persons "felt," "remembered," "believed," or "wanted" something. All these judgments rely heavily on folk psychology, often leveraging folk theory-of-mind concepts and applying them at the group level.

Emerging work by Lickel and others sheds light on the qualities of groups that underlie how folk psychology is applied to them (Lickel, Hamilton, Wieczorkowska, Lewis, Sherman, and Uhles 2000). Central to the application of an intentional stance to a group is the group's interdependence—the degree of interpersonal interaction among group members. Importantly, different kinds of groups achieve different levels of interdependence. For instance, intimacy groups (small, impermeable, long-lasting groups, such as families or circles of friends) often have higher levels of interdependence than social categories (which typically are large, long-lasting, and impermeable collections of people such as ethnic groups). Accordingly, folk perceivers are more willing to ascribe intentional terms such as "decided," "planned," and "wanted" to intimacy groups than to social categories (Lickel, Hamilton, and Sherman 1999). Lickel and his colleagues have also shown that many of the same qualities that lead to mentalistic descriptions of groups also support judgments of responsibility for groups: the more a group is seen as interdependent, the more folk perceivers are willing to assign responsibility to the group as a whole (Lickel, Schmader, and Hamilton 2000).

Inferring the attitudes and intentions of groups appears to rely on the same strategies used for inferring individual mental states: simulation/projection (Goldman 1989; Goldman, this volume) and theorizing (Gopnik and Wellman 1992). Ames (2000a) shows that each of these strategies has a role in the inference of beliefs and desires at the group level and the population level. Similarity theories guide how social projection—akin to simulation—is used. Perceivers who believe they are highly similar to a given group show a willingness to project their own beliefs and desires into their predictions of that group's beliefs and desires. Such belief-driven projection occurs whether or not the group is actually similar to the perceiver on the given stances. Further, when perceivers are led to consider how they are dissimilar from a target group, their use of social projection declines. Meanwhile, evaluative theories about groups help guide the inference of favorable and unfavorable attitudes. For instance, when Berkeley students inferred the frequency among Stanford students of a desire for money and power over companionship and affection (widely seen as an unfavorable attitude), they drew on their idiosyncratic beliefs about the goodness of Stanford students—in a word, their stereotypes. In short, perceivers infer the intentions and attitudes of social groups through a combination of simulation/projection and theorizing—an application of theory of mind to the group level.

Social Norms and Construal of Action

Agents are also judged in terms of identities that are relevant to social codes or rules of conduct (Schlenker 1997, Schlenker, Britt, Pennington, Murphy, and Doherty 1994). These rules have a deontic character; that is, they involve obligations, rights, and norms for proper behavior. For example, John is perceived not just as an individual but as a member of a particular group (e.g., an American citizen, a male). In addition to whatever dispositions such memberships might indicate, they lead us to see the individual as embedded in a deontic network including formal rights and obligations (e.g., those related to citizenship) and more implicit social norms (such as those related to gender stereotypes). For example, by virtue of his social identity, John has the right to vote, but he shouldn't wear a dress. Perceivers rely on such deontic considerations in their inferences and explanations.

For social psychologists, explaining social judgments in terms of agents' conceptions of social rules, norms, and obligations is commonplace. Less attention is given to how folk perceivers use such concepts in their lay explanations. Meanwhile, deontic considerations have been largely absent from accounts of developing theories of mind. This work has instead focused on individual-level representational explanations. Perceivers are seen as explaining a given agent's behavior by positing intentional states of the agent that are largely endogenous (that is, springing from within). Why did Julie go to the store? Because she had some desires and beliefs: she wanted milk and believed there was some at the store.

However, such a theoretical vocabulary of representational states does not fully capture deontic concerns. Why did Julie go to the store? A deontic explanation might be that her mother told her to. In some sense, this is intentional in that Julie is not an automaton: she *believed* her mother told her to go to the store, and she *wanted* to abide by her mother. Yet it seems worthwhile to recognize the uniquely social nature of these intentions. Folk inferences and explanations at the deontic level require a model of perceivers' recognizing others beyond the particular target agent—persons, groups, and societies that demand or prohibit certain kinds of behavior. Indeed, such contextual thinking could be seen in terms of Malle's (1999; this volume) model of folk intentional explanation, which highlights "reasons" (e.g., Al smiled at George because he wanted to be nice) and "causal history of reasons" (e.g., Al smiled at George because George was nice to him). Deontic explanations could be seen as a special kind of causal history of reason that is *someone else's* reason: Al smiled at George because his mother wanted him to be nice . . . and, it might go without saying, Al was compelled to do what his mother wanted him to do. The someone else in this case could be a particular person or a group or society as a whole. Thus, deontic explanations often take the form of a target adopting an intention that is someone else's (or some other collective's) intention.

Deontic reasoning about targets, then, is a kind of intentional inference invoking social context. Deontic concepts and intentions could be seen as different *stances* for viewing and explaining action (Dennett 1987). A question naturally arises about the conditions under which people engage in one or the other of these stances in their judgments and accounts. Past research suggests a number of possible factors: Norm-consistent behavior evokes deontic explanation, rule violations evoke intentional explanation; deontic reasoning is directed at familiar agents, intentional reasoning at strangers; deontic reasoning is used for the self, intentional reasoning for others (one way of describing the much-studied "actor/observer effect"). Further, perspectives from cultural psychology suggest that people may differ in the degree to which different forms of explanation are chronically accessible. Mental-state explanations may be more salient or may demand fewer cognitive resources in some cultures; deontic explanations may be preferred in other cultures.

Emerging developmental work is examining how deontic concepts are used in social thinking and the relationship between the deontic and intentional stances among children. Kalish (1998) has explored young children's understanding of the psychological processes involved in following a rule. When adults employ deontic explanations, they may implicitly assume that certain psychological events are occurring in the agent. Kalish's work suggests that developments within theory of mind may constrain children's appreciation of the psychological bases of social behavior. Young children may not apprehend the intentions underlying deontic constraints, such as an agent's awareness of a norm. Kalish and colleagues have also examined children's understanding of how social rules (as distinct from physical laws) are established. Kalish, Weissman, and Bernstein (in press) suggest that young children's conceptions of epistemic relations—the connections between representation and reality—limits their ability to understand some kinds of stipulations.

If theory of mind is to provide a full account of explanation, prediction, and judgment of behavior, it will have to expand its focus beyond issues of representation to include the study of the psychological states and processes that underlie deontic relationships. Although it may be the case that deontic explanations are "reducible" to intentional ones, treating them as synonymous in models of folk psychology omits important contextual components: norms and prohibitions, and the persons, groups, and societies that establish them. Theory-of-mind models could profit from embedding targets of folk explanation in social contexts of norms and obligations.

Folk Scientists Perform in Social Contexts: Interpersonal Factors and Intrapersonal Mechanisms

The topic of social sense making (how everyday perceivers understand the social world) has attracted different academic disciplines for different reasons. Social psychologists (e.g., Fritz Heider, Gustav Ichheiser, and Harold Kelley) were drawn to the topic of social inference in order to understand its consequences—the ways individuals respond to one another in interactions.[2] Accordingly, the notion of perceiver as scientist has been qualified to capture the role of inference as an expedient guide to practical action. For example, perceivers do not ascribe intentions to a potential aggressor out of detached interest in the truth; rather, intention inferences are relevant to judgments such as the assignment of responsibility, which, in turn, lays the groundwork for *actions* such as blaming, punishing, avoiding and so forth.

This emphasis on inference in the service of pragmatic action has led to various other metaphors, including viewing perceivers as lawyers (Hamilton 1980) and as politicians (Tetlock 1991). Further, the emphasis on consequences of social judgment has led to a concern for lapses in decision making and inference. Social psychologists are often drawn to the fallibilities of perceivers, such as stereotyping, overly dispositional attributions, and the effect of self-enhancement motives on reasoning. As a result, social psychologists have spent much research effort examining contextual drivers of performance rather than focusing on performance in contexts that enable participants to show their best judgment and competence.

Developmental psychologists, meanwhile, pursue somewhat different aims and accordingly adopt a different stance toward perceivers. Developmentalists have often studied the child's theory of mind (Wellman 1990; Gopnik and Meltzoff 1997) with an emphasis on understanding how human abilities unfold. These scholars often focus on documenting children's growing *competence* rather than tracking their everyday *performance* at social sense making. Developmental research on theory of mind often centers on what children at a given age are capable of at their finest moments (e.g., do 3- year-olds "have" a theory of mind?). Accordingly, research designs are crafted to facilitate the child's making use of the most elaborate theory that he or she possesses; there are few distractions and no tempting shortcuts. Major theory rivalries in developmental theory-of-mind work tend to be addressed by examining the timing, order, and breadth of emerging competencies rather than examining the effects of context on social inference performance.

In this section, we review selected social-psychological findings on how context affects the performance of social inference, focusing on two sets of context considerations: intrapersonal and interpersonal. Although our emphasis is on contexts, we begin by reviewing cognitive and motivational intrapersonal mechanisms. These are the proximal factors through which distal social contexts have their consequences; examining them points the way toward important context issues. We then move on to consider factors such as interaction goals and audiences.

Intrapersonal Factors
Social-cognitive psychologists have identified a number of intrapersonal factors that influence how perceivers weigh evidence and make use of knowledge when making inferences about others. In particular, researchers have investigated how various cognitive and motivational factors promote the use of *heuristic* versus *systematic* inference processes (Chaiken, Liberman, and Eagly 1989; Chaiken and Trope 1999). In heuristic processing, perceivers reason in a "top down" fashion from existing knowledge structures, such as crude generalizations or stereotypes, to infer traits or other qualities of a target person. This is often seen as a default kind of inference that requires little effort. In systematic, "bottom-up" processing, perceivers weigh a wider range of evidence (e.g., situational determinants

of the target's behavior, or the target's stereotype-inconsistent behavior) before reaching a conclusion about the target. This is generally regarded as a more effortful process and sometimes seen as a "correction" of initial heuristic inferences. However, it would be wrong to equate the heuristic/systematic distinction with notions of theory use and theory non-use. Both kinds of inferences tend to rely on some kinds of theories. Systematic processing seems to imply that an individual uses a broader range of theories, building on a broader range of evidence. Heuristic processing might be seen as reliance on less nuanced inferences based on scant evidence and cruder theories.

Cognitive Factors Influencing Heuristic vs. Systematic Processing

The primary cognitive factor influencing the use of heuristic versus systematic processing in social inference is *cognitive load*—that is, the degree to which a perceiver's attentional resources have been usurped by other mental tasks. Heuristic processes, because they represent relatively simple inferences from pre-existing beliefs, require less attention and effort to perform than do systematic processes. Thus, relatively resource-intensive systematic processes are particularly susceptible to disruption under high cognitive load.

Much of the evidence on this topic comes from studies of attitude inference. Gilbert, Pelham, and Krull (1988), for instance, asked perceivers to infer a target's attitude with regard to a controversial political topic from a speech given by the target. Gilbert et al. found that cognitively loaded perceivers made stronger inferences about the target's attitudes and tended to ignore evidence about constraints on the target (i.e., alternative explanations for the act). Sapped of attentional resources, these "busy" perceivers were unable to perform the systematic processing necessary to temper their attitude inferences and instead relied on a less effortful heuristic that people's behavior accurately reflects their dispositions.[3]

Cognitive load has been shown to increase reliance on stereotypes, and discourage the use of systematic processing, in other social judgments as well. Pendry and Macrae (1994), for instance, asked participants to form impressions of a woman based on passages describing her behavior, some of which contradicted participants' gender stereotypes. As in the attribution work described above, participants in a high-cognitive-load condition were less likely to "individuate" the target woman by considering her unique evidence. Cognitive load also appears to increase stereotypic information processing in other domains, such as age (Perry, Kulik, and Bourhis 1996) and race (Gordon and Anderson 1995).

Motivational Factors Influencing Heuristic vs. Systematic Processing
Motivation can affect the use of heuristic and systematic processes. A primary instance is accuracy motivation, the extent to which a perceiver is motivated to reach an accurate social judgment (Darke, Chaiken, Bohner, Einwiller, Erb, and Hazelwood 1998). Because they are insensitive to much of the information relevant to social inference, heuristic processes are more prone to error than systematic processes. Thus, accuracy-motivated perceivers should be more willing to expend the attention and effort required to perform social inference using systematic routes.

Various factors may increase or decrease perceivers' accuracy motivation. For instance, individuals high in need for cognitive closure may sacrifice an accurate inference for a quick and final one (Webster and Kruglanski 1994). Indeed, Dijksterhuis, van Knippenberg, Kruglanski, and Shaper (1996) found that participants high in "need for closure" were less willing to engage in the systematic process of attending to stereotype-inconsistent information when making inferences about properties of a group. In contrast, individuals high in "need for cognition," or the proclivity for elaborate information processing, tended to seek accurate inferences. Perceivers high in need for cognition do in fact expend more effort and engage in more systematic information processing than perceivers low in need for cognition (Cacioppo, Petty, and Morris 1983; Cacioppo and Petty 1982). Finally, "outcome dependency"—the extent to which the perceiver has a personal stake in reaching a correct inference—shapes accuracy motivation and helps determine which inference processes are employed. In studies of attribution (Vonk 1999) and stereotyping (Pendry and Macrae 1994), individuals who believe that they are in some way dependent on reaching a correct impression of a target (e.g., by the prospect of interacting with the target in the future) engage in more systematic processing and less heuristic thinking.

Intrapersonal factors such as cognitive load and motivation have a considerable impact on social judgment. Moreover, they draw attention to contextual aspects that might affect them—e.g., which kinds of situations increase cognitive load, or which contextual aspects increase need for closure. Developmental psychologists concerned with the use of theory of mind would do well to consider these factors, both as potential experimental confounds and as real-world phenomena shaping social judgment.

Interpersonal Factors

Factors in the structure of social interactions, such as power relationships, status, and conversational roles, exert an important influence on social inference by virtue of their effect on the cognitive and motivational variables discussed above. Social psychologists have revealed a number of important considerations about the contexts of lay scientists.

Interaction Role and Goals

Gilbert, Pelham, and Krull (1988) suggest that perceivers who are actively engaged in social interaction ("active perceivers") are, by virtue of this role, more cognitively loaded than perceivers who merely observe another's behavior ("passive perceivers"). Thus, active perceivers should be more likely to engage in heuristic processing and less likely to engage in systematic processing than passive perceivers. Evidence for this come from a pair of studies by Gilbert, Jones, and Pelham (1987), who found that perceivers given the active role of influencing their interaction partner performed less situational discounting (a systematic process) and made stronger dispositional attributions (a heuristic process) than their partners. A host of other researchers have examined interaction goals and find a variety of effects on person perception (Hilton, Fiske, Snyder, and Nisbett 1998), particularly centered on questions of expectancy confirmation.

Power

Another influential factor in the structure of social interaction is the perceiver's power and status relationship with respect to the target. Defining power as the ability to control another's fate, Susan Fiske (1993) suggested routes through which powerful individuals are led to perform more heuristic and less systematic processing than their subordinates. Individuals in positions of power (e.g., managers) have less of a personal stake in arriving at accurate impressions of their subordinates (e.g., employees, over whose fates managers exert more control than vice versa). In contrast, subordinates are highly outcome dependent in their impressions of their superiors. As we noted earlier, outcome dependency promotes systematic processing, so it is natural to expect lack of power over targets to increase the amount of systematic processing in social inference.

Indeed, Fiske (ibid.) reviews evidence that people in positions of power stereotype their subordinates more than subordinates stereotype their superiors. Fiske further notes that the powerful are more likely to be in positions of responsibility, and have more people competing for their attention, than their subordinates, and thus are chronically cognitively loaded. In keeping with work in attribution and stereotyping suggesting that cognitive load curtails systematic information processing, Fiske presents evidence that the powerful are too attentionally overloaded to avoid making overly dispositional and stereotypical inferences about their subordinates.

Other researchers have accumulated evidence along the same lines. Snodgrass (1985, 1992), for instance, has shown in a variety of studies with participants assigned to leader (teacher, boss) roles or subordinate (student, employee) roles, high-status perceivers are variously less accurate than low-status perceivers in their judgments of the other's emotions.

It seems clear that immediate social situations can exert a strong influence on how others are judged, including how perceivers infer agents' mental states. Interpersonal factors such as role, power, and expectancy influence how social inference unfolds—and these interpersonal factors often have their effects through intrapersonal process factors such as cognitive load and motivation.

Audience

People share many of their social understandings with others. Indeed, people often reach social understandings, such as explanations and impressions, for the specific purpose of sharing them with an audience. Who these others are and what they want to know shapes these understandings—at least at the level of discourse, and perhaps at the deeper level of private construal. Hilton (1990) has stressed the effect of conversational processes on the form and the content of shared explanations. Explanations, in this view, obey Gricean norms, and so explainers strive for relevance, parsimony, and truthfulness. Such qualities are an interactive product of the perceiver's construal of an event and the perceiver's construal of the audience's concerns and background knowledge. The extent to which such audience concerns intrude into private construals remains unresolved, but it seems clear that shared explanations are subject to the demands of an audience—an effect that should be of interest to any scholar concerned with how folk inferences are put to use in real life. For instance, recalling the earlier discussion of intentional and deontic stances, one could imagine explainers shifting stances depending on their perception of an audience's interest and background knowledge.

A Broader Context: Cultures Shape Folk Theories and Folk Theorizing

In recent years, theory-of-mind research has begun to consider the role of culture, in part drawing on ethnographic evidence to examine whether theory of mind is the same in all cultures. Both differences and similarities have emerged. Building on work by Wellman (1990, 1998) and Lillard (1998), we see cultures as sharing similar folk *framework* theories of belief-desire psychology but elaborating culturally distinct *specific* theories. Across cultures, most perceivers appear to share a basic set of assumptions and concerns (i.e., that others have mental lives; that guesses about others' mental states are useful in predicting action) but also differ in how certain concepts and relations are elaborated (e.g., different emotion categories).

Interestingly, a major theme of cultural difference emerges along the lines of one of the previous sections: some cultures view individuals as comparatively isolated agents (and make theory-of-mind judgments accordingly), whereas other cultures stress folk theories that embed persons in social contexts and focus on groups as agents. Cultures may also differ subtly in their concepts of intentionality and their epistemologies for inferring mental states.

Concepts of Group Agency
Emerging cultural research shows that perceivers in the East are more inclined to ascribe intentions, causality, and responsibility at the group level than perceivers in the West. This fits with various other psychological and ethnographic work and suggests an underlying Eastern folk psychology that grants a central role to groups. A launching point for this emerging work

is the question of whether the tendency to overattribute an act to personal dispositions (the "fundamental attribution error," described by Ichheiser, Jones, Ross, and others) is a product of individualism in North American culture. Various research reveals that this bias is less marked among perceivers in more collectivist East Asian cultures, and some scholars ascribe the difference to lay theories of individual behavior. Recently, researchers have turned to the question of whether lay theories concerning the behavior of groups also differ.

Ongoing research suggests that Confucian East Asian cultures regard groups as having stable properties that confer agency or autonomy on them. Some historical evidence for this is an emphasis on collective responsibility in traditional Chinese law. Starting from 746 B.C., the system of *yuan zuo* (holding offenders' superordinates, kinsmen, and neighbors responsible for their crime simply because they are related to the offenders) was widely practiced in China (Zhang 1984). The rationale underlying this practice was the belief that the would-be offender's in group had the obligation to monitor his or her behavior and therefore should have been able to prevent the crime. Such sentiment appears to continue today. Pursuing this notion, Morris (1993) asked American and Chinese survey respondents to predict whether particular groups would feel responsible after a negative outcome involving one of their members. As expected, Chinese respondents predicted more group feelings of responsibility.

In studies comparing judgments about groups made by East Asian and North American perceivers, a pattern of greater attribution by East Asians to dispositions of the group appears across a wide variety of particular cases (Chiu and Hong 1992; Morris 1993). In several studies relying on newspaper articles and surveys targeting at a range of events and outcomes (Menon, Morris, Chiu, and Hong 1999; Chiu, Morris, Hong, and Menon 2000), individual attributions were endorsed more by Americans and group attributions were endorsed more by Chinese. Menon et al. (1999, experiment 3) described negative outcomes (e.g., designing an unfair compensation system) as following the action of either an individual or group agent. Analyses focused on the extent to which internal stable factors (i.e., dispositions) were favored relative to other kinds of factors. Results showed an interaction effect of perceiver culture by kind of agent: American participants were more likely to endorse dispositional factors in the individual condition than the group condition, whereas Chinese participants were more likely to endorse dispositional factors in the group condition.

Another way to see the role of theories in interpretation is to contrast individuals identified as high versus low in need for closure, a dimension of cognitive style concerning the impulse to reach concrete conclusions quickly (Kruglanski 1996). High need for closure (NFC) is associated with greater reliance on stereotypes and other ready-made explanations to filter the facts of perception (Kruglanski 1996). In a striking result, Chiu et al. (2000) found that among North American participants NFC was associated with more dispositional attributions for individual acts and not associated with any particular type of attribution for group acts; among Hong Kong participants, however, NFC was not associated with any particular type of attribution for individual acts but was associated with dispositional attributions for group acts.

In sum, it appears that culture-specific theories guide the extension of folk psychology to groups. Group agency is a common notion in East Asian societies; it is less common in North American culture and also in developmental theory-of-mind research. This simultaneously suggests that cultural developmental work has the promise of revealing important cross-cultural differences in the content of folk theories and that certain forms of knowledge structures (i.e., defeasible, culturally driven theories) are involved in social inference.

Concepts of Intentionality and Mental States

Malle and Knobe's (1997a) work on the folk concept of "intentionality" shows that there is substantial agreement across perceivers on how acts can be arrayed in terms of their intentional nature. Grinding one's teeth, for instance, is consensually seen as less intentional than watering one's plants. Though this work has gone a long way toward revealing a crucial folk concept, the notion it documented may be culturally specific to the West in certain ways. Are there cultural differences in the seemingly basic idea of what is intentional?

A replication of Malle and Knobe's study in China and the United States (Ames and Fu 2000) showed that Eastern perceivers may view certain kinds of pro-social acts in a somewhat different intentional light. Perceivers in both countries showed considerable agreement in intentionality judgments across a variety of acts, including watering plants and grinding teeth. However, there were notable differences for pro-social acts, such as "helping someone who dropped the papers" and "agreeing to go with friends to eat somewhere you didn't like." Americans viewed these acts as substantially more intentional: American respondents rated a set of pro-social acts as having roughly the same intentionality as studying late and refusing a salesman's offer whereas Chinese respondents rated the same acts as having roughly the intentionality of being infatuated with someone or believing oneself has the flu.[4] It seems appropriate to interpret this difference in light of Confucian notions of social obligation: politeness and helping may be seen as more of a choice in the West and as more of an obligation in the East. Chinese may thus adopt a more deontic, rather than intentional, stance in explaining certain behaviors.

How is it that we know what others are thinking, feeling, and wanting? Recent work suggests that mental-state epistemologies may differ by culture. Knowles and Ames (2000a) suggest that Western cultures stress a "norm of authenticity" such that a person's external actions and displays should be consistent with his or her internal attitudes. "Straight talk" is a sought-after quality in the West. Americans often seem obsessed with communication, honesty, and "saying what they mean and meaning what they say." Eastern cultures may view such displays as impolite and possibly bizarre. The role of hosts in many Asian countries, for instance, is to intuit a guest's unspoken needs, whereas guests are often expected to defer and not betray self-centered desires.

Knowles and Ames (2000a) have collected initial evidence documenting such an epistemic difference in the United States and China. (For a discussion of epistemology as a cultural construct, see Peng, Ames, and Knowles 2000.) When asked how important various pieces of evidence are in determining what someone is thinking, Americans, on average, rated "what they say" as considerably more important than "what they do not say"; Chinese showed the reverse preference. The same pattern held for determining what someone is feeling or wanting. Such evidence suggests that mental-state inference is bound up with cultural norms about actions and cultural epistemologies about evidence.

Conclusions

Consider the case of Jack and his new acquaintance Janet. He needs to decide if she will be a good roommate, and he is puzzling over her recent gift of a house plant, an act of apparent kindness. How does Jack infer Janet's desires and intent? How does Jack explain her action? How does he form an impression of her? These questions of intention inference, explanation, and impression formation are closely linked, and all are clearly issues of folk psychology. In this chapter, we have reviewed a variety of observations from social and cultural psychology that can guide scholars to describe how a lay scientist such as Jack might answer the questions outlined above. Jack is likely to consider Janet's group memberships, such as her ethnicity, her gender, and her profession—and he will recruit his impressions of the attitudes and intentions of those groups. Jack will also consider Janet's actions against a background of norms and prohibitions: was she obliged to give him the plant? Observers should consider Jack's context too: In what ways might his position give him power, and how might that affect his judgment?

Other contextual elements are also important: Jack's outcome dependency in the case of a roommate is high, which might lead him to deliberate carefully. Yet Jack might be chronically low in need for cognition, raising the possibility of a more flippant conclusion. Perhaps Jack is under extreme stress and cognitive load, which might yield a more crude, dispositional judgment about Janet. If Jack's judgments are formed in the context of sharing them with a particular audience, his understanding of the audience's background knowledge and concerns are crucial to understand his shared explanations. Finally, Jack and Janet's culture is important. A Western Jack might explain Janet's act by focusing on her as an individual and on what she says; an Eastern Jack might rely more on contexts or groups as explanatory devices and on her nonverbal behaviors. In sum, Jack's project of understanding Janet is a rich folk-psychological effort that demands the acknowledgement of perceiver, actor, and cultural contexts.

Work in developmental theory of mind and in a variety of other disciplines approaches the issue of social perception as a question of lay scientists' drawing inferences from their theories and from available evidence. The social- and cultural-psychology considerations reviewed here—as highlighted in the case of Jack and Janet—help qualify and enrich the perceiver-as-scientist approach. By examining context issues related to targets, perceivers, and culture, scholarly models of perception become even more robust. It is worth noting that social and cultural psychology have not, by and large, embraced the theory-of-mind perspective in discussing social judgment. However, this appears to be changing (e.g., Malle 1999, this volume; Rosati et al, this volume; Kashima, McKintyre, and Clifford 1998)—and these disciplines have much to teach one another.

Insights and Aims
In contending that insights from social psychology may be valuable to developmental psychology and other disciplines, we are aware that the aims of research are often quite different. As we noted earlier, the theoretically relevant point for developmentalists is most often competence, not performance. However, it seems that the scholarship reviewed here, much of which focuses on performance, is valuable for developmentalists and others for a number of reasons. A first reason to attend to contextual factors relevant to children's behavior in inference tasks is the possibility that empirical evidence for competence or its absence may be misleading. Piaget, for instance, documented both kinds of errors in his conclusions about the unfolding of development. The evidence for competence, after all, is always a performance, and one performance can be confidently interpreted only against the background of other performances. Thus, understanding contextual variation in performance is in some sense necessary for understanding competence.

A second reason for attention to systematic contextual variation in performance is that findings can help distinguish between rival theories of development. For instance, the "theory-theory" account of development (Gopnik and Wellman 1992, Gopnik and Meltzoff 1997; Wellman 1990) differs from accounts based on innate modules (Leslie 1994b; Fodor 1986) in that it predicts that children growing up in different cultures should acquire different theories. The evidence reviewed in this chapter suggests as much, as indicated by the differing mental-state epistemologies noted by Knowles and Ames (2000a). Predictions about effects of many more proximal contextual factors also differ between accounts based on theories and those based on empathic simulation (Goldman 1993, this volume). For reasons that are well understood in the social-psychological literature, findings taken by simulation accounts as casting doubt on children's possession of theories may in fact merely point to contexts in which theories are relied on less. Indeed, it is more persuasive evidence for the theory-theory account if performance shifts as different conditions encourage perceivers to employ different knowledge structures in different ways. For instance, Ames's (2000a) work on the inference of group attitudes suggests that similarity theories govern when social projection is used.

A third reason for theory-of-mind developmentalists to incorporate insights from social psychology is a broadening of hypotheses about the content of children's theories. There may be many competences relevant to theories of development that have not been explored. For instance, some developmentalists have long suspected that young children understand collectivities or organizations. Lev Vygotsky, for one, argued that children cognize the mother-child organization before they cognize the self as individual. However, for a variety of reasons, developmentalists have conducted a massive number of studies on children's perceptions of individuals and comparatively few studies of their perceptions of groups. As we have shown here, groups differ in the way they are treated as intentional (Lickel et al. 1999), and cultures differ in the way they highlight groups as agents (Menon et al. 1999). Another underexplored area of competence is the development of similarity theories. As Ames (2000a) shows, beliefs about the similarity between oneself and a target person or group affect how social projection is employed in the inference of beliefs and desires; the developmental course of such similarity beliefs deserves attention.

In sum, the insights presented here are useful in pursuing the well-established aims of developmental theory-of-mind scholarship—that is, in exploring the development of competence. However, somewhat speculatively, we also suggest that developmental psychology may be ready for renewed attention to performance. Until children's competence was mapped, a science of performance was not possible. Yet the literature of social cognitive development has made so much progress in charting the rise in children's competence in the last decade that the time may be ripe for more research on performance. A systematic science of the conditions that moderate better or worse performance by children at a given level of competence might spawn useful theoretical insights. For example, how do motivation, audience, and agent group membership affect children's inference of others' thoughts at different points in development? Performance also bears upon practical questions. Contextual factors that help children make good use of their theories are factors that educators would want to understand. Practical implications also go beyond the realm of the cognitive, in that good performance in social understanding is critical to social adjustment and integration.

Final Thoughts

In many ways, perceivers are like scientists. In our ordinary lives, all of us constantly form theory-driven conclusions from a jumble of data—and much of this can be appropriately described with semi-rational models of evidence and inference rules. Many disciplines, including developmental theory-of-mind research, game theory, philosophy, and jurisprudence, have pursued this very route. Our argument here has not been a rejection of this approach. Indeed, it is hard to imagine describing social sense making without a "lay scientist" metaphor. Rather, we have sought to show that these models can be enriched by a consideration of the social contexts of *target agents* and *perceivers*—and, further, by a consideration of the broader *cultural* contexts that surround and inform the folk-psychological process of social sense making.

Acknowledgments

Charles W. Kalish was supported by a grant from the Spencer Foundation. Michael Morris was supported by research funds of the Stanford Graduate School of Business. We wish to thank Bertram Malle for comments on a draft of this chapter and, along with Lou Moses and Dare Baldwin, for organizing a stimulating interdisciplinary conference on intentions and intentionality.

Notes

1. "Theory of mind" is the collection of knowledge, often implicit, an ordinary perceiver possesses about the nature and working of minds. This is part of "folk psychology," the perceiver's broader set of folk beliefs about all things psychological. Many philosophers (e.g., Dennett (1987)) and developmentalists (e.g., Wellman

(1990)) view these beliefs (sometimes called ordinary, intuitive, lay, or folk theories) as playing a major role in social understanding.

2. It is worth recalling that Heider's classic 1958 book was titled *The Psychology of Interpersonal Relations* rather than *The Psychology of Interpersonal Perception*.

3. Note that the alternative explanation is deontic: the actor was "obliged" to give a speech contrary to his attitude because someone else asked him to. Whether cognitive load interferes with deontic explanations in general remains to be seen.

4. This seems to be a case of differences in what acts qualify as intentional rather than of differing definitions of the term. The concept of "intentional" was explicitly described to participants as "there was a *reason* for the action and that [the people] *chose* to do so" (Malle and Knobe 1997a).

16

Responsibility for Social Transgressions: An Attributional Analysis

Bernard Weiner

Attribution theorists have distinguished between the attribution process, which relates to how causal inferences are reached, and the attributional process, which concerns the effects of causal beliefs on action. This dichotomy within attribution theory corresponds quite well with an analysis of responsibility. Much thought and research considers the informational determinants of a person's inference of responsibility. These antecedents include well-known concepts, primarily derived from philosophy, such as free will, intention, foresight, mitigator, and controllability (Chandler, Sokol, and Hallett, this volume; Mele, this volume; Kaplan, this volume). Another body of thought and research examines the response to this inference. In a criminal context, for example, inferences of responsibility bear upon the severity of recommended punishment. As will be documented later in the chapter, the results of a judgment of responsibility also influence achievement appraisal, personal help giving, aggression, and a wide variety of other attitudes and behaviors.

The antecedent/consequent distinction can be combined with another classification category to further delineate the areas of thought about responsibility. This second classification dimension is anchored with the labels *self* and *other*. There are antecedents of responsibility inferences about the self and about others, and consequences that relate to the self versus those that are pertinent to others. Although overlapping, the antecedents are not identical for judgments about the self and others. Self-judgments are likely to be subject to hedonic biasing and defensive mechanisms, so that, for example, what is believed to be a mitigator when considering self-judgments might not have the same function when determining other-blame. And we know our own intentions but must infer the intents of others. Considering consequences, a responsibility inference for a personal transgression could evoke self-directed guilt or shame; if another is responsible for a transgression, the emotion experienced might be other-directed anger or irritation. Hence, on the basis of the above logic, there are four subdivisions within the study of responsibility: antecedents for self-related inferences as well as consequences for the self, and antecedents for other-related inferences as well as consequences for them.

In this chapter, I examine only the consequences of holding another responsible for a social transgression. The focus is on anger and sympathy, and on helping, punishment, and aggression, that is, on other-directed emotions and behaviors that to a great extent are determined by holding or not holding another person responsible for a misdeed.

A Theory of Social Conduct

My initial interest in achievement motivation provided the empirical foundation for a theory of social conduct and for reflections about social transgression. Achievement striving has fundamental moral aspects—social rules and norms dictate that we "should" try our hardest and "ought to" expend effort to reach socially valued goals. Hence, lack of effort as a cause of failure is punished more than is the absence of ability to perform a task. (For reviews, see Weiner 1986, 1995.) I suspect that this latter empirical law spans cultures, generations, and situations. Furthermore, persons judge it "fair" to punish a lack of effort that results in failure more than a lack of ability (Farwell and Weiner 1996).

But why should this be the case? Why punish lack of effort but not lack of ability (aptitude)? What is the intervening motivational process that determines how others react to failure? A first step in determining this process is to specify the underlying characteristics or properties of causes. That is, in what essential ways do effort and ability differ? A great deal of research has documented that there are three perceived underlying properties of causality (Weiner 1986): *locus*, *stability*, and *controllability*. Locus refers to the location of a cause, which is either within or outside of the actor. For example, both ability and effort are considered internal causes of failure, whereas the objective difficulty of a task or hindrance by others is an external cause. Causal stability refers to the duration of a cause. Some causes, such as math aptitude, are perceived as constant; others, such as chance, are considered unstable or temporary. Finally, causes such as effort are subject to volitional alteration, whereas others cannot be willfully changed. Luck and aptitude have this property. All causes can be located within this three-dimensional causal space. There is a great deal of agreement that, for example, aptitude is internal, stable, and uncontrollable, whereas effort is internal but controllable (with its perceived stability dependent on a variety of additional information).

Just as an internal cause need not be controllable by the person (e.g., lack of aptitude or height), a controllable cause need not be internal to the causal agent (e.g., failure may be due to teacher negligence, which is changeable by the teacher rather than by the failing student). However, if a cause is controllable by the actor, then by definition it must be internal to that individual. Just like causal locus, controllability again and again has been identified as a basic dimension or property of phenomenal causality (Weiner 1986, 1995).

For the construction of a theory of social behavior, the causal dimension of controllability is of prime importance. As already indicated, lack of effort is subject to volitional change and is regarded as an internal, controllable cause. If the cause of an event is controllable by others (that is, if it "could have been otherwise"), then in the absence of mitigators the person is regarded as responsible for the outcome of the event. On the other hand, low aptitude as a cause of achievement failure is construed as an uncontrollable cause. One does not choose one's aptitudes, and therefore one is not responsible for a failure given this cause (Weiner 1995). In sum, beliefs regarding the cause of failure determine whether the actor is responsible for an outcome. It is proposed here that, in instances of social transgression, this cognitive aspect of the larger motivational process proceeds from a focus on causes (Why did it happen? Was it personally controllable?) to an inference about the person (Is she responsible?).

Internal controllability is a component or determinant of responsibility. They are not to be equated. For example, if a student did not put forth effort in school because he had to take care of a sick parent, the lack of effort is nonetheless considered controllable, and the student intentionally did not study. However, he will not be held responsible because a justification is provided that serves a higher moral goal. Similarly, aggressive action can be carried out by an individual who could not distinguish right from wrong, in which case again there may be internal controllability and outcome intent, yet an inference of responsibility is not made.

On the Distinction between Intentionality and Responsibility

Inasmuch as this book centers on the concept of intentionality, whereas my approach centers on the concept of responsibility, it is appropriate to depart temporarily from the main subject of the chapter and examine the distinction between these two overlapping terms. First, I believe it is useful to differentiate between act intentionality and outcome intent. For example, one may intentionally not study (the act) yet not intend to fail (that is, one does not study in order to fail, or to reach the goal of failure). In a similar manner, one may intentionally shoot a gun to celebrate an event yet not intend the bodily harm that was the result of this behavior (that is, the goal was not to hurt another). Refusal to study and shooting the gun are considered controllable causes, and therefore the actor is likely to be held responsible for the unintended outcomes.

Carrying this line of reasoning one step further, if the outcome intent of the actor was to kill another (or to fail at a test), and if the actor intentionally brought this outcome about, then even more elevated responsibility judgments will be invoked, compared to the situation in which these outcomes were not intended (as illustrated in the different magnitude of punishment in murder versus manslaughter convictions). In the present attributional framework, outcome intent and controllability of the cause are both determinants of responsibility judgments. Of the two concepts, control is more central to responsibility judgments than is outcome intent, inasmuch as one cannot be held responsible for an uncontrollable cause but can be held responsible for an unintended outcome. Hence, although I wish to see another harmed, if I was pushed into that person by another and harm resulted, responsibility judgments would be withheld (although negative moral judgments concerning my wishes may be invoked). In addition, as already indicated, outcome intent along with causal controllability also may not result in a negative responsibility evaluation given the presence of mitigating circumstances (e.g., inability to distinguish right from wrong). In sum, causal control is a necessary but not a sufficient determinant of responsibility beliefs (there must also be the absence of mitigators), whereas outcome intent is neither a necessary nor a sufficient determinant of responsibility judgments. This being the case, controllability is a superordinate concept, and outcome intent a subordinate concept, with respect to responsibility.

There are, however, sets of behavior where it appears that individuals search for the act intentionality and the outcome intent of that behavior (i.e., reason for the action) in order to judge another (e.g., "Did he deliberately swing at me?" or "Did he want to harm me?"). In such cases, although the naive search is to understand the reason for the behavior (Malle, this volume), it is implicitly assumed that if the outcome intent was to harm then the action to do so was intended and the cause was controllable by the person. That is, in these cases the concepts of act intentionality, outcome intent, and controllability of the cause appear to merge or completely overlap.

From Cognition (Responsibility Inferences) to Emotion and Action

The path to action does not stop at responsibility. This "cold" inference process then has implications for a "hot" emotional process. There is an array of research from a cognitive appraisal perspective supporting the position that thoughts determine feelings. More specifically, if another is perceived as responsible for a negative event, then feelings of anger are aroused (Averill 1983; Reisenzein and Hoffman 1990; Roseman 1991). Imagine, for example, your feelings when your child is doing poorly at school because of a refusal to do homework, or when an athlete on a favorite team is loafing during a defeat. You are likely to be mad at your rebellious child and at the lackadaisical athlete. Anger is an accusation or a value judgment that follows from the belief that another person could and should have done something else.

In contrast to the linkage between responsibility and anger, the absence of responsibility given the personal plight of another is often associated with sympathy and the related (but not identical) emotions of pity and compassion. Thus, a person confined within a totalitarian state, athletic failure due to a physical handicap, and school failure due to a lack of aptitude are typical predicaments that elicit sympathy inasmuch as the person is not held responsible for his or her negative plight.

In addition to being emotional consequences that follow from thoughts about responsibility and nonresponsibility, anger and sympathy are considered stimuli or goads to subsequent action (Averill 1983; Weiner 1995).

That is, they provide bridges between thinking and conduct. Anger directs the person experiencing this emotion to "eliminate" the wrongdoer, to go toward that person and retaliate with some form of aggressive action, or to go away from that person to withhold some positive good. Anger, therefore, is viewed as an emotion that "pushes" or incites that person to undertake self-protective and retaliatory actions. Sympathy, on the other hand, directs the person to increase pro-social behaviors (such as help giving) and decrease anti-social conduct (including punishment and negative appraisal) (Eisenberg 1986).

A motivational sequence now has been outlined that explains why lack of effort is punished whereas lack of ability is not. In the two causal situations, the sequences are construed as follows:

failure → lack of effort is the cause → cause is controllable → person is responsible → anger → negative evaluation

failure → lack of ability is the cause → cause is not controllable → person is not responsible → sympathy → withhold negative evaluation

This motivational process is not confined to an explanation of achievement appraisal. A number of other observations also can be subsumed within the same conceptual framework. Figure 1 shows that reactions to the stigmatized, help giving, and aggression are also subject to a responsibility-based analysis. In all cases, first there is a search for why a state is present (Why is this person obese?) or why an event has occurred (Why did he hit that person?). If the actor is responsible for a negative state or act (such as needing help because of laziness or aggressing against someone intentionally), anger is experienced and the behavioral reaction is negative. On the other hand, persons stigmatized because of noncontrollable causes (such as genetic blindness or needing help because of missing school when ill) elicit sympathy and, in turn, pro-social behavior.

In all these situations, an appropriate metaphor to capture the reactions of the involved observer is that he or she is a judge presiding in a courtroom. The judge determines whether others are innocent or guilty and then passes sentences based on these beliefs and experienced emotions. Indeed, life may be considered a courtroom where dramas related to transgression

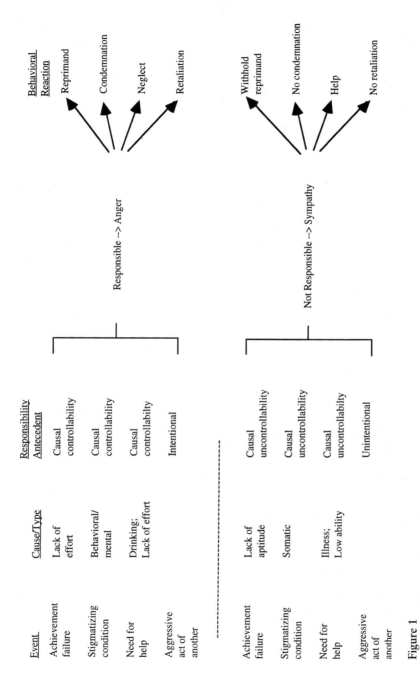

Figure 1

A responsibility-based theory of social conduct

are played out. The observer is a scientist in determining causal judgments, but then acts in a Godlike manner by reaching moral conclusions regarding right and wrong, good and evil.

Testing the Theory

The most extensive data putting this motivational sequence to test have been in the helping domain. Within this context, a number of investigations have assessed the controllability of and/or the responsibility for a need, the emotions of anger and/or sympathy, and some indicator of helping (quite often a judgment of aid rather than an actual behavioral event).

In a meta-analysis, we (Rudolph, Roesch, and Weiner 2000) identified 21 studies reporting the data that were required to test the theory. These investigations included more than 3700 subjects. The research participants came from numerous cultures (including the United States, Canada, Germany, and Japan), and the situations in which help was examined differed in a number of respects (e.g., lending class notes, helping someone on a subway, lending money, welfare payments, assisting someone with AIDS).

Table 1 shows the raw correlations between measures of causal controllability (which in these contexts is virtually synonymous with inferences of personal responsibility), sympathy, anger, and help giving. It is evident from table 1 that controllability relates negatively with sympathy (greater personal control for a need, less sympathy when asking for help), positively with anger, and negatively with help giving. All these relations are in the anticipated direction.

Table 2 shows the data for two path models based on these correlations. The path coefficients essentially reveal the relations between the variables with all other associations held constant. Model 1 gives the associations

Table 1
Weighted correlations among controllability, sympathy, anger, and help-giving. N ranged from 2100 to 3700. Data from Rudolph, Roesch, and Weiner 2000.

	Sympathy	Anger	Help giving
Controllability	−0.50	0.54	−0.30
Sympathy		−0.40	0.46
Anger			−0.38

Table 2
Path coefficients for two models of helping: with and without a direct path from control to help. N for each model = 2163. From Rudolph, Roesch, and Weiner 2000.

	Model 1	Model 2
Control-Sympathy	−0.50	−0.50
Control-Anger	0.55	0.55
Control-Help	0.01	—
Sympathy-Help	0.37	0.36
Anger-Help	−0.25	−0.24

when a direct path between controllability and help is specified, i.e., there is a proximal relation between thinking and helping. Model 2 shows the relations when this path is eliminated. Both models fit the data extremely well. However, it is clear that the associations in model 2 are virtually the same as in model 1. It is therefore more parsimonious not to specify a direct linkage between thoughts about controllability (and responsibility) and helping. In sum, the meta-analysis reveals a highly consistent representation across a large range of studies conducted in different cultures over 20 years, using different kinds of samples as well as disparate operationalizations of the independent and dependent variables, and showing that thoughts about responsibility influence feelings, which, in turn, determine behavior.

Current Research

I now turn to two of the research topics that currently have my attention: philosophies of punishment and individual differences in political ideology. The investigations to be reported were guided by the theory shown in figure 1 but are not construed as tests of the theory.

Philosophies of Punishment

Philosophers have pointed out that punishment is guided by two goals, one utilitarian and one retributive. Utilitarian goals consider the costs and the benefits of punishment; the focus is on the future, with aims reached through a reduction in the likelihood of the misdeed by the perpetrator and/or by others in society. Retribution pertains to a concern for a past wrong rather than the subsequent consequences of the punishment. That is, the goal is to avenge a past evil deed rather than to prevent future ones. Of course, most punishment may fulfill both purposes, but it is important nonetheless to consider the goals of the punishment and whether one aim is dominant.

How might the utilitarian/retribution distinction be related to causal beliefs and to inferences of responsibility? I propose that social transactions deemed controllable by the actor (i.e., those negative actions that result in inferences of personal responsibility) elicit anger and retributive responses. On the other hand, uncontrollable transgressions, which do not give rise to judgments of personal responsibility, are hypothesized to elicit sympathy and utilitarian goals. Stable causes are anticipated to exacerbate these reactions, so that, for example, greater retribution should be meted out to the lazy person and the repeated killer than to the student who did not try only on this occasion or to the criminal who volitionally killed only once.

In one illustrative study testing these ideas, we (Weiner, Graham, and Reyna 1997) gave scenarios to subjects describing three types of social transgressions. One transgression was a school failure; the other two depicted the criminal misdeeds of murder and burglary. Four vignettes were created for each transgression, obtained by factorially combining the controllability and the stability of the cause of the problem. For example, the controllable stable cause of school failure was described as laziness, whereas the controllable and unstable cause was phrased as "did not try on this occasion." Concerning the uncontrollable causes, the uncontrollable stable cause of failure was operationalized as lack of aptitude, whereas the uncontrollable unstable cause was lack of knowledge due to a late transfer into the class. Conceptually similar scenarios were created for murder and burglary.

Among the questions asked of the respondents was what amount of punishment should be given for this negative event. This was then followed by a description of retributive (because it is deserved) and utilitarian (to reduce the likelihood of this happening again) objectives of punishment. The participants indicated the extent to which their recommended punishment was for each of these two purposes or goals.

In figure 2, endorsement of retributive and utilitarian goals is plotted. The figure clearly indicates that when the cause of an aversive outcome is

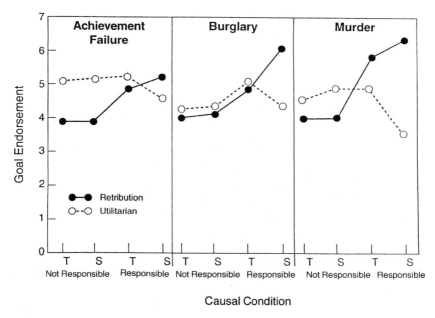

Figure 2
Endorsement of retributive versus utilitarian punishment goals as a function of controllability and stability of event causes (UT = uncontrollable, temporary; US = uncontrollable, stable; CT = controllable, temporary; CS = controllable, stable). From Weiner, Graham, and Reyna, 1997, p. 441.

uncontrollable, whether stable or unstable, punishment goals are less retributive (more utilitarian) than when the cause is controllable. Under controllable causality and stability, then, the goals of punishment are primarily retributive in each transgression context. Thus, one punishes the lazy student as well as the intentional murderer to "get back at them." Other research (Weiner, Graham, and Reyna 1997) documents that retributive desires are determined by inferences of responsibility, anger, and sympathy, whereas utilitarian goals are associated with expectations about recurrence of the misdeed.

Political Ideology
The concept of individualism incorporates a variety of beliefs related to personal responsibility and the positive effects of one's efforts on goal attainment. Individualism is found in Max Weber's theme of the Protestant

Ethic—through hard work success will be attained, whereas failure is caused by laziness and other moral shortcomings.

The belief in individualism is differentially represented in US politics, and indeed in part defines political identification. Conservatives are more likely to ascribe poverty to causes such as self-indulgence and laziness, whereas liberals tend to view the poor as victims of society (Skitka and Tetlock 1993). As a consequence of these perceptions and inferences, conservative motivation should be captured by the top half of the theory shown in figure 1, and they are anticipated to be less aid giving than their political counterparts, whereas the motivational process for liberals is better depicted by the bottom half of figure 1, resulting in more pro-social actions.

We all indeed recognize that conservatives and liberals differ in their approval of social spending and welfare, with conservatives more opposed and liberals more in favor of governmental support (Feather 1985; Kluegal and Smith 1986). In association with Lisa Farwell, I have been asking somewhat more detailed questions about the relations between political identification, inferences of responsibility, and endorsement of aid, especially asking how these associations are affected by knowledge that the cause of a need is either controllable or uncontrollable by the needy person (Farwell and Weiner 1996, 2000). Other questions driving our work have been the following: What do others predict the reactions of liberals and conservatives will be toward those who are or who are not responsible for their plights? And are these perceptions also influenced by personal political orientation? That is, do liberal and conservative persons differ in their beliefs about how other liberals and conservatives respond to those who are or who are not responsible for their needs?

To examine these questions, we created three need vignettes, each describing welfare recipients who either were unemployed, were obese, or had AIDS (Farwell and Weiner 2000). Two conditions within each stigma described the person as either responsible or not responsible for the problem (e.g., unemployed because of poor work habits versus unemployed because the employer went out of business). For all vignettes, subjects were asked to imagine that they were on the board of directors of a charitable organization and were asked how much financial assistance they would recommend (from least to most amount of money possible). They were also asked to predict how much assistance a liberal or a conservative member on the board would recommend. Additionally, the political identification of the participants was assessed.

The results from one representative study are shown in table 3. First look at the two left hand columns of table 3, which show how much individuals report they would allocate as a function of their own political leanings. As fully expected, all recommend more funding for those not responsible for their state of need. But although liberals and conservatives recommend equal funding to the "deserving" needy, liberals recommend more funding for the "undeserving" than do conservatives (5.49 versus 3.86 on an 11-point scale).

Now what are the perceptions of liberals and conservatives regarding what other liberals and conservatives would do? Table 3 shows that people expect liberals to be more generous than conservatives, whether or not the needy are responsible for their plight. However, conservative participants predicted that liberals would be more generous toward the responsible recipients than did others. In addition, given a responsible recipient, the assistance by liberals was overestimated by all ideological groups. Recall, however, that liberals indeed recommended more funding than did the other political groups, so that beliefs about liberals have a kernel of truth.

It is evident from table 3 that all political parties overestimated the stinginess of conservatives. This belief also has a kernel of truth with regard to the responsible needy, where conservatives indeed are wont to withhold help and are relatively "heartless." However, these inferences are not an exaggeration of a kernel of truth in regard to nonresponsible recipients.

The main message of this research, however, is not documentation of "accurate" or "inaccurate" stereotypes. Rather, what is essential is that

Table 3
Fund allocations as a function of personal ideology and perspective (self vs. imagined other). MOR: middle of road. Data from Farwell and Weiner 2000.

| | Own allocation | | Allocation predicted for | | | |
| | | | Liberal | | Conservative | |
	Responsible	Not	Responsible	Not	Responsible	Not
Liberal	5.49	9.01	6.11	8.99	2.47	7.68
MOR	4.20	8.99	5.99	8.73	2.76	7.63
Conservative	3.86	9.14	7.61	9.41	2.25	8.00

classification regarding the personal responsibility of others, in conjunction with the belief that responsibility is a determinant of distributive justice, sheds light on a variety of interesting questions.

Conclusion

An attributional approach to responsibility judgments views responsibility as an inference made after a causal judgment. Responsibility judgments are particularly likely in instances in which the cause of a transgression is perceived to be internal and controllable by the transgressing individual. This judgment then affects a number of behavioral reactions, including the likelihood of help giving, the severity and perceived purpose of punishment, and perceptions of other ideological groups. I think the attributional approach to responsibility provides a rich theoretical and empirical playground.

17

Moral Responsibility and the Interpretive Turn: Children's Changing Conceptions of Truth and Rightness

Michael J. Chandler, Bryan W. Sokol, and Darcy Hallett

Picture this: You are on Brighton Beach. Imagine hot sands, a striped tent, and children. Imagine that Punch and Judy are once again having at one another when suddenly Judy stumbles and falls into an awaiting box. Punch, driven to violence by centuries of slapstick abuse, seizes the opportunity, slams down the lid, and begins searching about for a bit of rope to tie the box shut before dumping the whole lot into the trash. Then—and this is the decisive moment—at just that instant when his back is turned, but still in full view of the audience, Judy manages to surreptitiously escape and quietly slips off into the wings. Punch, none the wiser, proceeds to tie shut what only we now appreciate to be an empty box and, with evident malice aforethought, tips it off the stage, thereby adding to the long list of attempted murders that somehow went wrong as a result of simple (or, if you will, "blameless") ignorance.

Imagine one more thing: You are a developmentalist who has been offered the opportunity to meet and talk with the young after-theater crowd of this, "the world's best-known puppet play" (Baird 1965, p. 93). What is there in the "Highly Moral Drama of Punch and Judy," as the play is traditionally called (Damon 1957, p. 5), that might provoke young school-age children to have something memorable to say about the human condition? What, in short, would you ask them?

In view of the current complexion of the field of developmental psychology, two general questions immediately suggest themselves. One of these, reserved for the young participants in our studies, would have to be about all those moral matters upon which the story so obviously turns: Just how bad is it really for Punch to be trashing what is, after all, only an empty box, and how much real weight is given—or ought to be given—to Punch's evident surplus of bad intentions? The other question (perhaps a matter for our own conscience) is whether this really is the sort of thing that young people should be watching in the first place?

According to Lord Hollifax, an early-nineteenth-century commentator, the answer to at least the second of these questions is clear enough: "In our corrupt state, common weaknesses and defects [of the sort that Punch exemplifies in spades] contribute more toward reconciling us to one another than all the precepts of the philosophers and divines." (Meyers 1971, p. 4) If, on such authority, one were to go on exposing young research subjects to this and other Punch and Judy shows, as we have done, then there would appear to be good reason to anticipate that their reactions might tell us something important about the development of moral reasoning—about children's beliefs about what is right and what is wrong.

Alternatively, you might, as Daniel Dennett (1978) did, see in this particular bit of puppet theater the "ideal" or "minimally complex" opportunity to get at children's earliest beliefs about belief. Clearly, as Dennett pointed out, all those children on Brighton Beach and elsewhere who ever found any humor in all this low comedy managed to do so just because they knew perfectly well (and in a way that Punch did not and could not know) that Judy had already gotten away "Scot free," and did so as a direct result of having already acquired at least a fledgling grasp of the possibility of false belief. Dennett's point about all this was and continues to be so compelling that his nostalgic recounting of this particular Punch and Judy episode went on to become the source model for a whole generation of paler, but now "standard," tests of children's developing theories of mind. Wimmer and Perner's (1983) now-classic "unexpected transfer" task, in which "Maxi" leaves his chocolate bar in one place only to have it moved in his absence; Baron-Cohen, Leslie, and Frith's (1985) more or less identical "Sally" task, involving a puppet whose marbles go missing; and, Perner, Leekam, and Wimmer's (1987) closely related "unexpected contents" task, that similarly tricks out subjects by substituting pencils for the candies ordinarily found in a Smarties tube, are all self-evidently derivative, and belong to the same Punch and Judy genre. That is, Maxi's confusion concerning the whereabouts of his chocolate, Sally's fruitless search for her marble, and all the children ever made to play the fool because someone had substituted pencils for their Smarties all amount to less comic stand-ins for Punch and his pointless efforts to push over a cliff what everyone but he knows to be an empty box. All that is missing is the laughter. Clearly, then, if you want a "litmus test" (Wellman 1990) of false-belief understanding, Punch, it would seem, is just the ticket.

What is not so obvious is why Punch's various efforts in the tying shut and pushing over departments should so readily prompt questions about moral development from some, questions about epistemic development from others, and questions about *both* from next to no one. That is, what is there about the balkanized nature of our current conceptual and disciplinary practices that, here and elsewhere, works so effectively to prevent us from automatically understanding both of these star-crossed matters as naturally existing within the same problem space? As a way of taking up such questions, this chapter begins with a brief look at the alleged "antinomy of truth and rightness" that continues to hold at arm's length studies of children's changing beliefs about belief and their developing conceptions of moral responsibility, goes on to entertain ways of building a much-needed conceptual bridge between these isolated islands of research, and finishes with a quick illustration of how Punch and Judy were enlisted in our own contributions to this bridging effort.

The Antinomy of Truth and Rightness

Some among us "do" moral development; others do something else, like study colder cognition, or people's conceptions of it. It is true, of course, that much of the available research having to do with moral matters is about moral *reasoning* and thus, in this technical sense, also qualifies as some rump part of the same aging "cognitive revolution" that once redrew the boundaries of psychology as a whole. At the same time, however, almost no one currently caught up in the business of working out the changing nature of children's beliefs, or beliefs about belief, is also seriously concerned with the study of their values, just as no one (or next to no one—see Wainryb and Ford 1998) in the business of studying moral development is also involved in the close examination of children's developing conceptions of epistemic life (Chandler, Sokol, and Wainryb 2000). Rather, for all practical purposes, these two research enterprises, with their separate learned societies and purpose-built journals, live in splendid isolation, so quarantined from one another that they might as well exist on separate planets.

Two divisive things, at least, share responsibility for these tatters in the frayed fabric of contemporary psychological thought, both of which will need some mending if the dangling threads of beliefs about truth and the unraveled beliefs about rightness are to be knit back up into something resembling a real sleeve. One of these is that the discipline has been all but reduced to silence on such matters by a phobic-like fear of somehow inadvertently committing the "naturalistic fallacy"—of foolishly crossing the black "is" wire with the white "ought" wire, thereby causing sparks of derision to emanate from those of our critics who claim a better understanding of Ohm's Law than our own. The second, which perhaps amounts to the same thing elevated to a slightly higher level of abstraction, is that matters of truth and matters of rightness are rumored not only to belong to two separate and watertight compartments but to occupy such distinct levels of abstraction that any attempt to bridge the two automatically amounts to a sort of category mistake. As a result, we are collectively inclined to pussyfoot about, gingerly making sure that we never do anything that might lead to our being indicted for having conflated what is and what ought to be the case.

Although no one seriously doubts the reasonableness or the utility of sustaining some sort of division between validity claims that are meant to be truth conditional and those that bear on matters of rightness and value, there is much contemporary debate about whether this distinction is nearly as iron-clad and unbridgeable as we have historically been led to believe. Habermas (1984), for example, persuasively argues that "objective" beliefs of the truth-conditional sort form only a minor subset of that larger, superordinate class of our convictions (including traditional notions of rightness and value), all of which deserve to be seen as more or less "valid" depending on the strength of the good reasons that can be marshaled in their defense. Similarly, Putnam (1987) insists that with the demise of logical empiricism all the classic divisions between a certain world of foundational "facts" and a subjective realm of controversial "values" must be rejected outright in favor of a more "relational" view (Overton 1998) that pictures all such forms of knowledge as existing along a common fact–value continuum. Searle (1969) and others (e.g., Baier 1958; Elgin 1989; Kuhn 1972) have contributed to the same point by drawing attention to the range of "institutional" or "social" facts that can be shown to clutter the supposedly empty space once imagined to quarantine "subjective" values from "brute" or "objective" facts. In light of all such contemporary accounts, the more traditional and ironclad dichotomy between what is subjectively (read arbitrarily) held out as "right" and what just "is" (objectively) the case lose their force, thereby reopening for negotiation all the old prescriptive obligations about keeping moral and epistemic matters at arm's length. In the midst of such renegotiations, it simply won't do to go on trying to hide out in imaginary places where beliefs and values are alleged to live chaste but spinster lives.

Even if all that has just been alluded to were not true—that is, even if contemporary philosophers were no less convinced than was Hume (1739) of the absolute necessity of avoiding anything that might risk conflating matters of "is" and "ought"—it still would not absolve psychologists and others concerned with the study of naive, or folk, or common-sense conceptions of mental life of their responsibility for understanding how matters of truth and rightness are intertwined in the ordinary practice of mental and social life. That is, all of us, along with the institutions and social practices we have created in order to manage our human affairs, regularly proceed as though these two domains were deeply connected, and, consequently, social scientists are obliged to take these connections seriously. (For further discussion, see Chandler, Sokol, and Wainryb 2000; Ames, Knowles, Morris, Kalish, Rosati, and Gopnik, this volume.)

Mistakes of Fact and Mistakes of Law

It is one thing to declare as contrary to our natures any restraining order that legislates against the joint consideration of beliefs about truth and rightness, and quite a different matter to work out the actual conceptual machinery necessary to allow for the proper study of their interrelations. That is, although as ordinary citizens we regularly show a vital interest in the interactions between what others believe is and ought to be the case, as social scientists we have traditionally made such a fetish out of isolating these moral and epistemic matters that we lack a proper language in which to discuss and explore the possible conditions of their coming together. As luck would have it, not every intellectual tradition has, as ours does, a long history of phobic-like fears of falling prey to some "naturalistic fallacy." In particular, the legal profession, with its standing obligation to help arbitrate disputes over what is right and what is true, has never enjoyed the luxury of treating matters of "is" and "ought" in pristine isolation, and so promises to be a potentially rich source of at least conceptual tools for possible use by researchers interested in getting into a related business. At least, this has been the conclusion of certain contemporary theorists of jurisprudence, such as Ronald Dworkin (1982, 1986) and social philosophers such as Jürgen Habermas (1984, 1996), who have worked to construct conceptual frameworks that allow for the joint consideration of moral and epistemic matters.

One aspect of such legal theories that shows special promise in assisting social scientists in thinking about the nature of the relation that obtains between children's developing beliefs about belief and their maturing conceptions of moral matters is the traditional courtroom distinction between "mistakes of fact" and "mistakes of law" (Black 1990, p. 1001). What, for our purposes, is the real nubbin of this otherwise complex legal distinction is that "mistakes of fact" refer to ways of getting things wrong that can be wholly laid at the door of ignorance-based false beliefs (e.g., one might well know all about the existing seat-belt law of the adjacent state but simply be ignorant of the fact of having inadvertently wandered across the state line, becoming in the process duty bound to buckle up). Mistakes of law, in contrast, are less about the availability of facts than about their possible meanings, but they turn on errors of interpretation regarding the legality, or perhaps the morality, of a given action (e.g., one might know all about the seat-belt law without imagining—even in a million years—that being parked in a lovers' lane actually qualifies someone as "conducting" an automobile).

Two rules of thumb for determining the culpability of others follow from this distinction. Specifically, simple misdeeds that arise as a result of not having clear access to all the relevant facts tend to be seen by the law, and by ordinary adults, as legitimately mitigated. In contrast, negatively sanctioned behaviors that stem from some misinterpretation of how the law might apply in this or that circumstance are generally seen as being altogether less excusable. (That is, though perhaps we all hope that the troubles of young lovers—with and without seat belts—are few, we all also likely share in the view that individuals' interpretations of the law, about buckling up and more, are more often than not suspect, and less an occasion for leniency than blameless ignorance.) This is understood to follow for the reason that if we venture some homespun interpretation of the law it behooves us to do a good job. Accordingly, failing to do so, by seizing on some interpretation that is poorly warranted by available evidence, is broadly understood to bring righteous approbation down on one's own head and is seen to be altogether more blameworthy than simply being blindsided by some stray fact.

If, on reflection, you find yourself generally in sympathy with this legalistic way of doing business, as we do, it is probably (and this is our hypothesis) because you, as an adult, along with various officers of the court, are operating in terms of the same tacit epistemology. That is, you and the legal system both judge the knowing process to be the work of active agents who are obliged to interpret the world around them in ways for which they are expected to take some responsibility. By this shared standard, "mistakes of fact," or at least all those forms of counterfactual belief that arise simply because one was inadvertently in the wrong place at the wrong time, are the active doings of an environment perpetrated upon people as patients, who, as a consequence, can be reasonably excused from responsibility for things about which they were innocently uninformed. In contrast, badly misreading one's circumstances and, as a consequence, behaving in some way that runs afoul of legal prohibitions and often attendant moral prohibitions (that is, making a "mistake of law") naturally invites recrimination.

For those acquainted with the burgeoning body of research literature detailing children's changing theories of mind, the rehearsal of this legal distinction should touch a familiar chord. That is, the parallel between the research findings concerning children's changing conceptions of mental life and these two adult rules of thumb for establishing relative degrees of culpability is, as we see it, clear enough. Recognition of a so-called mistake of fact, in particular, is just that parallel instance for an adult of what a card-carrying theorist of mind would label a demonstration of false-belief understanding—i.e., knowing that, as a result of simple ignorance, people can come to take as subjectively true things that are, in fact, objectively false. If, for example, there was a law against searching in the wrong place for one's missing chocolate, then Wimmer and Perner's (1983) much-imitated protagonist Maxi would deserve some relief from his legal responsibility for having inadvertently been in the wrong place at the wrong time when his chocolate was moved. On this logic, anyone capable of passing the now-standard "unexpected transfer" or "unexpected contents" tasks used to measure false-belief understanding ought to also be capable of using this insight as a tool for tempering his judgments about the legal and moral responsibilities owed by the ignorant. (See, e.g., Wimmer, Gruber, and Perner 1984, 1985.) It is important to note, however, that nothing in this description touches on those more genuinely interpretive matters that, in the cases to be presented here, relate to so-called mistakes of law.

The particular turn of the epistemic wheel that brings children closer to the interpretive issues associated with such mistakes of law is, we contend, their achievement of having come to what we have been calling an interpretive, or constructivistic, theory of mind (Carpendale and Chandler 1996; Chandler and Lalonde 1996; Chandler and Sokol 1999). That is, a proper understanding of a mistake of fact (or, as we have suggested, any standard false-belief scenario) requires no more than a simple understanding of the old cliché "Seeing is believing." Children old enough to have come to the simple realization that one has to at least "see" an event occur (or talk to someone who has) in order to know something about it, and who are equally capable of reversing this logic in such a way as to also appreciate that "not seeing" has the consequence of leaving one in the dark about particular matters, have all the cognitive prerequisites for understanding what it means to make a mistake of fact. In contrast, coming to understand that different people can reach legitimately different and sometimes wildly divergent views, even when they have seen everything there is to see about precisely one and the same thing, requires (in addition to simple false-belief understanding) some basic comprehension of interpretation, and how, in particular, the knowing process is informed by an active mind-to-world contribution on the part of human agents (Searle 1969). We and our immediate research colleagues are currently hip deep in a program of research aimed at determining when, in the usual course of their epistemic development, young children first come to the idea that the knowing process is fundamentally a constructive enterprise (Sokol and Chandler 1999). The thrust of what we have found so far is that 4- and 5-year-olds, who respond at ceiling on standard ignorance-based measures of false-belief understanding, nevertheless fail utterly to appreciate the possibility that two persons with precisely the same information at their disposal can still arrive at sharply different interpretations of such shared experiences. By 6 going on 8, however, as our research (e.g., Carpendale and Chandler 1996; Chandler and Lalonde 1996) suggests, young school-age children begin to negotiate this "interpretive turn" so and thus newly come to understand that two persons may interpret one and the same thing differently.

Once gifted with this newly emerging interpretive or constructivistic theory of mind, the way is opened up for such children to countenance the possibility that circumstances can and often do lead one into some ill-conceived interpretation that might constitute a mistake of law. That is, if misinterpretation is understood to be possible, then the prospect is seen to arise that one might well run afoul of the law by somehow putting the wrong spin on the events of one's experience. On these grounds, it seems reasonable that young persons mature enough to appreciate that people can act badly, either because they are ignorant of relevant facts or because they sometimes manage to misinterpret their circumstances, might side with adults in holding people more responsible for their misinterpretations than for their ignorance by judging mistakes of law more blameworthy than mistakes of fact.

Put concretely: It was our expectation that children who did and children who did not hold to an interpretive theory of mind would come to importantly different conclusions about the blameworthiness of others for misreading the circumstances in which they sometimes found themselves. In particular, we predicted that children who had already come to a constructivistic understanding of the knowing process would be epistemically well positioned to appreciate an important moral difference between mistakes of fact and mistakes of law and so would be quick to condemn anyone who, while attempting some homespun interpretation of the "facts," managed to get the important bits wrong. In contrast, it was anticipated that otherwise cognitively less mature individuals (i.e., individuals who continue to imagine that ignorance is the only intellectual crime) would still lack the ability to differentiate mistakes of fact and mistakes of law, and so would wrongly treat them as morally or legally equivalent. In view of these hypotheses, the classic Punch and Judy episode in which Punch trashes an empty box as a result of ignorance about Judy's real whereabouts will obviously get us only partway down the road to a better understanding of these equally moral and epistemic matters. Clearly, more than this simple measure of false-belief understanding is required.

Punch and Judy Redux—The Continuing Series

If (as both the law and ordinary conceptions of moral responsibility require) it is essential to distinguish behaviors that arise unwittingly as a result of simple ignorance from the more blameworthy actions that follow as a consequence of having actively misinterpreted what is required, and *if* (as available research demonstrates) we are not born into the world with either an appreciation of the possibility of false belief or a recognition that all knowledge is interpretive, *then* it follows that we have all come to an adult understanding of such common-sense legal and ethical matters only slowly and fitfully, and that we were, no doubt, once less competent at managing these distinctions than we are today. All of this sets the stage for an as-yet-unwritten developmental story, one chapter of which might be told by a close examination of children's responses to Punch's ill-conceived plan to get rid of Judy, box and all. What would obviously be missing from any such one-item test is the opportunity to determine whether all or only some of the children who already grasp the possibility of false belief are also capable of considering the prospect that Punch might make mistakes of law, owing to some failure on his part to properly interpret his circumstances.

Method

Stimulus Materials

Picture this: Instead of only one box, there are now two boxes on the stage. One is painted orange; the other is a similar, though differently colored, container into which Punch and Judy are industriously loading oranges. Punch again briefly leaves the stage, and in his absence Judy again manages to fall into a box—this time the one that she and Punch have been filling with oranges. "Help!" she cries, "I have fallen into *the orange box*." Punch, in search of any opportunity to do Judy in, (mis)interprets her cries to mean that she has fallen into the box painted orange, which he promptly, and with clearly stated lethal intentions, pushes over the edge of the stage. Plainly, what we have here is another bungled attempt at murder—an attempt that goes wrong this time not as a result of simple blameless igno-rance (a mistake of fact, if you will) but rather as a consequence of Punch's having carelessly misinterpreted Judy's open-ended claim regarding her whereabouts (a sort of mistake of law).

Balanced against these two "attempted murder" scenarios (let us call them scenes 1 and 2), which portrayed Punch as acting with malice afore-thought and as failing in his intention to do Judy in, two contrasting "acci-dental manslaughter" episodes (scenes 3 and 4) were also played out and captured on video. (See figure 1.) In these last two scenes, Punch acts out of good intentions but nevertheless ends up mistakenly throwing Judy into the trash. More specifically, scene 3 is effectively the mirror image of scene 1, in that, by again being in the wrong place at the wrong time, Punch is simply unaware of the fact that Judy has fallen into an on-stage box. On this occasion, however, and in the course of merely trying to tidy things up, he inadvertently pitches her out, along with what (as a result of blameless igno-rance) he falsely believes to be an empty crate. Scene 4 (the benevolent counterpart to the failed attempt at murder in scene 2) again involves two boxes. This time the stage contains a green box and also a white box; the latter is stamped with a large green numeral "1." Punch is again off stage when Judy accidentally falls into the green-colored box and begins calling for help by shouting "Check the green one!" Punch, eager to help, rushes in, interprets Judy's statement to mean that she is in the box designated by the green "1," and innocently attempts to "clear the decks" by trashing the green-colored box in which Judy is actually trapped.

Procedure and Response Measures

Except to say that we began by hiring an aging Punch and Judy "profes-sor" (as they traditionally call themselves) and videotaped his performance of the four scenes, which we then showed in a counterbalanced order to 25 adults and to 50 children between the ages of 5 and 7, enough has proba-bly been said about what was shown to whom.

Of the several questions that were put to the participants, two lines of inquiry are especially relevant to the present discussion. One line of inquiry was aimed at establishing who, from our sample of young school-age chil-dren, did or did not already possess some fledgling understanding of the constructivistic character of the knowing process and so deserved to be

Cause

	Error of Ignorance (Mistake of Fact)	Error of Interpretation (Mistake of Law)
Attempted Murder	Scene 1: Punch fails to "trash" Judy	Scene 2: Punch misinterprets "orange box"
Accidental Manslaughter	Scene 3: Punch unwittingly "trashes" Judy	Scene 4: Punch misinterprets "green one"

Crime

Figure 1
Scene-description table.

credited with something like the beginnings of an interpretive theory of mind. Second, we wanted to know, in much the same way that Piaget (1932) did, just how responsible (i.e., "bad") all of these participants judged Punch's actions to be by having them rate each of the four scenarios on a five-point "badness meter."

As a way of getting at the first of these matters, we closely questioned all the subjects as to whether they understood that, whenever there were two boxes on stage (interpretive scenes 2 and 4), both Punch and Judy were somehow within their rights in finding different meanings in the inherently ambiguous statements "I'm in the orange box" and "Check the green one." In addition, we queried the subjects directly as to whether all the responsibility for things' subsequently going badly could be fairly assigned to Judy for having been unclear as to her whereabouts , or to Punch because he had leaped to the wrong conclusion (e.g., "Was this mix-up about the boxes all Judy's fault, all Punch's fault, or perhaps a little bit of both?"). Because not every child who correctly answered the first of these questions also succeeded on the second, subjects responding correctly to both were characterized as "Fully Constructivistic"; those who answered just one correctly were labeled "Transitional"; those who succeeded on neither were labeled "Non-Constructivistic." Overall, 24 of the 48 child subjects who succeeded on a set of necessary control questions were scored as having a Non-Constructivistic theory of mind, 14 were labeled as Transitional, and 10 were categorized as having a Fully Constructivistic understanding of the knowing process. (Two children failed to correctly respond to the comprehension questions regarding the intentional/accidental nature of Punch's actions and were consequently excluded from the analysis.)

Although various other hypotheses were formulated and tested concerning how both children and adults might respond to these materials, the specific matter on which we particularly mean to focus your attention are the differential ways in which Non-Constructivistic, Transitional, and Fully Constructivistic subjects responded to the two "manslaughter" scenes (scenes 3 and 4). Because, as we see it, ordinary adults are a part of that moral community that originally authored the distinction between mistakes of fact and mistakes of law as a way of instrumenting our collective commitment to the view that persons evidencing different mental states are differently culpable, we reasoned that any adult standardly equipped with an *interpretive* theory of belief entitlement would understand and judge scenes

3 and 4 differently. That is, we reasoned that such routinely interpretive adult subjects would be more inclined to take a forgiving attitude toward Punch in scene 3 (where his error in assuming that he was trashing an empty box grew out of blameless or simple ignorance) than in scene 4 (where he failed to properly interpret Judy's plea for help). This follows because our ordinary adult conception of responsibility burdens us with the duty to prevent unintended outcomes when it is within our capacity to do so (Weiner, this volume). In scene 3, where Punch acted out of simple ignorance, there was nothing afoot that might have prompted him to pause before throwing out what he wrongly, but blamelessly, believed to be an empty box. (For a similar rationale, see Wimmer, Gruber, and Perner 1984.) In scene 4 (the scene with the two green boxes), anyone alert to the interpretive nature of the knowing process could ordinarily be expected to flag Judy's statement "Check the green one" as inherently ambiguous, and to require anyone hearing it to seek opportunities for clarification before going off half-cocked. His failure to do so, therefore, marks Punch's behavior as a form of reckless endangerment (Duff 1990) for which he can be legitimately held blameworthy, despite his otherwise good intentions. As it turned out, the collective response pattern of the 25 adults who agreed to help "norm" this procedure did in fact meet with these expectations. That is, as would have been expected by someone in the legal profession, they tended to treat Punch's being blindsided by an unexpected fact as a bona fide mitigating excuse, while insisting that when he ventured some homespun interpretation of the so-called facts he deserved being held responsible for having gotten things wrong.

Our predictions concerning the children who completed our procedures followed a similar logic. First, it was expected that those children who correctly understood the possibility of false belief but gave no indication of subscribing to even a Transitional understanding of interpretation could do little else than treat Punch as having simply been misinformed in scene 4. That is, by failing to appreciate that individuals make an active contribution to their own attempts at knowledge construction, such children would be in no position to regard Punch as having a positive duty to get to the bottom of any ambiguous communication; they were expected to treat both scenes 3 and 4 as equivalent cases of ignorance, and, consequently, to see Punch's actions as equally blameworthy in the two cases. The version of responsibility open to children such as these, who do not yet subscribe to an interpretive theory of mind, could scarcely be expected to include provisions for holding others liable for failing to resolve interpretive ambiguities that they do not themselves see. In contrast, children who were scored as having a Fully Constructivistic theory of mind were expected to perform as adults do, finding Punch more blameworthy in scene 4 (where he failed to proceed with appropriate caution) than in scene 3 (where he was none the wiser) Finally, subjects classified as Transitional were expected to fall midway between Non-Constructivistic and Fully Constructivistic subjects, by being more fickle or by finding only a more modest difference between these two scenes.

In short, then, we mean to argue that the role of intentionality in settling matters of responsibility depends on the particular theory of mind to which one subscribes. Children whose best understanding of mental life stops short of even a fledgling appreciation of the interpretive character of the knowing process, and who consequently imagine ignorance to be the worst of intellectual crimes, are hardly in a position to judge anyone harshly for failing to get to the bottom of some interpretive confusion that is lost on them. This limited vision of responsibility serves them well enough in scene 3 (where Punch's mistake is not having been everywhere at once) but fails them when the need for an interpretive stance arises, as it does in scene 4. In contrast, children with some insight into the interpretive nature of knowing are expected to have already made some measurable headway toward understanding that the duty to look before one leaps extends beyond the obligation to simply behave in some upstanding way and goes on to include responsibilities to deliberate, to inquire further, and to interpret ambiguous situations wisely. (See also Duff 1990.)

Results

Overall, the results from this first trial run with these new stimulus materials are quite promising. Some of these findings turn on the "attempted murder" scenarios (scenes 1 and 2), in which Punch acts out of bad intentions but in which, owing to his ignorance of the shifting circumstances, there are no negative material consequences of his actions. As such, these stories, and the responses that they prompt, revisits an older, but now largely moribund, debate about the role of intentions and consequences in the framing of children's moral judgments. (For reviews, see Karniol 1978, Keasey 1978, and Lapsley 1996.) For present purposes, at least two things must be said about this very substantial literature. One is that the large bulk of these earlier studies used only age as a subject-selection factor, leaving unsettled what more psychological matters might ultimately be responsible for actually explaining the age-graded changes that were observed. The other is that, while taking Piaget's (1932) original distinction between "objective" and "subjective" notions of moral responsibility as an initial point of departure, most of this previous research ended up glossing these potentially richer distinctions as a simpler and psychologically more empty contrast between behavioral "intentions" and "consequences," leaving no room for the epistemic considerations emphasized here. As a number of commentators (e.g., Chandler, Greenspan, and Barenboim 1973; Dean and Youniss 1991; Keasey 1978; Youniss and Damon 1992) have suggested, these cruder ways of putting the data have tended to weather badly (for one thing, even very young preschoolers have since been shown to recognize another's behavioral "intentions," or at least show some basic understanding of others' "motivational states"—see Astington, this volume; Chandler, Greenspan, and Barenboim 1973; Meltzoff, Gopnik, and Repacholi 1999; Wellman and Philips, this volume), with the result that the study of the place of subjectivity in our understanding of moral development has been prematurely forced out of fashion.

In opposition to this trend, it was reasoned in the present study that subjects who failed to understand Punch's confusion as traceable to either his own or Judy's interpretive actions (i.e., Non-Constructivistic subjects) would have something like an "objective" view of moral responsibility. In contrast, those who understood Punch's failures as a product of either Judy's lack of clarity or his own lack of diligence in seeking further instructions (i.e., both Transitional and Fully Constructivistic subjects) would harbor a more "subjective" view of responsibility. This is exactly what our findings suggest (figure 2). That is, the comparative badness ratings for these two groups produced diverging patterns of responses. Similar, then, to more classical findings (see Lapsley 1996 for an updated summary), participants rated as having a Non-Constructivistic theory of mind (and thus an objectively based view of responsibility) based their judgments of Punch's "badness" very heavily on whether Judy ended up being thrown in the trash

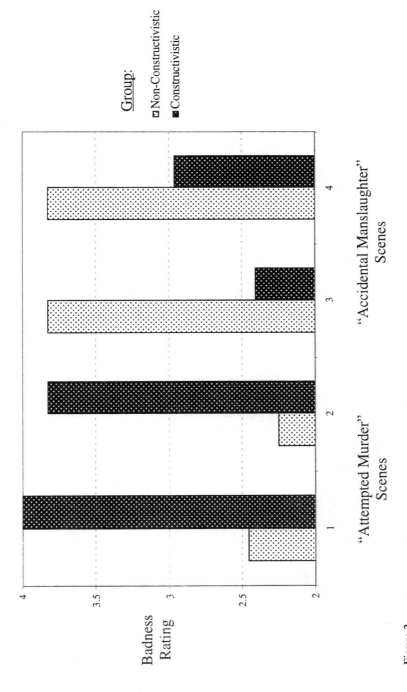

Figure 2
Children's badness ratings.

in scenes 3 and 4, giving only nominal (although not zero) consideration to Punch's benevolent intentions in these scenes. Alternatively, these same Non-Constructivistic subjects tended to be especially lenient in judging Punch in scenes 1 and 2, where, despite no shortage in his expression of murderous intentions, Judy ended up being accidentally spared as a result of Punch's ignorance or misinterpretation. In contrast, those children with even a minimal understanding of interpretation (and thus a more subjectively based view of responsibility) did just the opposite, condemning Punch for his bad intentions in the "attempted murder" scenes and minimizing his "badness" when, despite his good intentions, he ended up fairly accused of "accidental manslaughter." Importantly, these contrastive results were all statistically significant.

Because being coded as having a constructivistic or non-constructivistic theory of mind is itself significantly related to children's age, there is room to speculate that the evident connection between children's moral judgments and their epistemic stance may be an artifact of simply growing older. As it was, however, when age was factored out of the relationship between subjects' badness ratings and their theory of mind, the correlation was reduced in only modest ways, which suggests that the contribution of children's epistemic status to their moral judgments is largely independent of age.

Taken together, this first set of results goes some distance toward making the general case that the transition from an early "copy" theory of belief entitlement (which regards knowledge as the passive by-product of either simple exposure to or ignorance of all the relevant facts) to a more active, constructivistic stance (which obliges persons to take some responsibility for their own active interpretations of experience) has a significant impact on the way in which children frame their moral judgments. Coming to a more interpretive theory of mind appears to have the effect of especially alerting young subjects to the particular moral significance of such subjective factors as intention and avoidability in their assignment of responsibility. It is important to note, however, that this transition, at least as it involves the understanding of intention, is more a matter of degrees than an all-or-nothing process. That is, as these data indicate, even the children characterized as adhering to a non-constructivistic view still were able to comment properly on Punch's motivational states, or what he *wanted* (as required by the comprehension control questions), and to at least partially integrate this knowledge into their evaluations (i.e., their badness ratings differed significantly from both zero and ceiling in the relevant conditions). Without further research, the full nature of this difference between constructivistic and non-constructivistic subjects' use of intention information in their judgments remains unclear. The various chapters in this volume that distinguish between children's simpler conceptions of desire and their more fully fledged notions of intention (Astington; Malle and Knobe; Mele; Moses) provide at least one speculative possibility for explaining this difference. Still, what seems certain enough from our data is that an adult-like conception of intention and an interpretive view of knowledge both require an understanding of others as "epistemic agents" who lead active and interpretive mental lives. Failing to acknowledge the significance of agency at this mentalistic level results, then, not only in an under-developed conception of what intentions are, but also in the sort of objectivistic stance that the non-constructivistic children of our study assumed in their assignments of moral responsibility. This same point can be seen most clearly in the set of results dealing with children's ability to distinguish between potential mistakes of fact and mistakes of law.

With specific reference to our findings associated with participants' responses to the "accidental manslaughter" stories (scenes 3 and 4), where the mistake of fact and mistake of law distinction are most critical, the results obtained are again closely in line with our expectations. First, although there was no serious reason to doubt that all the adult subjects interviewed would prove to subscribe to a fully constructivistic theory of mind (as they in fact did), there was a real open question as to whether the particular stimulus materials in hand would allow them sufficient latitude to express whatever readiness they might have to judge interpretive mistakes of law more harshly than ignorance-driven mistakes of fact. As it turned out (figure 3), there was, as predicted, a highly significant $(t(24)=5.78, p<0.0001)$ difference in their badness ratings for scenes 3 and 4. Overall, these adult subjects tended to view Punch as much more blameworthy for harming Judy as a result of his having negligently misinterpreted her ambiguous pleas for help in scene 4 than for doing more or less the same thing out of simple ignorance in scene 3.

Essentially the same story is true for the 10 child subjects who were classified as already subscribing to a Fully Constructivistic theory of mind. As

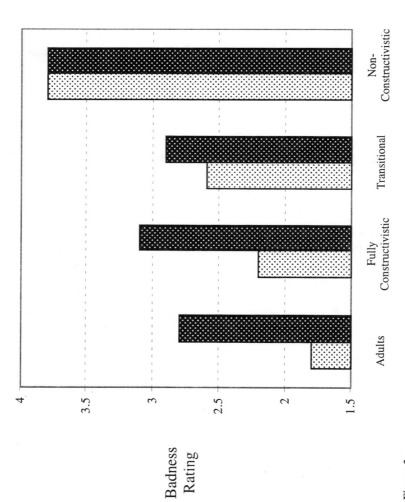

Figure 3
Ratings for "accidental manslaughter" scenes.

can be seen from figure 3, these subjects also judged Punch as significantly more blameworthy in scene 4 than in scene 3 ($t(9)=5.01$, $p<0.0004$]. In contrast, the 24 children who were classified as having a Non-Constructivistic theory of mind rated Punch's behavior in scenes 3 and 4 in exactly the same ways. Finally, as hypothesized, the 14 children categorized as Transitional did find Punch marginally more blameworthy in scene 4 than in scene 3 ($t(13) = 1.0$, $p = 0.17$), but the magnitude of this difference proved to be roughly one-third of that evident in the responses of their more fully constructivistic peers.

Conclusion

The new line of evidence brought forward in this chapter goes some distance toward making two points. First, our efforts show that it is not, after all, impossible to find empirical ways of studying how the course of children's moral and epistemic development might be deeply interpenetrating. Second, it already seems clear enough that children who have begun to round the interpretive turn that will eventually bring them to a full-fledged constructivistic view of knowledge appear to be beings of a sharply different moral order than those who haven't yet reached this point in development. Specifically, such young constructivistic thinkers appear to already have the epistemic eyes to see the essential distinction between mistakes of fact and mistakes of law that governs so much of our legal and moral system. If this is all true, then beliefs about truth and beliefs about rightness may not actually belong in the separate watertight compartments in which we have been pickling them for so many years.

Acknowledgments

The preparation of this chapter was supported by an operating grant from the Natural Sciences and Engineering Research Council of Canada to the first author, by an NSERC Graduate Fellowship to the second author, and by a University of British Columbia Graduate Fellowship to the third author.

18

Intentional Agency, Responsibility, and Justice

Leonard V. Kaplan

The liberal state allows a judge, or a jury if there is one, enough discretion to make a finding of guilt or innocence that is compatible with the intent element for criminal blame. However, judgments of intent and perceptions of justice are not always in harmony with each other (Kaplan 1995). In Melville's novella *Billy Budd,* for example, the protagonist, who intended a criminal act, arguably should have escaped liability in the name of justice because the context of the allegedly criminal act provided a powerful justification. Billy Budd acts out of uncontrollable righteous indignation when slaying a purveyor of evil. Thus, Budd represents goodness but is still hanged on the basis of his presumed intent. Similarly, Dürrenmatt's novels *The Judge and His Hangman* and *The Quarry* can be used to argue that the usual attribution of intent in the finding of criminal responsibility may conflict with intuitions of justice. Dürrenmatt's protagonist Barlach seeks justice for two suspected murderers (whom he cannot prove guilty) by manipulating one to kill the other, and his own intent for murder (executed by another person) may appear justified without any traditional rationalization (e.g., duress, necessity, or insanity).

This chapter assumes that judgments of intention, responsibility, and justice have been, are, and will continue to be in tension. The Platonic aspiration of integrating a citizen's obligation into communal and political organizations, culminating in just adjudication and state policy, remains an ideal. In the liberal state, *justice* refers to what the state should provide in accord with liberal principles: conditions for fair resolution of conflicts, for fair access to means of personal flourishing, and for sufficient prosocial motivation to result in both a general sense of autonomy and a commitment beyond the self to the community. The gap between just and unjust

outcomes is then explained by institutional failure. The unwelcome consequence is that the individual citizen will resist responding personally to the
injustice and suffering experienced by others, because the burden of providing justice and correcting injustice belongs to the state. The role of individual agents' intentions in bringing about justice might then appear
irrelevant; nevertheless, individuals' intentions are critical to many aspects
of the law.

The general aim of this chapter is to shed some light on how intention,
responsibility, and justice do not fit neatly together when made concrete in
today's liberal institutions. However, rather than explore legal conceptions
of these competing elements, I will explore their moral counterparts within
rival models of moral action. These models, though primarily normative,
provide fitting illustrations of the relationship among the individual's intentions, social norms of responsibility, and the corresponding patterns of justice. Moreover, several of these models focus on the paradigm of one agent's
becoming aware of the suffering of another and on the moral dilemma that
this situation poses. Thus, my discussion will also touch on the interpersonal nature of responsibility and the social-cognitive capacities that are
involved in it.

The interplay of intention and responsibility can be seen in the operation
of the criminal and tort systems in liberal societies. In American criminal
law, for example, full responsibility is ascribed when an agent acted with
intent. On the one hand, the requirements for a finding of intent are often
minimal, and some criminal-law theorists are concerned that this mini-
malism violates intuitions of justice. On the other hand, general excusing
conditions such as insanity, incapacity, and self-defense qualify the rule of
intent, and both the general rule and the exceptions are meant to foster
social justice and safety—social justice because those who accidentally create harm but otherwise intended to do good do not deserve as severe a punishment as those who deliberately plan a criminal act and execute it
intentionally, safety because intentionally acting criminals pose a greater
threat to society.

Whereas the law is concerned more with responsibility as liability, I will
explore the other side of normative responsibility: duty (more specifically,
the ethical duty to be responsive to another's needs). Criminal law is one
societal tool to prevent people from hurting one another, and thus it codi-

fies the negative duty of not doing harm. Ethical systems go beyond this negative goal and declare positive duties, such as to love, to respect, or even to aid one's fellow humans. Considerations of responsibility thus turn to the generally shared sense of what a person owes to another. Issues of intentional agency arise in the analysis of how the individual weighs his or her various motives (e.g., for self-preservation vs. altruistic concern) and how capable the individual is of acting autonomously. Moreover, issues of social cognition arise when we examine to what extent the individual is capable of recognizing the suffering of others and distinguishing it from deception or exploitation. Justice is, then, a function of the aggregated intentional actions of individuals in light of their ethical duty and in response to others in need, somehow complemented by the corrective intervention of institutions such as law and social welfare. Once more, my thesis is that these three elements—the individual's intentional agency, the shared sense of responsibility (now understood as ethical duty of interpersonal caring), and the community's achievement of justice—are in tension.

I want to consider three normative models of moral action that differ in how they flesh out the three parameters of intentional agency, responsibility, and justice as well as their interrelations. The choice of these models is admittedly idiosyncratic, but it aims at introducing the readership of this volume (most likely, cognitive scientists broadly understood) to another literature that predates these disciplines and still attracts scholarly and folk attention. In particular, this moral, humanistic, and theological literature has become integrated into legal discourse since the 1970s. Robert Cover (1975) suggested the necessity of reexamining theology for jurisprudence, and Roberto Unger (1975), the meta-theoretician of the Critical Legal Studies movement (which holds that law is just another moment of legitimated power in the liberal state) lamented to God the lack of justice in the contemporary legal order. The movement toward God was not mere rhetoric or postmodern irony; many law schools are now offering law and literature classes and law and theology classes influenced by Cover and Unger.

The first of the theories analyzed here is the liberal model of the economic person. Minimalist about the ethical duty of interpersonal caring, it demands from the individual only rational self-determined action and little for the attainment of justice. The second model, which can be traced back to Nietzsche and which is well exemplified in the work of Michel

Foucault, places all consequences of human action on individual actors but is at the same time skeptical about the autonomy of individual agency. The third model is exemplified by two scholars of theological ethics in the Judeo-Christian tradition. Both are fairly specific in defining the ethical duty of interpersonal caring but perhaps naive in their assumptions about individual agency and social cognition.

The Liberal Model of the Economic Person

The liberal state provides the economic model of responsibility and moral action as normative. The model centers on the proposition that the individual and the system will function best if people tend their own respective gardens. The hidden hand of the market, the theory goes, will respond to the law of supply and demand and create the abundant wealth and freedom that is central to liberal value. As long as the individual (who is portrayed as deliberative and as fully equipped with intentions and the capacity to act on them) maximizes his or her own profit, the individual will serve the entire community.

The economic agent will intend to take care of his or her own needs and perhaps of the needs of relatives, associates, and friends. Altruism as a value is allowed but not required, and it is constrained by private preference. Liberty and not interpersonal concern is the chief value. The maximization of personal preferences is constrained only by the duty to not hurt the other.

The American version of liberal law, even more than the versions of other capitalist economies, demands little of the individual to safeguard the other, even when the cost to the self is minimal and the protection for the other may be life saving. Minimization of interpersonal concern is reinforced by skepticism about the agent's capacity for accurate recognition of those who deserve concern. A man on the road who appears to be in distress may be part of a setup; those on social welfare who appear to be in need may deliberately exploit the system of foolish compassion; homeless young people may have freely chosen to abandon their parents' homes. The economic model assumes that individuals are well equipped with rationality and with intentional agency to pursue their own goals but poorly equipped to tell the needy from the greedy. In view of these assumptions, it should not be the individual's responsibility to take care of others (those few who really need it). Instead, the state is expected to pick up the justice burden.

Avineri's (1972) explication of Hegel's theory of the modern state illustrates the sources of this model in nineteenth-century liberalism and its culmination in the twentieth-century market economy. Hegel tried to posit the conditions under which the individual could flourish and still connect to an organic community that met individual needs and warranted a sense of commitment and belonging. Hegel took history and economic reality into account in attempting to solve the political-philosophical question of just human governance. He presupposed the market analyses of the political economists of the Scottish Enlightenment, and therefore he accepted the necessity of a divide between the private and the public sector that has since dominated liberal political theory.

The family, Hegel asserted, is the basic building block of the state. The family marks private social relations, and its love and emotional nourishment provide the psychological conditions for fully actualized human expressiveness. Marriage is covenant, not contract. Thus, the economic agent has a responsibility of altruism to the family. But the logic of public market relationships was one of mere self-interest. Here individuals contracted to their respective best advantages. This public aspect of social interaction, Hegel understood, would disrupt social relations because the market would necessarily create a poverty class despite the best efforts of all participants. This would happen for many reasons, including the volatility of technological dislocation. Since Hegel was concerned for all citizens of the state, he had to build in protections for those who were left impoverished. Hence, the state was assigned the role of providing justice for those economically bereft.

But Hegel was acutely aware of a further problem in the liberal mechanisms of social ordering: alienation. Why should one care for the other outside the family? And if one should, how could this be accomplished institutionally? Hegel suggested that individuals should belong to free associations that create solidarity beyond the family setting and bonds of expressiveness; together these would help ease the excessiveness of the market and merge organically into the fulfilled state.

The economic model of moral action, with its "tend your own garden ethos," has been furthered by the advance of market demands. Institutionally the professions have been forced (or at least they seem to feel compelled) to maximize profit: in law, for example, billable hours are far more important than public service. Economic necessity has reduced the effectiveness of the family as the general institution to fulfill the affective requirements of human nurture. No other institution, however, has replaced the family and its function.

Capitalism, as a political economy, has more than fulfilled expectations in creating enormous human wealth, which is probably distributed more widely than at any other time in human history. But, as Hegel (and others) foresaw, poverty and alienation within the bounds of the liberal state are continuing problems. The early-nineteenth-century division into public and private is under attack from left and right. The family is under debate, and the individual is isolated from the kinds of free associations that Hegel thought possible and necessary for both sociable and justice needs.

To recapitulate: The economic model puts great faith in the individual's capacity to rationally pursue goals and act intentionally. It defines the agent's responsibilities as mainly negative—to not harm or hinder others. And the model is skeptical about the individual's capacity to accurately perceive others in need. As a result of these three assumptions, the individual is not responsible for justice; the state is. And the state is also expected to attain justice without harming or hindering the individual's economic pursuits.

Not surprisingly, legal theorists from left and center have criticized the normative economic model as dehumanizing, and discontent with the actual manifestations of this model has engendered competing visions of moral action and responsibility. Many of these competing views have their roots in philosophy and in Western theology. They are as normative as the economic model, but their actual manifestations in the contemporary liberal state are more limited. An analysis of their assumptions with respect to intentional agency, responsibility, and the perception of the other illuminates how these basic categories are not only inescapable in ethical visions but also inescapably in tension.

Foucault and Postmodern Responsibility

Foucault's view of moral action builds on Nietzsche's understanding that humanity is alone in the world and that there is no foundation for human thought except that conventionally agreed upon. Humanity must therefore rise to the awareness that whatever happens in the human world is of human making and is within humanly shaped conceptions of responsibility.

In the most radical reading, Foucault denies humanity a metaphysical foundation for ethics or politics. Whereas Nietzsche pronounced the death of God (and the promise of a better human being freed from theological mystification), Foucault announced the death of the subject and of its assumptions of deliberation, intent, and autonomy. Such assumptions, he wrote, are merely socially constructed and cannot provide a solid foundation for ethics (Foucault 1997).

So why invoke Foucault as offering a theory of intention, responsibility, and justice? According to Thomas Keenan (1997), the skeptical aspect of Foucault's work—denying human agency—stands in conflict with another, perhaps more important aspect: Foucault's analysis of the interconnection between power and knowledge in society. According to Foucault, truth and knowledge are constructions of discourse, and discourse itself is dominated by disciplinary and institutional elites. Accordingly, knowledge is produced by an era's discourse and power structures; knowledge, in turn, regulates all institutions, be they asylums, prisons, or schools. The discourse of power also defines such concepts as human agency and responsibility; however, according to Foucault, these are illusory constructions, for there is no real freedom or agency within regulated social institutions.

Keenan argues that Foucault's analysis of this power-knowledge connection admits of intentional acts of social change, thereby casting doubt on the theoretical dismissal of autonomous agency. According to Keenan, postmodern responsibility lies in an understanding of the constructed nature of reality and of the potential for reconstruction of that reality into something better. Knowledge can be pried loose from power in order to alter power. Further, in his more direct social criticism, Foucault seemed to invoke the duty of bearing witness to injustice, taking a stance against injustice, and thus altering power through new discourse and action. Thus, not only Foucault's socio-political analysis but also his project of social reform (including his own political actions) presumed the very concepts of intentional agency that his metaphysical theory denies. Once more, these concepts seem inescapable.

Foucault adopted a sociological level of analysis, identifying institutional and social structures such as power, discourse, and knowledge. As a result,

Foucault has little to say about the interpersonal duty of one individual to another (especially another in need), and he does not address the intricate process of perceiving another, interpreting the other's actions and needs, and taking those into account when acting oneself. For Foucault, an individual's moral actions are situated within social institutions and the dominant discourse, not within the interpersonal dynamic of actual human encounters. Such an interpersonal frame lies at the core of the third model I would like to discuss, well represented by the theological ethics of Dietrich Bonhoeffer and Emmanuel Levinas.

Moral Action in Theological Ethics

In contrast to Foucault's skepticism toward human agency and a universal (i.e., discourse-transcending) responsibility, some ethical scholars have attempted to posit directly what moral responsibilities the citizen of the modern state has. In doing so, they not only offer moral prescriptions; they also presuppose intentional and social capacities in the individual that make moral action possible.

Bonhoeffer: Responsibility over Ethics

Bonhoeffer, one of the dazzling theological minds of the twentieth century, lived his theology. He was involved in the Abwehr's conspiracy to assassinate Hitler, and he was captured and executed. While captive, he wrote a good part of the fragmentary *Ethics*, presenting a case for the radical responsibility of every person to act in the face of injustice (Bonhoeffer 1995; see also Rasmussen 1998).

Bonhoeffer opened his analysis with the claim that ethics, as theorized in Western thought, had allowed good people to rationalize that their adherence to principles was sufficient protection from the ambiguities and messiness of human reality. Bonhoeffer can be read against the Kantian grain. Kant centers responsibility in the individual in the form of the categorical imperative—the universal ethic toward others. For Kant, then, the individual can and should act intentionally according to a fundamental ethical principle. Bonhoeffer holds that such a position is narcissistically grounded, and he denies the fundamental nature of the categorical imperative. Where the ethical Kantian justifies action in light of principles (to feel just and autonomous), Bonhoeffer demands more. He demands that one respond to the other in need without considering personal ethical costs or rationalized philosophical systems. The radical responsibility of the individual is always to another person, not to an ethical principle.

Bonhoeffer concedes, however, that the obligation to respond to the other is limited to the extraordinary. For the most part, people will live and should live within the bounds of what Bonhoeffer calls the three mandates: state, church, and family. Attending to these authorized institutions will regulate most moral action and relax much of the radical responsibility that Bonhoeffer demands.

But when faced with the abyss of injustice, an individual must respond without weighing alternatives. To save the other, one may have to sacrifice worldly laws and/or spiritual assurance. One must be willing to transgress in order to save the other from injustice. And so, despite "thou shalt not kill," Bonhoeffer himself took part in a conspiracy to assassinate Hitler, attempting murder in the face of injustice.

Bonhoeffer thus presumed that the individual has full intentional capacity to act morally, and that action should normally be guided by the responsibility to the three mandates. In extraordinary circumstances, however, a more radical duty is evoked that demands an immediate response to injustice, not just a response to mandates and rules. But what constitutes sufficient conditions of injustice to operate outside the normalizing mandates? Although the three mandates successfully and predictably regulate ordinary moral action in most situations, the extraordinary situations are hard to identify. By definition, the mandates provide no help with this identification, because the radical response may demand going against a mandate. There is a danger, then, that radical responsibility to the other is confounded with radical subjectivism. The assassination of Hitler and the assassination of Martin Luther King may be equally regarded as responses to extraordinary situations, albeit from very different ideological or personal viewpoints. Similarly, NATO's action against Serbian "ethnic cleansing" will be perceived by many as one of radical responsibility, but "pro-life" attacks on abortion clinics will divide perceivers in such assessment. An additional problem is that, even if injustice is identified, most will not heed the call for moral action but will instead assume the quiet guilt of omission. Intervention, so the rationalization goes, is typically dangerous and often ineffective.

There is perhaps some hope for the human capacity to recognize and respond to extraordinary situations. Social-psychological analyses suggest that, as long as the actor is alone, evasive rationalizations are rare, and interventions often occur without much deliberation; only when other potential actors are present is responsibility diffused (Latané and Darley 1969). Just as dozens of onlookers refrained from intervening when Kitty Genovese was murdered (in New York, in 1964), research participants in carefully planned experiments refrained from intervening in an emergency when others were around them (ibid.). Those who faced the emergency alone, however, intervened reliably and quickly.

Thus, humans may be capable of the radical responsibility that Bonhoeffer demands, but many forces counteract this kind of moral action against injustice. For example, there is the motivational constraint (the agent's perhaps rational reluctance to take significant risks in moral action), and there is the perceptual constraint (the limited human capacity to recognize injustice, or the disagreement over what constitutes injustice worthy of radical moral action). At the very least, if justice is left solely in the hands of individually acting moral citizens, error rates will be high—many injustices will not be reckoned, and some reckoned will not be fought.

Levinas and the Face of the Other
Levinas, a son of orthodox Jews with numerous rabbis as part of his heritage, was a philosopher, a teacher of adult Jewish education, a student of Husserl and Heidegger in his youth, the first to translate Heidegger into French, a fighter against Hitler, and a war prisoner. He built his philosophy out of Heideggerian ontology and Talmudic texts. All his work, if one had to summarize it briefly, could be reduced to the asymmetric responsibility of the moral agent to the call in need from the face of the other (Levinas 1981). Responsibility is asymmetric because one owes the other a response and care merely because of the other's existence; no "gift" should be expected in return.

In contrast to Foucault, Levinas grounds his analysis in an ancient, wonderfully bizarre set of Jewish texts: the Talmud, itself a commentary on the laws and stories revealed in the Torah. He follows a long philosophic tradition in Jewish thinking, bringing the tools of Greek philosophy as well as great literary texts such as Shakespeare and Dostoevski to his Talmudic studies of responsibility and justice issues. Levinas takes the position that the Talmud, as the work of rabbis, was evidence of human beings' trying to probe and reach God. God, however, has withdrawn from human reality, leaving only traces in the faces of others about the fact of God's withdrawal and presumed one-time presence.

Levinas offers a sketch of human development that may bring the individual closer to the withdrawing God. He suggests that existence starts in fear and must develop into autonomous atheism, which then allows the further development of a sense of agency and responsibility in the world. But Levinas argues that, ultimately, it is through the call for response from the face of the other (even a stranger) that one attains humanity—that one grows from atheistic autonomy to an understanding of the interpersonal obligation that inheres in human existence itself.

Thus, even though Levinas presupposes full intentional capacities in the individual, moral action lies in one's response to the call of the other. Ethical growth requires understanding of the illusory nature of individual autonomy—the individual does not directly intend moral action, but he or she is called to it. One can open oneself to the call, or one can avoid responsibility because of the harshness of its burden or because of the expectation that the liberal state will answer it. The (intentional and autonomous) decision to avoid responsibility, Levinas asserts, has a significant cost: the loss of the only potential trace to God. However, Levinas is aware of the "economics" of responding. Many faces call, and the world is invariably unjust. Globalization first heightens, then desensitizes awareness of human suffering. Even in the family, faces compete to demand response. Once again, the individual must be equipped with capacities to perceive and select from the demands of so many others—to distinguish the call of the psychopath or the con artist from that of the genuinely needy and oppressed.

Levinas knows that, owing to this selectiveness, individuals cannot do all that must be done. The state and its legal apparatus must provide conditions for justice and alleviate the radical call for individual moral action. But institutional welfare and the law are generally crude. Levinas does not specify the particular institutions that can shape and maintain structural injustice while still motivating the individual to personal ethical engagement. Ironically, justice as provided by the state may thwart responsiveness—or allow nonresponsiveness to rationalize itself—because the calls from those in need may be muted or may be directed toward institutions rather than individual moral agents.

Conclusion

Through the different lenses of the three models of moral action, the tension between individual intentions, responsibility, and justice plays out in different ways. The economic model puts its faith in the individual agent's rationality, constrained only by the duty to not stand in the way of others' freedom. Responsibility is conflated with the pursuit of one's own goals except in the obvious case of harming others. Moral action is then the absence of immorality, and injustice is the unfortunate residual that is left over from these equations—left for correction by the liberal state.

Foucault dismissed the agent's capacity for freedom and intentional action within the imprisoning constraints of power and discourse. For him, justice is not produced by an aggregate of individual actions; it emerges from the elitist discourse about justice. But despite taking this deeply relativistic and skeptical position, Foucault ends up encouraging a stance against injustice, reinvigorating (now implicitly) the concept of intentional action.

Bonhoeffer and Levinas equip the individual agent with intentionality but also demand a fundamental responsibility (i.e., ability to respond) to the fellow human. For them, moral action consists neither in rational goal pursuit nor in a stance against societal structures. They see the moral agent as interacting with and perceiving the social world, which sometimes calls for moral action far beyond the normal rules and standards. Levinas, especially, sees moral action as an interpersonal response to the other in need. With this interpersonal perspective comes the assumption that humans can recognize the other's mental life (e.g., true suffering or the authentic motive for a call in need)—an assumption that the economic model does not share.

Two conclusions seem warranted. On the ethical level, Foucault, Bonhoeffer, and Levinas share the insight that the liberal state is flawed, that justice is not guaranteed by the confluence of jurisprudence, individual rationality, and social rules of responsibility. It takes more to achieve justice, as long as justice is (optimistically) a duty imperfectly performed by the state or (pessimistically) a construct of discourse controlled by the state.

What more it takes varies by author. But (and this is the second conclusion) the ingredients for what more it takes will always include some assumptions about the agent's capacity to reason, to act intentionally, and to perceive and interpret the social world and other beings within it. In this circle of questions, philosophy and psychology, and ethics and social cognition, may meet, perhaps not to answer the same questions but to recognize the common assumptions they cannot escape.

Acknowledgments

Neil Komesar, Bernard Levinson, and Aviam Soifer contributed to whatever lucidity this chapter may possess. Carl Rasmussen has taught Law, Theology, and State with me at the University of Wisconsin School of Law and introduced me to the thought of Dietrich Bonhoeffer. Bertram Malle engaged me in this dialogue and shaped the chapter.

References

Aarts, J., and Aarts, F. 1991. Find and want: A corpus-based case study in verb complementation. In *The Verb in Contemporary English*, ed. B. Aarts and C. Meyer. Cambridge University Press.

Abelson, R. P., Dasgupta, N., Park, J., and Banaji, M. R. 1998. Perceptions of the collective other. *Personality and Social Psychology Review* 2: 243–250.

Adams, F. 1986. Intention and intentional action: The simple view. *Mind and Language* 1: 281–301.

Aloise, P. A. 1993. Trait confirmation and disconfirmation: The development of attribution biases. *Journal of Experimental Child Psychology* 55: 177–193.

Ames, D. R. 2000a. Strategies for social inference: The roles of evidence, implicit theories, and social projection in population-level judgments. Manuscript, University of California, Berkeley.

Ames, D. R. 2000b. Mental state inference in person perception: Everyday solutions to the problem of other minds. Manuscript, University of California, Berkeley.

Ames, D. R., and Fu, H. 2000. Conflicts of intentionality: Culture and the perception of endogenous/exogenous desires. Manuscript, University of California, Berkeley.

Anscombe, G. E. M. 1957. *Intention*. Blackwell.

Antaki, C. 1994. *Explaining and Arguing: The Social Organization of Accounts*. Sage.

Antony, L. 1989. Anomalous monism and the problem of explanatory force. *Philosophical Review* 98: 153–188.

Aristotle. 1962 (originally published ca. 330 B.C.). *The Nicomachean Ethics*. Macmillan.

Armstrong, D. M. 1981. The causal theory of mind. In *The Nature of Mind and Other Essays*. Cornell University Press.

Asch, S. E. 1952. *Social Psychology*. Prentice-Hall.

Aslin, R. N., Saffran, J. R., and Newport, E. L. 1998. Computation of conditional probability statistics by 8-month-old infants. *Psychological Science* 9: 321–324.

Astington, J. W. 1991. Intention in the child's theory of mind. In *Children's Theories of Mind*, ed. D. Frye and C. Moore. Erlbaum.

Astington, J. W. 1993. *The Child's Discovery of the Mind*. Harvard University Press.

Astington, J. W. 1999. The language of intention: Three ways of doing it. In *Developing Theories of Intention*, ed. P. Zelazo et al. Erlbaum.

Astington, J. W., and Gopnik, A. 1991. Developing understanding of desire and intention. In *Natural Theories of Mind*, ed. A. Whiten. Blackwell.

Astington, J. W., and Lee, E. 1991. What do children know about intentional causality? Presented at meeting of Society for Research in Child Development, Seattle.

Audi, R. 1973. Intending. *Journal of Philosophy* 70: 387–402.

Audi, R. 1986. Intending, intentional action, and desire. In *The Ways of Desire*, ed. J. Marks. Precedent.

Audi, R. 1988. Deliberative intentions and willingness to act: A reply to Professor Mele. *Philosophia* 18: 243–245.

Audi, R. 1991. Intention, cognitive commitment, and planning. *Synthese* 86: 361–378.

Audi, R. 1993. *Action, Intention, and Reason*. Cornell University Press.

Averill, J.R. 1983. Studies on anger and aggression. *American Psychologist* 38: 1145–1160.

Avineri, S. 1972. *Hegel's Theory of the Modern State*. Cambridge University Press.

Avrahami, J., and Kareev, Y. 1994. The emergence of events. *Cognition* 53: 239–261.

Baier, A. C. 1970. Act and intent. *Journal of Philosophy* 19: 648–658.

Baier, K. 1958. *Moral Point of View: A Rational Basis of Ethics*. Cornell University Press.

Baillargeon, R. 1995. A model of physical reasoning in infancy. In *Advances in Infancy Research*, volume 9, ed. C. Rovee-Collier and L. Lipsitt. Ablex.

Baillargeon, R., Graber, M., DeVos, J., and Black, J. C. 1990. Why do young infants fail to search for hidden objects? *Cognition* 36: 255–284.

Baird, B. 1965. *The Art of the Puppet*. Bonanza Books.

Baird, J. A. 1999. Young Children's Understanding of the Relation Between Actions and Intentions. Doctoral dissertation, University of Oregon.

Baird, J. A., Baldwin, D. A., and Malle, B. F. 2000. Parsing the behavior stream: Evidence for the psychological primacy of intention boundaries. Manuscript, University of Oregon.

Baird, J. A. and Moses, L. J. 2000. Do preschoolers appreciate that identical actions may be motivated by different intentions? Manuscript, University of Oregon.

Baldwin, D. A. 1993a. Early referential understanding: Infants' ability to recognize referential acts for what they are. *Developmental Psychology* 29: 832–843.

Baldwin, D. A. 1993b. Infants' ability to consult the speaker for cues to word reference. *Journal of Child Language* 20: 395–418.

Baldwin, D. A. 1995. Understanding the link between joint attention and language. In *Joint Attention*, ed. C. Moore and P. Dunham. Erlbaum.

Baldwin, D. A., and Baird, J. A. 1999. Action analysis: A gateway to intentional inference. In *Early Social Cognition*, ed. P. Rochat. Erlbaum.

Baldwin, D. A., Baird, J. A., Saylor, M. M., and Clark, M. A. In press. Infants detect structure in human action: A first step toward understanding others' intentions? *Child Development*.

Baldwin, D. A., Markman, E. M., and Melartin, R. L. 1993. Infants' ability to draw inferences about nonobvious object properties: Evidence from exploratory play. *Child Development* 64: 711–728.

Baldwin, D. A., and Moses, L. J. 1994. Early understanding of referential intent and attentional focus: Evidence from language and emotion. In *Origins of an Understanding of Mind*, ed. C. Lewis and P. Mitchell. Erlbaum.

Baldwin, D. A., and Moses, L. J. 1996. The ontogeny of social information gathering. *Child Development* 67: 1915–1939.

Bandura, A. 1997. *Self-Efficacy: The Exercise of Control*. Freeman.

Baron-Cohen, S. 1995. *Mindblindness: An Essay on Autism and Theory of Mind*. MIT Press.

Baron-Cohen, S., Leslie, A. M., and Frith, U. 1985. Does the autistic child have a "theory of mind"? *Cognition* 21: 37–46.

Barresi, J., and Moore, C. 1996. Intentional relations and social understanding. *Behavioral and Brain Sciences* 19: 107–154.

Bartsch, K., and Wellman, H. M. 1989. Young children's attribution of action to beliefs and desires. *Child Development* 60: 946–964.

Bartsch, K., and Wellman, H. M. 1995a. *Children Talk about the Mind*. Oxford University Press.

Bartsch, K., and Wellman, H. M. 1995b. Explanations and arguments. In K. Bartsch and H. W. Wellman, *Children Talk about the Mind*. Oxford University Press.

Bates, E., Benigni, L., Bretherton, I., Camaioni, L., and Volterra, V. 1979. *The Emergence of Symbols: Cognition and Communication in Infancy*. Academic Press.

Beardsley, M. 1978. Intending. In *Values and Morals*, ed. A. Goldman and J. Kim. Reidel.

Beardsley, M. 1980. Motives and Intentions. In *Action and Responsibility*, ed. M. Bradie and M. Brand. Applied Philosophy Program, Bowling Green State University.

Bennett, J. 1978. Some remarks about concepts. *Behavioral and Brain Sciences* 1: 557–560.

Black, H. C. 1990. *Black's Law Dictionary*, sixth edition. West.

Bogdan, R. 2000. *Minding Minds: Evolving a Reflexive Mind By Interpreting Others*. MIT Press.

Bonhoeffer, D. 1955. *Ethics*. Macmillan.

Brand, M. 1984. *Intending and Acting*. MIT Press.

Bratman, M. 1987. *Intention, Plans, and Practical Reason*. Harvard University Press.

Bratman, M. E. 1989. Replies to McCann and Velleman. Manuscript, Stanford University.

Bratman, M. E. 1993. Shared intention. *Ethics* 104: 97–113.

Bratman, M. E. 1997. Responsibility and planning. *Journal of Ethics* 1: 27–43.

Bratman, M. E. 1999. *Faces of Intention: Selected Essays on Intention and Agency*. Cambridge University Press.

Brazelton, T. B., and Tronick, E. 1980. Preverbal communication between mothers and infants. In *The Social Foundations of Language and Thought*, ed. D. Olson. Norton.

Brentano, F. C. 1874. *Psychology from an Empirical Standpoint*. Humanities Press, 1973.

Bretherton, I. 1991. Intentional communication and the development of an understanding of mind. In *Children's Theories of Mind*, ed. D. Frye and C. Moore. Erlbaum.

Bretherton, I., McNew, S., and Beeghly-Smith, M. 1981. Early person knowledge as expressed in gestural and verbal communication: When do infants acquire a "theory of mind"? In *Infant Social Cognition*, ed. M. Lamb and L. Sherrod. Erlbaum.

Brewer, M. B. 1988. A dual process model of impression formation. In *A Dual Process Model of Impression Formation*, ed. T. Srull and R. Wyer Jr. Erlbaum.

Bromberger, S. 1965. An approach to explanation. In *Analytical Philosophy*, second series, ed. R. Butler. Blackwell.

Brooks, R. 1999. Infant Understanding of Seeing as a Referential Event. Doctoral dissertation, Boston University.

Brooks, R., Caron, A. J., and Butler, S. C. 1998. Infant comprehension of looking as intentional behavior. Poster presented at Eleventh International Conference on Infant Studies, Atlanta.

Brooks, R., and Meltzoff, A. N. 2000. The role of eyes in studies of joint attention. Manuscript, University of Washington.

Bruner, J. S. 1975. From communication to language: A psychological perspective. *Cognition* 3: 255–287.

Bruner, J. S. 1981. Intention in the structure of action and interaction. In *Advances in Infancy Research*, volume 1, ed. L. Lipsett. Ablex.

Bruner, J. S. 1983. *Child's Talk: Learning to Use Language*. Norton.

Bruner, J. S. 1990. *Acts of Meaning*. Harvard University Press.

Bruner, J. S. 1999. The intentionality of referring. In *Development of Intention and Intentional Understanding in Infancy and Early Childhood*, ed. P. Zelazo et al. Erlbaum.

Bullock, T. H., Orkand, R., and Grinnell, A. 1977. *Introduction to Nervous Systems*. Freeman.

Buss, A. R. 1978. Causes and reasons in attribution theory: A conceptual critique. *Journal of Personality and Social Psychology* 36: 1311–1321.

Buss, D. M., and Craik, K. H. 1983. The act frequency approach to personality. *Psychological Review* 90: 105–126.

Butterworth, G. 1991. The ontogeny and phylogeny of joint visual attention. In *Natural Theories of Mind*, ed. A. Whiten. Blackwell.

Butterworth, G., and Cochran, E. 1980. Towards a mechanism of joint visual attention in human infancy. *International Journal of Behavioral Development* 3: 253–272.

Butterworth, G., and Grover, L. 1988. The origins of referential communication in human infancy. In *Thought without Language*, ed. L. Weiskrantz. Clarendon.

Butterworth, G., and Jarrett, N. 1991. What minds have in common is space: Spatial mechanisms serving joint visual attention in infancy. *British Journal of Developmental Psychology* 9: 55–72.

Byrne, R. W., and Whiten, A. 1986. *Machiavellian Intelligence: Social Expertise and the Evolution of Intellect in Monkeys, Apes, and Humans*. Oxford University Press.

Byrne, R. W., and Whiten, A. 1997. Machiavellian intelligence. In *Machiavellian Intelligence II*, ed. A. Whiten and R. Byrne. Oxford University Press.

Cacioppo, J. T. and Petty, R. E. 1982. The need for cognition. *Journal of Personality and Social Psychology* 42: 116–131.

Cacioppo, J. T., Petty, R. E., and Morris, K. J. 1983. Effects of need for cognition on message evaluation, recall, and persuasion. *Journal of Personality and Social Psychology* 45: 805–818.

Call, J., Hare, B. A., and Tomasello, M. 1998. Chimpanzee gaze following in an object-choice task. *Animal Cognition* 1: 89–99.

Call, J., and Tomasello, M. 1999. A nonverbal false belief task: The performances of children and great apes. *Child Development* 70: 381–395.

Carey, S. 1995. On the origin of causal understanding. In *Causal Cognition*, ed. D. Sperber et al. Oxford University Press.

Carpendale, J. I. and Chandler, M. J. 1996. On the distinction between false belief understanding and subscribing to an interpretive theory of mind. *Child Development* 67: 1686–1706.

Carpenter, M., Akhtar, N., and Tomasello, M. 1998. Fourteen through eighteen month old infants differentially imitate intentional and accidental actions. *Infant Behavior and Development* 21: 315–330.

Carpenter, M., Nagell, K., and Tomasello, M. 1998. *Social Cognition, Joint Attention, and Communicative Competence from 9 to 15 Months of Age*. Monographs of the Society for Research in Child Development serial no. 255.

Carruthers, P., and Smith, P. K., eds. 1996. *Theories of Theories of Mind*. Cambridge University Press.

Castañeda, H.-N. 1972. Intentions and intending. *American Philosophical Quarterly* 9: 139–149.

Chaiken, S., Liberman, A., and Eagly, A. H. 1989. Heuristic and systematic information processing within and beyond the persuasion context. In *Unintended Thought*, ed. J. Uleman et al. Guilford.

Chaiken, S., and Trope, Y. 1999. *Dual-Process Theories in Social Psychology.* Guilford.

Chandler, M. J., Greenspan, S., and Barenboim, C. 1973. Judgments of intentionality in response to video-taped and verbally presented moral dilemmas: The medium is the message. *Child Development* 44: 315–3206.

Chandler, M. J., and Lalonde, C. 1996. Shifting to an interpretive theory of mind: 5- to 7-year olds' changing conceptions of mental life. In *The Five to Seven Year Shift*, ed. A. Sameroff and M. Haith. University of Chicago Press.

Chandler, M. J., and Sokol, B. W. 1999. Representation once removed: Children's developing conceptions of representational life. In *Development of Mental Representation*, ed. I. Sigel. Erlbaum.

Chandler, M. J., Sokol, B. W., and Wainryb, C. 2000. Beliefs about truth and beliefs about rightness. *Child Development* 7: 91–97.

Cheney, D. L., and Seyfarth, R. M. 1990a. Attending to behaviour versus attending to knowledge: Examining monkeys attribution of mental states. *Animal Behaviour* 40: 742–753.

Cheney, D.L., and Seyfarth, R. M. 1990b. *How Monkeys See the World: Inside the Mind of Another Species.* University of Chicago Press.

Cheng, P. W., and Novick, L. R. 1990. A probabilistic contrast model of causal induction. *Journal of Personality and Social Psychology* 58: 545–567.

Chisholm, R. M. 1966. Freedom and action. In *Freedom and Determinism*, ed. K. Lehrer. Random House.

Chisholm, R. M. 1981. *The First Person: An Essay on Reference and Intentionality.* University of Minnesota Press.

Chiu, C., and Hong, Y. 1992. The effects of intentionality and validation on individual and collective responsibility attribution among Hong Kong Chinese. *Journal of Psychology* 3: 291–300.

Chiu, C., Hong, Y., and Dweck, C. S. 1997. Lay dispositionism and implicit theories of personality. *Journal of Personality and Social Psychology* 73: 19–30.

Chiu, C., Morris, M. W., Hong, Y., and Menon, T. 2000. Motivated cultural cognition: The impact of implicit cultural theories on dispositional attribution varies as a function of need for closure. *Journal of Personality and Social Psychology* 78: 247–259.

Clark, A. 1997. *Being There: Putting Brain, Body, and World Together Again.* MIT Press.

Clark, H. H. 1997. *Using Language.* Cambridge University Press.

Clark, H. H., and Brennan, S. E. 1991. Grounding in communication. In *Socially Shared Cognition*, ed. L. Resnick et al. American Psychological Association.

Clements, W., and Perner, J. 1994. Implicit understanding of belief. *Cognitive Development* 9: 377–395.

Clohessy, A., Posner, M. I., and Rothbart, M. K. 1992. Stability in anticipatory eye movement learning from four months to adulthood. Paper presented at International Conference on Infant Studies, Miami.

Collingwood, R. G. 1946. *The Idea of History*. Oxford University Press, 1993.

Collis, G. 1979. Describing the structure of social interaction in infancy. In *Before Speech*, ed. M. Bullowa. Cambridge University Press.

Corkum, V., and Moore, C. 1995. Development of joint visual attention in infants. In *Joint Attention*, ed. C. Moore and P. Dunham. Erlbaum.

Corkum, V., and Moore, C. 1998. The origins of joint visual attention in infants. *Developmental Psychology* 34: 28–38.

Cover, R. M. 1975. *Justice Accused: Antislavery and the Judicial Process*. Yale University Press.

Csibra, G., and Gergely, G. 1998. The teleological origins of mentalistic action explanation: A developmental hypothesis. *Developmental Science* 1, no. 2: 255–259.

Csibra, G., Gergely, G., Bíró, S., Koos, D., and Brockbank, M. In press. Goal attribution without agency cues: The perception of "pure reason" in infancy. *Cognition*.

Currie, G. 1995. Imagination and simulation: Aesthetics meets cognitive science. In *Mental Simulation*, ed. M. Davies and T. Stone. Blackwell.

Damon, S. F. 1957. *Punch and Judy*. Barre.

Darke, P. R., Chaiken, S., Bohner, G., Einwiller, S., Erb, H. P., and Hazlewood, J. D. 1998. Accuracy motivation, consensus information, and the law of large numbers: Effects on attitude judgment in the absence of argumentation. *Personality and Social Psychology Bulletin* 24: 1205–1215.

Darwall, S. 1983. *Impartial Reason*. Cornell University Press.

Dascal, M. 1997. Critique without critics? *Science in Context* 10: 39–62.

Dasser, V., Ulbaek, I., and Premack, D. 1989. Perception of intention. *Science* 243: 365–367.

Davidson, D. 1963. Actions, reasons, and causes. *Journal of Philosophy* 60: 685–700.

Davidson, D. 1980a. *Essays on Actions and Events*. Oxford University Press.

Davidson, D. 1980b. Intending. In D. Davidson, *Essays on Actions and Events*. Clarendon.

Davidson, D. 1980c. Psychology as philosophy. In D. Davidson, *Essays on Actions and Events*. Clarendon.

Davidson, D. 1985. Replies to Essays I–IX. In *Essays on Davidson*, ed. B. Vermazen and M. Hintikka. Clarendon.

Davies, M., and Stone, T., eds. 1995. *Mental Simulation: Evaluations and Applications*. Blackwell.

Davis, W. A. 1984. A causal theory of intending. *American Philosophical Quarterly* 21: 43–54.

Dean, A. L., and Youniss, J. 1991. The transformation of Piagetian theory by American psychology: The early competence issue. In *Criteria For Competence*, ed. M. Chandler and M. Chapman. Erlbaum.

Dennett, D. 1978a. Why the law of effect won't go away. In D. Dennett, *Brainstorms*. Bradford Books.

Dennett, D. C. 1978b. Beliefs about beliefs. *Behavioral and Brain Sciences* 1: 568–570.

Dennett, D. C. 1987. *The Intentional Stance*. MIT Press.

Desimone, R., and Duncan, J. 1995. Neural mechanisms of selective visual attention. *Annual Review of Neuroscience* 18: 193–222.

Dijksterhuis, A., van Knippenberg, A., Kruglanski, A. W., and Schaper, C. 1996. Motivated social cognition: Need for closure effects on memory and judgment. *Journal of Experimental Social Psychology* 32: 254–270.

Dipert, R. R. 1993. *Artifacts, Art, and Agency*. Temple University Press.

Dittrich, W. J., and Lea, S. E. G. 1994. Visual perception of intentional motion. *Perception* 23: 253–268.

Dretske, F. 1988. *Explaining Behavior: Reasons in a World of Causes*. MIT Press.

Duff, R. A. 1990. *Intention, Agency and Criminal Liability*. Blackwell.

Duhem, P. 1906. *The Aim and Structure of Physical Theory*. Princeton University Press, 1954

Dunn, J. 1991. Young children's understanding of other people: Evidence from observations within the family. In *Children's Theories of Mind*, ed. D. Frye and C. Moore. Erlbaum.

Duranti, A. 1988. Intentions, language, and social action in a Samoan context. *Journal of Pragmatics* 12: 13–33.

Dweck, C. S., Chiu, C., and Hong, Y. 1995. Implicit theories: Elaboration and extension of the model. *Psychological Inquiry* 6: 322–333.

Dworkin, R. 1982. Natural law revisited. *Florida Law Review* 34: 165–188.

Dworkin, R. 1986. *Law's Empire*. Harvard University Press.

Edwards, D., and Potter, J. 1993. Language and causation: A discursive action model of description and attribution. *Psychological Review* 100: 23–41.

Eisenberg, N. 1986. *Altruistic Emotion, Cognition, and Behavior*. Erlbaum.

Elgin, C. Z. 1989. The relativity of fact and the objectivity of value. In *Relativism*, ed. M. Krausz. University of Notre Dame Press.

Emery, N. J., Lorincz, E. N., Perret, D. I., Oran, M. W., and Baker, C. I. 1997. Gaze following and joint attention in rhesus monkeys (*Macaca mulatta*). *Journal of Comparative Psychology* 111: 286–293.

Erdmann, P. 1993. Die for . . . to-Konstruktion nach dem Verb want [The 'for . . . to' construction after the verb 'want']. *Zeitschrift für Anglistik und Amerikanistik* 41: 124–132.

Fadiga, L., Fogassi, L., Pavesi, G., and Rizzolatti, G. 1995. Motor facilitation during action observation: A magnetic stimulation study. *Journal of Neurophysiology* 73: 2608–2611.

Farwell, L., and Weiner, B. 1996. Self-perceptions of fairness in individual and group contexts. *Personality and Social Psychology Bulletin* 22: 868–881.

Farwell, L., and Weiner, B. 2000. Bleeding hearts and the heartless: Popular perceptions of liberal and conservative ideologies. *Personality and Social Social Psychology Bulletin* 26: 845–852.

Feather, N.T. 1985. Attitudes, values, and attributions: Explanations for unemployment. *Journal of Personality and Social Psychology* 48: 876–889.

Fein, S. 1996. Effects of suspicion on attributional thinking and the correspondence bias. *Journal of Personality and Social Psychology* 70: 1164–1184.

Feinfield, K. A., Lee, P. P., Flavell, E. R., Green, F. L., and Flavell, J. H. 1999. Young children's understanding of intention. *Cognitive Development* 14: 463–486.

Fincham, F. D., and Jaspars, J. M. 1980. Attribution of responsibility: From man the scientist to man as lawyer. In *Advances in Experimental Social Psychology*, volume 13, ed. L. Berkowitz. Academic Press.

Fischer, J. M. 1994. *The Metaphysics of Free Will*. Blackwell.

Fiske, S. T. 1993. Controlling other people: The impact of power on stereotyping. *American Psychologist* 48: 621–628.

Fiske, S. T. 1998. Stereotyping, prejudice, and discrimination. In *The Handbook of Social Psychology*, ed. D. Gilbert et al. McGraw-Hill.

Flavell, J. H. 1988. The development of children's knowledge about the mind: From cognitive connections to mental representations. In *Developing Theories of Mind*, ed. J. Astington et al. Cambridge University Press.

Flavell, J. H. 1999. Cognitive development: Children's knowledge about the mind. *Annual Review of Psychology* 50: 21–45.

Flavell, J. H., Flavell, E. R., Green, F. L., and Moses, L. J. 1990. Young children's understanding of fact beliefs and value beliefs. *Child Development* 61: 915–928.

Fodor, J. A. 1981. *Representations*. MIT Press.

Fodor, J. A. 1983. *Modularity of the Mind*. MIT Press.

Fodor, J. A. 1986. The modularity of mind. In *Meaning and Cognitive Structure*, ed. W. Demopoulos et al. Ablex.

Fodor, J. A. 1987. *Psychosemantics: The Problem of Meaning in the Philosophy of Mind*. MIT Press.

Fodor, J. 1992. A theory of the child's theory of mind. *Cognition* 44: 283–296.

Fodor, J. A., and Bever, T. G. 1965. The psychological reality of linguistic segments. *Journal of Verbal Learning and Verbal Behavior* 4: 414–420.

Fodor, J. A., and LePore, E. 1992. *Holism: A Shopper's Guide*. Blackwell.

Føllesdal, D. 1982. The status of rationality assumptions in interpretation and in the explanation of action. *Dialectica* 36: 301–316.

Foucault, M. 1997. *Ethics: Subjectivity and Truth*. New Press.

Freeman, N., and Lacohee, H. 1995. Making explicit 3-year-olds' implicit competence with their own false beliefs. *Cognition* 56: 31–60.

Freeman, W. 1997. Nonlinear neurodynamics of intentionality. *Journal of Mind and Behavior* 18: 291–304.

Frey, R. G., and Morris, C. W. 1991. Introduction. In *Liability and Responsibility*, ed. R. Frey and C. Morris. Cambridge University Press.

Gadamer, H.-G. 1989. *Truth and Method*, second revised edition. Crossroad.

Galilei, G. 1613. Letter to Castelli. In *Galileo at Work*, ed. S. Drake. University of Chicago Press, 1957.

Gallese, V., and Goldman, A. 1998. Mirror neurons and the simulation theory of mind-reading. *Trends in Cognitive Sciences* 2: 493–501.

Gallup, G. G., Jr. 1970. Chimpanzees: Self-recognition. *Science* 167: 86–87.

Gallup, G. G., Jr. 1982. Self-awareness and the emergence of mind in primates. *American Journal of Primatology* 2: 237–248.

Gentner, D., and Markman, A. B. 1997. Structure mapping in analogy and similarity. *American Psychologist* 52: 45–56.

Gergely, G., Nádasdy, Z., Csibra, G., and Bíró, S. 1995. Taking the intentional stance at 12 months of age. *Cognition* 56: 165–193.

Gibbs, R. 1999. *Intentions in the Experience of Meaning*. Cambridge University Press.

Gibbs, R. W., Jr. 1998. The varieties of intentions in interpersonal communication. In *Social and Cognitive Approaches to Interpersonal Communication*, ed. S. Fussell and R. Kreuz. Erlbaum.

Gilbert, D. T., Jones, E. E., and Pelham, B. W. 1987. Influence and inference: What the active perceiver overlooks. *Journal of Personality and Social Psychology* 52: 861–870.

Gilbert, D. T., Pelham, B. W., and Krull, D. S. 1988. On cognitive busyness: When person perceivers meet persons perceived. *Journal of Personality and Social Psychology* 54: 733–740.

Gilbert, M. 1989. *On Social Facts*. Routledge.

Givon, T. 1993. *English Grammar: A Function-Based Introduction*, volume II. John Benjamins.

Gleissner, B., Meltzoff, A. N., and Bekkering, H. 2000. Children's coding of human action: Cognitive factors influencing imitation in 3-year-olds. *Developmental Science* 3: 405–414.

Gnepp, J., and Chilamkurti, C. 1988. Children's use of personality attributions to predict other people's emotional and behavioral reactions. *Child Development* 59: 743–754.

Godfrey-Smith, P. 1996. *Complexity and the Function of Mind in Nature.* Cambridge University Press.

Goldman, A. 1970. *A Theory of Human Action.* Prentice-Hall.

Goldman, A. I. 1989. Interpretation psychologized. *Mind and Language* 4: 161–185.

Goldman, A. I. 1993. The psychology of folk psychology. *Behavioral and Brain Sciences* 16: 15–28.

Goody, E. N. 1995. Introduction: Some implications of a social origin of intelligence. In *Social Intelligence and Interaction,* ed. E. Goody. Cambridge University Press.

Gopnik, A. 1993. How we know our minds: The illusion of first-person knowledge. *Behavioral and Brain Sciences* 16: 1–14.

Gopnik, A. 1998. Explanation as orgasm. *Minds and Machines* 8: 101–118.

Gopnik, A., and Astington, J. W. 1988. Children's understanding of representational change and its relation to the understanding of false belief and the appearance-reality distinction. *Child Development* 59: 26–37.

Gopnik, A., and Meltzoff, A. N. 1997. *Words, Thoughts, and Theories.* MIT Press.

Gopnik, A., Meltzoff, A. N., and Kuhl, P. K. 1999. *The Scientist in the Crib: Minds, Brains, and How Children Learn.* Morrow.

Gopnik, A., and Slaughter, V. 1991. Young children's understanding of changes in their mental states. *Child Development* 62: 98–110.

Gopnik, A., and Wellman, H. M. 1992. Why the child's theory of mind really *is* a theory. *Mind and Language* 7: 145–171.

Gopnik, A., and Wellman, H. M. 1994. The theory theory. In *Mapping the Mind,* ed. L. Hirschfeld and S. Gelman. Cambridge University Press.

Gordon, R. A., and Anderson, K. S. 1995. Perceptions of race-stereotypic and race-nonstereotypic crimes: The impact of response-time instructions on attributions and judgments. *Basic and Applied Social Psychology* 16: 455–470.

Gordon, R. M. 1986. Folk psychology as simulation. *Mind and Language* 1: 158–171.

Greenwood, J. D., ed. 1991. *The Future of Folk Psychology: Intentionality and Cognitive Science.* Cambridge University Press.

Grice, H. P. 1957. Meaning. *Philosophical Review* 64: 377–388.

Grice, H. P. 1968. Utterer's meaning, sentence-meaning, and word-meaning. *Foundations of Language* 4: 225–242.

Grice, H. P. 1971. Intention and uncertainty. *Proceedings of the British Academy* 57: 263–279.

Grice, H. P. 1975. Logic and conversation. In *Syntax and Semantics 3,* ed. P. Cole and J. Morgan. Academic Press.

Habermas, J. 1984. *The Theory of Communicative Action,* volume 1: *Reason and the Rationalization of Society.* Beacon.

Habermas, J. 1996. Between Facts and norms: Contributions to a Discourse Theory of Law and Democracy. MIT Press.

Haidt, J., and Baron, J. 1996. Social roles and the moral judgement of acts and omissions. *European Journal of Social Psychology* 26: 201–218.

Haith, M. M. 1998. Who put the cog in infant cognition? Is rich interpretation too costly? *Infant Behavior and Development* 21: 167–179.

Haith, M. M., Hazan, C., and Goodman, G. S. 1988. Expectation and anticipation of dynamic visual events by 3.5-month-old infants. *Child Development* 59: 467–479.

Hamilton, V. L. 1978. Who is responsible? Towards a *social* psychology of responsibility attribution. *Social Psychology* 41: 316–328.

Hamilton, V. L. 1980. Intuitive psychologist or intuitive lawyer? Alternative models of the attribution process. *Journal of Personality and Social Psychology* 39: 767–772.

Hamilton, V. L., and Sanders, J. 1992. Human action and responsibility. In V. L. Hamilton and J. Sanders, *Everyday justice*. Yale University Press.

Hanson, N. R. 1958. *Patterns of Discovery*. Cambridge University Press.

Harman, G. 1976. Practical reasoning. *Review of Metaphysics* 29: 431–463.

Harman, G. 1978. Studying the chimpanzee's theory of mind. *Behavioral and Brain Sciences* 1: 591.

Harman, G. 1986. *Change in View*. MIT Press.

Harre, R., and Secord, P. F. 1972. *The Explanation of Social Behaviour*. Littlefield, Adams.

Harris, P. 1991. The work of the imagination. In *Natural Theories of Mind*, ed. A. Whiten. Blackwell.

Harris, P. 1992. From simulation to folk psychology: The case for development. *Mind and Language* 7: 120–144.

Harris, P. 1993. First-person current. *Behavioral and Brain Sciences* 16: 48–49.

Harris, P. 1995. Imagining and pretending. In *Mental Simulation*, ed. M. Davies and T. Stone. Blackwell.

Harris, P. 1996. Desires, beliefs, and language. In *Theories of Theories of Mind*, ed. P. Carruthers and P. Smith. Cambridge University Press.

Harris, P., and Kavanaugh, R. 1993. *Young Children's Understanding of Pretense*. Monographs of the Society for Research in Child Development, serial no. 237.

Hart, H. L. A. 1968. *Punishment and Responsibility: Essays in the Philosophy of Law*. Oxford University Press.

Heal, J. 1986. Replication and functionalism. In *Language, Mind, and Logic*, ed. J. Butterfield. Cambridge University Press.

Heider, F. 1944. Social perception and phenomenal causality. *Psychological Review* 51: 358–374.

Heider, F. 1958. *The Psychology of Interpersonal Relations*. Wiley.

Heil, J. 1991. Does cognitive psychology rest on a mistake? *Mind* 90: 321–342.

Hempel, C. G., Oppenheim, P. 1948. Studies in the logic of explanation. *Philosophy of Science* 15: 135–175.

Hendriks-Jansen, H. 1996. *Catching Ourselves in the Act: Situated Activity, Interactive Emergence, Evolution, and Human Thought*. MIT Press.

Hesslow, G. 1988. The problem of causal selection. In *Contemporary Science and Natural Explanation*, ed. D. Hilton. New York University Press.

Hewstone, M., and Jaspars, J. 1987. Covariation and causal attribution: A logical model of the intuitive analysis of variance. *Journal of Personality and Social Psychology* 53: 663–672.

Heyes, C. M. 1993. Anecdotes, training, trapping and triangulating: Do animals attribute mental states? *Animal Behaviour* 46: 177–188.

Hickling, A. K., and Wellman, H. W. 2000. The emergence of children's causal explanations and theories: Evidence from everyday conversation. Manuscript, University of Michigan.

Hilton, D. J. 1990. Conversational processes and causal explanation. *Psychological Bulletin* 107: 65–81.

Hilton, J. L., Fiske, S. T., Snyder, M., and Nisbett, R. E. 1998. Interaction goals and person perception. In *Attribution and Social Interaction*, ed. J. Darley et al. American Psychological Association.

Hirschberg, N. 1978. A correct treatment of traits. In *Personality*, ed. H. London. Wiley.

Hogrefe, G.-J., Wimmer, H., and Perner, J. 1986. Ignorance versus false belief: A developmental lag in attribution of epistemic states. *Child Development* 57: 567–582.

Holland, J. H., Holyoak, K. J., Nisbett, R. E., and Thagard, P. R. 1986. *Induction: Processes of Inference, Learning, and Discovery*. MIT Press.

Hong, Y., Morris, M. W., Chiu, C., and Benet-Martínez, V. 2000. Multicultural minds: A dynamic constructivist approach to culture and cognition. *American Psychologist* 55: 709–720.

Hood, B. M., Willen, J. D., and Driver, J. 1998. Adult's eyes trigger shifts of visual attention in human infants. *Psychological Science* 9: 131–134.

Hooper, R., and Drummond, K. 1990. Emergent goals at a relational turning point: The case of Gordon and Denise. *Journal of Language and Social Psychology* 9: 39–65.

Hume, D. 1739. *A Treatise of Human Nature*, second edition. Oxford University Press, 1978.

Hutchins, E. 1995. *Cognition in the Wild*. MIT Press.

Itakura, S. 1996. An exploratory study of gaze-monitoring in nonhuman primates. *Japanese Psychological Research* 38: 174–180.

Johnson, M. 1993. Constraints on plasticity. In *Brain Development and Cognition*, ed. M. Johnson. Blackwell.

Johnson, S. C. 2000. The recognition of mentalistic agents in infancy. *Trends in Cognitive Sciences* 4: 22–28.

Johnson, S., Slaughter, V., and Carey, S. 1998. Whose gaze will infants follow? The elicitation of gaze-following in 12-month-olds. *Developmental Science* 1: 233–238.

Jones, E. E. 1979. The rocky road from acts to dispositions. *American Psychologist* 34: 107–117.

Jones, E. E., and Davis, K. E. 1965. From acts to dispositions: The attribution process in person perception. In *Advances in Experimental Social Psychology*, volume 2, ed. L. Berkowitz. Academic Press.

Jones, E. E., and Nisbett, R. E. 1972. The actor and the observer: Divergent perceptions of the causes of behavior. In *Attribution*, ed. E. Jones et al. General Learning Press.

Kahn, R. 1996. In "Talk of the Town." *New Yorker*, October 4, 1996.

Kalish, C. 1998. Reasons and causes: Children's understanding of conformity to social rules and physical laws. *Child Development* 69: 706–720.

Kalish, C. 1999. Are children committed to the gambler's fallacy when reasoning about behavior? Paper presented at meetings of Society for Research in Child Development, Albuquerque.

Kalish, C., Weissman, M., and Bernstein, D. In press. Taking decisions seriously: Young children's understanding of conventional truth. *Child Development*.

Kaplan, L.V. 1995. The attenuation of evil, the unfairness of justice. In *Other Intentions, Cultural Contexts and the Attribution of Inner States*, ed. L. Rosen. School of American Research Press.

Karmiloff-Smith, A. 1992. *Beyond Modularity: A Developmental Perspective on Cognitive Science*. MIT Press.

Karniol, R. 1978. Children's use of intention cues in evaluating behavior. *Psychological Bulletin* 85: 76–85.

Kashima, Y., McKinture, A., and Clifford, P. 1998. The category of the mind: Folk psychology of belief, desire, and intention. *Asian Journal of Social Psychology* 1: 289–313.

Keasey, C. B. 1978. Children's developing awareness and usage of intentionality and motives. In *Nebraska Symposium on Motivation*, volume 25, ed. C. Keasey. University of Nebraska Press.

Keenan, T. 1997. *Fables of Responsibility: Aberrations and Predicaments in Ethics and Politics*. Stanford University Press.

Kelley, H. H. 1967. Attribution theory in social psychology. In *Nebraska Symposium on Motivation*, volume 15, ed. D. Levine. University of Nebraska Press.

Kelley, H. H. 1972. Causal schemata and the attribution process. In *Attribution*, ed. E. Jones et al. General Learning Press.

Kelso, J. A. S. 1995. *Dynamic Patterns: The Self-Organization of Brain and Behavior*. MIT Press.

Kidd, R. F., and Amabile, T. M. 1981. Causal explanations in social interaction: Some dialogues on dialogue. In *New Directions in Attribution Research*, volume 3, ed. J. Harvey et al. Erlbaum.

Kim, J. 1993. The non-reductivist's troubles with mental causation. In *Mental Causation*, ed. J. Heil and A. Mele. Oxford University Press.

Kluegal, J. R., and Smith, E. R. 1986. *Beliefs about Inequality*. Aldine.

Knowles, E., and Ames, D. 2000a. Culture and mental state epistemology: Limits to the norm of authenticity. Manuscript, University of California, Berkeley.

Knowles, E., and Ames, D. 2000b. Mental vs. consequential construal of personality traits. Manuscript, University of California, Berkeley.

Knowles, E., Morris, M., Hong, Y., and Chiu, C. 2000. Cultural theories and the process of causal judgment: Testing between alternative models of the role of culture by manipulating cognitive load. Manuscript. University of California, Berkeley.

Krauss, R. M., and Fussell, S. R. 1996. Social psychological models of interpersonal communication. In *Social Psychology*, ed. E. Higgins and A. Kruglanski. Guilford.

Kruglanski, A. W. 1989. *Lay Epistemics and Human Knowledge*. Plenum.

Kruglanski, A. W. 1975. The endogenous-exogenous partition in attribution theory. *Psychological Review* 82: 387–406.

Kruglanski, A. W. 1996. A motivated gatekeeper of our minds: Need-for-closure effects on interpersonal and group processes. In *Handbook of Motivation and Cognition*, volume 3, ed. R. Sorrentino and E. Higgins. Guilford.

Kuhl, P. K., and Meltzoff, A. N. 1982. The bimodal perception of speech in infancy. *Science* 218: 1138–1141.

Kuhl, P. K., and Meltzoff, A. N. 1984. The intermodal representation of speech in infants. *Infant Behavior and Development* 7: 361–381.

Kuhn, D., and Siegler, R., eds. 1997. *Handbook of Child Psychology*, Volume 2: *Cognition, Perception, and Language*, fifth edition. Wiley.

Kuhn, T. 1970. *The Structure of Scientific Revolutions*, second edition. University of Chicago Press.

Lapsley, D. K. 1996. *Moral Psychology*. Westview.

Latané, B., and Darley, J. M. 1969. Bystander "apathy." *American Scientist* 57: 244–268.

Lee, E. 1995. Young Children's Representational Understanding of Intention. Doctoral dissertation, University of Toronto (Ontario Institute for Studies in Education).

Lennon, K. 1990. *Explaining Human Action*. Open Court.

Leslie, A. M. 1982. The perception of causality in infants. *Perception* 11: 173–186.

Leslie, A. M. 1987. Pretense and representation: The origins of "theory of mind." *Psychological Review* 99: 412–426.

Leslie, A. M. 1994a. Pretending and believing: Issues in the theory of ToMM. *Cognition* 50: 211–238.

Leslie, A. M. 1994b. ToMM, ToBy, and Agency: Core architecture and domain specificity. In *Mapping the Mind*, ed. L. Hirschfeld et al. Cambridge University Press.

Leslie, A. M. 1995. A theory of agency. In *Causal Cognition*, ed. A. Premack et al. Clarendon.

Levenson, R. W., and Ruef, A. M. 1997. Physiological aspects of emotional knowledge and rapport. In *Empathic Accuracy*, ed. W. Ickes. Guilford.

Levinas, E. 1981. *Otherwise Than Being: Or Beyond Essence*. Kluwer.

Levinson, S. 1983. *Pragmatics*. Cambridge University Press.

Lewis, C., Freeman, N., Hagestadt, C., and Douglas, H. 1994. Narrative access and production in preschoolers' false belief reasoning. *Cognitive Development* 9: 397–424.

Lhermitte, F., Pilon, B., and Serdaru, M. 1986. Human autonomy and the frontal lobes: I. Imitation and utilization behavior: A neuropsychological study of 75 patients. *Annals of Neurology* 19: 326–334.

Lickel, B. A., Hamilton, D. L., and Sherman, S. J. 1999. Western conceptions of groups and the application of collectivist reasoning principles. Paper presented at Stanford Culture Conference.

Lickel, B., Hamilton, D. L., Wieczorkowska, G., Lewis, A., Sherman, S. J., and Uhles, N. 2000. Varieties of groups and the perception of group entitativity. *Journal of Personality and Social Psychology* 78: 223–246.

Lickel, B. A., Schmader T., and Hamilton, D. L. 2000. A case of collective responsibility: Who else is to blame for the Columbine High shootings? Manuscript in preparation.

Lillard, A. 1998. Ethnopsychologies: Cultural variations in theories of mind. *Psychological Bulletin* 123: 3–32.

Lillard, A. S., and Flavell, J. H. 1990. Young children's preference for mental state versus behavioral descriptions of human action. *Child Development* 61: 731–741.

Lillard, A. S. and Flavell, J. H. 1992. Young children's understanding of different mental states. *Developmental Psychology* 28: 626–634.

Livesley, W. J., and Bromley, D. B. 1973. *Person Perception in Childhood and Adolescence*. Wiley.

Locke, D., and Pennington, D. 1982. Reasons and other causes: Their role in attribution processes. *Journal of Personality and Social Psychology* 42: 212–223.

Lorenz, K. 1957. The nature of instinct: The conception of instinctive behavior. In *Instinctive Behavior*, ed. C. Schiller and K. Lashley. International University Press.

Lyons, W. 1995. *Approaches to Intentionality*. Clarendon.

Macphail, E. M. 1987. The comparative psychology of intelligence. *Behavioral and Brain Sciences* 10: 645–695.

Malle, B. F. 1994. Intentionality and Explanation: A Study in the Folk Theory of Behavior. Doctoral dissertation, Stanford University.

Malle, B. F. 1997. People's folk theory of behavior. In *Proceedings of the Nineteenth Annual Conference of the Cognitive Science Society*, ed. M. Shafto and P. Langley. Erlbaum.

Malle, B. F. 1998. F.Ex: Coding scheme for people's folk explanations of behavior. <http://darkwing.uoregon.edu/~bfmalle/fex.html>

Malle, B. F. 1999. How people explain behavior: A new theoretical framework. *Personality and Social Psychology Review* 3: 23–48.

Malle, B. F., and Ickes, W. 2000. Fritz Heider: Philosopher and psychologist. In *Portraits of Pioneers in Psychology*, volume 4, ed. G. Kimble and M. Wertheimer. American Psychological Association and Erlbaum.

Malle, B. F., and Knobe, J. 1997a. The folk concept of intentionality. *Journal of Experimental Social Psychology* 33: 101–121.

Malle, B. F., and Knobe, J. 1997b. Which behaviors do people explain? A basic actor-observer asymmetry. *Journal of Personality and Social Psychology* 72: 288–304.

Malle, B. F., Knobe, J., Nelson, S., and Stevens, S. 2001. A comprehensive study of actor-observer asymmetries in behavior explanation. Manuscript, University of Oregon.

Malle, B. F., Knobe, J., O'Laughlin, M. J., Pearce, G. E., and Nelson, S. E. 2000. Conceptual structure and social functions of behavior explanations: Beyond person-situation attributions. *Journal of Personality and Social Psychology* 79: 309–326.

Mandler, J. M. 1992. How to build a baby: II. Conceptual primitives. *Psychological Review* 99: 587–604.

Marshall, J. 1968. *Intention in Law and Society*. Funk and Wagnalls.

Maselli, M. D., and Altrocchi, J. 1969. Attribution of intent. *Psychological Bulletin* 71: 445–454.

Mataric, M. 1992. Integration of representation into goal-driven behavior-based robots. *IEEE Transactions on Robotics and Automation* 8: 304–312.

McClelland, J. L., and Plaut, D. C. 1999. Does generalization in infant learning implicate abstract algebra-like rules? *Trends in Cognitive Sciences* 3: 166–168.

McClure, J., and Hilton, D. 1997. For you can't always get what you want: When preconditions are better explanations than goals. *British Journal of Social Psychology* 36: 223–240.

McFarland, D. 1993. *Animal Behaviour*. Longman Scientific and Technical.

McGill, A. L. 1989. Context effects in judgments of causation. *Journal of Personality and Social Psychology* 57: 189–200.

Mele, A. R. 1988. Against a belief/desire analysis of intention. *Philosophia* 18: 239–242.

Mele, A. R. 1989. She intends to try. *Philosophical Studies* 54: 101–106.

Mele, A. R. 1992a. *Springs of Action: Understanding Intentional Behavior*. Oxford University Press.

Mele, A. R. 1992b. Acting for reasons and acting intentionally. *Pacific Philosophical Quarterly* 73: 355–374.

Mele, A. R. 1997a. *The Philosophy of Action*. Oxford University Press.

Mele, A. R. 1997b. Introduction. In *The Philosophy of Action*, ed. A. Mele. Oxford University Press.

Mele, A. R., and Moser, P. K. 1994. Intentional action. *Nous* 28: 39–68.

Mele, A. R., and Sverdlik, S. 1996. Intention, intentional action, and moral responsibility. *Philosophical Studies* 82: 265–287.

Meltzoff, A. N. 1988. Infant imitation after a 1-week delay: Long-term memory for novel acts and multiple stimuli. *Developmental Psychology* 24: 470–476.

Meltzoff, A. N. 1990. Foundations for developing a concept of self: The role of imitation in relating self to other and the value of social mirroring, social modeling, and self practice in infancy. In *The Self in Transition*, ed. D. Cicchetti and M. Beeghly. University of Chicago Press.

Meltzoff, A. N. 1995. Understanding the intentions of others: Re-enactment of intended acts by 18-month-old children. *Developmental Psychology* 31: 838–850.

Meltzoff, A. N. 1996. Understanding intentions in infancy. Paper delivered as part of an invited symposium entitled Children's Theory of Mind, XXVI International Congress of Psychology, Montreal.

Meltzoff, A. N. 1999. Origins of theory of mind, cognition, and communication. *Journal of Communication Disorders* 32: 251–269.

Meltzoff, A. N., and Borton, R. W. 1979. Intermodal matching by human neonates. *Nature* 282: 403–404.

Meltzoff, A. N., and Gopnik, A. 1993. The role of imitation in understanding persons and developing a theory of mind. In *Understanding Other Minds*, ed. S. Baron-Cohen et al. Oxford University Press.

Meltzoff, A. N., Gopnik, A., and Repacholi, B. M. 1999. Toddlers' understanding of intentions, desires, and emotions: Explorations of the dark ages. In *Developing Theories of Intention*, ed. P. Zelazo et al. Erlbaum.

Meltzoff, A. N., and Moore, M. K. 1977. Imitation of facial and manual gestures by human neonates. *Science* 198: 75–78.

Meltzoff, A. N., and Moore, M. K. 1983. Newborn infants imitate adult facial gestures. *Child Development* 54: 702–709.

Meltzoff, A. N., and Moore, M. K. 1989. Imitation in newborn infants: Exploring the range of gestures imitated and the underlying mechanisms. *Developmental Psychology* 25: 954–962.

Meltzoff, A. N., and Moore, M. K. 1992. Early imitation within a functional framework: The importance of person identity, movement, and development. *Infant Behavior and Development* 15: 479–505.

Meltzoff, A. N., and Moore, M. K. 1994. Imitation, memory, and the representation of persons. *Infant Behavior and Development* 17: 83–99.

Meltzoff, A. N., and Moore, M. K. 1995. Infants' understanding of people and things: From body imitation to folk psychology. In *The Body and the Self*, ed. J. Bermúdez et al. MIT Press.

Meltzoff, A. N., and Moore, M. K. 1997. Explaining facial imitation: A theoretical model. *Early Development and Parenting* 6: 179–192.

Meltzoff, A. N., and Moore, M. K. 1998. Object representation, identity, and the paradox of early permanence: Steps toward a new framework. *Infant Behavior and Development* 21: 201–235.

Menon, T., Ames, D., and Morris, M. W. 2001. Culture and lay theories of individuals and groups. To appear in *Personality and Social Psychology Review*.

Menon, T., Morris, M. W., Chiu, C., and Hong, Y. 1999. Culture and the construal of agency: Attribution to individual versus group dispositions. *Journal of Personality and Social Psychology* 76: 701–717.

Meyers, D. H. 1971. *The Last Days of Mr. Punch*. McCall.

Miller, J. G. 1986. Early cross-cultural commonalties in social explanation. *Developmental Psychology* 22: 514–520.

Miller, L. C. and Read, S. J. 1991. On the coherence of mental models of persons andrelationships: A knowledge structure approach. In *Cognition in Close Relationships*, ed. G. Fletcher et al. Erlbaum.

Mitchell, P., and Lacohee, H. 1991. Children's early understanding of false belief. *Cognition* 39: 107–127.

Moore, C. 1999. Gaze following and the control of attention. In *Early Social Cognition*, ed. P. Rochat. Erlbaum.

Moore, C., and Corkum, V. 1994. Social understanding at the end of the first year of life. *Developmental Review* 14: 349–372.

Moore, C., and Corkum, V. 1998. Infant gaze following based on eye direction. *British Journal of Developmental Psychology* 16: 495–503.

Moore, C., and Dunham, P., eds. 1995. *Joint Attention: Its Origin and Role in Development*. Erlbaum.

Morissette, P., Ricard, M., and Décarie, T. G. 1995. Joint visual attention and pointing in infancy: A longitudinal study of comprehension. *British Journal of Developmental Psychology* 13: 163–175.

Morris, M. W. 1993. Culture and cause: American and Chinese understandings of physical and social causality. *Dissertation Abstracts International* 54: 1725.

Morris, M. W., and Fu, H. In press. Dynamic approaches to cultural influences on interpersonal conflict resolution. *Social Cognition*.

Morris, M. W., and Larrick, R. 1995. When one cause casts doubt on another: A normative analysis of discounting in causal attribution. *Psychological Review* 102: 331–355.

Morris, M. W., Larrick, R. and Su, S. 1999. Misperceiving negotiation counterparts: Ascribing personality traits for situationally determined bargaining behaviors. *Journal of Personality and Social Psychology* 77: 52–67.

Morris, M. W., and Leung, K. 1999. Justice for all? Progress in research on cultural variation in the psychology of distributive and procedural justice. *Applied Psychology* 48: 100–132.

Morris, M. W., Nisbett, R. E. and Peng, K. 1995. Causal attribution across domains and cultures. In *Causal Cognition*, ed. G. Lewis et al. Clarendon.

Morris, M. W., and Peng, K. 1994. Culture and cause: American and Chinese attributions for social and physical events. *Journal of Personality and Social Psychology* 67: 949–971.

Morris, M. W., and Su, S. 1999. Social psychological obstacles in environmental conflict resolution. *American Behavioral Scientist* 42: 1322–1349.

Moses, L. J. 1993. Young children's understanding of belief constraints on intention. *Cognitive Development* 8: 1–25.

Moses, L., and Chandler, M. 1992. Traveler's guide to children's theories of mind. *Psychological Inquiry* 3: 286–301.

Moses, L. J., and Flavell, J. H. 1990. Inferring false beliefs from actions and reactions. *Child Development* 61: 929–945.

Moynihan, M. 1955. Some aspects of reproductive behaviour in the black-headed gull (*Larus ridibundus ridibundus L.*) and related species. *Behaviour* Suppl. 4: 1–201.

Nagel, T. 1970. *The Possibility of Altruism*. Oxford University Press.

Nagell, K., Olguin, R., and Tomasello, M. 1993. Processes of social learning in the imitative learning of chimpanzees and human children. *Journal of Comparative Psychology* 107: 174–186.

Nelson, S. E., and Malle, B. F. 2000. Explaining intentional actions: Explanations as modifiers of social perception and judgment. Poster presented at Annual Meeting of Western Psychological Association, Portland, Oregon.

Nelson-LeGall, S. A. 1985. Motive-outcome matching and outcome foreseeability: Effects on attribution of intentionality and moral judgments. *Developmental Psychology* 21: 323–337.

Newtson, D. 1973. Attribution and the unit of perception of ongoing behavior. *Journal of Personality and Social Psychology* 28: 28–38.

Newtson, D. 1976. Foundations of attribution: The perception of ongoing behavior. In *New Directions in Attribution Research*, ed. J. Harvey et al. Erlbaum.

Newtson, D., and Engquist, G. 1976. The perceptual organization of ongoing behavior. *Journal of Experimental Social Psychology* 12: 436–450.

Newtson, D., Engquist, G., and Bois, J. 1977. The objective basis of behavior units. *Journal of Personality and Social Psychology* 35: 847–862.

Nichols, S., and Stich, S. 2000. Reading one's own mind: A cognitive theory of self-awareness. Manuscript, Rutgers University.

Nichols, S., Stich, S., Leslie, L., and Klein, D. 1996. Varieties of off-line simulation. In *Theories of Theories of Mind*, ed. P. Carruthers, and P. Smith. Cambridge University Press.

Nisbett, R. E., Caputo, C., Legant, P., and Marecek, J. 1973. Behavior as seen by the actor and as seen by the observer. *Journal of Personality and Social Psychology* 27: 154–164.

O'Laughlin, M., and. Malle, B. F. 2000. How people explain actions performed by groups and individuals. Manuscript, University of Oregon.

Ochs, E. 1984. Clarification and culture. In *Georgetown University Roundtable on Language and Linguistics*, ed. D. Schiffirn. Georgetown University Press.

Overton, W. F. 1998. Developmental psychology: Philosophy, concepts, and methodology. In *Theoretical Models of Human Development*, volume 1, ed. R. Lerner. Wiley.

Parkinson. B. 1995. *Ideas and Realities of Emotion*. Routledge.

Pears, D. 1984. *Motivated Irrationality*. Oxford University Press.

Pears, D. 1985. Intention and Belief. In *Essays on Davidson*, ed. B. Vermazen and M. Hintikka. Clarendon.

Pendry, L. F., and Macrae, C. N. 1994. Stereotypes and mental life: The case of the motivated but thwarted tactician. *Journal of Experimental Social Psychology* 30: 303–325.

Peng, K., Ames, D. R., and Knowles, E. D. 2000. Culture and human inference: Perspectives from three traditions. In *Handbook of Cross-Cultural Psychology*, ed. D. Matsumoto. Oxford University Press.

Perner, J. 1991. *Understanding the Representational Mind*. MIT Press.

Perner, J. 1996. Simulation as explicitation of predication-implicit knowledge about the mind: Arguments for a simulation-theory mix. In *Theories of Theories of Mind*, ed. P. Carruthers and P. Smith. Cambridge University Press.

Perner, J., Baker, S., and Hutton, D. 1994. Prelief: The conceptual origins of belief and pretence. In *Children's Early Understanding of Mind*, ed. C. Lewis and P. Mitchell. Erlbaum.

Perner, J., Leekam, S., and Wimmer, H. 1987. Three-year-olds' difficulty with false belief: The case for a conceptual deficit. *British Journal of Developmental Psychology* 5: 125–137.

Perner, J., Stummer, S., and Lang, B. 1999. Executive functions and theory of mind: Cognitive complexity or functional dependence? In *Developing Theories of Intention*, ed. P. Zelazo et al. Erlbaum.

Perry, E. L., Kulik, C. T., and Bourhis, A. C. 1996. Moderating effects of personal and contextual factors in age discrimination. *Journal of Applied Psychology* 81: 628–647.

Phillips, A. T., and Wellman, H. M. In preparation. Infants' attention to action-connectedness. Manuscript, University of Michigan.

Phillips, A. T., and Wellman, H. M. 2000. Infants' understanding of object-directed action. Manuscript, University of Michigan.

Phillips, A. T., Wellman, H. M., and Spelke, E. S. 2000. Infants' ability to connect gaze and emotional expression to intentional action. Manuscript, University of Michigan.

Phillips, W. 1994. Understanding Intention and Desire by Children with Autism. Doctoral dissertation, University of London.

Phillips, W., Baron-Cohen, S., and Rutter, M. 1998. Understanding intention in normal development and in autism. *British Journal of Developmental Psychology* 16: 337–348.

Piaget, J. 1932. *The Moral Judgment of the Child*. Free Press, 1965.

Piaget, J. 1952. *The Origins of Intelligence in Children*. International Universities Press.

Piaget, J. 1954. *The Construction of Reality in the Child*. Basic Books.

Piaget, J. 1962. *Play, Dreams and Imitation in Childhood*. Norton.

Port, R., and Van Gelder, T., eds. 1995. *Mind in Motion: Dynamics, Behavior, and Cognition*. MIT Press.

Povinelli, D. J. 1993. Reconstructing the evolution of mind. *American Psychologist* 48: 493–509.

Povinelli, D. J. 1994. Comparative studies of mental state attribution: A reply to Heyes. *Animal Behaviour* 48: 239–241.

Povinelli, D. J. 1996. *Growing Up Ape*. Monographs of the Society for Research in Child Development, serial no. 247.

Povinelli, D. 1999. Social understanding in chimpanzees: New evidence from a longitudinal approach. In *Developing Theories of Intention*, ed. P. Zelazo et al. Erlbaum.

Povinelli, D. J. In press. *Folk Physics for Apes*. Oxford University Press.

Povinelli, D. J., Bering, J., and Giambrone, S. 2000. Toward a science of other minds: Escaping the argument by analogy. *Cognitive Science* 24: 509–541.

Povinelli, D. J., Bierschwale, D. T., and Cech, C. G. 1999. Comprehension of seeing as a referential act in young children, but not juvenile chimpanzees. *British Journal of Developmental Psychology* 17: 37–60.

Povinelli, D. J., and Eddy, T. J. 1996a. *What Young Chimpanzees Know about Seeing*. Monographs of the Society for Research in Child Development, serial no. 247.

Povinelli, D. J., and Eddy, T. J. 1996b. Chimpanzees: Joint visual attention. *Psychological Science* 7: 129–135.

Povinelli, D. J., and Eddy, T. J. 1997. Specificity of gaze-following in young chimpanzees. *British Journal of Developmental Psychology* 15: 213–222.

Povinelli, D. J., and Giambrone, S. 1999. Inferring other minds: Failure of the argument by analogy. *Philosophical Topics* 27: 167–201.

Povinelli, D. J., and Prince, C. G. 1998. When self met other. In *Self-Awareness*, ed. M. Ferrari and R. Sternberg. Guilford.

Premack, D. 1988. "Does the chimpanzee have a theory of mind" revisited. In *Machiavellian Intelligence*, ed. R. Byrne and A. Whiten. Oxford University Press.

Premack, D. 1990. The infant's theory of self-propelled objects. *Cognition* 36: 1–16.

Premack, D., and Premack, A. J. 1995. Intention as psychological cause. In *Causal Cognition*, ed. D. Sperber et al. Clarendon.

Premack, D., and Woodruff, G. 1978. Does the chimpanzee have a theory of mind? *Behavioral and Brain Sciences* 1: 515–526.

Putnam, H. 1987. *The Many Faces of Realism*. Open Court.

Quine, W. V. O. 1953. *From a Logical Point of View*. Harvard University Press.

Rasmussen, C. 1998. Justice, justification, and responsibility in Bonhoeffer's Ethics. In *Transgression, Punishment, Responsibility and Forgiveness*, ed. A. Weiner and L. Kaplan. University of Wisconsin Law School.

Read, S. J. 1987. Constructing causal scenarios: A knowledge structure approach to causal reasoning. *Journal of Personality and Social Psychology* 52: 288–302.

Read, S. J., and Marcus-Newhall, A. 1993. Explanatory coherence in social explanations: A parallel distributed processing account. *Journal of Personality and Social Psychology* 65: 429–447.

Reaux, J. E., Theall, L. A., and Povinelli, D. J. 1999. A longitudinal investigation of chimpanzees' understanding of visual perception. *Child Development* 70: 275–290.

Reber, A. S., and Anderson, J. R. 1970. The perception of clicks in linguistic and nonlinguistic messages. *Perception and Psychophysics* 8: 81–89.

Reeder, G. D., and Brewer, M. B. 1979. A schematic model of dispositional attribution in interpersonal perception. *Psychological Review* 86: 61–79.

Reisenzein, R., and Hoffman, T. 1990. An investigation of the dimension of cognitive appraisal in emotion using the repertory grid technique. *Motivation and Emotion* 14: 1–26.

Repacholi, B. M., and Gopnik, A. 1997. Early reasoning about desires: Evidence from 14- and 18-month-olds. *Developmental Psychology* 33: 12–21.

Rholes, W. S., and Ruble, D. N. 1984. Children's understanding of dispositional characteristics of others. *Child Development* 55: 550–560.

Rholes, W. S., Newman, L. S., and Ruble, D. N. 1990. Understanding self and other: Developmental and motivational aspects of perceiving persons in terms of invariant dispositions. In *Handbook of Motivation and Cognition*, ed. E. Higgins and R. Sorrentino. Guilford.

Ripstein, A. 1987. Explanation and empathy. *Review of Metaphysics* 40: 465–482.

Rizzolatti, G., Fadiga, L., Gallese, V., and Fogassi, L. 1996. Premotor cortex and the recognition of motor actions. *Cognitive Brain Research* 3: 131–141.

Rochat, P., Morgan, R., and Carpenter, M. 1997. Young infants' sensitivity to movement information specifying social causality. *Cognitive Development* 12: 537–561.

Roese, N., and Morris, M. W. 1999. Impression valence constrains social explanation: The case of discounting versus conjunction effects. *Journal of Personality and Social Psychology* 77: 437–448.

Rosaldo, M. 1982. The things we do with words: Ilongot speech acts and speech act theory in philosophy. *Language in Society* 11: 203–237.

Rosati, A. D. 2000. Attributions, intentions, and trait concepts in childhood. Manuscript. University of California, Berkeley.

Roseman, I. J. 1991. Appraisal determinants of discrete emotions. *Cognition and Emotion* 5: 161–200.

Rosenbaum, P. S. 1970. A principle governing deletion in English sentential complementation. In *Readings in English Transformational Grammar*, ed. R. Jacobs and P. Rosenbaum. Ginn.

Ross, L., and Nisbett, R. E. 1991. *The Person and the Situation: Perspectives of Social Psychology*. McGraw-Hill.

Ruble, D. N., and Dweck, C. S. 1995. Self-perceptions, person conceptions, and their development. Review of personality and social psychology 15: 109–139.

Rudolph, U. R., Roesch, S. C., and Weiner, B. 2000. Responsibility and help-giving: A meta-analysis. Manuscript, University of Chemnitz.

Rundle, B. 1997. *Mind in Action*. Oxford University Press.

Russell, J. 1996. *Agency*. Psychology Press.

Russell, J., Mauthner, N., Sharpe, S., and Tidswell, T. 1991. The "windows task" as a measure of strategic deception in preschoolers and autistic subjects. *British Journal of Developmental Psychology* 9: 331–349.

Sabbagh, M. A. 1999. Communicative intentions and language: Evidence from right-hemisphere damage and autism. *Brain and Language* 70: 29–69.

Saffran, J. R., Aslin, R. N., and Newport, E. L. 1996. Statistical learning by 8-month-old infants. *Science* 274: 1926–1928.

Sagar, H. A. and Schofield, J. W. 1980. Racial and behavioral cues in Black and White children's perceptions of ambiguously aggressive acts. *Journal of Personality and Social Psychology* 39: 590–598.

Scaife, M., and Bruner, J. S. 1975. The capacity for joint visual attention in the infant. *Nature* 253: 265–266.

Schaffer, H. R. 1984. *The Child's Entry into a Social World*. Academic Press.

Schank, R. C. and Abelson, R. P. 1977. *Scripts, Plans, Goals and Understanding: An Inquiry into Human Knowledge Structures*. Erlbaum.

Schlenker, B. R. 1997. Personal responsibility: Applications of the triangle model. *Research in Organizational Behavior* 19: 241–301.

Schlenker, B. R., Britt, T. W., Pennington, J., Murphy, R., and Doherty, K. 1994. The triangle model of responsibility. *Psychological Review* 101: 632–652.

Schlick, M. 1966. When is a man responsible? In *Free Will and Determinism*, ed. B. Erofsky. Harper and Row.

Schmidt, C. F. 1976. Understanding human action: Recognizing the plans and motives of other persons. In *Cognition and Social Behavior*, ed. J. Carroll, and J. Payne. Erlbaum.

Schueler, G. F. 1995. *Desire: Its Role in Practical Reason and the Explanation of Action*. MIT Press.

Schult, C. A. 1996. Intended Actions and Intentional States: Young Children's Understanding of the Causes of Human Actions. Doctoral dissertation, University of Michigan.

Schult, C. A. 1999. Children's ability to identify intentions and desires. Presented at the meetings of Society for Research in Child Development, Albuquerque.

Schult, C. A., and Wellman, H. M. 1997. Explaining human movements and actions: Children's understanding of the limits of psychological explanation. *Cognition* 62: 291–324

Schwitzgebel, E. 1997. Words about Young Minds: The Concepts of Theory, Representation, and Belief in Philosophy and Developmental Psychology. Doctoral dissertation, University of California, Berkeley.

Schwitzgebel, E. 1999. Representation and desire: A philosophical error with consequences for theory-of-mind research. *Philosophical Psychology* 12: 157–180.

Scott, M. B., and Lyman, S. M. 1968. Accounts. *American Sociological Review* 33: 46–62.

Searle, J. R. 1969. *Speech Acts: An Essay in the Philosophy of Language*. Cambridge University Press.

Searle, J. R. 1983. *Intentionality: An Essay in the Philosophy of Mind*. Cambridge University Press.

Searle, J. R. 1984. *Minds, Brains, and Science*. Harvard University Press.

Searle, J. R. 1990. Collective intentions and actions. In *Intentions in Communication*, ed. P. Cohen et al. Free Press.

Searle, J. R. 1992. *The Rediscovery of the Mind*. MIT Press.

Searle, J. R. 1995. *The Construction of Social Reality*. Free Press.

Semin, G. R., and Manstead, A. S. R. 1983. *The Accountability of Conduct: A Social Psychological Analysis*. Academic Press.

Shaver, K. G. 1985. *The Attribution of Blame*. Springer-Verlag.

Shultz, T. R. 1980. Development of the concept of intention. In *The Minnesota Symposium on Child Psychology*, volume 13, ed. W. Collins. Erlbaum.

Shultz, T. R., and Shamash, F. 1981. The child's conception of intending act and consequence. *Canadian Journal of Behavioural Science* 13: 368–372.

Shultz, T. R., and Wells, D. 1985. Judging the intentionality of action-outcomes. *Developmental Psychology* 21: 83–89.

Shultz, T. R., Wells, D., and Sarda, M. 1980. The development of the ability to distinguish intended actions from mistakes, reflexes, and passive movements. *British Journal of Social and Clinical Psychology* 19: 301–310.

Skitka, L. J., and Tetlock, P. E. 1993. Providing public assistance: Cognitive and motivation processes underlying liberal and conservative policy preferences. *Journal of Personality and Social Psychology* 65: 1205–1223.

Slugoski, B. R., Lalljee, M., Lamb, R., and Ginsburg, G. P. 1993. Attribution in conversational context: Effect of mutual knowledge on explanation-giving. *European Journal of Social Psychology* 23: 219–238.

Small, M. Y. 1990. *Cognitive Development*. Harcourt Brace Jovanovich.

Smith, L. B., and Heise, D. 1992. Perceptual similarity and conceptual structure. In *Percepts, Concepts and Categories*, ed. B. Burns. Elsevier.

Snodgrass, S. E. 1985. Women's intuition: The effect of subordinate role on interpersonal sensitivity. *Journal of Personality and Social Psychology* 49: 146–155.

Snodgrass, S. E. 1992. Further effects of role versus gender on interpersonal sensitivity. *Journal of Personality and Social Psychology* 62: 154–158.

Sokol, B. W., and Chandler, M. J. 1999. Children's beliefs about truth and rightness: The relationship between moral reasoning and an interpretive theory of mind. Manuscript, University of British Columbia, Vancouver.

Spelke, E. S. 1998. Where perceiving ends and thinking begins: The apprehension of objects in infancy. In *Perceptual Development in Infancy*, ed. A. Yonas. Erlbaum.

Spelke, E. S., and Newport, E. L. 1998. Nativism, empiricism, and the development of knowledge. In *Handbook of Child Psychology*, volume 1, ed. W. Damon and R. Lerner. Wiley.

Spelke, E. S., Breinlinger, K., Macomber, J., and Jacobson, K. 1992. Origins of knowledge. *Psychological Review* 99: 605–632.

Spellman, B. A. 1997. Crediting causality. *Journal of Experimental Psychology* 126: 323–348.

Sperber, D., and Wilson, D. 1986. *Relevance: Communication and cognition*. Harvard University Press.

Stern, D. N. 1985. *The Interpersonal World of the Infant: A View from Psychoanalysis and Developmental Psychology*. Basic Books.

Stich, S., and Nichols, S. 1992. Folk psychology: Simulation or tacit theory? *Mind and Language* 7: 35–71.

Stich, S. P., and Nichols, S. 1995. Second thoughts on simulation. In *Mental Simulation*, ed. M. Davies and T. Stone. Blackwell.

Su, S. K., Chiu, C., Hong, Y., Leung, K., Peng, K., and Morris, M. W. 1999. Self organization and social organization: U.S. and Chinese constructions. In *The Psychology of the Social Self*, ed. T. Tyler and R. Kramer. Erlbaum.

Taylor, C. 1964. *The Explanation of Behavior*. Routledge and Kegan Paul.

Taylor, M. 1996. A theory of mind perspective on social cognitive development. In *Handbook of Perception and Cognition*, ed. R. Gelman and T. Au. Academic Press.

Taylor, S. E. 1981. A categorization approach to stereotyping. In *Cognitive Processes in Stereotyping and Intergroup Behavior*, ed. D. Hamilton. Erlbaum.

Tedeschi, J. T., and Reiss, M. 1981. Verbal strategies as impression management. In *The Psychology of Ordinary Social Behaviour*, ed. C. Antaki. Academic Press.

Tetlock, P. E. 1991. An alternative metaphor in the study of judgment and choice: People as politicians. *Theory and Psychology* 4: 451–475.

Thalberg, I. 1972. *Enigmas of Agency: Studies in the Philosophy of Human Action*. Humanities Press.

Thalberg, I. 1984. Do our intentions cause our intentional actions? *American Philosophical Quarterly* 21: 249–260.

Theall, L. A., and Povinelli, D. J. 1999. Do chimpanzees tailor their gestural signals to fit the attentional states of others? *Animal Cognition* 2: 207–214.

Thelen, E., and Smith, L. 1995. *A Dynamic Systems Approach to the Development of Cognition and Action*. MIT Press.

Thommen, A., Dumas, A., Erskine, J., and Reymond, J. 1998. Perception and conceptualization of intentionality in children. *British Journal of Developmental Psychology* 16: 255–272.

Tinbergen, N. 1951. *The Study of Instinct*. Clarendon.

Tomasello, M. 1995. Joint attention as social cognition. In *Joint Attention*, ed. C. Moore and P. Dunham. Erlbaum.

Tomasello, M. 1999. Having intentions, understanding intentions, and understanding communicative intentions. In *Developing Theories of Intention*, ed. P. Zelazo et al. Erlbaum.

Tomasello, M. In press. Perceiving intentions and learning words in the second year of life. In *Language Acquisition and Conceptual Development*, ed. M. Bowerman and S. Levinson. Cambridge University Press.

Tomasello, M., and Barton, M. E. 1994. Learning words in nonostensive contexts. *Developmental Psychology* 30: 639–650.

Tomasello, M., Call, J., and Gluckman, A. 1997. Comprehension of novel communicative signs by apes and human children. *Child Development* 68: 1067–1080.

Tomasello, M., Call, J., and Hare, B. 1998. Five primate species follow the visual gaze of conspecifics. *Animal Behavior* 55: 1063–1069.

Tomasello, M., Kruger, A. C., and Ratner, H. H. 1993. Cultural learning. *Behavioral and Brain Sciences* 16: 495–552.

Trevarthen, C. 1980. The foundations of intersubjectivity: Development of interpersonal and cooperative understanding in infants. In *The Social Foundations of Language and Thought*, ed. D. Olson. Norton.

Trope, Y. 1986. Identification and inferential processes in dispositional attribution. *Psychological Review* 93: 239–257.

Turnbull, W. 1986. Everyday explanation: The pragmatics of puzzle resolution. *Journal for the Theory of Social Behavior* 16: 141–160.

Turnbull, W., and Slugoski, B. 1988. Conversational and linguistic processes in causal attribution. In *Contemporary Science and Natural Explanation*, ed. D. Hilton. Harvester.

Unger, R. M. 1975. *Knowledge and Politics*. Free Press.

Van Gelder, T. 1995. What cognition might be, if not computation? *Journal of Philosophy* 92: 345–381.

Van Overwalle, F. 1998. Causal explanation as constraint satisfaction: A critique and a feedforward connectionist alternative. *Journal of Personality and Social Psychology* 74: 312–328.

Velleman, J. D. 1989. *Practical Reflection*. Princeton University Press.

Velleman, J. D. 1997. How to share an intention. *Philosophical and Phenomenological Research* 57: 29–50.

von Hippel, W., Sekaquaptewa, D., and Vargas, P. 1995. On the role of encoding processes in stereotype maintenance. In *Advances in Experimental Social Psychology*, volume 27, ed. M. Zanna. Academic Press.

Vonk, R. 1999. Effects of outcome dependency on correspondence bias. *Personality and Social Psychology Bulletin* 25: 382–389.

von Wright, G. H. 1971. *Explanation and Understanding*. Cornell University Press.

Wainryb, C., and Ford, S. 1998. Young children's evaluations of acts based on beliefs different from their own. *Merrill Palmer Quarterly* 44: 484–503.

Wallace, R. J. 1994. *Responsibility and the Moral Sentiments*. Harvard University Press.

Webster, D. M., and Kruglanski, A. W. 1994. Individual differences in need for cognitive closure. *Journal of Personality and Social Psychology* 67: 1049–1062.

Weiner, B. 1985. An attributional theory of achievement motivation and emotion. *Psychological Review* 92: 548–573

Weiner, B. 1986. *An Attributional Theory of Motivation and Emotion*. Springer-Verlag.

Weiner, B. 1995. *Judgments of Responsibility: A Foundation For a Theory of Social Conduct*. Guilford.

Weiner, B., Graham, S., and Reyna, C. 1997. An attributional examination of retributive versus utilitarian philosophies of punishment. *Social Justice Research* 10: 431–452.

Wellman, H. M. 1990. *The Child's Theory of Mind*. MIT Press.

Wellman, H. M. 1993. Early understanding of mind: The normal case. In *Understanding Other Minds*, ed. S. Baron-Cohen et al. Oxford University Press.

Wellman, H. 1998. Culture, variation, and levels of analysis in folk psychologies: Comment on Lillard 1998. *Psychological Bulletin* 123: 33–36.

Wellman, H. M., and Banerjee, M. 1991. Mind and emotion: Children's understanding of the emotional consequences of beliefs and desires. *British Journal of Developmental Psychology* 9: 191–124.

Wellman, H. M., Cross, D., and Watson, J. K. In press. Meta-analysis of theory of mind development: The truth about false-belief. *Child Development*.

Wellman, H. M, Hickling, A. K, and Schult, C. A. 1997. Young children's psychological, physical, and biological explanations. In *The Emergence of Core Domains of Thought*, ed. H. Wellman and K. Inagaki. Jossey-Bass.

Wellman, H. M., Phillips, A. T. and Rodriguez, T. 2000. Young children's understanding of perception, desire, and emotion. *Child Development* 71: 895–912.

Wellman, H. M., and Woolley, J. D. 1990. From simple desires to ordinary beliefs: The early development of everyday psychology. *Cognition* 35: 245–275.

White, P. A. 1991. Ambiguity in the internal/external distinction in causal attribution. *Journal of Experimental Social Psychology* 27: 259–270.

Whiten, A., and Byrne, R. W, eds. 1997. *Machiavellian Intelligence II: Extensions and Evaluations*. Cambridge University Press.

Williams, B. 1993. Recognizing responsibility. In B. Williams, *Shame and Necessity*. University of California Press.

Wilson, G. 1989. *The Intentionality of Human Action*. Stanford University Press.

Wilson, J. Q. 1997. *Moral Judgment: Does the Abuse Excuse Threaten Our Legal System?* HarperCollins.

Wimmer, H., Gruber, S., and Perner, J. 1984. Young children's conception of lying: Lexical realism—moral subjectivism. *Journal of Experimental Child Psychology* 37: 1–30.

Wimmer, H., Gruber, S., and Perner, J. 1985. Young children's conception of lying: Moral intuition and the denotation and connotation of "to lie." *Developmental Psychology* 21: 993–995.

Wimmer, H., and Hartl, M. 1991. Against the Cartesian view on mind: Young children's difficulty with own false beliefs. *British Journal of Developmental Psychology* 9: 125–128.

Wimmer, H., and Perner, J. 1983. Beliefs about beliefs: Representation and constraining function of wrong beliefs in young children's understanding of deception. *Cognition* 13: 103–128.

Winter, L., and Uleman, J. S.1984. When are social judgments made? Evidence for the spontaneousness of trait inferences. *Journal of Personality and Social Psychology* 47: 237–252.

Woodward, A. L. 1998. Infants selectively encode the goal object of an actor's reach. *Cognition* 69: 1–34.

Woodward, A. L. 1999. Infants' ability to distinguish between purposeful and non-purposeful behaviors. *Infant Behavior and Development* 22: 145–160.

Woodward, A. L. 2000. Infants' developing understanding of the link between looker and object. Manuscript, University of Chicago.

Woodward, A. L., Phillips, A. T., and Spelke, E. S. 1993. Infants' expectations about the motion of animate versus inanimate objects. In *Proceedings of the Fifteenth Annual Conference of the Cognitive Science Society*. Erlbaum.

Woodward, A. L., and Sommerville, J. A. 2000. Twelve-month-old infants interpret action in context. *Psychological Science* 11: 73–77.

Wyer, R. S., and Srull, T. K. 1989. *Memory and Cognition in Its Social Context.* Erlbaum.

Youniss, J., and Damon, W. 1992. Social construction in Piaget's theory. In *Piaget's Theory*, ed. H. Beilin and P. Pufall. Erlbaum.

Yuill, N. 1997. Children's understanding of traits. In *The Development of Social Cognition*, ed. S. Hala et al. Psychology Press and Erlbaum.

Yuill, N., and Pearson, A. 1998. The development of bases for trait attribution: Children's understanding of traits as causal mechanisms based on desire. *Developmental Psychology* 34: 574–586.

Yuill, N., and Perner, J. 1988. Intentionality and knowledge in children's judgments of actor's responsibility and recipient's emotional reaction. *Developmental Psychology* 24: 358–365.

Zaibert, L. A. In press. Collective intentions and collective intentionality. *American Journal of Economics and Sociology.*

Zeedyk, M. 1996. Developmental access of intentionality: Towards integration. *Developmental Review* 16: 416–461.

Zelazo, P. D., Astington, J. W., and Olson, D. R., eds. 1999. *Developing Theories of Intention: Social Understanding and Self-Control.* Erlbaum.

Zhang, J. 1984. Exploratory investigations on the characteristics of the judicial system in feudal China. *Theses of Law in China* 1: 245–266.

Authors

Daniel R. Ames
Department of Psychology
University of California, Berkeley

Janet Wilde Astington
Institute of Child Study
Ontario Institute for Studies in Education
University of Toronto

Jodie A. Baird
Institute of Child Study
University of Toronto

Dare A. Baldwin
Department of Psychology
University of Oregon

Rechele Brooks
Department of Psychology
University of Washington

Michael J. Chandler
Department of Psychology
University of British Columbia

Raymond W. Gibbs Jr.
Department of Psychology
University of California, Santa Cruz

Alvin I. Goldman
Department of Philosophy
University of Arizona

Alison Gopnik
Department of Psychology
University of California, Berkeley

José J. Guajardo
Department of Psychology
University of Chicago

Darcy Hallett
Department of Psychology
University of British Columbia

Charles W. Kalish
Department of Educational Psychology
University of Wisconsin, Madison

Leonard V. Kaplan
School of Law
University of Wisconsin, Madison

Joshua Knobe
Department of Philosophy
Princeton University

Eric D. Knowles
Department of Psychology
University of California, Berkeley

Bertram F. Malle
Department of Psychology
University of Oregon

Alfred R. Mele
Department of Philosophy
Florida State University

Andrew N. Meltzoff
Department of Psychology
University of Washington

Michael W. Morris
Graduate School of Business
Stanford University

Louis J. Moses
Department of Psychology
University of Oregon

Ann T. Phillips
Center for Human Growth and Development
University of Michigan, Ann Arbor

Daniel J. Povinelli
Institute of Cognitive Science
University of Louisiana

Andrea D. Rosati
Department of Psychology
University of California, Berkeley

G. F. Schueler
Philosophy Department
University of New Mexico

Bryan W. Sokol
Department of Psychology
University of British Columbia

Jessica A. Sommerville
Department of Psychology
University of Chicago

Bernard Weiner
Department of Psychology
University of California, Los Angeles

Henry M. Wellman
Center for Human Growth and Development
University of Michigan

Amanda L. Woodward
Department of Psychology
University of Chicago

Index